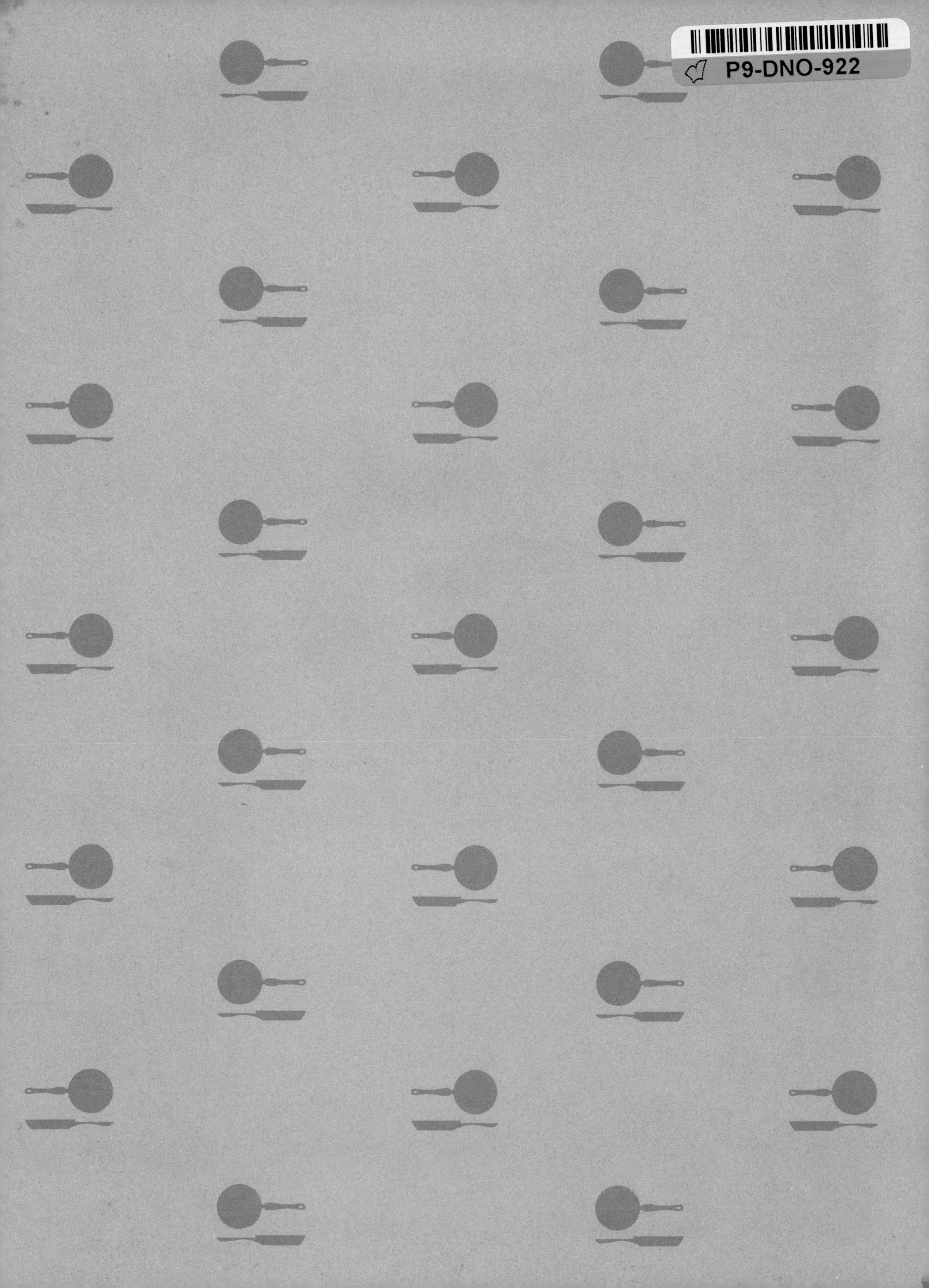

The Treasury of
CREATIVE COOKING

By The Editors of Consumer Guide®

Louis Weber, C.E.O.
Publications International, Ltd.
7373 N. Cicero Avenue
Lincolnwood, IL 60646

Cover photography by Sacco Productions, Ltd./Chicago

8 7 6 5 4 3 2 1

ISBN 1-56173-526-4

Pictured on the front cover (*clockwise from bottom left*): Poached Salmon with Basil Mayonnaise and Pea-Pod Medley (*page 372*), Serbian Lamb Sausage Kabobs (*page 38*), Plum Sweet and Spicy Chicken (*page 194*), Spicy Sweet Potato Muffins (*page 330*), Chocolate Yogurt Cake (*page 222*), Chocolate Pistachio Fingers (*page 578*), Orange & Chocolate Ribbon Cookies (*page 571*), Chocolate Cherry Cookies (*page 569*), Ham & Cheese Quesadillas (*page 335*), Hot Chinese Chicken Salad (*page 142*) and Pasta Delight (*page 114*).

Inset photo on front cover: Gourmet Gala Cheesecake with Orange Rum Sauce (*page 226*).

Microwave ovens vary in wattage and power output; cooking times given with microwave directions in this book may need to be adjusted.

The Treasury of

CREATIVE COOKING

By The Editors of Consumer Guide®

Publications International, Ltd.

CONTENTS

Your Guide to Creative Cooking

THE TREASURY OF CREATIVE COOKING is just that—a great collection of recipes to bring creative new ideas into your kitchen. Each recipe has been kitchen-tested to assure delicious, successful results. You'll find classics as well as many novel creations sure to become family favorites for years to come.

Cooks today want easy-to-follow recipes suitable for everyday or for entertaining. Whether fancy or casual, you like to gather with family and friends for exceptional meals. That's why we've selected recipes especially for cooks like you. We know how busy your life-style is and that you want recipes you can count on. This collection is unique in that it focuses on those areas of cooking proven to be the most popular with most people. From this multitude of popular recipes, you are bound to find just what you are looking for.

As you glance through the book, the variety of recipes is apparent. First, we've included an elegant segment showcasing award-winning recipes. The great-tasting recipes in the Award-Winning Appetizers, Pasta, Chicken and Cakes & Desserts chapters were gathered from a variety of recipe contests and cook-offs across America. These contest winners represent some of the very best offerings in cookery—original dishes created by home cooks like you. Each recipe has its own mouth-watering, beautiful photograph and lists the name of the winner and the contest they entered. We've selected the most delicious appetizers, superb salads, delectable pasta dishes, succulent chicken suppers and decadent desserts for you to try.

We've also included a special selection of breakfast and brunch dishes sure to get you to rise 'n' shine. Whether you're having company for a special brunch or you want a quick breakfast on those hectic weekdays—this chapter has many inventive morning meals.

The 30-Minute Meals section is chock-full of recipes that fit into your busy schedule. Each menu has a beautiful full-color photograph as well as a detailed game plan to successfully guide you through each step of the meal preparation. We've included complete meals with poultry, meat and seafood you can prepare in 30 minutes or less!

In addition, you'll find great hamburger innovations. Ground beef is a mainstay in the American diet. And now, more than ever before, with leaner ground beef readily available, you can enjoy quick, economical and versatile meals with less fat! This delightful chapter will add new specialties to your current favorites.

When you have time to be creative, choose gourmet specialties with the international flair of Italy and China. Since Italian and Chinese cuisines are universally enjoyed, we've included two special cooking class chapters with step-by-step photographs and easy instructions for fabulous Italian and Chinese dishes. You'll be as confident as an international chef in no time!

And to top off any imaginative meal, who wouldn't want to include America's favorite flavor—chocolate! Our Chocolate Lover's Cookies & Brownies chapter will satisfy your cravings for chocolate treats and cookies in dozens of luscious ways.

As wonderful as these recipes are, you'll find that this book is appealing to browse through as well. Just by looking at the large full-color photographs throughout the book, meal planning will be a snap. And with a treasury of recipes this comprehensive, you'll always have just the right recipe at your fingertips. So start creating—and enjoying—the savory results!

Award-Winning APPETIZERS

Scampi alla "Fireman Chef" (page 20)

SENSATIONAL SOUPS

Does chopping or slicing onions make you cry? It is probably due to an enzyme called alliinase. When exposed to the air through peeling or chopping it can irritate the tear ducts causing your eyes to water. Sometimes chilling the onion before cutting can reduce the effects of alliinase.

Picante Onion Soup

♦ Joyce Lee Sproul from Pembroke Pines, Florida was the grand prize winner in the Pace® Picante Sauce "Pick Up the Pace" Recipe Contest sponsored by Pace Foods, Inc.

Makes 6 servings

3 cups thinly sliced onions
1 clove garlic, minced
¼ cup butter or margarine
2 cups tomato juice
1 can (10½ ounces) condensed beef broth
1 soup can water
½ cup Pace® picante sauce
1 cup unseasoned croutons (optional)
1 cup (4 ounces) shredded Monterey Jack cheese (optional)
Additional Pace® picante sauce

Place onions, garlic and butter in 3-quart saucepan. Cook over medium-low heat about 20 minutes, stirring frequently, until onions are tender and golden brown. Stir in tomato juice, broth, water and ½ cup picante sauce; bring to a boil. Reduce heat and simmer, uncovered, 20 minutes. Ladle soup into bowls and sprinkle with croutons and cheese. Serve with additional picante sauce.

Note: 2⅔ cups ready-to-serve beef broth may be substituted for the condensed beef broth and water.

"Dearhearts" Seafood Bisque

♦ Michele Myers from San Jose, California was the first place winner at the Castroville Artichoke Festival Recipe Contest, Castroville, California.

Makes 6 servings

2 tablespoons olive oil
1 onion, finely chopped
3 pounds fresh baby artichoke hearts, outer leaves removed, leaf tips trimmed and hearts cut into quarters
2 cups chicken broth
½ cup white wine
1 pound mixed shellfish (shrimp, crab, scallops), cleaned and shells removed
1 cup heavy cream
2 tablespoons chopped parsley
1 teaspoon salt
½ teaspoon ground nutmeg
¼ teaspoon white pepper

Heat oil in large saucepan; add onion and cook gently for 5 minutes or until softened. Add artichokes, broth and wine. Cover and simmer 20 to 30 minutes or until artichokes are tender and a leaf pulls away easily. Process mixture in food processor or blender until smooth. Return soup to saucepan. Stir in shellfish, cream, parsley, salt, nutmeg and pepper. Simmer very gently, uncovered, over low heat 5 to 10 minutes. Do not boil or shellfish will become tough.

Peeling Tomatoes

To peel tomatoes, place them, one at a time, in a saucepan of simmering water for about 10 seconds. (Add about 30 seconds if they are not fully ripened.) Then immediately plunge them into a bowl of cold water for another 10 seconds. The skins will peel off easily with a knife. Do not add more than one tomato to the water at a time or the temperature will drop rapidly and the tomatoes will stew before their skins can be removed.

Golden Tomato Soup

♦ Kim Plotzky from Stamford, Connecticut was the sixth place winner in the *Weight Watcher's Magazine* recipe contest sponsored by the Florida Tomato Committee.

Makes 8 servings

4 teaspoons reduced-calorie margarine
1 cup chopped onion
2 cloves garlic, coarsely chopped
½ cup chopped carrots
¼ cup chopped celery
8 medium-size tomatoes, blanched, peeled, seeded and chopped
6 cups chicken broth
1 ounce uncooked rice
2 tablespoons tomato paste
1 tablespoon Worcestershire sauce
¼ to ½ teaspoon black pepper
½ teaspoon dried thyme
5 drops hot pepper sauce

Melt margarine in large Dutch oven over medium-high heat. Add onion and garlic; cook and stir 1 to 2 minutes or until tender. Add carrots and celery; cook 7 to 9 minutes or until tender, stirring frequently. Stir in tomatoes, broth, rice, tomato paste, Worcestershire sauce, pepper, thyme and hot pepper sauce. Reduce heat to low; cook about 30 minutes, stirring frequently.

Remove from heat and let cool about 10 minutes. In food processor or blender, process soup in small batches until smooth. Return soup to Dutch oven; simmer 3 to 5 minutes or until heated through. Garnish as desired.

Sherried Oyster and Brie Soup

♦ Judith Mettlin from Snyder, New York was a prize winner at the St. Mary's County National Oyster Cook-Off in Leonardtown, Maryland.

Makes 4 servings

1 quart select Maryland oysters with liquor
2 tablespoons butter or margarine
1 pound fresh mushrooms, thinly sliced
½ cup minced shallots
2 tablespoons fresh lemon juice
2 tablespoons all-purpose flour
3 cups beef broth
1 cup cream sherry, reduced to ½ cup*
4 ounces Brie cheese, rind trimmed
1 cup milk
1 cup heavy cream
Salt and pepper to taste
Chives, for garnish

Drain oysters and reserve liquor; set aside. Melt butter in large saucepan over medium-high heat. When foam subsides, stir in mushrooms, shallots and lemon juice; cook and stir 2 minutes. Sprinkle with flour; cook and stir 1 minute more. Add broth and reduced sherry. Bring to a boil; reduce heat and simmer 20 minutes.

Add Brie and stir to melt. Stir in reserved oyster liquor, milk and cream; season with salt and pepper. Heat until very hot. Do not boil. Remove from heat and add oysters. Cover and let stand until oysters are just plumped. Garnish with chives.

**To reduce, simmer over medium heat until slightly thickened and reduced to desired amount.*

Black-Eyed Pea Soup

♦ Joe Bayer from Dallas, Texas was the fourth place winner at the Black-Eyed Pea Jamboree, Athens, Texas.

Makes 12 to 16 servings

2 pounds fresh East Texas Black-Eyed Peas*
½ pound bacon, diced
4 medium-size onions, thinly sliced
4 carrots, thinly sliced
8 quarts water
2 cups thinly sliced celery
2 large potatoes, peeled and grated
2 whole jalapeño peppers
4 bay leaves
½ teaspoon dried thyme
1 meaty ham bone
Salt and pepper to taste

Clean and drain black-eyed peas; set aside. Combine bacon, onions and carrots in large saucepan. Cook and stir over medium-high heat until onions are golden. Add black-eyed peas, water, celery, potatoes, jalapeño peppers, bay leaves, thyme and ham bone. Season with salt and pepper. Cover; simmer over low heat 3 to 4 hours. Remove and discard whole jalapeños and bay leaves. Cut meat from ham bone and return meat to saucepan. Adjust seasonings; reheat if necessary.

**Fresh black-eyed peas are often available in supermarkets in the produce section. If desired, substitute 1 pound dried black-eyed peas, cooked, for the fresh.*

Elegant Starters

Clarifying Butter

Clarified butter is what remains after removing protein and milk solids from butter. It is simple to make and has the advantage of cooking at high temperatures without burning. Melt the butter over low heat. Skim off the white foam that forms on top, then strain the clear, golden clarified butter through cheesecloth into a container. Discard the milky residue at the bottom of the pan. You can make a large quantity of clarified butter at one time. It will keep, covered, in the refrigerator for up to 2 months.

Scampi alla "Fireman Chef"

♦ Jim Neil from Gilroy, California was a finalist in the Gilroy Garlic Festival Recipe Contest, Gilroy, California. Courtesy of the Gilroy Garlic Festival Association's *Garlic Lover's Cookbook.*

Makes 8 first-course servings

1½ pounds large prawns, peeled and deveined (about 16)
⅓ cup clarified butter
4 tablespoons minced garlic
6 green onions, thinly sliced
¼ cup dry white wine
Juice of 1 lemon (about 2 tablespoons)
8 large sprigs parsley, finely chopped
Salt and freshly ground pepper to taste
Lemon slices and parsley sprigs, for garnish

Rinse prawns and set aside. Heat clarified butter in large skillet over medium heat. Cook garlic 1 to 2 minutes or until softened but not brown. Add prawns, green onions, wine and lemon juice; cook until prawns turn pink and firm, 1 to 2 minutes on each side. Do not overcook. Just before serving add chopped parsley and season with salt and pepper. Serve on individual shell-shaped or small gratin dishes, garnished with slice of lemon and fresh parsley sprig.

Caviar is a luxury few can afford on a regular basis. Good beluga sturgeon caviar can be outrageously priced and is usually beyond most people's entertaining budget. Now Whitefish caviar, also called golden caviar, is widely available and often priced quite reasonably. The tiny, bright yellow eggs come from Great Lakes Whitefish. This roe is processed similarly to salmon and beluga sturgeon caviar and then flash-frozen for freshness. All types of caviar are best when served very cold and should never be cooked.

Chilled Seafood Lasagna with Herbed Cheese

♦ Marc Waltzer was a prize winner in the Wisconsin Milk Marketing Board Supermarket Chef Showcase.

Makes 24 first-course or 8 entrée servings

2 cups Wisconsin ricotta cheese
1½ cups Wisconsin mascarpone cheese*
2 tablespoons lemon juice
1 tablespoon minced fresh basil
1 tablespoon minced fresh dill
1 tablespoon minced fresh tarragon
¼ teaspoon white pepper
8 lasagna noodles (2 inches wide), cooked and drained
1 pound lox
4 ounces Whitefish caviar, gently rinsed

Place ricotta cheese, mascarpone cheese, lemon juice, herbs and pepper in food processor container; process until well combined. Line terrine mold with plastic wrap, allowing wrap to come over sides of pan. Layer 1 noodle, ½ cup of the cheese mixture, 2 ounces lox and 2 rounded teaspoons caviar in pan. Repeat layers with remaining ingredients, ending with noodle. Cover; refrigerate several hours or until firm. Carefully remove from mold and remove plastic wrap. Garnish with strips of lox rolled to look like roses and fresh herb sprigs. Slice with warm knife.

Note: Can be prepared without terrine mold. Layer lasagna on plastic wrap. Cover and wrap with foil.

**Mascarpone cheese is a soft, delicate cheese with a buttery-rich flavor and is similar in consistency to whipped cream cheese.*

Cheddar Chili Tomato Pots

♦ Marge Walker from Indianapolis, Indiana won first prize in the Appetizer category of the "Sargento® Cheese Makes the Recipe" contest.

Makes 6 first-course servings

6 medium-size tomatoes
3½ cups (14 ounces) Sargento® Fancy Shredded Sharp Cheddar Cheese, divided
2 cans (4 ounces each) chopped mild green chilies, well-drained
½ teaspoon dried oregano
½ teaspoon minced garlic
6 tablespoons sour cream
3 green onions, sliced
Breadsticks, for serving

Preheat oven to 325°F. Grease shallow baking dish. Cut ½-inch slice from top of each tomato; scoop out pulp and seeds, leaving ¼-inch shell (reserve pulp for another use such as salads or sauces). Invert tomatoes on paper towel-lined plate and let drain 20 minutes. Combine 3 cups of the cheese, the chilies, oregano and garlic in medium-size bowl. Divide mixture evenly among tomato shells. Arrange tomato shells in prepared dish; bake 20 minutes. To serve, top with sour cream, remaining ½ cup cheese and the green onions. Serve with breadsticks.

Flounder Ravioli with Mustard-Tomato Sauce

♦ Susan Weisberg from Pleasantville, New Jersey was a prize winner in the "Fabulous Fishing for Compliments" Recipe Contest sponsored by the New Jersey Department of Agriculture, Fish and Seafood Development Program.

Makes 4 first-course servings

½ pound fresh flounder, cut into chunks
1 egg, separated
⅓ cup buttermilk
2 tablespoons minced parsley
1 package (16 ounces) wonton skins
2 tablespoons virgin olive oil, divided
2 large tomatoes, seeded and chopped
¼ cup minced onion
1 large garlic clove, minced
1 cup *each* white wine and water
1½ tablespoons *each* prepared yellow and spicy brown mustard
4 tablespoons butter, cut into pieces

Process flounder, egg white and buttermilk in food processor or blender until well combined. Stir in parsley; season with salt and pepper. Place heaping teaspoonful of fish mixture in center of wonton skin; moisten edges with beaten egg yolk. Top with another wonton skin and press to seal, working out any air bubbles. Repeat with remaining wonton skins.

Heat 1 tablespoon olive oil in large skillet; add tomatoes and cook briefly. Remove with slotted spoon; set aside. Heat remaining 1 tablespoon oil in skillet; cook onion until tender. Add garlic and cook about 2 minutes. Add wine, scraping up any brown bits. Add water; bring to a boil. Reduce heat; simmer until reduced to ½ cup. Whisk mustards into wine mixture until well blended. Gradually whisk in butter. Reduce heat to low. Season with salt and pepper; add reserved tomatoes. Cook until heated through.

Cook ravioli, a few at a time, in boiling salted water for 5 minutes; drain. Top ravioli with sauce. Garnish as desired.

This surefire method to hard cook eggs comes from the American Egg Board. Place the desired number of eggs in a single layer in a saucepan. Add enough water to come at least 1 inch above the eggs. Cover and quickly bring water just to boiling. Turn off heat. If necessary, remove the pan from the burner to prevent further boiling. Let eggs stand, covered, in the hot water 15 to 17 minutes. Immediately run cold water over eggs or put them in ice water until completely cooled.

Avocado Egg Salad ▸

♦ Daryl Urzen from Pennsylvania won second place in the Adult Division of the National Egg Cooking Contest sponsored by the American Egg Board.

Makes 6 first-course servings

2 tablespoons mayonnaise
2 tablespoons sour cream
1 tablespoon lemon juice
½ teaspoon salt
¼ teaspoon hot pepper sauce
2 avocados, peeled, pitted and chopped
1 cup chopped tomatoes
½ cup chopped red onion
6 hard-cooked eggs, chopped
¼ cup chopped parsley or cilantro

Combine mayonnaise, sour cream, lemon juice, salt and hot pepper sauce in large bowl. Add avocados, tomatoes, onion, eggs and parsley. Toss lightly until well combined. Cover; refrigerate. Serve on spinach leaves.

Zesty Wild Rice Salad ▸

♦ Michele Eklund from Minnesota was a prize winner in the Wild Rice Food Show at the Minnesota State Wild Rice Festival, Kelliher, Minnesota.

Makes about 8 first-course servings

5 cups cooked wild rice
2 cups frozen cooked shrimp, thawed *or* 1 can (9¼ ounces) tuna, drained and flaked
½ cup chopped broccoli
½ cup chopped cauliflower
½ cup cubed cheese
¼ cup diced red bell pepper
¼ cup diced green bell pepper
¼ cup Italian dressing

Combine wild rice, shrimp, broccoli, cauliflower, cheese and peppers in large bowl. Cover; refrigerate. Just before serving, toss gently with dressing. Serve on lettuce leaves.

Mushrooms Mary Louise

♦ Terrance Smith from Newark, Delaware was the first place winner at the Mushroom Cook-Off sponsored by the Pennsylvania Fresh Mushroom Program, Kennett Square, Pennsylvania.

Makes 4 first-course servings

28 medium-size fresh mushroom caps, divided
8 tablespoons butter, melted and divided
2 ounces scallops, diced
3 medium-size raw shrimp, peeled, deveined and diced
2 ribs celery, sliced
¼ cup finely chopped onion
6 soft-shell clams, shucked and diced, juices reserved
⅓ cup white wine
⅔ cup bread crumbs
1 cup hollandaise sauce*

Preheat oven to 350°F. Grease 4 (6-inch) casserole dishes. Slice 4 of the mushroom caps. Melt 1 tablespoon of the butter in large skillet. Add sliced mushrooms; cook and stir until tender. Set aside. Place scallops, shrimp, celery and onion in same skillet with remaining 7 tablespoons butter. Cook over medium heat about 2 minutes or until seafood is fully cooked. Add clams with reserved juices to skillet and simmer 1 minute. Add white wine, then remove from heat. Fold in bread crumbs; set aside. (The mixture will become firm as it stands.)

Place 6 mushroom caps in each prepared casserole dish. Cover mushrooms with stuffing mixture. Bake 10 minutes. Remove from oven and place reserved mushrooms on top of each casserole. Top each with ¼ cup of hollandaise sauce and return to oven just to heat through. Serve hot, garnished as desired.

**Use your favorite recipe.*

Since 1970 the people of Athens, Texas have staged the Black-Eyed Pea Jamboree. It's a wildly popular annual celebration that draws crowds of people to join in the fun and games and beat their feet to the sounds of country music. The high point is the judging of the reci-peas, and the winners agree to cook up enough of their concoctions to feed 500 people. Imagine the scene when a winner once produced a Pea-tini, which was (you guessed it) a martini sporting a black-eyed pea on a toothpick!

Plentiful "P's" Salad

◆ Anna Ardinger from Dallas, Texas was a second place winner in the salad category of the Black-Eyed Pea Jamboree, Athens, Texas.

Makes 12 first-course servings

4 cups cooked and drained black-eyed peas
2 cups cooked and drained rotini pasta
1 medium-size red bell pepper, chopped
1 medium-size green bell pepper, chopped
1 medium-size purple onion, chopped
2 tablespoons chopped parsley
4 slices Provolone cheese, chopped
4 slices pepperoni or salami, chopped
1 jar (2 ounces) pimiento
1 jar (4½ ounces) whole mushrooms, drained
2 tablespoons dry Italian salad dressing mix
½ teaspoon salt
¼ teaspoon black pepper
½ cup wine vinegar
¼ cup sugar
¼ cup vegetable oil

Combine black-eyed peas, pasta, peppers, purple onion, parsley, Provolone cheese, pepperoni, pimiento and mushrooms in large bowl; set aside.

Combine salad dressing mix, salt and pepper in small bowl. Add vinegar and sugar; mix well. Stir in oil. Add to black-eyed pea mixture; toss lightly until well combined. Cover; refrigerate at least 2 hours before serving. Garnish as desired.

Note: Other vegetables such as cauliflower, broccoli, carrots or celery can be added.

Jumbo Shells Seafood Fancies

♦ Edith Lehr from Wishek, North Dakota was the second place winner in the Appetizing Appetizers Pasta Contest sponsored by the North Dakota Wheat Commission and the North Dakota Mill, Bismark, North Dakota.

Makes 8 first-course servings

1 package (16 ounces) uncooked jumbo-size pasta shells
1 can (7½ ounces) crabmeat, drained, flaked and cartilage removed
1 can (2½ ounces) tiny shrimp, drained
1 cup (4 ounces) shredded Swiss cheese
½ cup salad dressing or mayonnaise
2 tablespoons thinly sliced celery
1 tablespoon finely chopped onion
1 tablespoon finely chopped pimiento
Celery leaves, for garnish

Add shells gradually to 6 quarts boiling salted water; cook until tender, yet firm. Drain; rinse with cold water, then drain again. Invert on paper towel-lined plate to cool. Combine crabmeat, shrimp, cheese, salad dressing, celery, onion and pimiento in medium-size bowl. If mixture seems too dry, add more salad dressing. Spoon mixture into cooled shells; cover and refrigerate until chilled. Garnish with celery leaves.

FOREIGN FLAIR

Taco Dip

♦ Beth Gostisha was a prize winner in the Wisconsin Milk Marketing Board Supermarket Chef Showcase.

Makes 10 servings

12 ounces cream cheese, softened
½ cup dairy sour cream
2 teaspoons chili powder
1½ teaspoons ground cumin
⅛ teaspoon ground red pepper
½ cup salsa
2 cups shredded lettuce or lettuce leaves
1 cup (4 ounces) shredded Wisconsin Cheddar cheese
1 cup (4 ounces) shredded Wisconsin Monterey Jack cheese
½ cup diced plum tomatoes
⅓ cup sliced green onions
¼ cup sliced ripe olives
¼ cup pimiento-stuffed green olives
Tortilla chips and blue corn chips

Combine cream cheese, sour cream, chili powder, cumin and red pepper in large bowl; mix until well blended. Stir in salsa. Spread onto 10-inch serving platter lined with lettuce. Top with cheeses, tomatoes, green onions and olives. Serve with chips.

Serbian Lamb Sausage Kabobs

♦ Jane Witty Gould from Elizabeth, New Jersey was a prize winner in the "Food Editors' Choice" Recipe Contest sponsored by the American Lamb Council.

Makes 10 servings

1 pound lean ground lamb
1 pound lean ground beef
1 small onion, finely chopped
2 cloves garlic, minced
1 tablespoon hot Hungarian paprika
1 small egg, slightly beaten
Salt and freshly ground black pepper to taste
Red, green and yellow bell peppers, cut into squares
Rice pilaf (optional)

Combine lamb, beef, onion, garlic, paprika and egg in large bowl; season with salt and pepper. Shape meat mixture into small (about 1-inch) oblong sausages. Place on waxed paper-lined jelly-roll pan and freeze 30 to 45 minutes or until firm; do not freeze completely.

Alternately thread sausages and peppers onto metal skewers. Grill over medium-hot coals 5 to 7 minutes. Turn kabobs taking care not to knock sausages off. Continue grilling 5 to 7 minutes longer or until meat is done. If desired, serve with rice pilaf. Garnish as desired.

Note: The seasonings may be adjusted, but the key to authenticity is the equal parts beef and lamb and the garlic and paprika. You may use sweet paprika if you prefer a milder taste.

Peeling Garlic Cloves

To quickly peel whole garlic cloves, place the desired number of cloves in a small glass custard cup. Microwave at HIGH (100% power) until slightly softened, 5 to 10 seconds for 1 clove or 45 to 55 seconds for a whole head. Then just slip the garlic out of its skin; nothing could be easier! If the cloves are to be minced, trim off the ends and crush with the bottom of a heavy saucepan or the flat side of a large knife. The peels can then be easily removed.

Patrician Escargots

♦ Pat Trinchero from Gilroy, California won third prize in the Great Garlic Recipe Contest sponsored by the Fresh Garlic Association in association with the Gilroy Garlic Festival, Gilroy, California.

Makes 4 servings

4 heads garlic,* separated into cloves and peeled
½ cup olive oil
½ cup butter
1 onion, finely chopped
1 teaspoon finely chopped fresh rosemary *or* **½ teaspoon dried rosemary**
¼ teaspoon ground thyme
2 dashes ground nutmeg
Salt and pepper to taste
24 large canned snails, drained
½ cup chopped parsley
24 large fresh mushrooms
12 pieces thin-sliced white bread

Finely chop garlic. Heat oil and butter in large skillet over medium heat until butter is melted. Add garlic, onion, rosemary, thyme and nutmeg; season with salt and pepper. Reduce heat to low and add snails and parsley; simmer for 30 minutes, stirring occasionally.

Preheat oven to 350°F. Remove stems from mushrooms. Arrange mushroom caps upside down in 2-inch-deep baking dish; place 1 snail in each mushroom cap. Pour garlic mixture over snails; cover with foil and bake 30 minutes. While snails are baking, remove crusts from bread slices. Toast each slice and cut diagonally into 4 triangles. Serve with escargots.

**The whole garlic bulb is called a head.*

Picante Black Bean Soup

♦ Katheryn Gonzales from Park Forest, Illinois won first prize in the Soups and Stews category of the Pace® Picante Sauce "Pick Up the Pace" Recipe Contest sponsored by Pace Foods, Inc.

Makes 6 to 8 servings

4 slices bacon, diced
1 large onion, chopped
1 clove garlic, minced
2 cans (15 ounces each) black beans, undrained
1 can (about 14 ounces) beef broth
1¼ cups water
¾ cup Pace® picante sauce
½ to 1 teaspoon salt
½ teaspoon oregano leaves, crushed
Sour cream
Additional Pace® picante sauce and crackers

Cook bacon over medium-high heat in large saucepan until crisp. Remove to paper towels; set aside. Add onion and garlic to drippings; cook and stir 3 minutes. Add beans, broth, water, 3/4 cup picante sauce, salt and oregano. Cover and simmer 20 minutes. Ladle into soup bowls; dollop with sour cream. Sprinkle with reserved bacon. Serve with additional picante sauce and crackers.

Arrowroot is a thickening agent coming from a plant native to West India. It has almost no taste and more thickening power than flour or cornstarch. Since it thickens at lower temperatures it can be used in delicate sauces. If arrowroot is unavailable cornstarch can be substituted using 1½ teaspoons of cornstarch for every 1 teaspoon of arrowroot.

Both oriental sesame oil, a strong-tasting oil made from sesame seeds, and rice wine vinegar, a mild, slightly sweet vinegar, can be found in the imported (Oriental) section of the supermarket or in specialty food shops.

Microwave Oriental Relish Dip

♦ Mr. Lynn Whately from Double Springs, Alabama was the fifth place winner in the *Weight Watcher's Magazine* recipe contest sponsored by the Florida Tomato Committee.

Makes 16 servings

1 cup peeled chopped tomato
¼ cup soy sauce
¼ cup drained canned crushed pineapple
1 tablespoon sugar
1 tablespoon finely chopped red bell pepper
1 tablespoon finely chopped green onion
1 tablespoon minced garlic
2 teaspoons fresh lemon juice
1½ teaspoons grated fresh ginger
2 teaspoons rice wine vinegar
1 teaspoon sesame oil
1 teaspoon arrowroot
4 cups plain low-fat yogurt
1 cup creamy peanut butter
8 cups assorted fresh vegetables

Combine tomato, soy sauce, pineapple, sugar, red pepper, onion, garlic, lemon juice and ginger in 1-quart glass measuring cup. Microwave at HIGH (100% power) 8 minutes; stir every 2 minutes. Stir in rice wine vinegar and sesame oil. Microwave 2 to 3 minutes or until ingredients are reduced to 1 cup. Stir in arrowroot. Cool slightly. Store relish covered in glass container in refrigerator.

To make dip: Combine relish with yogurt and peanut butter in large bowl; mix until well blended. Serve with assorted vegetables.

To make one serving of dip: Combine ¼ cup plain low-fat yogurt, 1 tablespoon peanut butter and 1 tablespoon relish. Serve with ½ cup assorted vegetables.

Notes: Relish is also great mixed with reduced-calorie mayonnaise and used as a sandwich spread or salad dressing.

Microwave ovens vary in wattage and power output; cooking times may need to be adjusted.

SNACK TIME

Popcorn is believed to be the world's oldest form of corn, at least 7,000 years old. The Native Americans brought popcorn to the first Thanksgiving in 1621 and amazed the Pilgrims by heating it up with a little oil and transforming the hard inedible kernels into a delicious fluffy white snack.

Fall Harvest Popcorn

♦ Peggy Meuli from Hope, Kansas was the first place winner in the Appetizers category in the annual recipe contest sponsored by the *Reflector-Chronicle*, Abilene, Kansas.

Makes 2½ quarts

2 quarts freshly popped popcorn, unsalted
2 cans (1¾ ounces each) shoestring potatoes (3 cups)
1 cup salted mixed nuts
¼ cup butter or margarine, melted
1 teaspoon dill weed
1 teaspoon Worcestershire sauce
½ teaspoon lemon-pepper seasoning
¼ teaspoon garlic powder
¼ teaspoon onion powder

Preheat oven to 325°F. Combine popcorn, shoestring potatoes and nuts in large roasting pan. Set aside. Combine butter, dill, Worcestershire sauce, lemon-pepper seasoning, garlic powder and onion powder in small bowl; pour over popcorn mixture, stirring until evenly coated. Bake 8 to 10 minutes, stirring once. Cool completely; store in airtight containers.

HERE'S A LITTLE SOMETHING...

Canned chilies should be rinsed in cold water before using. Much of the "fire" is in the seeds and canning liquid. The hotness of chilies is rated on a scale of 1 to 200—with 1 being the mildest. A jalapeño chili, hot enough to burn your mouth, bring tears to your eyes and make your hair curl, rates only 15 on this scale! Taste all chilies very warily if you are a novice.

Southwestern Chili Rellenos

♦ Dan Gerlock was a prize winner in the Wisconsin Milk Marketing Board Supermarket Chef Showcase.

Makes 6 servings

2 tablespoons olive oil
½ teaspoon white pepper
½ teaspoon salt
½ teaspoon ground red pepper
¼ teaspoon ground cloves
4 cans (4 ounces each) whole green chilies, drained, seeded
1½ cups (6 ounces) shredded Wisconsin Cheddar cheese
1½ cups (6 ounces) Wisconsin Monterey Jack cheese
1 package (16 ounces) egg roll skins
1 egg yolk
1 teaspoon water
Vegetable oil

Combine olive oil and seasonings in small bowl. Add chilies; toss to coat. Let stand 1 hour. Combine cheeses in another small bowl.

For each chili rellenos, place 1 chili in center of 1 egg roll skin; top with ¼ cup cheese mixture. Brush egg roll skin with combined egg yolk and water. Fold two opposite edges over filling, overlapping edges; press together. Press together ends, enclosing filling.

Heat about 3 inches of peanut oil in large heavy saucepan over medium-high heat until oil reaches 375°F; adjust heat to maintain temperature. Fry chili rellenos, a few at a time, in hot oil 2 to 3 minutes or until golden brown. Drain on paper towels.

The size of an olive is no indication of its flavor. Some tiny varieties are bitter while others are quite mild, and the same is true for the large ones. Green olives are harvested before they are fully ripe; black olives have ripened on the tree. Both kinds must be cured in brine in order to be fit to eat.

Oven-Fried California Quesadillas

♦ Sally Vog from Springfield, Oregon was the first place winner in the Appetizers and Snacks category of the Pace® Picante Sauce 40th Anniversary Recipe Contest sponsored by Pace Foods, Inc.

Makes 32 appetizers

2½ cups (10 ounces) shredded Monterey Jack cheese
1 jar (6 ounces) marinated artichoke hearts, drained and chopped
1 can (2¼ ounces) sliced ripe olives, drained
⅔ cup Pace® picante sauce
½ cup chopped toasted almonds
¼ cup loosely packed, chopped cilantro
8 flour tortillas (7- to 8-inch)
3 tablespoons butter or margarine, melted
Additional Pace® picante sauce and lime wedges

Preheat oven to 450°F. Combine cheese, artichokes, olives, ⅔ cup picante sauce, the almonds and cilantro in large bowl; mix well. Brush one side of 4 tortillas with butter; place buttered side down on baking sheet. Place 1 cup cheese mixture on each tortilla; spread to within ¾ inch of edge; top each with remaining tortillas, pressing firmly. Brush tops of tortillas with butter.

Bake about 10 minutes or until tops are lightly browned. Remove from oven; let stand 3 to 5 minutes. Cut each quesadilla into 8 wedges. Serve with additional picante sauce and lime wedges.

Fresh herbs are used to delicately accent and enhance the flavor of food. Until recently the only fresh herb available at supermarkets was parsley, but now hot-house variety herbs of all kinds are available year-round. The flavor in herbs comes from aromatic essential oils that are released by chopping or heating. When herbs are dried these flavorful oils become concentrated so when substituting dried herbs for fresh use about one third as much.

Dynasty Duckling Pizza Imperiale

♦ Tillie A. Astorino from North Adams, Massachusetts was the first place winner at the Concord National Duckling Cook-Off sponsored by Concord Farms®.

Makes about 16 servings

4 cups cooked rice
½ cup ground pecans or hazelnuts
1 egg, beaten
2½ cups (20 ounces) shredded Swiss cheese, divided
½ cup grated Parmesan cheese, divided
2 tablespoons olive oil
1 whole Concord Farms® duck breast, halved, boned, skinned and cut into bite-size pieces
1 small sweet onion, cut into thin rings
1 small green pepper, cut into thin rings
1 small red pepper, cut into thin rings
4 ounces fresh mushroom caps, thinly sliced
½ cup pitted ripe olives, sliced
1⅓ cups pizza sauce
1 teaspoon *each* Italian seasoning, fresh chopped mint and fresh chopped basil

Preheat oven to 375°F. Combine rice, pecans, egg, ½ cup of the Swiss cheese and ¼ cup of the Parmesan cheese in large bowl. Grease 12-inch pizza pan. Evenly press rice mixture onto bottom and up side of pan to create ½-inch rim. Bake 10 to 12 minutes; set aside to cool.

Heat olive oil over medium heat in large skillet. Add duck, onion, peppers, mushrooms and olives. Cook and stir 5 to 7 minutes.

Spread pizza sauce over cooled rice crust. Layer 1 cup of the Swiss cheese, the duckling mixture, Italian seasoning, mint and basil on pizza sauce. Top with remaining 1 cup Swiss cheese and ¼ cup Parmesan. Bake 15 to 20 minutes. Let cool slightly. Garnish as desired.

Baked Garlic Bundles

♦ Mark Douglas from Riverside, California was the second place winner in the Great Garlic Recipe Contest sponsored by the Fresh Garlic Association in association with the Gilroy Garlic Festival, Gilroy, California.

Makes 24 to 27 appetizers

½ of 16-ounce package frozen phyllo dough, thawed
¾ cup butter, melted
3 large heads fresh garlic,* separated into cloves and peeled
½ cup walnuts, finely chopped
1 cup Italian-style bread crumbs

Preheat oven to 350°F. Remove phyllo from package; unroll and place on waxed paper. With a pizza cutter or sharp knife, cut phyllo crosswise into 2-inch wide strips. Cover with another sheet of waxed paper and a damp cloth. (Caution: Phyllo dries out quickly if not covered.) Lay 1 strip at a time on a flat surface and brush immediately with melted butter. Place 1 clove of garlic at 1 end. Sprinkle about 1 teaspoon walnuts along length of strip. Roll up garlic clove in strip, tucking in side edges as you go. Brush with more butter. Roll in bread crumbs. Repeat until all but smallest garlic cloves are used. Place bundles on rack in shallow roasting pan and bake 20 minutes.

**This whole garlic bulb is called a head.* *See page 40 for helpful tips on peeling garlic.*

Cheesy Sun Crisps

♦ Mrs. Orlen Sheldon from Washburn, North Dakota was the second place winner in the Sunflower Council Recipe Contest sponsored by the National Sunflower Association.

Makes 4 to 5 dozen crackers

2 cups (8 ounces) shredded Cheddar cheese
½ cup grated Parmesan cheese
½ cup sunflower oil margarine, softened
3 tablespoons water
1 cup all-purpose flour
¼ teaspoon salt (optional)
1 cup uncooked quick oats
⅔ cup roasted, salted sunflower kernels

Beat cheeses, margarine and water in large bowl until well blended; add flour and salt; mix well. Stir in oats and sunflower kernels; mix until well combined. Shape dough into 12-inch-long roll; wrap securely. Refrigerate about 4 hours (dough may be stored up to 1 week in refrigerator).

Preheat oven to 400°F. Lightly grease cookie sheets. Cut roll into ⅛- to ¼-inch slices; flatten each slice slightly. Place on prepared cookie sheets. Bake 8 to 10 minutes or until edges are light golden brown. Remove immediately; cool on wire rack.

PARTY PLEASERS

Fresh ginger is completely different from dry ginger powder both in appearance and flavor. Resembling a gnarled, tan-colored root, fresh ginger adds its own pungency and aroma to foods and is used extensively in the dishes of the Far East. Store fresh ginger indefinitely by peeling and cutting it into small chunks. Put it in a glass jar and add enough dry sherry to cover. Store, covered, in the refrigerator.

Hot 'n' Honeyed Chicken Wings

♦ Mary Lou Newhouse from South Burlington, Vermont won first prize in the Snacks and Appetizers category of the Pace® Picante Sauce "Pick Up the Pace" Recipe Contest sponsored by Pace Foods, Inc.

Makes about 34 appetizers

3 pounds chicken wings
¾ cup Pace® picante sauce
⅔ cup honey
⅓ cup soy sauce
¼ cup Dijon-style mustard
3 tablespoons vegetable oil
2 tablespoons grated fresh ginger
½ teaspoon grated orange peel
Additional Pace® picante sauce

Cut off and discard wing tips; cut each wing in half at joint. Place in 13 x 9-inch baking dish. Combine 3/4 cup picante sauce, honey, soy sauce, mustard, oil, ginger and orange peel in small bowl; mix well. Pour over chicken wings. Cover and refrigerate at least 6 hours or overnight. Preheat oven to 400°F. Place chicken wings and sauce in single layer on foil-lined 15 x 10-inch jelly-roll pan. Bake 40 to 45 minutes or until brown. Serve warm with additional picante sauce. Garnish as desired.

Deep Fried Stuffed Shells

♦ Clarice Moberg from Redstone, Montana was a winner in the Appetizing Appetizers Pasta Contest sponsored by the North Dakota Wheat Commission and the North Dakota Mill, Bismark, North Dakota.

Makes 8 servings

16 uncooked jumbo-size pasta shells
2 eggs, divided
1 can (6½ ounces) tuna, drained and flaked ***or*** **1 can (6 ounces) crabmeat, drained, flaked and cartilage removed**
1 cup (4 ounces) shredded Cheddar or Swiss cheese
1 medium-size tomato, peeled, seeded and chopped
2 tablespoons sliced green onion
½ teaspoon dried basil, crushed
⅛ teaspoon black pepper
1 tablespoon water
1 cup dry bread crumbs
Vegetable oil, for frying
Tartar sauce, for serving

Add shells gradually to 6 quarts boiling salted water and cook until tender, yet firm. Drain; rinse with cold water, then drain again. Set aside to cool.

Slightly beat 1 egg; combine with tuna, cheese, tomato, green onion, basil and pepper in medium-size bowl. Stuff cooked shells with tuna mixture.

Beat remaining 1 egg with water in small bowl. Dip each stuffed shell in egg mixture and roll in bread crumbs. Heat 2 inches oil in large heavy saucepan over medium-high heat until oil reaches 365°F; adjust heat to maintain temperature. Fry shells, a few at a time, in hot oil 1½ to 2 minutes or until golden brown. Drain on paper towels. Serve with tartar sauce. Garnish as desired.

Scallops à la Schaller

♦ Veronica Schrader from Cranbury, New Jersey was a prize winner in the "Fabulous Fishing for Compliments" Recipe Contest sponsored by the New Jersey Department of Agriculture, Fish and Seafood Development Program.

Makes 4 servings

1 pound bacon, cut in half crosswise
2 pounds small sea scallops
½ cup olive oil
½ cup dry vermouth
2 tablespoons chopped parsley
1 teaspoon garlic powder
1 teaspoon black pepper
½ teaspoon onion powder
Dash of oregano
Salad greens, for serving

Wrap 1 bacon piece around each scallop; if necessary secure with wooden toothpick. Place wrapped scallops in baking dish. Combine olive oil, vermouth, parsley, garlic powder, pepper, onion powder and oregano in small bowl. Pour over scallops. Cover and refrigerate at least 4 hours.

Remove scallops from marinade. Arrange on broiler pan. Broil, 4 inches from heat, 7 to 10 minutes or until bacon is brown. Turn over and brown other side for about 5 minutes. Remove wooden toothpicks. Arrange on platter lined with greens. Garnish as desired.

Carrots have been around since ancient times, but were not widely used until the Middle Ages. At that time, they were red, purple or black in color. It wasn't until the 16th century that a yellow strain became popular. By the next century, in Holland, it had evolved into the familiar orange vegetable we know today.

Twelve Carat Black-Eyed Pea Relish

♦ Lauralyn Murphy from Dallas, Texas was the third place winner at the Black-Eyed Pea Jamboree, Athens, Texas.

Makes 2 to 3 pints

1 cup vinegar
¼ cup vegetable oil
2 cans (15 ounces each) black-eyed peas, drained
12 small carrots, steamed until crisp-tender, coarsely chopped
1 sweet onion, finely chopped
1 green bell pepper, finely chopped
1 cup sugar
¼ cup Worcestershire sauce
2 teaspoons black pepper
2 teaspoons salt (optional)
2 dashes ground red pepper

Combine vinegar and oil in small saucepan. Bring to a boil. Combine black-eyed peas, carrots, onion, green pepper, sugar, Worcestershire sauce, black pepper, salt and ground red pepper in large bowl. Pour oil mixture over vegetable mixture. Cover and refrigerate at least 24 hours to allow flavors to blend. Store covered in glass containers in refrigerator. Serve cold; garnish as desired.

Sour cream will curdle if it becomes too hot and there are no culinary tricks that will restore it. Always add sour cream at the end of the cooking time and heat it only until it is warm, not hot, and never to a boil.

Sesame-Sour Cream Meatballs

♦ Marella Presler from Gackle High School was a winner in the North Dakota High School Beef Bash sponsored by the North Dakota CattleWomen and the North Dakota Beef Commission in cooperation with the State Board for Vocational Education.

Makes 4 dozen meatballs

1½ pounds ground beef
⅔ cup minced onion
½ cup fresh bread crumbs
1 egg
¼ cup milk
½ teaspoon salt
⅛ teaspoon black pepper
⅛ teaspoon ground ginger
2 tablespoons vegetable oil
2 tablespoons butter or margarine
½ cup beef broth
Sesame-Sour Cream Sauce (recipe follows)
Toasted sesame seeds

Combine ground beef, onion, bread crumbs, egg, milk, salt, pepper and ginger in large bowl. Shape into 1-inch meatballs. Heat oil and butter over medium heat in skillet. Add meatballs and brown on all sides. Add broth. Cover and simmer 5 to 10 minutes. Prepare Sesame-Sour Cream Sauce. Place hot meatballs in serving bowl; top with sauce. Sprinkle with toasted sesame seeds. Garnish as desired.

Sesame-Sour Cream Sauce: Melt 2 tablespoons butter or margarine in small saucepan. Blend in 2 tablespoons all-purpose flour, ½ teaspoon ginger and ¼ teaspoon salt. Cook until bubbly. Add ½ cup beef broth. Cook until thickened, stirring constantly. Add 1 tablespoon soy sauce and 2 tablespoons toasted sesame seeds. Remove from heat; pour into small bowl. Add ¾ cup sour cream, stirring until smooth.

Chilled Seafood Antipasta

♦ T.J. Planteck from Skillman, New Jersey was a prize winner in the "Fabulous Fishing for Compliments" Recipe Contest sponsored by the New Jersey Department of Agriculture, Fish and Seafood Development Program.

Makes 8 servings

12 ounces scallops, cleaned
7 tablespoons olive oil, divided
2 teaspoons lemon juice
1 pound cod fillets, cut into cubes
1 tablespoon *each* sugar and dry minced onion
1 teaspoon salt
½ teaspoon *each* garlic powder, freshly ground black pepper and crushed red pepper
1 cup fresh basil leaves, divided
1 can (6 ounces) small ripe olives, pitted, drained
1 jar (5¾ ounces) Spanish green olives, drained
1 jar (4½ ounces) whole mushrooms, drained
1 can (8½ ounces) artichoke hearts, drained
12 ounces white Cheddar cheese, cut into 1-inch chunks
1 cup vegetable oil
⅔ cup vinegar

Cook and stir scallops and 4 tablespoons of the olive oil in large saucepan over high heat 2 to 4 minutes or just until opaque; remove. Stir in lemon juice; set aside. Repeat with remaining 3 tablespoons oil and the cod; remove.

Combine sugar, onion, salt, garlic powder, black pepper and red pepper in small bowl. Place ½ cup basil in 13 x 9-inch dish; sprinkle with half the sugar mixture. Add seafood; layer with olives, mushrooms, artichokes and cheese. Top with remaining sugar mixture and basil. Combine vegetable oil and vinegar; pour over seafood. Cover; refrigerate overnight. Remove and discard basil leaves if desired. Place seafood mixture onto lettuce-lined platter. Garnish as desired.

Award-Winning
PASTA

Spinach Stuffed Manicotti (page 84)

SUPERB SALADS

When pasta is served with legumes all the essential amino acids are present, making it a good choice for a vegetarian meal.

Seafood Pea-Ista Salad

♦ Kathy Lewis from Murchison, Texas was the second place winner at the Black-Eyed Pea Jamboree in Athens, Texas.

Makes 4 to 6 servings

½ cup mayonnaise or salad dressing
¼ cup zesty Italian salad dressing
2 tablespoons grated Parmesan cheese
2 cups canned green or yellow black-eyed peas, rinsed
8 ounces corkscrew pasta, cooked, rinsed and drained
1½ cups chopped imitation crabmeat (about 8 ounces)
1 cup broccoli flowerets, partially cooked
½ cup chopped green pepper
½ cup chopped tomato
¼ cup sliced green onions

Combine mayonnaise, Italian salad dressing and cheese in large bowl; blend well. Add peas, pasta, imitation crabmeat, broccoli, pepper, tomato and onions; toss gently to mix. Cover; refrigerate at least 2 hours.

Ingredients are added to give pasta its color. Beets and tomatoes make a reddish color, carrots make an orange color, spinach makes a green color and squid ink makes a black color.

Rainbow Pasta Salad

♦ Jodi Magrum from Braddock, North Dakota was the fourth place winner in the Sensational Salads Pasta Contest sponsored by the North Dakota Wheat Commission.

Makes 4 servings

8 ounces uncooked tricolor corkscrew pasta, cooked, rinsed, drained and cooled
2 cans (4½ ounces each) medium shrimp, drained *or* ½ pound cooked fresh shrimp, peeled
½ cup chopped walnuts (optional)
¼ cup French salad dressing
¼ cup mayonnaise
2 tablespoons sliced pimiento-stuffed green olives
1 teaspoon finely chopped onion
Lettuce leaves
Grape clusters (optional)
Lemon peel strips (optional)

Combine pasta, shrimp, walnuts, salad dressing, mayonnaise, olives and onion in large bowl; toss gently to coat. Cover; refrigerate at least 2 hours. Serve over lettuce. Garnish with grapes and lemon peel.

The artichoke, long considered a mysterious delicacy, is available all year. Artichokes have a subtle, sweet and somewhat nutty flavor. During spring months artichokes should be bright green. They may appear bronzed in winter. Don't worry, these artichokes are "winter-kissed" by frost, which doesn't affect flavor.

Pasta Salad in Artichoke Cups

♦ Richard Hansen was a finalist in the Castroville Artichoke Festival, Castroville, California.

Makes 6 servings

5 cloves garlic
½ cup white wine
6 medium artichokes for cups
1 lemon, cut into halves
1 tablespoon *plus* 1 teaspoon olive oil, divided
Chicken broth
Basil Vinaigrette Dressing (recipe follows)
8 ounces uncooked corkscrew pasta or pasta twists, cooked, rinsed and drained
½ teaspoon dried basil leaves, crushed
2 cups sliced cooked artichoke hearts (not marinated)

Simmer garlic and wine in small saucepan 10 minutes. Meanwhile, cut bottoms of artichokes flat and remove outer leaves. Cut 1 inch from tops; snip tips from remaining leaves and rub ends with lemon. Add artichokes, wine-garlic mixture and 1 tablespoon oil to 2 inches boiling chicken broth in large saucepan. Cover; simmer 25 to 30 minutes or until leaves pull easily from base. Drain.

Prepare Basil Vinaigrette Dressing. Sprinkle pasta with remaining 1 teaspoon oil and basil.

Combine pasta, sliced artichoke hearts and 1 cup dressing in large bowl; toss gently to coat. Carefully, spread outer leaves of whole artichokes; remove the small heart leaves and scoop out the fuzzy choke. Fill with pasta mixture. Cover; refrigerate until serving time. Serve with remaining dressing. Garnish as desired.

Basil Vinaigrette Dressing: Combined ⅓ cup wine vinegar, 2 tablespoons Dijon mustard and 3 minced garlic cloves in blender or food processor. Cover; pulse until garlic is well mixed. Add ¾ cup coarsely cut fresh basil leaves; pulse mixture to blend. With motor running, slowly pour in 1 cup olive oil. Add salt and pepper to taste.

Chicken Salad Deluxe

♦ Julie Billstein from Shoreville, Minnesota was a first place winner in the Sensational Salads Pasta Contest sponsored by the North Dakota Wheat Commission.

Makes 20 servings

1¼ cups prepared buttermilk salad dressing
½ cup mayonnaise
3 tablespoons half-and-half
1¾ teaspoons Beau Monde seasoning
1 teaspoon salt
½ teaspoon pepper
5 whole chicken breasts (about 2 pounds), skinned, cooked and cubed
10 ounces uncooked 100% semolina medium shell macaroni, cooked, rinsed, drained and cooled
3 cups diced celery
2½ cups seedless green grapes, cut lengthwise into halves
1 package (12 ounces) slivered almonds, reserve 1 tablespoon for garnish
2 cans (2.25 ounces each) sliced water chestnuts, drained
½ cup chopped onion
Lettuce leaves
Parsley (optional)
Sliced star fruit (optional)
Cantaloupe slices

Combine salad dressing, mayonnaise, half-and-half, seasoning, salt and pepper in small bowl; blend well. Cover; refrigerate overnight to blend flavors.

Combine chicken, shells, celery, grapes, almonds, water chestnuts and onion in large bowl. Pour dressing over salad; toss gently to coat. Serve on lettuce. Garnish with reserved almonds, parsley and star fruit. Serve with cantaloupe slices.

Rotini Salad

♦ Diane Amble from Sarles, North Dakota was the fifth place winner in the Sensational Salads Pasta Contest sponsored by the North Dakota Wheat Commission.

Makes 8 to 10 servings

2 to 3 stalks broccoli
10 ounces uncooked rotini, cooked, rinsed, drained and cooled
1 can (6 ounces) small pitted ripe olives, drained
10 to 12 cherry tomatoes, cut into halves
½ medium red onion, thinly sliced
½ cup Italian salad dressing
1 to 2 tablespoons grated Parmesan cheese (optional)
Freshly ground black pepper
Carrot strips (optional)

Cut flowerets from broccoli. Peel stalks; cut into chunks. Cook broccoli in boiling salted water in medium saucepan over medium-high heat just until broccoli is bright green and tender-crisp. Drain; rinse under cold water and drain thoroughly. Combine broccoli, rotini, olives, tomatoes, onion and salad dressing in large bowl. Add cheese. Season to taste with pepper. Toss gently to coat. Cover; refrigerate at least 2 hours. Garnish with carrot strips.

ENTICING ENTREES

Peeling Garlic Cloves

To quickly peel whole garlic cloves, place the desired number of cloves in a small glass custard cup. Microwave at HIGH (100% power) until slightly softened, 5 to 10 seconds for 1 clove or 45 to 55 seconds for a whole head. Then just slip the garlic out of its skin; nothing could be easier! For more information on peeling cloves by a range-top method, see page 130.

Sweet Garlic with Chicken Pasta

♦ Chefs Suvit and Gordon from Washington, D.C. were semifinalists in the "Use Your Noodle" contest sponsored by the National Pasta Association.

Makes 6 to 8 servings

8 ounces garlic, minced
5½ tablespoons olive oil
1½ pounds shiitake mushrooms, sliced
2 cups fresh plum tomatoes, diced
1 cup chopped green onions
1 teaspoon crushed red pepper
2 cups chicken broth
1½ pounds chicken breasts, grilled, skinned, boned and diced
1 package (16 ounces) uncooked bow tie noodles, cooked, rinsed and drained
4 ounces cilantro, chopped and divided

Cook and stir garlic in hot oil in large skillet over medium-high heat until lightly browned. Add mushrooms, tomatoes, green onions and crushed red pepper. Cook and stir 2 minutes more. Add broth; simmer mixture to reduce slightly. Add chicken, noodles and ½ of the cilantro; heat through. Garnish with remaining cilantro.

Pasta that is "al dente" is tender but firm. Overcooked pasta is soft and shapeless.

Spinach Stuffed Manicotti

♦ Chef Toni Piccinini from San Francisco, California was a semifinalist in the "Use Your Noodle" recipe contest sponsored by the National Pasta Association.

Makes 4 servings

1 teaspoon dried rosemary leaves, crushed
1 teaspoon dried sage leaves, crushed
1 teaspoon dried oregano leaves, crushed
1 teaspoon dried thyme leaves, crushed
1 teaspoon chopped garlic
1½ teaspoons olive oil
1½ cups canned or fresh tomatoes, chopped
1 package (10 ounces) frozen spinach, cooked, drained and squeezed dry
4 ounces ricotta cheese
1 slice whole wheat bread, torn into coarse crumbs
2 egg whites, lightly beaten
8 uncooked manicotti shells, cooked, rinsed and drained
Yellow pepper rings (optional)
Sage sprig (optional)

Cook and stir rosemary, sage, oregano, thyme and garlic in oil in small saucepan over medium heat about 1 minute; do not let herbs turn brown. Add tomatoes; reduce heat to low. Simmer 10 minutes, stirring occasionally.

Combine spinach, cheese and bread crumbs in medium bowl. Fold in egg whites. Stuff manicotti with spinach mixture. Place ⅓ of the tomato mixture on bottom of 13×9-inch pan. Arrange manicotti in pan. Pour remaining tomato mixture over manicotti. Cover with foil. Bake in preheated 350°F. oven 30 minutes or until bubbly. Garnish with yellow pepper rings and sage sprig.

Tacos in Pasta Shells

♦ Mary Anne Alexander from Charlotte, North Carolina was third place winner in the Dairylicious Pasta Dishes contest sponsored by the Southeast United Dairy Industry Association, Inc., Atlanta, Georgia.

Makes 4 to 6 servings

1¼ pounds ground beef
1 package (3 ounces) cream cheese with chives, cubed and softened
1 teaspoon salt
1 teaspoon chili powder
18 uncooked jumbo pasta shells, cooked, rinsed and drained
2 tablespoons butter, melted
1 cup prepared taco sauce
1 cup (4 ounces) shredded Cheddar cheese
1 cup (4 ounces) shredded Monterey Jack cheese
1½ cups crushed tortilla chips
1 cup dairy sour cream
3 green onions, chopped
Leaf lettuce (optional)
Small pitted ripe olives (optional)
Cherry tomatoes (optional)

Cook beef in large skillet over medium-high heat until brown, stirring to separate meat; drain fat. Reduce heat to medium-low. Add cream cheese, salt and chili powder; simmer 5 minutes.

Toss shells with butter; fill with beef mixture. Arrange shells in buttered 13×9-inch pan. Pour taco sauce over each shell. Cover with foil. Bake in preheated 350°F. oven 15 minutes. Uncover; top with Cheddar cheese, Monterey Jack cheese and chips. Bake 15 minutes more or until bubbly. Top with sour cream and onions. Garnish with lettuce, olives and tomatoes.

Spaghetti Rolls

♦ Christine Fried from Mandan, North Dakota was a prize winner in the Beef Cook-Off contest sponsored by the North Dakota CattleWomen and the North Dakota Beef Commission.

Makes 4 servings

1½ pounds ground beef
1 tablespoon vegetable oil
1 tablespoon onion powder
1 teaspoon salt
½ teaspoon pepper
2 cups spaghetti sauce, divided
1 cup (4 ounces) shredded pizza-flavored cheese blend or mozzarella cheese
1 package (8 ounces) uncooked manicotti shells, cooked, rinsed and drained

Cook beef in oil in large skillet over medium-high heat until brown, stirring to separate meat; drain fat. Stir in onion powder, salt and pepper. Stir in 1 cup of the spaghetti sauce; cool and set aside.

Reserve ½ cup of the ground beef mixture. Combine remaining beef mixture with cheese in large bowl. Stuff into manicotti. Arrange in greased 13×9-inch pan. Combine remaining spaghetti sauce with reserved beef mixture in small bowl; blend well. Pour over manicotti. Cover with foil. Bake in preheated 350°F. oven 20 to 30 minutes or until hot. Garnish as desired.

Oregano grows in profusion in the Mediterranean, spilling down the hillsides and filling the air with fragrance. Literally translated, it means "joy of the mountain."

Shrimp in Angel Hair Pasta Casserole

♦ William Sarnecky from Chester, Virginia was a first place winner in the Dairylicious Pasta Dishes contest sponsored by the Southeast United Dairy Industry Association, Inc., Atlanta, Georgia.

Makes 6 servings

1 tablespoon butter
2 eggs
1 cup half-and-half
1 cup plain yogurt
½ cup (4 ounces) shredded Swiss cheese
⅓ cup crumbled feta cheese
⅓ cup chopped parsley
¼ cup chopped fresh basil *or* 1 teaspoon dried basil leaves, crushed
1 teaspoon dried oregano leaves, crushed
1 package (9 ounces) uncooked fresh angel hair pasta
1 jar (16 ounces) mild, thick and chunky salsa
1 pound medium shrimp, peeled and deveined
½ cup (4 ounces) shredded Monterey Jack cheese
Snow peas (optional)
Plum tomatoes stuffed with cottage cheese (optional)

With 1 tablespoon butter, grease 12×8-inch pan. Combine eggs, half-and-half, yogurt, Swiss cheese, feta cheese, parsley, basil and oregano in medium bowl; mix well. Spread ½ of the pasta on bottom of prepared pan. Cover with salsa. Add ½ of the shrimp. Cover with remaining pasta. Spread egg mixture over pasta and top with remaining shrimp. Sprinkle Monterey Jack cheese over top. Bake in preheated 350°F. oven 30 minutes or until bubbly. Let stand 10 minutes. Garnish with snow peas and stuffed plum tomatoes.

It is said that in Sicily, the housewives used to roll freshly made pasta onto knitting needles to dry, creating spiral shapes.

Beef Oriental

♦ Coreen Hoffert was a prize winner in the Beef Bash contest sponsored by the North Dakota CattleWomen and the North Dakota Beef Commission.

Makes 4 servings

1 pound ground beef
7 green onions, diagonally sliced into 2-inch pieces
3 tablespoons soy sauce
¼ teaspoon ground ginger
2 to 3 ribs celery, diagonally sliced into 1-inch pieces
8 mushrooms, sliced
1 package (20 ounces) frozen pea pods, rinsed under hot water and drained
1 can (8 ounces) tomato sauce
3 cups uncooked corkscrew pasta, cooked and drained
3 fresh tomatoes, cut into wedges
1 cup (4 ounces) shredded Cheddar cheese, divided
1 green pepper, cut into thin slices

Cook beef, onions, soy sauce and ginger in wok over medium-high heat until meat is brown, stirring to separate meat. Push mixture up the side of the wok. Add celery and mushrooms; stir-fry 2 minutes. Push up the side. Add pea pods and tomato sauce; cook 4 to 5 minutes, stirring every minute. Add pasta, tomatoes and ¾ cup of the cheese. Stir gently to combine all ingredients. Cook 1 minute. Add green pepper; sprinkle remaining cheese over top. Reduce heat to low; cook until heated through.

Noodles originated in Germany in the 13th century. Noodles derive their name from the German word "Nudeln" that means a pasta product made with eggs and shaped in ribbons.

Shrimp Noodle Supreme

♦ Glenda Beecher from Wray, Georgia was a finalist in the Dairylicious Pasta Dishes contest sponsored by the Southeast United Dairy Industry Association, Inc., Atlanta, Georgia.

Makes 6 servings

1 package (8 ounces) uncooked spinach noodles, hot cooked and drained
1 package (3 ounces) cream cheese, cubed and softened
1½ pounds medium shrimp, peeled and deveined
½ cup butter, softened
Salt and pepper to taste
1 can (10¾ ounces) condensed cream of mushroom soup
1 cup dairy sour cream
½ cup half-and-half
½ cup mayonnaise
1 tablespoon chopped chives
1 tablespoon chopped parsley
½ teaspoon Dijon mustard
¾ cup (6 ounces) shredded sharp Cheddar cheese
Tomato wedges (optional)
Parsley sprigs (optional)
Lemon slices (optional)
Paprika (optional)

Combine noodles and cream cheese in medium bowl. Spread noodle mixture in bottom of greased 13×9-inch glass casserole. Cook shrimp in butter in large skillet over medium-high heat until pink and tender, about 5 minutes. Season to taste with salt and pepper. Spread shrimp over noodles.

Combine soup, sour cream, half-and-half, mayonnaise, chives, chopped parsley and mustard in another medium bowl. Spread over shrimp. Sprinkle Cheddar cheese over top. Bake in preheated 325°F. oven 25 minutes or until hot and cheese melts. Garnish with tomato, parsley sprigs, lemon slices and paprika.

String Pie

♦ Melanie Cunningham was a prize winner in the Beef Bash contest sponsored by the North Dakota CattleWomen and the North Dakota Beef Commission.

Makes 6 to 8 servings

1 pound ground beef
½ cup chopped onion
¼ cup chopped green pepper
1 jar (15½ ounces) spaghetti sauce
8 ounces spaghetti, hot cooked and drained
⅓ cup grated Parmesan cheese
2 eggs, beaten
2 teaspoons butter
1 cup cottage cheese
½ cup (2 ounces) shredded mozzarella cheese

Cook beef, onion and green pepper in large skillet over medium-high heat until meat is brown, stirring to separate meat. Drain fat. Stir in spaghetti sauce; mix well. Combine spaghetti, Parmesan cheese, eggs and butter in large bowl; mix well. Place in bottom of 13×9-inch pan. Spread cottage cheese over top. Pour sauce mixture over cottage cheese. Sprinkle mozzarella cheese over top. Bake in preheated 350°F. oven until cheese melts, about 20 minutes.

Cheesy Chicken Roll-Ups

♦ Sheila Megill from Greenville, South Carolina was a finalist in the Dairylicious Pasta Dishes contest sponsored by the Southeast United Dairy Industry Association, Inc., Atlanta, Georgia.

Makes 6 servings

1 medium onion, diced
4 ounces fresh mushrooms, sliced
¼ cup butter
3 chicken breast halves, skinned, boned and cut into bite-sized pieces
¾ cup dry white wine
½ teaspoon dried tarragon leaves, crushed
½ teaspoon salt
½ teaspoon pepper
6 uncooked lasagna noodles, cooked, drained and each cut lengthwise into halves
1 package (8 ounces) cream cheese, cubed and softened
½ cup heavy cream
½ cup dairy sour cream
1½ cups (6 ounces) shredded Swiss cheese, divided
1 cup (4 ounces) shredded Muenster cheese, divided
3 tablespoons toasted sliced almonds
Chopped parsley (optional)

Cook and stir onion and mushrooms in melted butter in large skillet over medium-high heat until tender. Add chicken, wine, tarragon, salt and pepper; bring to a boil. Reduce heat to low; simmer 10 minutes.

Curl each lasagna noodle half into a circle; arrange in greased 13×9-inch pan. Using a slotted spoon, fill center of lasagna rings with chicken mixture. To remaining liquid in skillet, add cream cheese, heavy cream, sour cream, ¾ cup of the Swiss cheese and ½ cup of the Muenster cheese. Cook and stir until cheeses melt; do not boil. Pour over lasagna rings. Sprinkle remaining cheeses and almonds on top. Bake in preheated 325°F. oven 35 minutes or until bubbly. Sprinkle with parsley. Garnish as desired.

Polish Sausage is also called kielbasa. It is garlicky flavored and consists mainly of seasoned pork, although beef and veal are often added. It is commonly sold in long links that are smoked and precooked, ready to heat and serve. The method for making kielbasa has remained virtually unchanged for more than five hundred years and sausage connoisseurs consider it perfection.

Polish Reuben Casserole

♦ Darlene Lutz from New England, North Dakota was third place winner in "Casseroles of the Century" Pasta Contest sponsored by the North Dakota Wheat Commission.

Makes 8 to 10 servings

2 cans (10¾ ounces each) condensed cream of mushroom soup
1⅓ cups milk
½ cup chopped onion
1 tablespoon prepared mustard
2 cans (16 ounces each) sauerkraut, rinsed and drained
1 package (8 ounces) uncooked medium-width noodles
1½ pounds Polish sausage, cut into ½-inch pieces
2 cups (8 ounces) shredded Swiss cheese
¾ cup whole wheat bread crumbs
2 tablespoons butter, melted

Combine soup, milk, onion and mustard in medium bowl; blend well. Spread sauerkraut in greased 13×9-inch pan. Top with uncooked noodles. Spoon soup mixture evenly over top. Top with sausage, then cheese. Combine crumbs and butter in small bowl; sprinkle over top. Cover pan tightly with foil. Bake in preheated 350°F. oven 1 hour or until noodles are tender. Garnish as desired.

LUSCIOUS LASAGNA

Mozzarella is a soft white cheese that melts easily. In southern Italy, where it originated, it is made from the milk of buffaloes. In other parts of Italy and in North America, it is made from cows' milk.

Lazy Lasagna

♦ Mrs. B.J. Thompson from Devils Lake, North Dakota was a finalist in the North Dakota Dairy Cookoff sponsored by the North Dakota Dairy Promotion Commission.

Makes 8 to 10 servings

1 pound ground beef
1 jar (32 ounces) spaghetti sauce
1 pound cottage cheese
8 ounces dairy sour cream
8 uncooked lasagna noodles
3 packages (6 ounces each) sliced mozzarella cheese (12 slices)
½ cup grated Parmesan cheese
1 cup water

Cook beef in large skillet over medium-high heat until meat is brown, stirring to separate meat; drain fat. Add spaghetti sauce. Reduce heat to low. Heat through, stirring occasionally; set aside. Combine cottage cheese and sour cream in medium bowl; blend well.

Spoon 1½ cups of the meat sauce in bottom of 13×9-inch pan. Place ½ of the uncooked noodles over sauce, then ½ of the cheese mixture, 4 slices of the mozzarella, ½ of the remaining meat sauce and ¼ cup of the Parmesan cheese. Repeat layers starting with the noodles. Top with remaining 4 slices of mozzarella cheese. Pour water around the sides of the pan. Cover tightly with foil. Bake in preheated 350°F. oven 1 hour. Uncover; bake 20 minutes more or until bubbly. Let stand 15 to 20 minutes. Garnish as desired.

Brooklyn, New York has the distinction of being the home to the first commercial pasta plant in the United States. It was founded in 1848.

Lasagna Supreme

♦ Michelle Watson from Sapulpa, Oklahoma was a finalist in the A-OK Cook Off sponsored by various Oklahoma agricultural organizations, Oklahoma City, Oklahoma.

Makes 8 to 10 servings

½ pound ground Oklahoma beef
½ pound mild Italian sausage
½ cup chopped onion
2 cloves garlic, minced
1 can (16 ounces) tomatoes, undrained and cut up
1 can (6 ounces) tomato paste
2 teaspoons dried basil, crushed
1 teaspoon dried marjoram, crushed
1 can (4 ounces) sliced mushrooms, drained
2 eggs
1 pound cream-style cottage cheese
¾ cup grated Parmesan cheese, divided
2 tablespoons parsley flakes
½ teaspoon salt
½ teaspoon pepper
8 ounces uncooked lasagna noodles, cooked, rinsed and drained
2 cups (8 ounces) shredded Cheddar cheese
3 cups (12 ounces) shredded mozzarella cheese
Mixed salad (optional)

Cook meats, onion and garlic in large skillet over medium-high heat until meat is brown, stirring to separate meat; drain fat. Add tomatoes with juice, tomato paste, basil and marjoram. Reduce heat to low. Cover; simmer 15 minutes, stirring often. Stir in mushrooms; set aside.

Beat eggs in large bowl; add cottage cheese, ½ cup of the Parmesan cheese, parsley, salt and pepper. Mix well. Place ½ of the noodles in bottom of greased 13×9-inch pan. Spread ½ of the cheese mixture over noodles, then ½ of the meat mixture and ½ of the Cheddar and mozzarella cheeses. Repeat layers. Sprinkle with remaining ¼ cup Parmesan cheese. Bake in preheated 375°F. oven 40 to 45 minutes or until bubbly. Let stand 10 minutes. Serve with mixed salad.

Note: Lasagna may be assembled, covered and refrigerated. Bake in preheated oven 60 minutes or until bubbly.

Luscious Vegetarian Lasagna

♦ Ted Quanrud from Bismarck, North Dakota was a finalist in the North Dakota Dairy Cookoff sponsored by the North Dakota Dairy Promotion Commission.

Makes 6 to 8 servings

1 can (14½ ounces) tomatoes, undrained
1 can (12 ounces) tomato sauce
1 teaspoon dried oregano leaves, crushed
1 teaspoon dried basil leaves, crushed
Dash black pepper
1 large onion, chopped
1½ teaspoons minced garlic
2 tablespoons olive oil
2 small zucchini, chopped
8 ounces mushrooms, sliced
1 large carrot, chopped
1 green pepper, chopped
1 cup (4 ounces) shredded mozzarella cheese
2 cups 1% milkfat cottage cheese
1 cup grated Parmesan or Romano cheese
8 ounces uncooked lasagna noodles, cooked, rinsed and drained
Parsley sprigs (optional)

Simmer tomatoes with juice, tomato sauce, oregano, basil and black pepper in medium saucepan over low heat. Cook and stir onion and garlic in hot oil in large skillet over medium-high heat until onion is golden. Add zucchini, mushrooms, carrot and green pepper. Cook and stir until vegetables are tender, 5 to 10 minutes. Stir vegetables into tomato mixture; simmer 15 minutes. Combine mozzarella, cottage and Parmesan cheeses in large bowl; blend well.

Spoon about 1 cup sauce in bottom of 12×8-inch pan. Place a layer of noodles over sauce, then ½ of the cheese mixture and ½ of the remaining sauce. Repeat layers of noodles, cheese mixture and sauce. Bake in preheated 350°F. oven 30 to 45 minutes or until bubbly. Let stand 10 minutes. Garnish with parsley.

Substitution: Other vegetables may be added or substituted for the ones listed above.

Apple Lasagna

♦ Rhonda Jordahl from Fargo, North Dakota was third place winner in the Delicious Desserts Pasta Contest sponsored by the North Dakota Wheat Commission.

Makes 12 to 15 servings

2 cups (8 ounces) shredded Cheddar cheese
1 cup ricotta cheese
1 egg, lightly beaten
¼ cup granulated sugar
1 teaspoon almond extract
2 cans (20 ounces each) apple pie filling
8 uncooked lasagna noodles, cooked, rinsed and drained
6 tablespoons all-purpose flour
6 tablespoons packed brown sugar
¼ cup quick-cooking oats
½ teaspoon ground cinnamon
Dash ground nutmeg
3 tablespoons margarine
1 cup dairy sour cream
⅓ cup packed brown sugar

Combine Cheddar cheese, ricotta cheese, egg, granulated sugar and almond extract in medium bowl; blend well. Spread 1 can apple pie filling over bottom of greased 13×9-inch pan. Layer ½ of the noodles over filling, then spread cheese mixture over noodles. Top with remaining noodles, then remaining can of apple pie filling.

Combine flour, 6 tablespoons brown sugar, oats, cinnamon and nutmeg in small bowl. Cut in margarine until crumbly. Sprinkle over apple pie filling. Bake in preheated 350°F. oven 45 minutes. Cool 15 minutes.

Meanwhile, prepare garnish by blending sour cream and ⅓ cup brown sugar in small bowl until smooth. Cover; refrigerate.

To serve, cut lasagna into squares and garnish with sour cream mixture.

SAVORY SAUCES

Fettuccine with Duckling and Roasted Red Peppers

♦ Sharyn Lane from Coral Springs, Florida was second place winner in the Concord National Duckling Cookoff sponsored by Concord Farms®, Concord, North Carolina.

Makes 4 main-dish or 8 appetizer servings

1 Concord Farms® Duckling (4½ to 5½ pounds), thawed and quartered
Garlic powder
Onion salt
2 tablespoons butter or margarine, melted
1½ tablespoons all-purpose flour
1¼ cups heavy cream
2 tablespoons grated Parmesan cheese
1 pound uncooked fettuccine, hot cooked and drained
½ cup prepared roasted red peppers, drained
¼ cup chopped walnuts
¼ cup sliced pitted ripe olives

Place duckling, skin side up, on rack in shallow pan. Sprinkle with garlic powder and onion salt. Cook in 350°F. oven about 1½ hours or until internal temperature registers 185°F. when tested with a meat thermometer. Cool; remove bones and skin. Cut duckling into bite-sized pieces; set aside.

Combine butter and flour in medium saucepan; blend well. Cook 1 minute over medium heat. Gradually stir in cream. Stir in cheese. Cook until sauce thickens, stirring constantly.

Place fettuccine in large bowl. Add duckling, peppers, walnuts and olives. Pour sauce over fettuccine; toss gently to coat. Garnish as desired.

A handy tip from the California Tomato Advisory Board: To hasten ripening, place an apple in a paper bag with an unripe tomato.

Fresh Tomato Pasta Andrew

♦ Dahlia Haas from Los Angeles, California was the first place winner in the California Fresh Market Tomato Advisory Board Contest, Los Angeles, California.

Makes 2 main-dish or 4 appetizer servings

1 pound fresh tomatoes, cut into wedges
1 cup packed fresh basil leaves
2 cloves garlic, chopped
2 tablespoons olive oil
8 ounces Camenzola cheese *or* 6 ounces ripe Brie plus 2 ounces Stilton cheese, each cut into small pieces
Salt and white pepper to taste
4 ounces uncooked angel hair pasta, vermicelli or other thin pasta, hot cooked and drained
Grated Parmesan cheese

Place tomatoes, basil, garlic and oil in covered food processor or blender; pulse on and off until ingredients are coarsely chopped, but not pureed. Combine tomato mixture and Camenzola cheese in large bowl. Season to taste with salt and white pepper. Add pasta; toss gently until cheese melts. Serve with Parmesan cheese. Garnish as desired.

Leftover pasta can be frozen and reheated or microwaved. Refrigerated pasta can be freshened by rinsing with hot or cold water, depending on how you plan to use it.

Pasta Delight

♦ Chef Cherif Brahmi from Dallas, Texas was a semifinalist in the "Use Your Noodle" contest sponsored by the National Pasta Association.

Makes 4 to 6 servings

1 medium zucchini, sliced
1 tablespoon olive oil
2 tablespoons chopped shallots
2 cloves garlic, chopped
1 medium tomato, diced
2 tablespoons chopped fresh basil *or*
½ teaspoon dried basil, crushed
2 tablespoons grated Parmesan cheese
12 ounces uncooked penne pasta, hot cooked and drained

Cook and stir zucchini in hot oil in large skillet over medium-high heat. Reduce heat to medium. Add shallots and garlic; cook 1 minute. Add tomato; cook and stir 45 seconds. Add basil and cheese. Pour vegetable mixture over penne in large bowl; toss gently to mix.

The scallop has two shells like oysters and clams, but unlike them it swims in the water and moves along the ocean floor. A large muscle, sometimes called the eye, controls the movements of the shell. It is this muscle that opens and closes the shell and is the only part of the scallop that is usually eaten in North America.

Scallops with Vermicelli

♦ Maria Hannis from Plainfield, New Jersey was a finalist in the "Fishing for Compliments Recipe Contest" sponsored by the New Jersey Department of Agriculture.

Makes 4 servings

1 pound bay scallops
2 tablespoons fresh lemon juice
2 tablespoons chopped parsley
1 onion, chopped
1 clove garlic, minced
2 tablespoons olive oil
2 tablespoons butter, divided
1½ cups canned Italian tomatoes, undrained and cut up
2 tablespoons chopped fresh basil *or* ½ teaspoon dried basil, crushed
¼ teaspoon dried oregano leaves, crushed
¼ teaspoon dried thyme leaves, crushed
2 tablespoons heavy cream
Dash ground nutmeg
12 ounces uncooked vermicelli, hot cooked and drained

Rinse scallops. Combine scallops, lemon juice and parsley in glass dish. Cover; marinate in refrigerator while preparing sauce.

Cook and stir onion and garlic in oil and 1 tablespoon of the butter in large skillet over medium-high heat until onion is tender. Add tomatoes with juice, basil, oregano and thyme. Reduce heat to low. Cover; simmer 30 minutes, stirring occasionally.

Drain scallops. Cook and stir scallops in remaining 1 tablespoon butter in another large skillet over medium heat until scallops are opaque, about 2 minutes. Add cream, nutmeg and tomato sauce.

Pour sauce over vermicelli in large bowl; toss gently to coat. Garnish as desired.

Penne with Artichokes

♦ Chef Angelo Nicelli from Chicago, Illinois was a prize winner in the "Use Your Noodle" contest sponsored by the National Pasta Association.

Makes 4 to 6 servings

1 package (10 ounces) frozen artichokes
1¼ cups water
2 tablespoons lemon juice
5 cloves garlic, minced
2 tablespoons olive oil, divided
2 ounces sun-dried tomatoes, drained
2 small dried hot red peppers, crushed
2 tablespoons chopped parsley
¼ teaspoon salt
¼ teaspoon pepper
¾ cup fresh bread crumbs
1 tablespoon chopped garlic
12 ounces uncooked penne, hot cooked and drained
1 tablespoon grated Romano cheese

Cook artichokes in water and lemon juice in medium saucepan over medium heat until tender. Cool artichokes, then cut into quarters. Reserve artichoke liquid.

Cook and stir the 5 whole cloves garlic in 1½ tablespoons oil in large skillet over medium-high heat until golden. Reduce heat to low. Add artichokes and tomatoes; simmer 1 minute. Stir in artichoke liquid, red peppers, parsley, salt and pepper. Simmer 5 minutes.

Meanwhile, cook and stir bread crumbs and 1 tablespoon chopped garlic in remaining ½ tablespoon oil. Pour artichoke sauce over penne in large bowl; toss gently to coat. Sprinkle with bread crumb mixture and cheese.

Pasta should be cooked at a fast boil. This method circulates the pasta so that it cooks more evenly.

Spinach Pesto

♦ Penny Lockhart was the third place winner in the Great Garlic Recipe Contest, sponsored by the Fresh Garlic Association and the Gilroy Garlic Festival, Gilroy, California.

Makes 2 cups sauce

1 bunch fresh spinach, washed, dried and chopped
1 cup fresh parsley leaves, stems removed
⅔ cup grated Parmesan cheese
½ cup walnut pieces
6 cloves fresh garlic, crushed
4 flat anchovy filets
1 tablespoon dried tarragon leaves, crushed
1 teaspoon dried basil leaves, crushed
1 teaspoon salt
½ teaspoon pepper
¼ teaspoon anise or fennel seed
1 cup olive oil
Hot cooked spaghetti, pasta twists or shells
Mixed salad (optional)

Place all ingredients except oil and pasta in covered food processor. Process until mixture is smooth. With motor running, add oil in thin stream. Adjust seasonings, if desired. Pour desired amount over pasta; toss gently to coat. Serve with mixed salad. Garnish as desired.

Note: Sauce will keep about 1 week in a covered container in the refrigerator.

Wrap fresh ginger in a plastic bag and store in the refrigerator crisper for up to 2 weeks. To use fresh ginger, rinse and scrub outer skin before peeling with a sharp knife or vegetable peeler.

An Early Spring Pasta

◆ Chef Gregory Funk from Philadelphia, Pennsylvania was a semifinalist in the "Use Your Noodle" contest sponsored by the National Pasta Association.

Makes 4 to 6 servings

1 cup Oriental Dressing (recipe follows)
8 ounces cooked turkey breast, cut into julienne strips
4 ounces carrots, cut into julienne strips
4 ounces asparagus, diagonally sliced into 1-inch pieces
4 ounces spinach, chopped
12 ounces uncooked linguine, hot cooked and drained

Heat Oriental Dressing in large saucepan over high heat to a boil. Add turkey, carrots, asparagus and spinach; reduce heat to medium. Cook 2 to 3 minutes. Pour sauce over linguine in large bowl; toss gently to coat.

Oriental Dressing

1 large onion, sliced
1 cup water
¼ cup *each* soy sauce and rice vinegar
1 tablespoon *each* garlic and ginger root, minced
1 tablespoon *each* sesame oil and lemon juice
1½ teaspoons *each* sugar and pepper
1½ teaspoons hot pepper sauce
2 tablespoons cornstarch
¼ cup water

Spread onion on large baking pan. Heat in preheated 400°F. oven until edges are dark brown, about 15 minutes. Puree onion in covered food processor. Place onion and remaining ingredients except cornstarch and ¼ cup water in medium saucepan. Bring to a boil. Combine cornstarch and ¼ cup water in cup until smooth. Gradually stir into dressing mixture. Heat until mixture boils, stirring constantly. Reduce heat to low; simmer 2 to 3 minutes.

PASTA POTPOURRI

The word orzo actually means barley, even though the shape of this pasta looks more like rice. It is available in the pasta sections of large supermarkets.

Quick Beef Soup

♦ Aloiuse Michlitsch from Flasher, North Dakota was a prize winner in the North Dakota Beef Cook-Off sponsored by the North Dakota CattleWomen and the North Dakota Beef Commission.

Makes 6 servings

1½ pounds lean ground beef
1 cup chopped onion
2 cloves garlic, finely chopped
1 can (28 ounces) tomatoes, undrained
6 cups water
6 beef bouillon cubes
¼ teaspoon pepper
½ cup uncooked orzo
1½ cups frozen peas, carrots and corn vegetable blend
French bread (optional)

Cook beef, onion and garlic in large saucepan over medium-high heat until beef is brown, stirring to separate meat; drain fat.

Puree tomatoes with juice in covered blender or food processor. Add tomatoes, water, bouillon cubes and pepper to meat mixture. Bring to a boil; reduce heat to low. Simmer, uncovered, 20 minutes. Add orzo and vegetables. Simmer 15 minutes more. Serve with French bread.

Wisconsin Swiss Linguine Tart

♦ Michael Hove was a winner in the Supermarket Chef's Showcase sponsored by the Wisconsin Milk Marketing Board.

Makes 8 servings

½ cup butter, divided
2 cloves garlic, minced
30 thin French bread slices
3 tablespoons all-purpose flour
1 teaspoon salt
¼ teaspoon white pepper
Dash ground nutmeg
2½ cups milk
¼ cup grated Wisconsin Parmesan cheese
2 eggs, beaten
8 ounces fresh linguine, cooked and drained
2 cups (8 ounces) shredded Wisconsin Swiss cheese, divided
⅓ cup sliced green onions
2 tablespoons minced fresh basil *or* 1 teaspoon dried basil leaves, crushed
2 plum tomatoes, each cut lengthwise into eights

Melt ¼ cup butter in small saucepan over medium heat. Add garlic; cook 1 minute. Brush 10-inch pie plate with butter mixture. Line bottom and side of pie plate with bread, allowing up to 1-inch overhang. Brush bread with remaining butter mixture. Bake in preheated 400°F. oven 5 minutes or until lightly browned.

Melt remaining ¼ cup butter in medium saucepan over low heat. Stir in flour and seasonings. Gradually stir in milk; cook, stirring constantly, until thickened. Add Parmesan cheese. Stir some of the sauce into eggs; stir back into sauce. Set aside. Combine linguine, 1¼ cups of the Swiss cheese, onions and basil in large bowl. Pour sauce over linguine mixture; toss to coat. Pour into crust. Arrange tomatoes on top; sprinkle with remaining ¾ cup Swiss cheese. Bake in preheated 350°F. oven 25 minutes or until warm; let stand 5 minutes. Garnish as desired.

Most pastas are prepared with wheat flours or other cereal grains and water. If an egg is added to this mix, the product is then called a noodle.

Shaker Chicken and Noodle Soup

♦ Lorraine Bourgois from Bismarck, North Dakota was a runner-up in the Savory Soups Pasta Contest sponsored by the North Dakota Wheat Commission.

Makes 15 servings

13 cups chicken broth, divided
¼ cup dry vermouth
¼ cup butter or margarine
1 cup heavy cream
1 package (12 ounces) frozen or dry egg noodles
1½ cups water
¾ cup all-purpose flour
2 cups diced cooked chicken
Salt and pepper to taste
¼ cup finely chopped parsley (optional)

Combine 1 cup broth, vermouth and butter in small saucepan. Bring to a boil and cook until liquid is reduced to ¼ cup and has a syrupy consistency. Stir in cream; set aside.

Bring remaining broth to a boil in Dutch oven. Add noodles and cook until just tender. Combine water and flour in medium bowl until smooth. Stir into broth mixture. Boil for 2 minutes, stirring constantly. Stir in reserved cream mixture; add chicken. Season to taste with salt and pepper. Heat just to serving temperature. Do not boil. Sprinkle with parsley. Garnish as desired.

Note: This soup freezes well.

Peeling Garlic Cloves

To peel whole garlic cloves, trim off the ends and drop cloves into boiling water for 5 to 10 seconds. Immediately plunge into cold water, then drain. The peels should slip right off. If the cloves are to be minced, trim off the ends and crush with the bottom of a heavy saucepan or the flat side of a large knife. The peels can then be easily removed. *For information on peeling cloves by microwave oven method, see page 82.*

Spinach-Garlic Pasta with Garlic-Onion Sauce

♦ Ira Jacobson from Oakland, California was third place winner in the Great Garlic Recipe Contest, sponsored by the Fresh Garlic Association in association with the Gilroy Garlic Festival, Gilroy, California.

Makes 2 to 4 servings

SPINACH-GARLIC PASTA

1½ cups all-purpose flour, divided
2 eggs *plus* 4 yolks
1 tablespoon olive oil
½ pound fresh spinach, blanched, squeezed dry and finely chopped
6 large cloves fresh garlic, crushed and finely chopped
½ teaspoon salt

GARLIC-ONION SAUCE

½ cup butter
1 tablespoon olive oil
1 pound Vidalia or other sweet onions, sliced
⅓ cup chopped fresh garlic (about 12 large cloves)
1 tablespoon honey (optional)
¼ cup Marsala wine
Grated Parmesan cheese (optional)

For pasta, place 1 cup flour in large bowl. Make well in center; place eggs, yolks and olive oil in well. Add spinach, garlic and salt. Mix, working in more flour as needed. Knead until dough is smooth. Cover with plastic wrap. Let rest 15 to 30 minutes. Roll dough to desired thickness with pasta machine. Cut into desired width. Cook in boiling water about 2 minutes; drain.

For sauce, heat butter and oil in large skillet over medium heat. Add onions and garlic; cover and cook until soft. Add honey; reduce heat to low. Cook, uncovered, 30 minutes, stirring occasionally. Add wine; cook 5 to 10 minutes more. Pour sauce over pasta; toss gently to coat. Serve with cheese. Garnish as desired.

Almond Crunch Macaroni Custard

♦ Linda Jung from Norwich, North Dakota was first place winner in the Delicious Desserts Pasta Contest sponsored by the North Dakota Wheat Commission.

Makes 9 servings

CUSTARD
2 eggs
1 cup milk
½ cup packed brown sugar
¼ cup all-purpose flour
¼ cup butter, softened
1½ teaspoons almond extract
½ cup uncooked ring macaroni, cooked and drained

ALMOND TOPPING
½ cup slivered almonds
⅓ cup packed brown sugar
2 tablespoons butter, softened
1 tablespoon milk

For custard, combine all custard ingredients except macaroni in covered blender. Blend on medium speed 2 minutes. Fold macaroni into milk mixture in large bowl. Spoon into greased and floured 8-inch square pan. Bake in preheated 350°F. oven 40 to 45 minutes or until set.

For almond topping, mix all topping ingredients in small bowl. Spread over custard. Broil 2 to 3 minutes or until topping is bubbly and golden brown. Garnish as desired.

Award-Winning
CHICKEN

Bittersweet Farm Chicken (page 174)

(page 174)

Appetizers & Salads

Peeling Garlic Cloves

To peel whole garlic cloves, trim off the ends and drop cloves into boiling water for 5 to 10 seconds. Immediately plunge into cold water, then drain. The peels should slip right off. If the cloves are to be minced, trim off the ends and crush with the bottom of a heavy saucepan or the flat side of a large knife. The peels can then be easily removed.

Garlicky Gilroy Chicken Wings

♦ Winifred Harano from Los Angeles, California was the first place winner in the Great Garlic Recipe Contest, sponsored by the Fresh Garlic Association in association with the Gilroy Garlic Festival, Gilroy, California.

Makes about 6 appetizer servings

2 pounds chicken wings (about 15 wings)
3 heads fresh garlic,* separated into cloves and peeled
1 cup plus 1 tablespoon olive oil, divided
10 to 15 drops Tabasco pepper sauce
1 cup grated Parmesan cheese
1 cup Italian-style bread crumbs
1 teaspoon black pepper

Preheat oven to 375°F. Disjoint chicken wings, removing tips. (If desired, save tips to make chicken stock.) Rinse wings; pat dry. Place garlic, 1 cup oil and the pepper sauce in food processor or blender container; cover and process until smooth. Pour garlic mixture into small bowl. Combine cheese, bread crumbs and black pepper in shallow dish. Dip wings into garlic mixture, then roll, one at a time, in crumb mixture until thoroughly coated. Brush shallow nonstick pan with remaining 1 tablespoon oil; arrange wings in a single layer. Drizzle remaining garlic mixture over wings; sprinkle with remaining crumb mixture. Bake 45 to 60 minutes or until brown and crisp. Garnish as desired.

**The whole garlic bulb is called a head.*

Mozzarella is a soft white cheese that melts easily. In southern Italy, where it originated, it is made from the milk of buffaloes. In other parts of Italy and in North America, it is made from cows' milk.

Chicken Pizza

♦ Mary Cerami of California was a prize winner in the National Chicken Cooking Contest, sponsored by the National Broiler Council.

Makes 8 appetizer servings

1 package (8 ounces) refrigerated crescent dinner rolls
2 whole chicken breasts, split, skinned and boned
¼ cup vegetable oil
1 large onion, sliced into thin rings
1 large green bell pepper, sliced into thin rings
½ pound fresh mushrooms, sliced
½ cup pitted ripe olives, sliced
1 can (10½ ounces) pizza sauce with cheese
1 teaspoon garlic salt
1 teaspoon dried oregano
¼ cup grated Parmesan cheese
2 cups (8 ounces) shredded mozzarella cheese

Preheat oven to 425°F. Separate crescent dough into 8 triangles. Press triangles into lightly oiled 12-inch pizza pan, covering it completely. Cut chicken into 1-inch pieces. Heat oil in large skillet over medium-high heat. Add chicken, onion, green pepper, mushrooms and olives. Cook and stir about 5 minutes or until chicken is cooked. Spread pizza sauce over dough. Spoon chicken mixture evenly over sauce. Sprinkle with garlic salt, oregano and Parmesan cheese. Top with mozzarella cheese. Bake 20 minutes or until crust is golden brown.

Dipper's Nuggets Chicken

♦ Norma Young from Arkansas was a prize winner in the National Chicken Cooking Contest, sponsored by the National Broiler Council.

Makes 8 appetizer servings

2 whole chicken breasts, split, skinned and boned
Vegetable oil
1 egg
⅓ cup water
⅓ cup all-purpose flour
2 teaspoons sesame seeds
1½ teaspoons salt
Dipping Sauces (recipes follow)
Red onion rings, for garnish

Cut chicken into 1-inch pieces. Heat 3 inches oil in large heavy saucepan over medium-high heat until oil reaches 375°F; adjust heat to maintain temperature. Meanwhile, beat egg and water in large bowl until well mixed. Add flour, sesame seeds and salt, stirring to form smooth batter. Dip chicken pieces into batter, draining off excess. Fry chicken, a few pieces at a time, in hot oil about 4 minutes or until golden brown. Drain on paper towels. Serve with Dipping Sauces; garnish with onion rings.

Dipping Sauces

Nippy Pineapple Sauce: Mix 1 jar (12 ounces) pineapple preserves, ¼ cup prepared mustard and ¼ cup prepared horseradish in small saucepan. Cook and stir over low heat 5 minutes.

Dill Sauce: Combine ½ cup sour cream, ½ cup mayonnaise, 2 tablespoons finely chopped dill pickle and 1 teaspoon dill weed in small bowl. Cover; refrigerate 1 hour.

Royalty Sauce: Combine 1 cup catsup, 6 tablespoons butter or margarine, 2 tablespoons vinegar, 1 tablespoon brown sugar and ½ teaspoon dry mustard in small saucepan. Cook and stir over low heat 5 minutes.

Hot Chinese Chicken Salad

♦ Fayne Lutz from New Mexico was a prize winner in the National Chicken Cooking Contest, sponsored by the National Broiler Council.

Makes 4 servings

8 chicken thighs, skinned, boned and cut into bite-sized pieces
1/4 cup cornstarch
1/4 cup vegetable oil
1 large ripe tomato, cut into pieces
1 can (4 ounces) water chestnuts, drained and sliced
1 can (4 ounces) sliced mushrooms, drained
1 cup coarsely chopped green onions
1 cup diagonally sliced celery
1/4 cup soy sauce
1 teaspoon monosodium glutamate
1/8 teaspoon garlic powder
2 cups finely shredded iceberg lettuce
Orange slices, for garnish
Hot cooked rice

Dredge chicken, one piece at a time, in cornstarch. Heat oil in wok or large skillet over medium-high heat. Add chicken; stir-fry about 3 minutes or until browned. Add tomato, water chestnuts, mushrooms, green onions, celery, soy sauce, monosodium glutamate and garlic powder. Cover; simmer 5 minutes. Place lettuce on large serving plate. Top with chicken mixture; garnish with orange slices. Serve immediately with rice.

Roasting and Peeling Peppers

Place peppers on a rack in a broiler pan 3 to 5 inches from heat source, or hold over an open gas flame on the end of a long-handled metal fork. Roast peppers, turning often, until blistered and charred on all sides. Transfer to a plastic bag; seal bag and let stand 15 to 20 minutes to loosen the skins. Remove loosened skins with a paring knife. Cut peppers in half and remove the seeds and stems.

Grilled Chicken, Corn & Avocado Salad

♦ Philippa Farrar from Santa Barbara, California was a finalist at the California Avocado Festival Cook-Off, Carpinteria, California.

Serves 4

2 tablespoons lime juice
2 tablespoons vinegar
1 cup olive oil
1 small bunch cilantro, divided
1 clove garlic, peeled
2 green onions, cut into 1-inch pieces
Salt and black pepper to taste
6 ears fresh corn,* silk and husks intact
2 whole chicken breasts, split and boned
2 Anaheim or poblano peppers,* roasted, peeled and diced
1 large red bell pepper,* roasted, peeled and diced
2 large avocados, peeled, pitted and diced
Crisp salad greens

Pour lime juice and vinegar into food processor or blender container. With processor on, slowly add oil. Add ¾ of the cilantro leaves; process until leaves are finely chopped. Add garlic, green onions, salt and black pepper; process until onions are chopped. Set dressing aside.

Roast corn in husks on covered grill over medium-hot heat about 25 minutes or until tender. Cool slightly, then remove husks and silk. Cut corn from cobs; set aside.

Season chicken with salt and black pepper. Grill or broil skin side 8 minutes. Turn and cook 5 minutes more or until chicken is tender; keep warm.

Toss corn with roasted peppers, avocados and desired amount of dressing in large bowl. Arrange chicken on serving plate lined with greens. Garnish with remaining cilantro. Serve with corn mixture; pass remaining dressing.

**Two cups frozen corn, cooked, 1 can (4 ounces) chopped green chilies, drained, and 1 jar (7 ounces) roasted red peppers, drained, may be substituted for the fresh corn and peppers.*

The same grapes that are eaten fresh are used for making wine and raisins. Though seedless grapes are by far the most popular, especially the white Thompson variety, those who grow them are convinced that the ones with seeds have a better flavor. In the industry there are rumors that new varieties will be coming along that are three to four times larger than those in the markets today.

Lagoon Chicken Salad

♦ Gloria Kirchman from Minnesota was a prize winner in the National Chicken Cooking Contest, sponsored by the National Broiler Council.

Makes 4 to 6 servings

1½ cups unsweetened apple juice
2 whole chicken breasts
3 cups cooked rice
1½ cups seedless green grapes, halved
1 cup chopped unpeeled apple
½ cup chopped celery
¾ cup slivered almonds, divided
½ cup chopped water chestnuts
1 cup mayonnaise
½ teaspoon seasoned salt
¼ teaspoon ground cinnamon
Fresh spinach leaves
Apple slices, for garnish

Bring apple juice to a simmer in deep saucepan over medium heat; add chicken. Cover; simmer about 30 minutes or until tender. Remove chicken from pan; cool. (Reserve broth for another use, if desired.) Remove and discard skin and bones; dice chicken.

Gently toss chicken with rice, grapes, apple, celery, ½ cup of the almonds and the water chestnuts in large bowl. Combine mayonnaise, seasoned salt and cinnamon in small bowl; add to chicken mixture and toss lightly. Cover; refrigerate at least 30 minutes. To serve, spoon chicken mixture onto spinach-lined platter. Sprinkle with remaining ¼ cup almonds; garnish with apple slices.

Montmorency Cherry Chicken Salad

♦ Linda Burke from Williamsville, New York was a finalist in the Cherry Creations Recipe Contest, sponsored by the New York Cherry Growers Association.

Serves 6

3 nectarines or peaches, divided
2 cups tart red Montmorency cherries, pitted*
3 cups cooked cubed chicken
1½ cups sliced celery
2 tablespoons sliced green onions
1 cup mayonnaise
¼ cup sour cream
2 tablespoons honey
1 teaspoon lemon juice
¼ to ½ teaspoon curry powder
⅛ teaspoon ground ginger
Salt to taste
½ cup toasted slivered almonds, divided
Boston or Bibb lettuce leaves

Slice 1 of the nectarines; combine with cherries, chicken, celery and green onions in large bowl. Combine mayonnaise, sour cream, honey, lemon juice, curry powder, ginger and salt in small bowl, mixing well. Pour mayonnaise mixture over chicken mixture; toss to coat. Cover; refrigerate until chilled. Just before serving, stir in all but 1 tablespoon of the almonds. Arrange chicken salad on lettuce-lined salad plates. Slice remaining 2 nectarines; garnish with nectarines and almonds.

**Fresh, canned or frozen cherries may be used. Thaw frozen cherries. Drain canned and thawed cherries before using.*

Making Mayonnaise

When making mayonnaise, it is essential to add the oil gradually to the egg yolks in order for the mixture to thicken properly. If the oil is added too quickly, the mayonnaise will be runny and the oil will separate from the yolks.

When mixing mayonnaise by hand, start beating in the oil a drop or two at a time until you have incorporated 2 or 3 tablespoons. Then, while beating constantly, begin to add the oil in a thin, steady stream.

When using a food processor or blender, substitute 1 whole egg for the 2 yolks; this makes the mayonnaise more stable and less likely to separate. Turn the machine on and add the oil a teaspoon at a time. After 1/4 cup has been added, pour the oil in a thin, steady stream while processing continuously.

Rainbow Chicken Salad

♦ Pamela Stross from Colorado was a prize winner in the National Chicken Cooking Contest, sponsored by the National Broiler Council.

Makes 4 to 6 servings

2 cups water
2 whole chicken breasts
1 teaspoon salt
1/4 teaspoon pepper
Orange-Mustard Mayonnaise (recipe follows)
1 head romaine lettuce
2 avocados, peeled, pitted and sliced lengthwise
2 grapefruit, peeled and sectioned
Juice of 1 lemon
4 navel oranges, peeled and sectioned
1 red onion, sliced into rings
Orange zest, for garnish

Bring water to a simmer in deep saucepan over medium heat; add chicken, salt and pepper. Cover; simmer about 30 minutes or until tender. While chicken is cooking, prepare Orange-Mustard Mayonnaise. Remove chicken from pan; cool. (Reserve broth for another use, if desired.) Remove and discard skin and bones from chicken; cut into thin slices and set aside.

Arrange lettuce on platter with stalks toward center. Alternately arrange avocados and grapefruit around edge of lettuce; sprinkle with lemon juice. Arrange oranges and onion inside avocados and grapefruit. Arrange chicken in center. Spoon some Orange-Mustard Mayonnaise over chicken; garnish with orange zest. Serve with remaining mayonnaise.

Orange-Mustard Mayonnaise: Beat 2 egg yolks with 2 teaspoons Dijon-style mustard and 1 teaspoon lemon juice in medium-sized bowl. Gradually add 1 cup olive oil, beating in a drop or two at a time with a wire whisk. After 3 tablespoons have been added, pour in a thin, steady stream, beating constantly, until mixture thickens. Stir in grated peel of 1 orange, juice from 1/2 orange and salt and pepper to taste.

One-Dish Meals

Marinating chicken in a bath of flavorful liquids provides a twofold benefit: it infuses the chicken with a wonderful flavor and also increases its tenderness. Place the chicken in a plastic bag or shallow glass or stainless steel container. Pour the marinade over the chicken; cover and refrigerate for a few minutes, hours or overnight. The longer it marinates, the more flavor it will have. Turn the chicken occasionally so the marinade penetrates evenly.

Chicken Picante

♦ Sally Vog from Oregon was a prize winner in the National Chicken Cooking Contest, sponsored by the National Broiler Council.

Makes 6 servings

½ cup medium-hot chunky taco sauce
¼ cup Dijon-style mustard
2 tablespoons fresh lime juice
3 whole chicken breasts, split, skinned and boned
2 tablespoons butter or margarine
Chopped cilantro, for garnish
Plain yogurt

Combine taco sauce, mustard and lime juice in large bowl. Add chicken, turning to coat. Cover; marinate in refrigerator at least 30 minutes.

Melt butter in large skillet over medium heat until foamy. Remove chicken from marinade; reserve marinade. Add chicken to skillet; cook about 10 minutes or until brown on both sides. Add marinade; cook about 5 minutes or until chicken is tender and marinade glazes chicken. Remove chicken to serving platter. Boil marinade over high heat 1 minute; pour over chicken. Garnish with cilantro. Serve with yogurt.

Sauerkraut is chopped cabbage that has been salted and fermented. It is German in origin and literally means "sour cabbage." This does not mean you should ignore the expiration date on the package. Sauerkraut that has gone sour is not the same thing as cabbage that has been intentionally fermented and salt-pickled.

Baked Chicken Reuben

♦ Marcia Adams from Indiana was a prize winner in the National Chicken Cooking Contest, sponsored by the National Broiler Council.

Makes 6 to 8 servings

4 whole chicken breasts, split, skinned and boned
1/4 teaspoon salt
1/8 teaspoon pepper
1 can (16 ounces) sauerkraut, well drained
4 (6×4-inch) slices Swiss cheese
1 1/4 cups Thousand Island salad dressing

Preheat oven to 325°F. Place chicken in a single layer in greased baking pan. Sprinkle with salt and pepper. Press excess liquid from sauerkraut; spoon over chicken. Arrange cheese slices over sauerkraut. Pour dressing evenly over the top. Cover pan with aluminum foil. Bake about 1 1/2 hours or until chicken is tender.

Green onion brushes make a pretty garnish. Trim roots and most of the green tops from green onions. Make parallel cuts, about 1½ inches long, along the length of each onion at the root end or both ends. Fan out the cuts to form a brush. If desired, place the brushes in a bowl of ice water for several hours so they open and curl.

Chicken Cherry-Yaki Stir-Fry

♦ Marion C. Boesl from Williamsville, New York was first place winner in the Cherry Creations Recipe Contest, sponsored by the New York Cherry Growers Association.

Serves 4

1½ cups tart red cherries, pitted (frozen or canned)
2 whole chicken breasts, split, skinned and boned
2 tablespoons teriyaki sauce
2 tablespoons dry sherry
1 tablespoon lemon juice
3 (¼-inch) slices fresh ginger
1 tablespoon cornstarch
2 to 3 tablespoons peanut or vegetable oil
6 green onions, diagonally sliced into 1-inch pieces
2 small carrots, thinly sliced
2 cups snow peas
4 ounces sliced water chestnuts, drained
2 ounces Chinese rice stick noodles, cooked *or* 2 cups hot cooked rice
¼ cup slivered toasted almonds, for garnish
4 green onion brushes, for garnish

Thaw cherries if frozen. Drain cherries, reserving juice; set aside. Cut chicken into bite-sized cubes. Combine teriyaki sauce, sherry, lemon juice and ginger in small bowl; stir in chicken. Cover; marinate in refrigerator 1 hour, stirring once or twice.

Drain chicken, reserving marinade. Discard ginger. Blend reserved cherry juice into cornstarch; stir in marinade and set aside. Heat 2 tablespoons oil in wok or large skillet over high heat. Add sliced green onions, carrots and snow peas; stir-fry 2 to 3 minutes or until crisp-tender. Remove vegetables from wok; add more oil to wok, if needed. Add chicken; stir-fry 2 to 3 minutes or until tender. Push chicken away from center of wok; add cornstarch mixture. Cook and stir until thickened and bubbly. Stir in chicken, cherries, vegetables and water chestnuts; heat through. Serve over noodles. Garnish with almonds and green onion brushes.

Rick's Good-As-Gold Chili

♦ Rick Christman from Mobridge, South Dakota was a prize winner at the Golden Chili Pepper Awards, sponsored by the American Spice Trade Association.

Makes 4½ cups

⅓ cup water
¼ cup instant minced onion
2 teaspoons instant minced garlic
½ cup vegetable oil
1½ pounds skinned and boned chicken breasts
1 can (15 ounces) tomato sauce
¾ cup beer
½ cup chicken broth
2 tablespoons chili powder
2 teaspoons ground cumin
1 teaspoon dried oregano, crushed
1 teaspoon soy sauce
1 teaspoon Worcestershire sauce
¾ teaspoon salt
½ teaspoon paprika
½ teaspoon ground red pepper
¼ teaspoon turmeric
⅛ teaspoon rubbed sage
⅛ teaspoon dried thyme, crushed
⅛ teaspoon dry mustard

Combine water, onion and garlic in small bowl; let stand for 10 minutes to soften. Heat oil in large skillet until hot. Add chicken, a few pieces at a time; cook until golden brown, about 5 minutes on each side. Remove and drain on paper towels. Cool slightly; cut into ¼-inch cubes and set aside. Pour off all but 2 tablespoons oil from skillet; heat oil until hot. Add softened onion and garlic; cook and stir about 5 minutes or until golden. Add remaining ingredients and chicken; mix well. Bring to a boil; reduce heat and simmer about 20 minutes, stirring occasionally, until sauce thickens slightly. Garnish as desired.

Chicken Timatar

♦ Raymonde Woodward from Enosburg Falls, Vermont was the third prize winner in the Delmarva Chicken Cooking Contest, Georgetown, Delaware.

Makes 6 servings

4 tablespoons vegetable oil
2 medium-size onions, chopped
6 cloves garlic, very finely chopped
4 whole cardamom pods *or* 1/4 teaspoon ground cardamom
1 (1-inch) piece fresh ginger, very finely chopped
1 (1-inch) cinnamon stick
1 teaspoon cumin seeds *or* 1/4 teaspoon ground cumin
1 bay leaf
6 whole chicken legs (thighs attached), skinned
3 medium-size tomatoes, chopped
1/2 teaspoon salt
1/2 teaspoon black pepper
1/8 teaspoon ground red pepper
2 tablespoons all-purpose flour
3 tablespoons water

Heat oil in large skillet or Dutch oven over medium-high heat. Add onions, garlic, cardamom, ginger, cinnamon, cumin and bay leaf. Reduce heat to medium; cook and stir 5 minutes. Add chicken, tomatoes, salt and black and red peppers. Bring to a boil, then reduce heat to low. Cover tightly; simmer 30 minutes or until chicken is tender, turning after 15 minutes. Combine flour and water; stir into tomato mixture. Cook and stir 5 minutes or until thickened. Remove cardamom pods, cinnamon stick and bay leaf before serving.

Boning a Chicken Breast

1. For easier handling, freeze the chicken until it is firm, but not hard. Remove the skin.

2. For each breast half, use a sharp knife to make three or four arched cuts between the meat and the bone, lifting the meat away with your free hand. (Or, slip your fingers between the meat and the bone and work the meat free without the aid of a knife.)

3. When the meat and bone are separated, remove the heavy white tendon that runs along the length of the breast. This will prevent the meat from shrinking as it cooks.

Chicken Mexicana

♦ Adrienne Sloboden from Puyallup, Washington was the grand prize winner in the Pace® Picante Sauce Young Cooks Recipe Contest, sponsored by Pace Foods, Inc.

Makes 4 servings

2 whole chicken breasts, split, skinned and boned
1/4 teaspoon garlic salt
2 tablespoons butter or margarine
1/2 cup sliced green onions with tops (1/2-inch slices)
1/2 cup chopped green bell pepper
2 to 3 cups hot cooked rice
1 cup Pace® picante sauce
4 ounces pasteurized process cheese spread, diced
Additional Pace® picante sauce

Sprinkle chicken with garlic salt. Melt butter in large skillet over medium heat. Add chicken; cook 5 minutes. Turn chicken over; add green onions and green pepper around edge of skillet. Cook 5 minutes more or until chicken is tender. Place rice on serving platter. Remove chicken and vegetables from skillet and arrange over rice; keep warm.

Add 1 cup picante sauce and the cheese spread to skillet. Cook and stir until cheese is melted and sauce is hot. Pour cheese sauce over chicken and vegetables. Garnish as desired. Serve with additional picante sauce.

Commercial poultry seasonings vary widely in flavor, depending on the company that produces them. Many are blends of three or more herbs, including parsley, thyme, sage, rosemary and marjoram.

Apple Curry Chicken

♦ Mary Oatway from Augusta, Maine was a finalist in the Delmarva Chicken Cooking Contest, Georgetown, Delaware.

Makes 4 servings

2 whole chicken breasts, split, skinned and boned
1 cup apple juice, divided
¼ teaspoon salt
Dash of pepper
1½ cups plain croutons
1 medium-size apple, chopped
½ cup finely chopped onion
¼ cup raisins
2 teaspoons brown sugar
1 teaspoon curry powder
¾ teaspoon poultry seasoning
⅛ teaspoon garlic powder

Preheat oven to 350°F. Lightly grease shallow baking dish. Arrange chicken breasts in a single layer in prepared pan. Combine ¼ cup of the apple juice, the salt and pepper in small bowl. Brush all of the mixture over chicken. Combine croutons, apple, onion, raisins, sugar, curry powder, poultry seasoning and garlic powder in large bowl. Stir in remaining ¾ cup apple juice; spread over chicken. Cover; bake about 45 minutes or until chicken is tender. Garnish as desired.

Stir-Frying Techniques

Follow these simple steps for successful stir-frying:

1. Prepare all the ingredients in advance, including cleaning, cutting, measuring and combining.

2. Cut the meat and vegetables into uniform sizes and shapes to ensure even cooking.

3. Make sure the oil is hot before adding any food to the pan. (The best oils to use for stir-frying are peanut, corn and soybean oils.)

4. Keep the food in constant motion, tossing and stirring it with a flat metal or wooden spatula. This prevents it from burning and also seals in the flavor.

Stir-Fried Chicken

♦ Hope Boyd from McAlester, Oklahoma was a prize winner at the A-OK Cook-Off, sponsored by various Oklahoma agricultural organizations, Oklahoma City, Oklahoma.

Makes about 6 servings

2 whole chicken breasts, split, skinned and boned
2 tablespoons vegetable oil
1 cup diagonally sliced celery
1 medium-size carrot, diagonally sliced
1 medium-size green bell pepper, cut into thin strips
1 cup sliced mushrooms
½ small onion, thinly sliced
1 teaspoon salt
¼ teaspoon ground ginger
1 can (16 ounces) bean sprouts, drained
1 can (5 ounces) water chestnuts, drained and sliced
¼ cup water
2 teaspoons cornstarch
2 tablespoons soy sauce
3 cups hot cooked rice
¾ cup peanuts

Slice chicken crosswise into ¼-inch strips. Heat oil in wok or large skillet over high heat. Add celery, carrot, green pepper, mushrooms, onion, salt and ginger. Stir-fry about 3 minutes or until vegetables are crisp-tender; remove from wok and keep warm. Add chicken to wok; stir-fry 3 to 5 minutes or until tender. Return vegetables to wok; stir in bean sprouts, water chestnuts and water. Blend cornstarch with soy sauce until smooth, then gradually stir into chicken and vegetables. Cook, stirring constantly, until thickened. Mound rice onto serving platter; spoon chicken and vegetables over rice. Sprinkle with peanuts; serve immediately.

Chicken with Lime Butter

♦ Karen Johnson from Kansas was a prize winner in the National Chicken Cooking Contest, sponsored by the National Broiler Council.

Makes 6 servings

3 whole chicken breasts, split, skinned and boned
1/2 teaspoon salt
1/2 teaspoon pepper
1/3 cup vegetable oil
Juice of 1 lime
1/2 cup butter
1 teaspoon minced chives
1/2 teaspoon dill weed

Sprinkle chicken with salt and pepper. Heat oil in large skillet over medium heat. Add chicken; cook until light brown, about 3 minutes per side. Cover; reduce heat to low. Cook 10 minutes or until chicken is tender. Remove chicken to serving platter; keep warm.

Discard oil from skillet. Add lime juice; cook over low heat until juice begins to bubble, about 1 minute. Add butter, 1 tablespoon at a time, stirring until butter becomes opaque and forms a thickened sauce. Remove from heat; stir in chives and dill weed. Spoon sauce over chicken; serve immediately. Garnish as desired.

Contestants at the Delmarva Chicken Cooking Contest come not only from Delaware, Maryland and Virginia (the vast area that gave the competition its DEL-MAR-VA name), but from all over the country. They are lured by the big prize money and the publicity that always surrounds one of the largest of the food festivals.

Olympic Seoul Chicken

♦ Muriel Brody from Cumberland, Rhode Island was the first prize winner in the Delmarva Chicken Cooking Contest, Georgetown, Delaware.

Serves 4

1/4 cup white vinegar
3 tablespoons soy sauce
2 tablespoons honey
1/4 teaspoon ground ginger
2 tablespoons peanut oil
8 chicken thighs, skinned
10 cloves garlic, coarsely chopped
1/2 to 1 teaspoon crushed red pepper
2 ounces Chinese rice stick noodles, cooked *or* **2 cups hot cooked rice**

Combine vinegar, soy sauce, honey and ginger in small bowl; set aside. Heat oil in large skillet over medium-high heat. Add chicken; cook about 10 minutes or until evenly browned on both sides. Add garlic and red pepper; cook, stirring, 2 to 3 minutes. Drain off excess fat. Add vinegar mixture. Cover; reduce heat and simmer about 15 minutes or until chicken is tender. Uncover and cook about 2 minutes or until sauce has reduced and thickened. Serve with noodles and desired vegetables.

Forty-Clove Chicken Filice

♦ Val Filice from Gilroy, California was a finalist in the Gilroy Garlic Festival Recipe Contest, Gilroy, California. Courtesy of the Gilroy Garlic Festival Association's *Garlic Lover's Cookbook.*

Makes 4 to 6 servings

1 (3-pound) frying chicken, cut into serving pieces
40 cloves fresh garlic, peeled* and left whole
½ cup dry white wine
¼ cup dry vermouth
¼ cup olive oil
4 ribs celery, thickly sliced
2 tablespoons finely chopped parsley
2 teaspoons dried basil
1 teaspoon dried oregano
Pinch of crushed red pepper
1 lemon
Salt and black pepper to taste

Preheat oven to 375°F. Place chicken pieces, skin side up, in a single layer in shallow baking pan. Combine garlic, wine, vermouth, oil, celery, parsley, basil, oregano and red pepper in medium-sized bowl; mix thoroughly. Sprinkle garlic mixture over chicken pieces. Remove zest from lemon in thin strips; place zest throughout pan. Squeeze juice from lemon and pour over the top. Season with salt and black pepper. Cover pan with aluminum foil. Bake 40 minutes. Remove foil and bake another 15 minutes. Garnish as desired.

**See page 136 for helpful tips on peeling garlic.*

SAVORY SUPPERS

Always use tongs to turn chicken pieces over during cooking. This prevents the skin from being pierced, keeping the natural juices sealed inside the skin.

Bittersweet Farm Chicken

♦ Ann Combs from New Hampshire was a prize winner in the National Chicken Cooking Contest, sponsored by the National Broiler Council.

Makes 4 servings

½ cup all-purpose flour
1 teaspoon salt
¼ teaspoon pepper
1 (3½- to 4-pound) frying chicken, cut into serving pieces
8 tablespoons butter or margarine, divided
¼ cup lemon juice
¼ cup orange-flavored liqueur
¼ cup honey
2 tablespoons orange zest
1 tablespoon soy sauce
Whole cooked baby carrots

Preheat oven to 350°F. Combine flour, salt and pepper in large plastic bag. Add chicken pieces, a few at a time, to bag; shake to coat completely with flour mixture. Melt 4 tablespoons of the butter in large baking pan. Roll chicken in butter to coat all sides; arrange skin side down in a single layer in pan. Bake 30 minutes.

Meanwhile, melt remaining 4 tablespoons butter in small saucepan over medium heat. Stir in lemon juice, liqueur, honey, orange zest and soy sauce; reserve 2 tablespoons of the mixture. Remove chicken from oven; turn pieces over. Pour remaining honey mixture over chicken. Continue baking, basting occasionally, 30 minutes or until chicken is glazed and tender. Toss reserved honey mixture with cooked carrots; serve with chicken. Garnish as desired.

Apricot Chicken Oriental

♦ Harriet Kuhn of Patterson, California was a prize winner in the Apricot Sweepstakes at the Patterson Apricot Fiesta, sponsored by the Apricot Advisory Board, Walnut Creek, California.

Makes 4 servings

1 tablespoon butter or margarine
2 whole chicken breasts, split, skinned and boned
1 jar (10 ounces) apricot preserves
1 cup water
½ cup soy sauce
1 can (8 ounces) sliced water chestnuts, drained and liquid reserved
12 dried apricots, coarsely chopped
1 teaspoon ground ginger
1 teaspoon garlic powder
Apricot Rice (recipe follows)
3 ribs celery, diagonally sliced
2 cups sliced mushrooms
1 bunch green onions, sliced
1 package (6 ounces) frozen pea pods
1 red or green bell pepper, cut into strips

Melt butter in large skillet over medium heat. Add chicken; cook until brown on both sides. Stir in preserves, water, soy sauce, liquid from water chestnuts, apricots, ginger and garlic powder. Simmer 40 minutes or until chicken is tender. Meanwhile, prepare Apricot Rice. Add celery, mushrooms, green onions, pea pods, red pepper and water chestnuts to skillet; cook and stir 5 minutes or until heated through. Serve chicken and vegetables over rice. Garnish as desired.

Apricot Rice: Combine 2½ cups water, ¼ cup finely chopped dried apricots and ¼ teaspoon salt in medium-sized saucepan. Bring to a boil; stir in 1 cup long-grain rice. Cover; reduce heat and simmer 20 minutes. Remove from heat; let stand 5 minutes.

Curry powder is formed by blending together a number of spices, including turmeric, cardamom, cumin, pepper, cloves, cinnamon, nutmeg and sometimes ginger. Chilies give it heat and ground dried garlic provides depth of taste. Curry blends vary depending on their use. Milder powders are used for fish and eggs; stronger ones season meats and poultry. There are also regional variations. Store curry powder away from the heat of the stove to preserve its full strength and pungency.

Curried Chicken Rolls

♦ Barbara Long from Wyoming was a prize winner in the National Chicken Cooking Contest, sponsored by the National Broiler Council.

Makes 4 servings

2 whole chicken breasts, split, skinned and boned
½ teaspoon salt
⅛ teaspoon pepper
1 tablespoon butter or margarine
½ medium-size onion, finely chopped
¾ cup cooked rice
¼ cup raisins
1 tablespoon chopped parsley
1 teaspoon curry powder
1 teaspoon brown sugar
½ teaspoon poultry seasoning
Pinch of garlic powder
1 tablespoon vegetable oil
½ cup dry white wine
1 teaspoon instant chicken bouillon granules

Pound chicken breasts between 2 pieces of plastic wrap to ⅜-inch thickness; sprinkle with salt and pepper. Melt butter in medium-sized skillet over medium heat. Add onion; cook and stir about 3 minutes or until soft. Remove from heat. Add rice, raisins, parsley, curry powder, brown sugar, poultry seasoning and garlic powder; mix well. Divide rice mixture into 4 equal portions. Spoon 1 portion onto each chicken breast. Roll up chicken jelly-roll fashion; secure with wooden toothpicks. Heat oil in large skillet over medium heat; add chicken rolls. Cook about 15 minutes or until brown on all sides. Add wine and bouillon. Cover; simmer 30 minutes or until chicken is tender. Garnish as desired.

Serving Suggestion: Additional rice stuffing may be prepared and served alongside the chicken rolls. Bake the extra stuffing in a covered casserole at 350°F until heated through.

Fresh Gazpacho Chicken

♦ Gloria Piantek from Skillman, New Jersey was a second prize winner in the Delmarva Chicken Cooking Contest, Georgetown, Delaware.

Makes 4 servings

1/4 cup all-purpose flour
1 1/2 teaspoons salt, divided
1/2 teaspoon paprika
1/4 teaspoon black pepper, divided
2 whole chicken breasts, split
1/4 cup vegetable oil
2 1/2 cups tomato juice
1/2 cup finely chopped, seeded tomatoes
1/2 cup finely chopped carrots
1/2 cup finely chopped celery
1/2 cup finely chopped onion
1/2 cup finely chopped green pepper
1/2 cup finely chopped, peeled, seeded cucumber
1/2 cup red wine vinegar
1/4 cup olive oil
5 teaspoons Worcestershire sauce
5 dashes hot pepper sauce
2 cloves garlic, crushed
Hot cooked rice

Combine flour, 1 teaspoon of the salt, the paprika and 1/8 teaspoon of the black pepper in shallow dish. Add chicken, one piece at a time, dredging to coat. Heat vegetable oil in large skillet over medium heat; add chicken. Cook about 10 minutes or until brown on both sides; drain off oil. Combine remaining ingredients, *except* rice, in large bowl. Stir in remaining 1/2 teaspoon salt and 1/8 teaspoon black pepper. Reserve 1 cup of the tomato mixture; cover and refrigerate. Pour remaining tomato mixture over chicken in skillet. Cover; cook over medium heat, turning occasionally, about 30 minutes or until chicken is tender. Arrange chicken on serving platter; spoon about 1 cup pan juices over chicken. Serve with chilled tomato mixture and rice. Garnish as desired.

A member of the parsley family, dill weed is the dried soft feathery leaves of the dill plant. Dill is the cornerstone of Scandinavian cooking, where it turns up in everything from scrambled eggs to fish, cucumbers and sandwiches. Central European and Russian cooks also prefer it above other herbs. Its distinctive flavor can easily dominate a dish so you may want to use it sparingly at first.

Calorie-Wise Dill Chicken

♦ Anna Bodisch from Coplay, Pennsylvania was a finalist in the National Chicken Cooking Contest, sponsored by the National Broiler Council.

Makes 4 servings

1 cup plain low-fat yogurt
1½ cups regular wheat germ
½ cup chopped almonds
2 teaspoons dried dill weed
½ teaspoon salt
¼ teaspoon pepper
12 chicken drumsticks
Nonstick vegetable cooking spray

Preheat oven to 350°F. Place yogurt in shallow bowl. Combine wheat germ, almonds, dill weed, salt and pepper in another shallow bowl. Dip chicken drumsticks, one at a time, into yogurt, then roll in wheat germ mixture to coat. Line baking sheet with aluminum foil; spray with nonstick vegetable cooking spray. Arrange chicken in a single layer on baking sheet. Bake about 50 minutes or until chicken is tender. Garnish as desired.

Chicken Avocado Melt

♦ Marjorie Fortier from Connecticut was a prize winner in the National Chicken Cooking Contest, sponsored by the National Broiler Council.

Makes 4 servings

2 whole chicken breasts, split, skinned and boned
2 tablespoons cornstarch
1 teaspoon ground cumin
1 teaspoon garlic salt
1 egg, slightly beaten
1 tablespoon water
1/3 cup yellow cornmeal
3 tablespoons vegetable oil
1 firm ripe avocado, peeled and sliced
1 1/2 cups (6 ounces) shredded Monterey Jack cheese
1/2 cup sour cream
1/4 cup sliced green onion tops
1/4 cup chopped red bell pepper

Preheat oven to 350°F. Pound chicken breasts between 2 pieces of plastic wrap to 1/4-inch thickness. Combine cornstarch, cumin and garlic salt in shallow dish. Add chicken, dredging to coat. Combine egg and water in small bowl. Place cornmeal in shallow dish. Dip chicken into egg mixture, then roll in cornmeal to coat. Heat oil in large skillet over medium heat. Add chicken; cook 2 minutes on each side. Remove chicken to shallow baking pan. Arrange avocado slices over chicken; sprinkle with cheese. Bake about 15 minutes or until chicken is tender and cheese melts. Transfer chicken to serving platter. Top with sour cream; sprinkle with green onions and red pepper.

Chicken in Lemon Sauce

♦ Nelda Smith from Oklahoma was a prize winner in the National Chicken Cooking Contest, sponsored by the National Broiler Council.

Makes 8 servings

1/4 cup butter or margarine
4 whole chicken breasts, split, skinned and boned
2 tablespoons dry white wine
1/2 teaspoon grated lemon peel
2 tablespoons lemon juice
1/4 teaspoon salt
1/8 teaspoon white pepper
1 cup heavy cream
1/3 cup grated Parmesan cheese
1 cup sliced mushrooms
Red grapes and lemon peel, for garnish

Melt butter in large skillet over medium heat; add chicken. Cook, turning, about 10 minutes or until chicken is brown and tender. Remove chicken to ovenproof serving dish. Discard butter from skillet. Add wine, lemon peel and lemon juice to skillet; cook and stir over medium heat 1 minute. Stir in salt and white pepper. Gradually pour in cream, stirring constantly, until hot; *do not boil.* Pour cream sauce over chicken; sprinkle with cheese and mushrooms. Broil chicken about 6 inches from heat source until lightly browned. Garnish with grapes and lemon peel.

COME FOR DINNER

If you skin and debone your own chicken breasts, be sure to reserve both the bones and skin. Let these scraps collect in a plastic bag in your freezer and soon you'll have enough to make flavorful homemade chicken stock.

Curried Chicken Calcutta

♦ Alice Cory from King of Prussia, Pennsylvania won honorable mention in the Delmarva Chicken Cooking Contest, Georgetown, Delaware.

Makes 4 servings

1/4 cup all-purpose flour
1/2 teaspoon curry powder
1/2 teaspoon ground cinnamon
1/2 teaspoon ground ginger
1/4 teaspoon garlic powder
2 whole chicken breasts, split, skinned and boned
1/4 cup vegetable oil
1 cup plain yogurt
2 tablespoons lime juice
Peel of 1 lime, grated
Lime slices and mint sprigs, for garnish

Combine flour, curry powder, cinnamon, ginger and garlic powder in shallow dish. Add chicken, one piece at a time, dredging to coat. Heat oil in large skillet over medium heat. Add chicken; cook until brown on both sides. Cover; reduce heat to low and cook 15 minutes or until chicken is tender.

Combine yogurt and lime juice in small saucepan. Cook over low heat, stirring constantly, until warm. Arrange chicken on serving platter. Spoon about one half of the yogurt sauce over chicken; sprinkle with grated lime peel and garnish with lime slices and mint. Pass remaining sauce.

Here is a valuable tip to keep in mind in case you should find yourself dying of thirst on a desert island: Eat a cucumber. It is 96 percent water and maintains a lower temperature than the air around it. In fact, it was to have a year-round supply of cucumbers that hothouses were first built.

Chicken with Cucumbers and Dill

♦ Frank Mullin from Washington, D.C. was a third prize winner in the Delmarva Chicken Cooking Contest, Georgetown, Delaware.

Makes 4 servings

2 whole chicken breasts, split, skinned and boned
1 teaspoon salt, divided
¾ teaspoon pepper, divided
4 tablespoons butter or margarine, divided
2 cucumbers, peeled, seeded and cut into ¼-inch slices
½ teaspoon dill weed
¼ cup lemon juice
Lemon slices, for garnish

Sprinkle chicken breasts with ½ teaspoon of the salt and ½ teaspoon of the pepper. Melt 2 tablespoons of the butter in large skillet over medium heat; add chicken. Cook about 8 minutes or until chicken is brown on both sides; remove and keep warm. Melt remaining 2 tablespoons butter in same skillet. Add cucumbers; stir to coat. Sprinkle remaining ½ teaspoon salt and ¼ teaspoon pepper over cucumbers; cook 2 minutes. Stir in dill weed. Push cucumbers to side of skillet.

Return chicken and any collected juices to skillet. Cook 2 minutes or until chicken is tender. Place chicken on serving platter; arrange cucumbers around chicken. Cook juices in skillet until light brown. Pour lemon juice and pan juices over chicken. Garnish with lemon slices.

Mustard is one of the most frequently eaten condiments in the world. Although it has been around since the beginning of time, it is only recently that we have begun to glimpse the infinite number of varieties that are available. Dijon mustard is smooth and piquant with a slightly hot undertone and is made in Dijon, France. Dijon-style mustard is its American counterpart. Chinese mustard is more pungent than Dijon and can be so fiery hot that it will bring tears to your eyes if eaten in large amounts. German mustard is milder, sweeter and darker than Dijon or Chinese mustards—the perfect accompaniment to a good sausage.

Chicken with Fruit and Mixed Mustards

♦ Marjorie Farr from Rockville, Maryland was second prize winner in the Delmarva Chicken Cooking Contest, Georgetown, Delaware.

Makes 4 servings

½ cup Dijon-style mustard
½ cup Bavarian or other German mustard
1 tablespoon Chinese mustard
⅓ cup honey
⅓ cup light cream
2 whole chicken breasts, split, skinned and boned
½ teaspoon salt
¼ teaspoon pepper
2 tablespoons butter or margarine
4 kiwifruit, peeled and sliced
2 cups melon balls (honeydew and cantaloupe)
¼ cup mayonnaise
Mint sprigs, for garnish

Combine mustards, honey and cream in medium-sized bowl. Spoon half of the mustard sauce into large glass bowl; reserve remainder. Sprinkle chicken with salt and pepper; place in glass bowl, turning to coat with mustard sauce. Cover; marinate in refrigerator 30 minutes, turning often.

Heat butter in large skillet over medium heat until foamy. Add chicken; cook about 7 minutes on each side or until brown and tender. Remove chicken to cutting board and cut across the grain into thin slices. Arrange chicken and fruit on serving platter.

Place reserved mustard sauce in small saucepan; whisk in mayonnaise. Heat thoroughly over medium heat. Drizzle some sauce over chicken. Garnish platter with mint sprigs. Pass remaining sauce.

Plum Sweet and Spicy Chicken

♦ Joan McCormick from Virginia was a prize winner in the National Chicken Cooking Contest, sponsored by the National Broiler Council.

Makes 4 servings

½ teaspoon white pepper
½ teaspoon ground ginger
½ teaspoon ground cinnamon
¼ teaspoon ground cloves
1 (3½- to 4-pound) frying chicken
4 tablespoons soy sauce, divided
2 tablespoons honey
½ cup plum jelly
¼ cup chutney
2 teaspoons sugar
2 teaspoons vinegar

Combine white pepper, ginger, cinnamon and cloves in small dish. Rub inside of chicken with half of the spice mixture. Stir 1 tablespoon of the soy sauce into remaining spice mixture; rub on outside of chicken. Cover chicken; refrigerate 1 hour.

Place chicken, breast side up, on rack in wok over 2 inches of boiling water. Cover; steam 1 hour, adding water to wok as needed.

Preheat oven to 350°F. Remove chicken to shallow baking pan. Bake about 15 minutes or until leg moves freely when twisted; remove from oven. *Increase oven temperature to 450°F.* Combine remaining 3 tablespoons soy sauce and the honey; brush on chicken. Combine plum jelly, chutney, sugar and vinegar; spread on chicken. Bake 10 minutes longer or until brown and tender. Let chicken stand 15 minutes before carving. Garnish as desired.

Stuffed Chicken with Apple Glaze

♦ Ruth Dykes from Beltsville, Maryland was a first prize winner in the Delmarva Chicken Cooking Contest, Georgetown, Delaware.

Makes 4 servings

1 (3½- to 4-pound) frying chicken
½ teaspoon salt
¼ teaspoon pepper
2 tablespoons vegetable oil
1 package (6 ounces) chicken-flavored stuffing mix, plus ingredients to prepare mix
1 cup chopped apple
¼ cup chopped walnuts
¼ cup raisins
¼ cup thinly sliced celery
½ teaspoon grated lemon peel
½ cup apple jelly
1 tablespoon lemon juice
½ teaspoon ground cinnamon

Preheat oven to 350°F. Sprinkle inside of chicken with salt and pepper; rub outside with oil. Prepare stuffing mix according to package directions in large bowl. Add apple, walnuts, raisins, celery and lemon peel; mix thoroughly. Stuff body cavity loosely with stuffing.* Place chicken in baking pan; cover loosely with aluminum foil and roast 1 hour.

Meanwhile, combine jelly, lemon juice and cinnamon in small saucepan. Simmer over low heat 3 minutes or until blended. Remove foil from chicken; brush with jelly mixture. Roast, uncovered, brushing frequently with jelly glaze, 30 minutes or until meat thermometer inserted into thickest part of thigh registers 185°F. Let chicken stand 15 minutes before carving.

**Bake any leftover stuffing in a covered casserole alongside chicken until heated through.*

Roast Chicken & Kiwi with Raspberry Glaze

♦ Stephen Abel from Rehoboth Beach, Delaware was a first prize winner in the Delmarva Chicken Cooking Contest, Georgetown, Delaware.

Makes 4 servings

2 (3½- to 4-pound) frying chickens, cut into halves
1 teaspoon salt
¼ teaspoon pepper
½ cup butter or margarine, melted
Raspberry Glaze (recipe follows)
Kiwifruit, peeled and sliced

Preheat oven to 400°F. Sprinkle chicken with salt and pepper. Place, skin side up, in a single layer in large shallow pan; brush with butter. Roast, basting frequently with butter, about 45 minutes or until chicken is tender. Drain off fat. While chicken is cooking, prepare Raspberry Glaze. Spoon glaze over chicken; top with kiwi slices. Spoon glaze from bottom of pan over chicken and kiwi. Bake about 3 minutes or until kiwi and chicken are well glazed.

Raspberry Glaze: Combine 1 cup seedless raspberry preserves, ½ cup white port wine and grated peel of 1 lemon in small saucepan. Cook over low heat about 5 minutes or until slightly thick.

Award-Winning CAKES & DESSERTS

CAKES

DESSERTS

Maple Sweetheart (page 280)

The Classics

Chiffon Cake

♦ Catherine A. Melvin from Edgar, Nebraska was a finalist in the Cakes category at the Nebraska State Fair, Lincoln, Nebraska.

Makes one 10-inch tube cake

5 eggs, separated
½ teaspoon cream of tartar
2¼ cups sifted all-purpose flour
1½ cups sugar
1 tablespoon baking powder
1 teaspoon salt
¾ cup water
½ cup vegetable oil
1 teaspoon vanilla
1 teaspoon almond extract
Strawberries, kiwifruit and whipped cream for garnish (optional)

Preheat oven to 325°F. Beat egg whites with cream of tartar at high speed with electric mixer until stiff peaks form. Set aside. Sift together dry ingredients into large bowl. Make a well in flour mixture. Add egg yolks, water, oil and flavorings; mix well. Fold in egg white mixture. Immediately pour into ungreased 10-inch tube pan. Bake 55 minutes. *Increase oven temperature to 350°F.* Continue baking 10 minutes or until cake springs back when lightly touched with finger. Invert pan and allow cake to cool completely before removing from pan. Garnish as desired.

Cherry-Pineapple Upside-Down Cake

♦ Charlotte Scott from Rock Island, Illinois was a finalist in the "Bake-a-Cake" category in the Blue Ribbon Culinary Contest at the Illinois State Fair, Springfield, Illinois.

Makes one 9-inch cake

1¼ cups sifted cake flour
2 teaspoons baking powder
¼ teaspoon salt
½ cup (1 stick) butter or margarine, softened, divided
¾ cup granulated sugar
1 egg, beaten
½ cup milk
1 teaspoon vanilla
¾ cup packed brown sugar
1 (20-ounce) can crushed pineapple, well drained
1 (16-ounce) can sour pie cherries, drained
Fresh mint leaves for garnish (optional)

Preheat oven to 350°F. Combine flour, baking powder and salt; set aside. Beat together ¼ cup of the butter and the granulated sugar in large bowl until light and fluffy. Blend in egg. Add flour mixture alternately with milk, beating well after each addition. Blend in vanilla. Melt the remaining ¼ cup butter in 9-inch ovenproof skillet or 9-inch cake pan. Stir in brown sugar; spread to cover bottom of skillet. Cover with pineapple. Reserve a few cherries for garnish, if desired. Spoon remaining cherries over pineapple; top with batter. Bake 50 minutes or until wooden pick inserted in center comes out clean. Cool in pan on wire rack 10 minutes. Loosen edges and turn upside down onto cake plate. Garnish with reserved cherries and mint, if desired.

Sweet Zucchini Spice Cake

♦ Sharon Norlander from Albuquerque, New Mexico was a finalist in the Cakes category at the New Mexico State Fair, Albuquerque, New Mexico.

Makes one 2-layer cake

3 cups grated peeled zucchini (approximately 1 pound)
1 cup ground walnuts
1 cup flaked coconut
4 eggs
1 cup vegetable oil
2 tablespoons vanilla
2½ cups granulated sugar
3 cups all-purpose flour
2 teaspoons ground cinnamon
1½ teaspoons baking soda
1 teaspoon baking powder
1 teaspoon salt
Pineapple Cream Cheese Icing (recipe follows)

Preheat oven to 350°F. Grease and flour 2 (10-inch) round cake pans. Combine zucchini, walnuts and coconut; set aside. Beat together eggs, oil and vanilla in large bowl until well blended. Beat in granulated sugar. Gradually add combined dry ingredients, beating well after each addition. Stir in zucchini mixture. Pour evenly into prepared pans. Bake 35 to 40 minutes or until wooden pick inserted in centers comes out clean. Cool layers in pans on wire racks 10 minutes. Loosen edges and remove to racks to cool completely. Fill and frost with Pineapple Cream Cheese Icing.

Pineapple Cream Cheese Icing: Beat together 1 (8-ounce) package softened cream cheese and ½ cup (1 stick) softened margarine in large bowl until creamy. Add 1 (8-ounce) can drained crushed pineapple. Gradually add 1 pound (approximately 4½ cups) sifted powdered sugar, beating until smooth and of spreading consistency.

Buttermilk Pound Cake

♦ Winifred Merrill from Beverly, Massachusetts was a first place winner in the Topsfield Fair Baking Competition, sponsored by the Essex Agricultural Society, Topsfield, Massachusetts.

Makes two 9×5-inch loaves

3 cups sifted all-purpose flour
½ teaspoon baking powder
½ teaspoon baking soda
½ teaspoon salt
1 cup (2 sticks) butter or margarine, softened
2 cups superfine sugar
2 eggs
1 teaspoon vanilla
1 teaspoon lemon extract
1 cup buttermilk
Starfruit and strawberry slices for garnish (optional)
Lemon or orange zest for garnish (optional)

Preheat oven to 350°F. Grease and flour 2 (9×5-inch) loaf pans. Combine flour, baking powder, baking soda and salt; set aside. Beat together butter and sugar in large bowl until light and fluffy. Add eggs, one at a time, beating well after each addition. Blend in flavorings. Add flour mixture alternately with buttermilk, beating well after each addition. Pour evenly into prepared pans. Bake 35 to 40 minutes or until wooden pick inserted in centers comes out clean. Cool loaves in pans on wire racks 10 minutes. Loosen edges and remove to racks to cool completely. Garnish as desired.

Boston Cream Pie

♦ Sarah Cuozzo from Boxford, Massachusetts was a first place winner in the Topsfield Fair Baking Competition, sponsored by the Essex Agricultural Society, Topsfield, Massachusetts.

Makes one 9-inch cake

⅓ cup shortening
1 cup granulated sugar
1 egg
1 teaspoon vanilla
1¼ cups all-purpose flour
1½ teaspoons baking powder
½ teaspoon salt
¾ cup milk
Filling (recipe follows)
Glaze (recipe follows)

Preheat oven to 350°F. Grease and flour 1 (9-inch) round cake pan. Beat together shortening and sugar in large bowl until light and fluffy. Blend in egg and vanilla. Add combined dry ingredients to sugar mixture alternately with milk, beating well after each addition. Pour into prepared pan. Bake 35 minutes or until wooden pick inserted in center comes out clean. Cool in pan 10 minutes. Loosen edges and remove to rack to cool completely. When cool, split cake horizontally in half to make 2 thin layers. To assemble, spoon Filling over bottom half of cake on cake plate; cover with top half of cake layer. Spread top with Glaze; let cool. Serve when glaze is completely set. Refrigerate.

Filling: Combine ⅓ cup granulated sugar, 2 tablespoons cornstarch and ¼ teaspoon salt in 2-quart saucepan. Gradually stir in 1½ cups milk. Cook over medium heat, stirring constantly, until mixture thickens and comes to boil. Boil 1 minute, stirring constantly. Gradually stir small amount of hot mixture into 2 slightly beaten egg yolks; mix thoroughly. Return to hot mixture in pan. Return to boil; boil 1 minute, stirring constantly. *(Do not overcook.)* Remove from heat; stir in 2 teaspoons vanilla. Cool to room temperature. Chill.

Glaze: Combine 2 (1-ounce) squares unsweetened chocolate and 3 tablespoons butter in medium saucepan; stir over low heat until melted. Remove from heat; stir in 1 cup powdered sugar and ¾ teaspoon vanilla. Stir in 1 to 2 tablespoons water, a teaspoonful at a time, until glaze is of desired consistency. Cool slightly.

White Buttermilk Cake

♦ Inez Mortley from Albuquerque, New Mexico was a finalist in the Cakes category at the New Mexico State Fair, Albuquerque, New Mexico.

Makes one 2- or 3-layer cake

3 cups sifted cake flour
1 teaspoon baking soda
½ teaspoon salt
1 cup shortening
2 cups granulated sugar, divided
1 cup buttermilk
2 teaspoons clear vanilla
½ teaspoon almond extract
6 egg whites, at room temperature
1 teaspoon cream of tartar
Creamy Frosting (recipe follows)

Preheat oven to 350°F. Grease and flour 2 (9-inch) or 3 (8-inch) round cake pans. Combine flour, baking soda and salt; set aside. Beat together shortening with 1⅓ cups of the granulated sugar in large bowl until light and fluffy. Add flour mixture alternately with buttermilk, beating well after each addition. Blend in flavorings. Beat egg whites in separate bowl at medium speed with electric mixer until foamy. Add cream of tartar; beat at high speed until soft peaks form. Gradually beat in the remaining ⅔ cup granulated sugar, beating until stiff peaks form; fold into flour mixture. Pour evenly into prepared pans. Bake 30 to 35 minutes or until wooden pick inserted in centers comes out clean. Cool layers in pans on wire racks 10 minutes. Loosen edges and remove to racks to cool completely. Fill and frost with Creamy Frosting.

Creamy Frosting: Combine 3 tablespoons all-purpose flour and 1 cup milk in medium saucepan; stir over low heat until thickened. Cool. Beat 1 cup (2 sticks) softened butter in large bowl until creamy. Add 1 cup powdered sugar; beat until fluffy. Blend in 1 teaspoon vanilla. Add flour mixture; beat until thick and smooth.

Angel Food Cake

♦ Nancy Turner from St. Clair Shores, Michigan was a prize winner in the Cakes category at the Michigan State Fair, Detroit, Michigan.

Makes one 10-inch tube cake

1¼ cups cake flour, sifted
1⅓ cups plus ½ cup sugar, divided
12 egg whites
1¼ teaspoons cream of tartar
¼ teaspoon salt
1 teaspoon vanilla
¼ teaspoon almond extract
Fresh strawberries for serving (optional)

Preheat oven to 350°F. Sift together flour with ½ cup of the sugar 4 times. Beat egg whites with cream of tartar, salt and flavorings in large bowl at high speed with electric mixer until stiff peaks form. Gradually add the remaining 1⅓ cups sugar, mixing well after each addition. Fold in flour mixture. Pour into ungreased 10-inch tube pan. Bake 35 to 40 minutes or until cake springs back when lightly touched with finger. Invert pan and allow cake to cool completely in pan before removing from pan. Serve with strawberries, if desired.

THE CHOCOLATE COLLECTION

Devil's Food Cake with Ricotta Frosting

♦ Margaret A. Cyrus from New Orleans, Louisiana was a finalist in a cookbook and recipe contest sponsored by *The Times-Picayune*, New Orleans, Louisiana.

Makes one 2-layer cake

1 cup shortening
3 cups granulated sugar
3 eggs
2 cups buttermilk
1 teaspoon baking soda
3 cups all-purpose flour
6 tablespoons cocoa
1½ teaspoons ground cinnamon
¼ teaspoon ground cloves
1 tablespoon vanilla
Ricotta Frosting (recipe follows)

Preheat oven to 350°F. Grease and flour 2 (9-inch) square baking pans. Beat together shortening and granulated sugar in large bowl until light and fluffy. Add eggs, one at a time, beating well after each addition. Gradually add buttermilk to soda, mixing well. Sift together flour, cocoa and spices; add to egg mixture alternately with buttermilk mixture, beating well after each addition. Blend in vanilla. Pour evenly into prepared pans. Bake 25 minutes or until wooden pick inserted in centers comes out clean. Cool layers in pans on wire racks 10 minutes. Loosen edges and remove to racks to cool completely. Fill and frost with Ricotta Frosting.

Ricotta Frosting: Beat together 2½ pounds ricotta cheese, 1 teaspoon almond extract and 1½ cups powdered sugar until smooth. Add 1 finely chopped (8-ounce) chocolate bar with almonds; mix well.

Zucchini Chocolate Cake

♦ Mrs. Val Sypal from Brainard, Nebraska was a finalist in the Zucchini Cakes category at the Nebraska State Fair, Lincoln, Nebraska.

Makes one 13×9-inch cake

½ cup (1 stick) margarine or butter, softened
½ cup vegetable oil
1⅔ cups granulated sugar
2 eggs
1 teaspoon vanilla
½ teaspoon chocolate flavoring
2½ cups all-purpose flour
¼ cup cocoa
1 teaspoon baking soda
½ teaspoon salt
½ cup buttermilk
2 cups shredded zucchini
1 (6-ounce) package semisweet chocolate chips
½ cup chopped nuts

Preheat oven to 325°F. Grease and lightly flour 13×9-inch baking pan. Beat together margarine, oil and sugar in large bowl until light and fluffy. Add eggs, one at a time, beating well after each addition. Blend in flavorings. Combine dry ingredients. Add to creamed mixture alternately with buttermilk, beating well after each addition. Stir in zucchini. Pour into prepared pan. Sprinkle with chocolate chips and nuts. Bake 55 minutes or until wooden pick inserted in center comes out clean; cool on wire rack. Cut into squares. Frost with your favorite chocolate frosting, if desired.

Black Forest Cake

♦ Lynn Morford from Sherman, Illinois was a finalist in the "Bake-a-Cake" category in the Blue Ribbon Culinary Contest at the Illinois State Fair, Springfield, Illinois.

Makes one 3-layer cake

2 cups plus 2 tablespoons all-purpose flour
1½ teaspoons baking powder
¾ teaspoon baking soda
¾ teaspoon salt
2 cups granulated sugar
¾ cup cocoa
3 eggs
1 cup milk
½ cup vegetable oil
1 tablespoon vanilla
Cherry Topping (recipe follows)
Frosting (recipe follows)

Preheat oven to 350°F. Grease and flour 2 (9-inch) round cake pans. Cover bottoms with waxed paper. Combine dry ingredients in large bowl. Add eggs, milk, oil and vanilla; beat until well blended. Pour evenly into prepared pans. Bake 35 minutes or until wooden pick inserted in centers comes out clean. Cool layers in pans on wire racks 10 minutes. Loosen edges and remove to racks to cool completely. While cake is baking, prepare Cherry Topping; cool. Split cooled cakes horizontally in half to make 4 layers. Tear 1 layer into crumbs; set aside. Reserve 1½ cups Frosting for decorating cake; set aside. To assemble, place 1 layer on cake plate. Spread with 1 cup frosting; top with ¾ cup cherry topping. Top with second cake layer; repeat layers of frosting and cherry topping. Top with third cake layer. Frost sides of cake with remaining frosting. Pat reserved crumbs into frosting on sides of cake; pipe reserved 1½ cups frosting around top and bottom edges of cake. Spoon remaining cherry topping onto top of cake. Refrigerate.

Cherry Topping: Drain 2 (20-ounce) cans tart pitted cherries, reserving ½ cup juice. Combine reserved juice, cherries, 1 cup granulated sugar and ¼ cup cornstarch in 2-quart saucepan. Cook over low heat until thickened, stirring constantly. Stir in 1 teaspoon vanilla. Cool; set aside.

Frosting: Beat together 3 cups whipping cream and ⅓ cup powdered sugar in chilled bowl at high speed with electric mixer until stiff peaks form.

Chocolate Yogurt Cake

♦ Mrs. George Hulett from Shively, Kentucky was a finalist in the Cakes category at the Kentucky State Fair, Louisville, Kentucky.

Makes one 2-layer cake

⅔ cup shortening
1¾ cups granulated sugar
2 eggs
1 teaspoon Cognac vanilla or vanilla
2½ cups sifted cake flour
1½ teaspoons baking soda
½ teaspoon salt
1 cup (8 ounces) plain yogurt
½ cup boiling water
½ cup cocoa
Filling (recipe follows)
Fluffy Cocoa Frosting (recipe follows)
Additional chopped hazelnuts for garnish (optional)
Toasted flaked coconut for garnish (optional)

Preheat oven to 350°F. Grease and flour 2 (9-inch) round cake pans. Beat together shortening and sugar until light and fluffy. Add eggs, one at a time, beating well after each addition. Blend in vanilla. Combine flour, baking soda and salt. Add to shortening mixture alternately with yogurt, beating well after each addition. Gradually add boiling water to cocoa, stirring until well blended; cool slightly. Add to batter; beat until well blended. Pour evenly into prepared pans. Bake 35 minutes or until wooden pick inserted in centers comes out clean. Cool layers in pans on wire racks 10 minutes. Loosen edges and remove to racks to cool completely. To assemble, place 1 cake layer on cake plate; spread with Filling. Top with second cake layer. Frost with Fluffy Cocoa Frosting. Garnish as desired.

Filling: Combine ½ cup Fluffy Cocoa Frosting (recipe follows), 2 tablespoons chopped frozen cherries, thawed, ¼ cup flaked coconut and ¼ cup chopped toasted hazelnuts, mixing until well blended.

Fluffy Cocoa Frosting: Combine 4 cups powdered sugar and ¾ cup cocoa; set aside. Beat ½ cup (1 stick) softened unsalted butter in large bowl until creamy. Add half of the cocoa mixture; beat until fluffy. Blend in ¼ cup evaporated milk and 1 teaspoon Cognac vanilla or vanilla. Gradually add the remaining powdered sugar mixture, beating until well blended. Add additional ¼ cup evaporated milk; beat until frosting is of spreading consistency. (Additional evaporated milk may be added, if desired, for a softer frosting.)

DECADENT CHEESECAKES

Turtle Pecan Cheesecake

♦ Linda Bland from Edwardsville, Illinois was a finalist in the Baked Desserts Using Dairy Products category at the Illinois State Fair, Springfield, Illinois.

Makes one 9-inch cheesecake

2 cups crushed chocolate cookies or vanilla wafers (approximately 8 ounces cookies)
¼ cup (½ stick) butter, melted
2½ (8-ounce) packages cream cheese, softened
1 cup sugar
1½ tablespoons all-purpose flour
¼ teaspoon salt
1 teaspoon vanilla
3 eggs
2 tablespoons whipping cream
Caramel Topping (recipe follows)
Chocolate Topping (recipe follows)
1 cup chopped toasted pecans

Preheat oven to 450°F. Combine cookie crumbs and butter; press onto bottom of 9-inch springform pan. Beat cream cheese in large bowl until creamy. Add sugar, flour, salt and vanilla; mix well. Add eggs, one at a time, beating well after each addition. Blend in cream. Pour over crust. Bake 10 minutes. *Reduce oven temperature to 200°F;* continue baking 35 to 40 minutes or until set. Loosen cake from rim of pan; cool before removing rim of pan. Drizzle with Caramel Topping and Chocolate Topping. Refrigerate. Sprinkle with pecans just before serving.

Caramel Topping: Combine ½ (14-ounce) bag caramels and ⅓ cup whipping cream in small saucepan; stir over low heat until smooth.

Chocolate Topping: Combine 1 (4-ounce) package German sweet chocolate, 1 teaspoon butter and 2 tablespoons whipping cream in small saucepan; stir over low heat until smooth.

Gourmet Gala Cheesecake with Orange Rum Sauce

♦ Eleanor Ostman and Ron Aune entered this prize-winning recipe at the March of Dimes Gourmet Gala in Minneapolis, Minnesota.

Makes one 10-inch cheesecake

4 (8-ounce) packages cream cheese, softened
½ cup (1 stick) butter, softened
2 cups (16 ounces) sour cream
1¼ cups sugar
2 tablespoons cornstarch
2 teaspoons lemon juice
1 teaspoon vanilla
5 eggs, at room temperature
Orange Rum Sauce (recipe follows)

Preheat oven to 375°F. Thoroughly grease 10-inch springform pan. Beat together cream cheese and butter in large bowl until creamy. Blend in sour cream. Add sugar, cornstarch, lemon juice and vanilla; beat until well blended. Add eggs, one at a time, beating well after each addition. Pour into prepared pan. Place springform pan in a larger pan; add enough water to come halfway up outside of springform pan. Bake 1 hour or until set. Turn off oven. Let cheesecake cool in oven 1 hour with oven door slightly open. Remove cheesecake from oven; let stand on wire rack 2 hours. Loosen cake from rim of pan; cool completely before removing rim of pan. Refrigerate at least 6 hours before serving. Serve with Orange Rum Sauce.

Orange Rum Sauce: Using a zester or vegetable peeler, remove only orange portion of peel from each of 3 oranges. Cut into very thin slivers to make ½ cup. Squeeze juice from oranges; strain. (There should be enough juice to make 1 cup. If necessary, add enough water to juice to measure 1 cup.) Place juice and orange peel in small saucepan; simmer over low heat 5 minutes. Add ½ cup corn syrup, ¼ cup sugar and ¼ cup dark rum; stir until the sugar dissolves. Increase heat to high; bring to a boil. Reduce heat to medium; boil 20 minutes or until liquid becomes syrupy. Remove from heat; cool thoroughly. Stir in ¼ cup chopped macadamia nuts.

Orange Cappuccino Cheesecake

♦ Shirley Britt from Lincoln, Illinois was a finalist in the Baked Desserts Using Dairy Products category at the Illinois State Fair, Springfield, Illinois.

Makes one 9-inch cheesecake

1½ cups finely chopped nuts
1 cup plus 2 tablespoons sugar, divided
3 tablespoons butter, melted
4 (8-ounce) packages cream cheese, softened
3 tablespoons all-purpose flour
4 eggs
1 cup sour cream
1 tablespoon instant coffee powder
¼ teaspoon ground cinnamon
¼ cup orange juice
1 teaspoon grated orange peel
Cinnamon sugar for garnish (optional)
Whipped cream and orange zest for garnish (optional)

Preheat oven to 325°F. Combine nuts, 2 tablespoons of the sugar and the butter; press onto bottom of 9-inch springform pan. Bake 10 minutes. Remove from oven. *Increase oven temperature to 450°F.* Beat together cream cheese, the remaining 1 cup sugar and the flour in large bowl until well blended. Add eggs, one at a time, beating well after each addition. Blend in sour cream. Add coffee powder and cinnamon to orange juice; stir until coffee is dissolved. Gradually add juice mixture with orange peel to cream cheese mixture, mixing until well blended. Pour over crust. Bake 10 minutes. *Reduce oven temperature to 250°F;* continue baking 1 hour. Loosen cake from rim of pan; cool before removing rim of pan. Refrigerate. Sprinkle top of cheesecake with cinnamon sugar, if desired. Garnish as desired.

Perfect Pies

Mississippi Mist Pie

♦ Helen Peach from Meridian, Mississippi was the second place winner at the Dairylicious Pie Recipe Contest sponsored by the Southeast United Dairy Industry Association, Inc., Atlanta, Georgia.

Makes 6 to 8 servings

2 cups vanilla wafer crumbs (about 50 wafers)
5 tablespoons butter or margarine, melted
2 pints fresh strawberries
1 package (8 ounces) light cream cheese, softened
1 can (14 ounces) sweetened condensed milk
½ cup fresh lime juice (about 6 to 8 limes)
1 tablespoon green creme de menthe liqueur
1 cup whipping cream
3 tablespoons sugar
½ teaspoon vanilla
Lime slice, for garnish

Combine crumbs and butter in small bowl. Press firmly on bottom and up side of 9-inch pie plate. Refrigerate until firm.

Reserving 3 strawberries for garnish, cut off stem ends of remaining berries so they are no more than 1 inch tall. Arrange, cut ends down, on crust; refrigerate. Beat cream cheese until smooth. Add sweetened condensed milk; beat well. Add lime juice and liqueur; blend well. Pour into prepared crust, covering strawberries. Refrigerate at least one hour.

Whip cream until soft peaks form. Gradually add sugar and vanilla and whip until stiff and glossy. Using pastry bag with decorating tip, pipe lattice design on top of pie. Garnish with reserved strawberries and lime slice.

Lemons are rarely eaten on their own, but they are probably used more than any other fruit, in everything from flavoring beverages and pies to adding zest to vegetables, fish and poultry. They can even prevent some fruits (such as apples and bananas) from turning brown when sliced. Fresh lemons are found in supermarkets year-round and bottled lemon juice is also widely available. To get the most juice from your lemons, warm to room temperature and press down as you roll them on the countertop with the palm of your hand before squeezing. To remove peel in strips, use a very sharp knife or vegetable peeler (or a special gadget called a lemon zester). Remove only the colored part of the peel. If necessary, scrape any white left on peels before adding to recipe.

Heavenly Sinful Lemon Chiffon Pie

♦ Toni Canfill was the second place winner in the Junior division of the Citrus Pie Contest at the National Orange Show, San Bernardino, California.

Makes one 9-inch pie

CRUST

1 cup all-purpose flour
¼ cup sugar
1 tablespoon grated lemon peel
½ cup butter
1 egg yolk, slightly beaten
½ teaspoon vanilla
1 teaspoon lemon juice

FILLING

4 eggs,* separated
1 cup sugar, divided
⅓ cup lemon juice
2 tablespoons grated lemon peel
½ teaspoon unflavored gelatin
¼ teaspoon salt
Whipped cream and lemon peel, for garnish

Preheat oven to 400°F. To make crust, combine flour, ¼ cup sugar and 1 tablespoon lemon peel in medium bowl. Cut in butter until mixture resembles coarse crumbs. Stir in egg yolk, vanilla and 1 teaspoon lemon juice. Press evenly in 9-inch pie plate; trim and flute edge. Prick dough and line with foil. Fill with dried beans, uncooked rice or pie weights and bake 10 minutes. Remove foil lining and beans; cool completely on wire rack.

To make filling, beat 4 egg yolks in small bowl. Combine with ½ cup of the sugar, ⅓ cup lemon juice, 2 tablespoons lemon peel and the gelatin in top of double boiler. Cook over boiling water 5 minutes or until thickened, stirring constantly. Remove from heat. Beat egg whites and salt in large bowl until soft peaks form. Gradually add remaining ½ cup sugar, beating until stiff and glossy. Fold egg white mixture into lemon mixture; pour into cooled crust. Refrigerate until set. Garnish with whipped cream and lemon peel.

**Use clean, uncracked eggs.*

Peanut butter seems to be a staple of most young lives and often continues to be a favorite into adulthood (although not many will admit to it). By the last day of high school, the average student will have eaten 1500 peanut butter-and-jelly sandwiches. And enough peanut butter is consumed annually by Americans of all ages to cover the floor of the Grand Canyon!

Norma Gene's Peanut Butter Creme Pie

♦ Norma Gene Anderson from Crete, Nebraska was a finalist in the Miscellaneous Cream Pie category at the Nebraska State Fair, Lincoln, Nebraska.

Makes 6 to 8 servings

1 9-inch unbaked single pie crust
¾ cup granulated sugar, divided
3 tablespoons cornstarch
1 tablespoon all-purpose flour
⅛ teaspoon salt
3 eggs, separated
3 cups milk
2 teaspoons butter or margarine
1 teaspoon vanilla
½ cup crunchy peanut butter
¾ cup powdered sugar
¼ teaspoon cream of tartar

Preheat oven to 425°F. Prick dough and line with foil. Fill with dried beans, uncooked rice or pie weights; bake 10 to 15 minutes or until lightly brown. Remove foil and beans. Cool completely on wire rack. In 2-quart saucepan, stir together ½ cup of the granulated sugar, the cornstarch, flour and salt. Add egg yolks and milk; stir with wire whisk until well blended. Bring to a boil over medium heat, stirring constantly. Continue cooking and stirring 2 minutes or until thick. Remove from heat. Stir in butter and vanilla.

Reduce oven temperature to 375°F. Cut peanut butter into powdered sugar until mixture resembles coarse crumbs. Sprinkle ⅓ of the peanut butter crumbs over bottom of pie crust. Spoon ½ of the milk mixture over crumbs. Sprinkle with another ⅓ of the crumbs, top with remaining pudding. Combine cream of tartar and egg whites in medium bowl. Beat egg whites at high speed until soft peaks form. Gradually add remaining ¼ cup granulated sugar, beating until stiff and glossy. Spread over pudding and seal to edge of crust. Sprinkle remaining peanut butter crumbs around edge. Bake 8 to 10 minutes or until meringue is golden. Cool completely on wire rack.

Topsy Turvy Apple Pie

♦ Beverly McDevitt from Livonia, Michigan was a finalist in the General Public category of the Apple-Cooking Cooking Contest, sponsored by the Michigan Apple Committee, DeWitt, Michigan.

Makes 6 to 8 servings

1 unbaked 9-inch double pie crust
¼ cup butter or margarine, softened
½ cup pecan halves
½ cup packed brown sugar
4 large Granny Smith apples, peeled, cored and sliced
1 tablespoon lemon juice
1 tablespoon all-purpose flour
½ cup granulated sugar
1 teaspoon ground cinnamon
1 teaspoon ground nutmeg
Dash of salt

Preheat oven to 400°F. Roll out half of pie crust dough on lightly floured surface to circle 1 inch larger than inverted pie plate. Set aside. Spread butter evenly on bottom and up side of 9-inch pie plate. Press pecans, rounded side down, into butter. Pat brown sugar over pecans. Press dough in pie plate over brown sugar. Place apples in large bowl; sprinkle with lemon juice. Combine flour, granulated sugar, cinnamon, nutmeg and dash of salt in small bowl. Add to apples; toss. Turn into pie crust; spread evenly to keep top level. Roll out remaining dough on lightly floured surface to 1 inch larger than pie plate. Place over apples; fold edge under and flute. Cut slits for steam to escape. Bake 50 minutes. Remove from oven; cool 5 minutes. Invert onto serving plate.

Brown sugar is a mixture of granulated sugar and molasses that adds a rich flavor to baked goods. Dark brown sugar has more molasses added and will actually give foods a darker color. Light brown sugar has a milder flavor and lighter color than the dark variety. Whatever the type, brown sugar is moist and clingy when fresh but can easily dry out. Adding a slice of apple or bread to the box or bag will restore moisture.

Making Caramel Flowers

These caramel flowers are easy to make and add that special touch to any dessert. Place one fresh, soft caramel on a very lightly floured surface. Pressing down firmly, roll the caramel out to a 1-inch square. Roll the flattened caramel into a cone to resemble a flower.

"Just in Case" Pie

♦ Christa I. Schmitt from Sykesville, Maryland won first place in the Chocolate Baked Goods category in the Chocolate Recipe Contest sponsored by Lexington Market, Inc., Baltimore, Maryland.

Makes 6 to 8 servings

Chocolate-Pecan Crust (recipe follows)
1 envelope unflavored gelatin
¼ cup cold water
1¾ cups whipping cream, divided
1 cup semisweet chocolate chips
2 eggs*
1 teaspoon vanilla
1 cup caramels (about 24)
2 tablespoons butter or margarine
Caramel flowers, for garnish

Prepare Chocolate-Pecan Crust; set aside. Sprinkle gelatin over water in small saucepan; let stand 1 minute. Stir over low heat until gelatin is completely dissolved, about 3 minutes. Stir in 1 cup of the cream. Heat just to a boil; immediately pour into a food processor or blender. Add chocolate chips and process until chocolate is completely melted, about 1 minute. Continue processing and add ½ cup of the cream, the eggs and vanilla. Pour into large bowl; refrigerate about 15 minutes or until thickened. Combine caramels, remaining ¼ cup of the cream and the butter in small saucepan. Simmer over low heat, stirring occasionally, until completely melted and smooth. Pour into prepared crust; let stand about 10 minutes. Beat thickened gelatin mixture until smooth. Pour over caramel layer; refrigerate 3 hours or until firm. Garnish with caramel flowers.

**Use clean, uncracked eggs.*

Chocolate-Pecan Crust: Preheat oven to 350°F. Combine 2 cups chocolate wafer cookie crumbs, ¾ cup finely chopped pecans and ½ cup melted butter or margarine in small bowl. Press on bottom and up side of 9-inch deep-dish pie plate, forming a high rim. Bake 10 minutes. Cool completely before filling.

The secret to creating a superbly tender pie crust is to add a small amount of acid, such as lemon juice, vinegar, sour cream or even crème fraîche, to the pastry dough along with the liquid.

Nutty Chocolate Sour Cream Pie

♦ Sharon Roach from Lincoln, Illinois was a finalist in the Pies category of the Blue Ribbon Culinary Contest at the Illinois State Fair, Springfield, Illinois.

Makes 6 to 8 servings

Flaky Pie Crust (recipe follows)
4 eggs
⅔ cup packed brown sugar
⅔ cup sour cream
¼ cup honey
1 teaspoon vanilla-nut flavoring
⅛ teaspoon salt
2 cups chopped pecans
1 cup semisweet chocolate chips

Prepare Flaky Pie Crust; set aside. Preheat oven to 350°F. Combine eggs, brown sugar, sour cream, honey, vanilla-nut flavoring and salt in large bowl; beat well. Stir in pecans and chocolate chips. Pour into prepared crust. Bake 40 to 45 minutes; cool completely on wire rack.

Flaky Pie Crust

1 egg, beaten
5 tablespoons cold water
1 teaspoon vinegar
1 teaspoon salt
1 cup shortening
3 cups all-purpose flour

Combine egg, water, vinegar and salt in medium bowl; set aside. Cut shortening into flour in large bowl until mixture resembles coarse crumbs. Add egg mixture; toss with fork until mixture holds together. Press together to form ball. Roll out on lightly floured surface to circle 1 inch larger than inverted 9-inch pie plate. Press in pie plate. Trim and flute edge.

DAYDREAM DESSERTS

Because these meringue treats are left in the oven for eight to twelve hours, you can make them in the evening and they will be done by morning. Hence the Howell family's nickname for them—"Go to Bed Cookies."

Chocolate Chip & Mint Meringue Cookies

♦ Katherine Howell from Royal Oak, Michigan was a prize winner in the Cookies category at the Michigan State Fair, Detroit, Michigan.

Makes about 4 dozen cookies

3 egg whites
½ teaspoon cream of tartar
Pinch of salt
¾ cup sugar
4 drops green food coloring
4 drops mint extract
1 package (6 ounces) miniature chocolate chips

Preheat oven to 375°F. Grease and lightly flour 2 cookie sheets. Beat egg whites with cream of tartar and salt until foamy. Gradually add sugar, 2 tablespoons at a time and beat until soft peaks form. Stir in food coloring and mint extract. Gently fold in chocolate chips. Drop by teaspoonfuls 1 inch apart onto prepared pans. Place in preheated oven, then turn off oven and let stand in oven with door closed 8 to 12 hours.

Carrot Cake

♦ Grace Meadows from Taylorville, Illinois was a finalist in the "Bake-A-Cake" category of the Blue Ribbon Culinary Contest at the Illinois State Fair, Springfield, Illinois.

Makes 8 to 10 servings

4 eggs
1½ cups vegetable oil
2 cups all-purpose flour
2 cups sugar
2 teaspoons baking soda
2 teaspoons baking powder
2 teaspoons ground cinnamon
¼ teaspoon salt
3 cups grated carrots
1½ cups coarsely chopped pecans or walnuts
Cream Cheese Icing (recipe follows)

Preheat oven to 350°F. Grease and flour 13 x 9-inch baking pan. Beat eggs and oil in small bowl. Combine flour, sugar, baking soda, baking powder, cinnamon and salt in large bowl. Add egg mixture; mix well. Stir in carrots and pecans. Pour into prepared pan. Bake 30 to 35 minutes or until wooden pick inserted into center comes out clean. Cool completely on wire rack. Spread with Cream Cheese Icing.

Cream Cheese Icing: Combine 1 box (16 ounces) powdered sugar, 1 package (8 ounces) cream cheese, softened, ½ cup margarine, softened and 1 teaspoon vanilla in medium bowl. Beat until smooth.

Spumoni is a Sicilian ice cream that is usually flavored with ground almonds and some type of fruit, such as cherries or lemons. It is lightened with whipped cream or egg whites and is a refreshing ending to a spicy Italian meal.

Simple Spumoni

♦ Jane Saribay from Pahala Elementary School in Pahala, Hawaii was a prize winner in a contest run by home economics teachers across the United States, sponsored by the Cherry Marketing Institute, Inc., Okemos, Michigan.

Makes about 1 quart

2 cups whipping cream
⅔ cup (7 ounces) sweetened condensed milk
½ teaspoon rum extract
1 can (21 ounces) cherry pie filling
½ cup chopped almonds
½ cup miniature chocolate chips

Combine cream, sweetened condensed milk and rum extract in large bowl; refrigerate 30 minutes. Remove from refrigerator and beat just until soft peaks form. Do not overbeat. Fold in cherry pie filling, almonds and chocolate chips. Transfer to 8 × 8-inch pan. Cover and freeze about 4 hours or until firm. Scoop out to serve. Garnish as desired.

Chocolate Chip Cake

♦ Darren Roach from Lincoln, Illinois was a finalist in the "Bake-A-Cake" category of the Blue Ribbon Culinary Contest at the Illinois State Fair, Springfield, Illinois.

Makes 8 to 10 servings

2 cups all-purpose flour
1 cup packed dark brown sugar
½ cup granulated sugar
1 tablespoon baking powder
1 teaspoon salt
½ teaspoon baking soda
½ cup shortening
1¼ cups milk
3 eggs
½ cup semisweet chocolate chips, finely chopped
1½ teaspoons vanilla
¼ cup finely chopped walnuts
Butterscotch Filling (recipe follows)
Chocolate Chip Glaze (recipe follows)

Preheat oven to 350°F. Grease and flour two 9-inch round baking pans. Combine all ingredients except walnuts, Butterscotch Filling and Chocolate Glaze in large bowl, mixing at low speed 30 seconds and scraping bowl constantly. Beat at high speed 3 minutes, scraping bowl occasionally. Pour into prepared pans. Bake 40 to 45 minutes or until wooden pick inserted into center comes out clean. Cool completely on wire rack.

Spread 1 cake layer with Butterscotch Filling; sprinkle with walnuts. Top with second cake layer and pour Chocolate Chip Glaze over top of cake. Garnish with additional walnuts if desired.

Butterscotch Filling: Combine ½ cup packed light brown sugar, ¼ cup cornstarch and ¼ teaspoon salt in medium saucepan. Add ½ cup water; cook over medium heat until mixture comes to a boil, stirring constantly. Boil and stir 1 minute. Stir in 1 tablespoon butter; cool.

Chocolate Chip Glaze: Combine ½ cup semisweet chocolate chips, 2 tablespoons butter and 1 tablespoon light corn syrup in small saucepan. Cook over low heat until chocolate melts, stirring constantly. Cool slightly.

Long, long ago, a proper pound cake was made from a pound of butter, a pound of flour, a pound of eggs and a pound of sugar. Modern cooks have modified this formula. Today, all the same ingredients are used, but the proportions have changed considerably. While pound cake cannot be classified as a health food, a well-made one is a comforting thing to have, especially when it is toasted and topped with black cherry preserves.

Sour Cream Pound Cake

♦ Jeanette Martin from Jacksonville, Illinois was a finalist in the "Bake-A-Cake" category of the Blue Ribbon Culinary Contest at the Illinois State Fair, Springfield, Illinois.

Makes 10 to 12 servings

1 cup butter, softened
2¾ cups sugar
1 tablespoon vanilla
2 teaspoons grated orange peel
6 eggs
3 cups all-purpose flour
½ teaspoon salt
¼ teaspoon baking soda
1 cup sour cream
Citrus Topping (recipe follows)

Preheat oven to 325°F. Grease 10-inch tube pan. Beat butter in large bowl until creamy; gradually add sugar, beating until light and fluffy. Beat in vanilla and orange peel. Add eggs, one at a time, beating 1 minute after each addition. Combine flour, salt and baking soda in small bowl. Add to butter mixture alternately with sour cream beginning and ending with flour mixture. Pour into prepared pan. Bake 1 hour and 15 minutes or until wooden pick inserted into center comes out clean. Spoon Citrus Topping over hot cake; cool in pan 15 minutes. Remove from pan to wire rack; cool completely.

Citrus Topping

⅓ cup slivered orange peel
2 teaspoons salt
⅓ cup orange juice
½ cup sugar, divided
⅓ cup lemon juice
1 teaspoon vanilla

Combine orange peel and salt in medium saucepan. Add enough water to cover; boil 2 minutes. Drain. Add orange juice and ¼ cup of the sugar; simmer 10 minutes. Add remaining ¼ cup sugar, the lemon juice and vanilla; stir until smooth.

Apricot Squares

♦ Alma Lauer from Abilene, Kansas was the first place winner in the Cookie category in the annual recipe contest sponsored by the *Reflector-Chronicle,* Abilene, Kansas.

Makes about 2 dozen squares

1 cup butter, softened
½ cup granulated sugar
½ teaspoon vanilla
2 cups all-purpose flour
1 jar (12 ounces) apricot jam
2 egg whites
½ teaspoon almond extract
1 cup powdered sugar
½ cup slivered almonds

Preheat oven to 350°F. Cream butter, granulated sugar and vanilla in large bowl until fluffy. Stir in flour; blend well. Spread in ungreased 13 x 9-inch baking pan. Bake 15 minutes. Cool completely on wire rack.

Spread jam over cooled crust. Beat egg whites and almond extract in medium bowl until soft peaks form. Gradually add powdered sugar and beat until stiff and glossy. Spread mixture over jam. Sprinkle with almonds. Bake at 350°F 15 to 20 minutes. Cool completely on wire rack. Cut into 2-inch squares.

GLORIOUS CHOCOLATE

Grand Marnier is one of the most popular orange-flavored liqueurs and is widely enjoyed in America. It comes from an infusion of the finest cognac with the peels of luscious Curaçao oranges. Some other orange-flavored liqueurs include Triple Sec, Cointreau and Curaçao.

Grand Marnier Brownies

♦ Mary P. Murphy from Hampton, New Hampshire was the first place winner in the Topsfield Fair Baking Competition sponsored by the Essex Agricultural Society, Topsfield, Massachusetts.

Makes about 2 dozen brownies

2 squares (1 ounce each) unsweetened chocolate
2 cups sugar
½ cup vegetable oil
½ cup Grand Marnier liqueur or other orange-flavored liqueur
¼ cup chocolate-flavored syrup
4 eggs, beaten
3 tablespoons unsweetened cocoa
2 teaspoons grated orange peel
1 teaspoon orange juice
1¼ cups all-purpose flour
1 teaspoon baking powder
1 package (12 ounces) semisweet chocolate chips, divided
2 tablespoons shortening
Orange peel strips, for garnish

Preheat oven to 350°F. Grease 13 × 9-inch pan. Melt unsweetened chocolate in top of double boiler over hot, not boiling, water. Remove from heat and mix in sugar, oil, liqueur, syrup, eggs, cocoa, orange peel and juice. Stir in flour, baking powder and 1⅓ cups of the chocolate chips. Spread batter evenly in prepared pan. Bake 22 minutes; do not overbake.

As soon as brownies are removed from oven, melt remaining ⅔ cup chocolate chips and shortening in top of double boiler over hot, not boiling water; stir until smooth. Spread hot chocolate mixture over warm brownies. Cool completely in pan on wire rack. Cut into 2-inch squares. Garnish with orange peel strips if desired.

Unsweetened cocoa is formed by extracting most of the cocoa butter from pure chocolate and grinding the remaining chocolate solids into a powder. "Dutch process" cocoa is unsweetened cocoa that has been treated with an alkali, giving it a darker appearance and a slightly less bitter flavor. In recipes, do not substitute sweetened cocoa, the type that is used for making hot chocolate, for unsweetened cocoa.

Chocolate Almond Ladyfinger Crown

♦ Jill Earl from Baltimore, Maryland won second place in the Chocolate Specialties category of the Chocolate Recipe Contest sponsored by Lexington Market, Inc., Baltimore, Maryland.

Makes about 12 servings

2 envelopes unflavored gelatin
1¼ cups sugar, divided
¾ cup unsweetened cocoa
4 eggs,* separated
2¼ cups milk
⅓ cup almond-flavored liqueur
2 packages (3 ounces each) ladyfingers, split
1½ cups whipping cream, whipped
Almond Cream (recipe follows)
Sliced almonds, for garnish

Mix gelatin with 1 cup of the sugar and the cocoa in medium saucepan. Blend in egg yolks beaten with milk and let stand 1 minute. Stir over low heat until gelatin is completely dissolved, about 5 minutes. Using a wire whisk, beat until completely blended, then stir in liqueur. Pour into large bowl and refrigerate, stirring occasionally, until mixture mounds slightly when dropped from spoon. Meanwhile, line bottom and side of 9-inch springform pan with ladyfingers; refrigerate.

Beat egg whites in large bowl until soft peaks form. Gradually add remaining ¼ cup sugar and beat until stiff and glossy. Fold egg whites into gelatin mixture, then fold in whipped cream. Pour mixture into prepared pan and refrigerate until firm. To serve, remove side of pan. Garnish with Almond Cream and sliced almonds.

Almond Cream: Beat ½ cup whipping cream with 1 tablespoon powdered sugar in small bowl until stiff and glossy. Fold in 1 tablespoon almond-flavored liqueur.

**Use clean, uncracked eggs.*

Mousse is a French word meaning froth or foam. It can be sweet or savory, but is always light and airy due to the addition of beaten egg whites and/or cream. When most people think of a mousse, they think of chocolate. Not so long ago chocolate mousse was on almost every menu and most accomplished cooks had at least two recipes for it. Like all the best desserts, it is made with eggs, sugar, cream and, of course, chocolate.

Chocolate Mousse Pie

♦ Terri Kaiser from West Haven, Connecticut was the first place winner in the No-Bake category in the Pie Contest, sponsored by *The Hartford Courant*, Hartford, Connecticut.

Makes 10 servings

1 package (8½ ounces) chocolate wafer cookies, finely crushed
½ cup butter, melted
16 ounces semisweet chocolate chips (about 2⅔ cups)
6 eggs,* separated
2 eggs,* whole
5 cups whipping cream, divided
⅓ cup plus ¼ cup powdered sugar, divided
2 teaspoons vanilla, divided
¼ cup miniature chocolate chips
Fresh raspberries and mint leaves, for garnish

Combine crumbs and butter in medium bowl. Press on bottom and up side of 9-inch springform pan; set aside.

Melt chocolate chips in top of double boiler over hot, not boiling, water. Beat egg yolks with the 2 whole eggs. Add to hot melted chocolate; mix well. Beat egg whites in large bowl until stiff peaks form; set aside. Whip 3 cups of the cream in large bowl until soft peaks form. Gradually add ⅓ cup of the sugar and 1 teaspoon of the vanilla; whip until stiff and glossy. Fold chocolate mixture into whipped cream. Fold beaten egg whites and ¼ cup miniature chocolate chips into cream mixture. Pour into prepared crust and refrigerate at least 3 hours. (Pour any extra filling into individual dishes.)

Whip remaining 2 cups cream in large bowl until soft peaks form. Gradually add remaining ¼ cup sugar and 1 teaspoon vanilla. Spread over chilled pie. To serve, remove side of pan and garnish with raspberries and mint leaves.

**Use clean, uncracked eggs.*

Not really chocolate at all because it lacks chocolate liquor (the main component in unsweetened chocolate), white chocolate is cocoa butter with added sugar, milk and flavorings (often vanilla or vanillin). It is more delicate than other chocolates and burns easily. So melt it carefully using a double boiler and stirring constantly.

To make white chocolate triangles, spread melted white chocolate into a rectangle on a waxed paper-lined baking sheet. Refrigerate until set but not hard. With tip of a knife make a diagonal score cutting rectangle into two triangles. Refrigerate until firm.

Chocolate Bombe

♦ Pat Miceli from Baltimore, Maryland won third place in the Chocolate Recipe Contest sponsored by Lexington Market, Inc., Baltimore, Maryland.

Makes about 8 servings

1 package (12 ounces) semisweet chocolate chips
5 whole eggs,* divided
3 egg whites,*
1¼ cups sugar, divided
1 cup flour
1 teaspoon baking soda
1 cup unsweetened cocoa
1 cup water
¼ cup vegetable oil
Melted white chocolate, for garnish

Melt chocolate chips in top of double boiler over hot, not boiling, water. Beat 3 of the whole eggs and add to chocolate. Continue to cook, stirring constantly, until mixture starts to bubble and thicken. Beat 3 egg whites in large bowl until soft peaks form. Gradually add ¼ cup of the sugar and beat until stiff and glossy. Fold whites into chocolate mixture. Pour into oiled 2- to 3-quart mold or bowl; cover and refrigerate 4 hours.

Preheat oven to 375°F. Grease and flour 8- or 9-inch round baking pan. Sift flour with baking soda. Beat the remaining 2 whole eggs and 1 cup sugar in medium bowl until creamy. Stir in cocoa and flour mixture. Add water and oil; mix until smooth. Pour batter into prepared pan. Bake 18 to 20 minutes or until wooden pick inserted into center comes out clean. Cool 10 minutes in pan. Loosen edge and remove to wire rack; cool completely.

Unmold mousse onto cake. Cover with plastic wrap and refrigerate at least 4 hours. Drizzle with melted white chocolate before serving.

**Use clean, uncracked eggs.*

Soufflé Making Tips

To ensure perfect soufflés, start by choosing the right dish. Choose a porcelain or ceramic dish with straight sides made just for soufflés. To extend the side and support the soufflé use a waxed paper "collar." Fold a sheet of waxed paper in half lengthwise and carefully tape it to the dish, overlapping ends.

Gently fold beaten egg whites into soufflé mixture just until combined. Too much agitation can cause the egg whites to break down and the soufflé to fall.

Black Forest Soufflé

♦ Angie Leialoha Oliveros from Pahala, Hawaii was a prize winner in a contest run by home economics teachers across the United States sponsored by the Cherry Marketing Institute, Inc., Okemos, Michigan.

Makes about 10 servings

3 eggs,* separated
2 cups milk
2 envelopes unflavored gelatin
¾ cup sugar, divided
4 squares (1 ounce each) semisweet chocolate
2 teaspoons rum extract
1½ teaspoons vanilla
2 cups whipping cream, divided
1 can (21 ounces) cherry pie filling
⅓ cup chopped almonds
Maraschino cherries and chocolate curls, for garnish

Tape a 3-inch-wide greased and floured waxed paper or parchment paper "collar" around rim of 1-quart soufflé dish, greased side in. Beat egg yolks and milk in small bowl. Mix gelatin with ½ cup of the sugar in medium saucepan. Add egg mixture; let stand 1 minute. Stir over low heat until gelatin is completely dissolved, about 5 minutes. Add chocolate; stir constantly until melted. Beat until thoroughly blended. Stir in rum extract and vanilla. Pour into large bowl and refrigerate, stirring occasionally, until mixture mounds slightly when dropped from spoon.

Beat egg whites in large bowl until soft peaks form. Gradually add remaining ¼ cup sugar and beat until stiff and glossy. Fold into gelatin mixture. Whip 1½ cups of the cream in medium bowl until stiff peaks form; fold into gelatin mixture. Fold in cherry pie filling and almonds. Pour mixture into prepared dish and refrigerate until set. To serve, whip remaining ½ cup cream until stiff peaks form. Remove collar and decorate with whipped cream, maraschino cherries and chocolate curls.

**Use clean, uncracked eggs.*

Chocolate Chiffon Cake

♦ Jeanette Monahan from Albuquerque, New Mexico was a finalist in the Cakes category at the New Mexico State Fair, Albuquerque, New Mexico.

Makes about 12 servings

1 bar (4 ounces) sweet baking chocolate
½ cup hot water
5 eggs, separated
⅔ cup sugar
1 cup all-purpose flour
1 teaspoon baking powder
½ teaspoon salt
1 teaspoon vanilla
Powdered sugar

Preheat oven to 350°F. Melt chocolate in hot water; set aside. Beat egg whites in large bowl until soft peaks form. Gradually add sugar and beat until stiff and glossy; set aside. Combine melted chocolate mixture, egg yolks, flour, baking powder, salt and vanilla in small bowl; beat 1 minute with electric mixer. Carefully fold chocolate mixture into egg whites until blended. Pour into ungreased 10-inch tube pan. Bake 45 to 50 minutes or until top springs back when lightly touched. Invert in pan; cool completely. Remove from pan; sprinkle with powdered sugar.

FRUIT FANTASIES

Acini di Pepe Fruit Pudding

♦ Verda Seeklander from Hazelton, North Dakota was the second place winner in the Delicious Desserts category of the Pasta Contest sponsored by the North Dakota Wheat Commission.

Makes 8 servings

1 cup acini di pepe or other small pasta, cooked and drained
¾ cup milk
1 can (20 ounces) crushed pineapple in juice, drained, reserving ½ cup juice
2 eggs, well beaten
½ cup granulated sugar
½ teaspoon grated lemon peel
½ teaspoon ground cinnamon (optional)
⅔ cup packed brown sugar
⅔ cup finely chopped walnuts
¼ cup all-purpose flour
6 tablespoons butter or margarine
Whipped topping, for serving

Cook acini di pepe according to package directions; drain well. Preheat oven to 375°F. Grease 8 × 8-inch baking pan. Combine pasta, milk, reserved ½ cup pineapple juice, the eggs, granulated sugar, lemon peel and cinnamon in large bowl. Spoon mixture into prepared pan. Top with pineapple.

Combine brown sugar, walnuts and flour in small bowl; cut in butter until mixture resembles coarse crumbs. Sprinkle over pineapple. Bake 60 minutes or until knife inserted into center comes out clean. Serve warm or cold with whipped topping.

Note: Any type of fruit canned in fruit juice may be used, such as fruit cocktail, peaches, pears, etc.

Cobblers, pandowdies, buckles, grunts and slumps are all old-fashioned fruit desserts that have lost none of their charm with the passing of generations. The fruit can be anything from huckleberries and blueberries to apples and peaches. Cobblers are usually baked in a deep dish and often have a pastry crust and/or a biscuit-like topping. This version has a crunchy brown sugar and oatmeal topping.

Crunch Peach Cobbler

♦ Gladys Montgomery from Orangevale, California was a prize winner in the Peach Cobbler Contest at the California State Fair.

Makes about 6 servings

1 can (29 ounces) *or* 2 cans (16 ounces each) cling peach slices in syrup
1/3 cup plus 1 tablespoon granulated sugar, divided
1 tablespoon cornstarch
1/2 teaspoon vanilla
1/2 cup packed brown sugar
2 cups all-purpose flour, divided
1/3 cup uncooked rolled oats
1/4 cup margarine or butter, melted
1/2 teaspoon ground cinnamon
1/2 teaspoon salt
1/2 cup shortening
4 to 5 tablespoons cold water
Whipped cream, for serving

Drain peach slices, reserving 3/4 cup syrup. Combine 1/3 cup of the granulated sugar and the cornstarch in small saucepan. Slowly add reserved peach liquid, stirring to make sauce smooth; add vanilla. Cook over low heat, stirring constantly, until thickened. Set aside.

Combine brown sugar, 1/2 cup of the flour, the oats, margarine and cinnamon in small bowl; stir until crumbly. Set aside.

Preheat oven to 350°F. Combine remaining 1 1/2 cups flour, 1 tablespoon granulated sugar and the salt in small bowl. Cut in shortening until mixture resembles coarse crumbs. Sprinkle water, 1 tablespoon at a time, over flour mixture and toss lightly until mixture holds together. Press together to form ball. Roll out on floured surface to 10-inch square. Press on bottom and about 1 inch up sides of 8 × 8-inch baking dish.

Layer peaches, sauce and crumb topping over crust. Bake 45 minutes. Serve warm or at room temperature with whipped cream.

Apricot Roll-Ups

♦ Harriet Kuhn from Patterson, California was the Apricot Sweepstakes winner at the Patterson Apricot Fiesta, sponsored by the Apricot Advisory Board, Walnut Creek, California.

Makes 20 to 26 roll-ups

4 cups dried apricots
1 can (12 ounces) apricot-pineapple nectar
1½ cups water
½ cup sugar
2 tablespoons lemon juice
1 tablespoon quick-cooking tapioca
2 cups finely chopped walnuts
1 package (7 ounces) shredded coconut
1 package egg roll wrappers
Vegetable oil, for frying
Sour cream and chocolate sauce, for dipping

Combine apricots, nectar, water, sugar and lemon juice in large saucepan; bring to a boil. Remove from heat; cover and let stand 1 hour. Drain, reserving liquid. Finely chop apricots. Combine apricots, reserved liquid and tapioca in same saucepan; bring to a boil, stirring constantly. Remove from heat and let stand 20 minutes. Stir in walnuts and coconut.

For each roll-up, place about 2 heaping tablespoons of the apricot mixture on lower half of egg roll wrapper. Moisten left and right edges with water. Fold bottom edge up to just cover filling. Fold left and right edges ½ inch over; roll up jelly-roll fashion. Moisten top edge and seal.

Heat about 2 inches oil in heavy skillet to 370°F. Fry roll-ups, a few at a time, seam side down in hot oil until golden brown; turn as necessary. Drain on paper towels. Serve with bowls of sour cream and chocolate sauce for dipping.

Bees have been producing honey for more than 5 million years, and it has been harvested for almost 3 million. A worker bee will toil for an entire lifetime to make 1/12 teaspoon of honey (about 3 drops). Darker honeys are stronger in flavor than lighter honeys.

Apples 'n' Honey Nut Tart

♦ Mary King of Concordia, Kansas was a grand prize winner in the Dessert category of the "Celebrate! Kansas Food" Recipe Contest.

Makes 8 to 10 servings

1¼ cups all-purpose flour
⅓ cup wheat germ
⅓ cup packed brown sugar
½ teaspoon salt
¾ teaspoon grated orange peel, divided
½ cup cold butter, cut into pieces
1 egg, beaten
1 cup pecans, coarsely chopped
⅓ cup golden raisins
8 tablespoons honey, divided
2 tablespoons butter, melted
½ teaspoon ground cinnamon
4 cups peeled, cored, ¼-inch-thick apple slices
⅓ cup orange marmalade
⅔ cup whipping cream

Combine flour, wheat germ, sugar, salt and ½ teaspoon of the orange peel in large bowl. Cut in ½ cup cold butter until mixture resembles coarse crumbs. Stir in egg until well blended; press in bottom and up side of 9-inch tart pan with removable bottom. Freeze until very firm, about 30 minutes.

Preheat oven to 350°F. Sprinkle pecans and raisins on chilled crust. Combine 6 tablespoons of the honey, the 2 tablespoons melted butter, remaining ¼ teaspoon orange peel, the cinnamon and apple slices in large bowl; stir to coat apples. Arrange apple slices in circular pattern on top of pecans and raisins. Drizzle any honey mixture left in bowl over apples. Bake 50 to 55 minutes or until apples are tender. Heat marmalade until warm; brush over apples. Cool; remove side of tart pan. Whip cream until soft peaks form. Add remaining 2 tablespoons honey and whip until stiff and glossy. Serve with tart.

Note: If desired, sprinkle 1 cup granola over top of tart after it has been glazed with marmalade.

We have come a long way on the road to culinary evolution since the days, when we refused to eat kiwifruit, because we thought they were small suede potatoes. But we are no longer fooled by the fuzzy brown skin. We know it hides the succulent, emerald-green flesh that often is described as a combination of melon, pineapple and strawberry.

Raspberry Cheesecake Blossoms

♦ Vienna Taylor from Richmond, Virginia was a finalist in the Dairy Dessert Recipe Contest, sponsored by the Southeast United Dairy Industry Association, Atlanta, Georgia.

Makes 12 servings

8 sheets phyllo dough
¼ cup butter, melted
½ cup cottage cheese
1 package (8 ounces) cream cheese, softened
1 egg
½ cup plus 3 tablespoons sugar, divided
4 teaspoons lemon juice, divided
½ teaspoon vanilla
3 packages (10 ounces each) frozen raspberries, thawed and drained, reserving syrup
Fresh raspberries and sliced kiwifruit, for garnish

Preheat oven to 350°F. Grease 12 (2½-inch) muffin cups. Layer 4 sheets of phyllo dough on waxed paper, brushing each sheet with melted butter. Repeat with remaining 4 sheets, forming separate stack. Cut each stack in half lengthwise and then in thirds crosswise, to make a total of 12 squares. Gently fit each stacked square into prepared muffin cup, forming 4-petaled blossom.

Process the cheeses, egg, 3 tablespoons of the sugar, 1 teaspoon of the lemon juice and the vanilla in a food processor or blender until smooth. Divide evenly among blossom cups. Bake 10 to 15 minutes or until lightly browned. Carefully remove from muffin cups to cool.

Bring reserved raspberry syrup to a boil in small saucepan. Cook until reduced to ¾ cup, stirring occasionally. Purée thawed raspberries in food processor or blender; press through sieve to remove seeds. Combine raspberry purée, syrup, remaining ½ cup sugar and 3 teaspoons lemon juice. Refrigerate.

To serve, spoon raspberry sauce onto 12 dessert plates. Place cheesecake blossom on each plate. Top with fresh raspberries and arrange kiwifruit in sauce to resemble leaves.

GRAND FINALES

The first meringue was created by a Swiss pastry chef named Gastaparini in the early eighteenth century. He named his new dessert Mehryngen in honor of the snow-clad Alpine village where he spent his boyhood. Gradually the spelling of the word was simplified until it became meringue.

Angel Cream Dessert

♦ Sharon Roach from Lincoln, Illinois was a finalist in the Baked Desserts Using Dairy Foods category at the Illinois State Fair, Springfield, Illinois.

Makes 8 servings

3 egg whites
⅛ teaspoon salt
1½ cups sugar, divided
1 teaspoon baking powder
1½ teaspoons vanilla, divided
1 cup crumbled saltine crackers*
½ cup chopped pecans
1 package (3 ounces) cream cheese, softened
1 cup mini marshmallows
½ cup whipped cream
½ cup sour cream
¼ cup chopped maraschino cherries
Assorted fresh fruit, for serving

Preheat oven to 350°F. Grease 8-inch round baking pan. Beat egg whites and salt until soft peaks form. Combine 1 cup of the sugar and the baking powder; gradually beat into egg whites. Add 1 teaspoon of the vanilla and beat until stiff and glossy. Fold in crackers and pecans. Pour into prepared pan. Bake 30 minutes. Turn off oven and let stand in oven 10 minutes. Remove from oven and cool completely; center will fall. Remove from pan.

Combine cream cheese with remaining ½ cup sugar and ½ teaspoon vanilla. Gently fold in marshmallows, whipped cream, sour cream and cherries. Spread over cooled base and refrigerate. Serve with fresh fruit if desired.

**Saltines should be crumbled with hand so they are not too fine.*

In French, "coeur à la crème" means "heart with cream." Coeur à la crème is a classic dessert often made in specially shaped wicker baskets or heart-shaped porcelain molds with holes in the bottom. After the cheese mixture is placed in the cheesecloth-lined baskets or molds, the holes allow the liquid (whey) in the cheeses to drain off. You can find coeur à la crème molds in specialty food shops.

Coeur à la Crème

♦ James St. Clair was a prize winner at the March of Dimes Gourmet Gala in Boston, Massachusetts.

Makes 6 servings

1 package (8 ounces) cream cheese, softened
1 cup small curd cottage cheese
1 cup whipping cream
⅓ cup powdered sugar
2 teaspoons vanilla
1 pint fresh strawberries, hulled
2 tablespoons orange-flavored liqueur

Blend cream cheese and cottage cheese in food processor or blender. In small chilled bowl, whip cream with sugar and vanilla until stiff peaks form. Fold whipped cream into cheese mixture. Line 6 coeur à la crème molds with moist cheesecloth. Divide cheese mixture evenly between molds. Place on platter and refrigerate until thoroughly chilled.

Process strawberries and liqueur in food processor or blender until puréed. To serve, spoon strawberry sauce onto small dessert plates; invert each coeur à la crème onto sauce.

Every April in Vermont, when the snow is often still thick on the ground, a great maple festival takes place. There are maple-glazed doughnuts, maple-sugar candy, pancakes drenched in maple syrup and as much maple fudge to eat as a body can bear. And, of course, there's a cooking contest where the winner is crowned Mrs. Maple, the Maple Queen.

Maple Sweetheart

♦ Jeannine Dandurand was the winner of the Mrs. Maple award at the Vermont Maple Festival, St. Albans, Vermont.

Makes about 10 servings

1 package (3 ounces) ladyfingers, split
2 tablespoons unflavored gelatin
¼ cup cold water
½ cup real maple syrup
5 eggs*
1½ cups heavy cream
Dark brown sugar and whipped cream, for garnish

Line sides of 9-inch springform pan with ladyfingers. Sprinkle gelatin over water in small saucepan; let stand 1 minute. Stir over low heat until gelatin is completely dissolved, about 5 minutes.

Bring maple syrup in heavy saucepan to a boil; continue boiling until it reaches 230°F on a candy thermometer. Meanwhile, beat eggs in large bowl until light and fluffy. Gradually add hot syrup in thin stream, beating until mixture starts to cool. Stir in gelatin. Refrigerate about 30 minutes or until mixture mounds slightly when dropped from spoon.

In medium bowl, whip cream until stiff peaks form; fold into thickened mixture. Pour into prepared pan and refrigerate 2 hours until firm. To serve, remove side of pan and garnish with brown sugar and additional whipped cream.

**Use clean, uncracked eggs.*

Making Vanilla Sugar

To make vanilla sugar, place 1 or 2 vanilla beans in a small canister of granulated sugar. Keep the canister tightly closed for a few weeks or until the sugar is infused with the flavor of vanilla. You can continue to replenish the sugar in the canister until the beans lose their flavoring power. Substitute vanilla sugar for plain sugar whenever a sweet vanilla flavor is desired.

Crème Brûlée

♦ Sue Wylie was a prize winner at the March of Dimes Gourmet Gala in Lexington, Kentucky.

Makes 6 servings

2 cups whipping cream
1 tablespoon vanilla sugar
4 egg yolks, beaten
¾ cup sieved brown sugar*

Preheat oven to 350°F. Heat cream in top of covered double boiler over hot, not boiling, water 5 to 7 minutes or until hot but not scalding. Remove from heat and add vanilla sugar; stir until dissolved. Gradually beat egg yolks into hot cream. Pour into 7½-inch pie plate or 6 small ovenproof bowls. Set plate or bowls in pan of hot water. Bake on middle rack of oven 50 to 60 minutes or until set. (The custard may still look runny, but it will continue to set up after being removed from oven.) Refrigerate until well chilled.

Preheat broiler. Sprinkle ¼-inch-thick layer of brown sugar over top of custard. Broil 6 inches from heat, rotating occasionally, to brown the sugar evenly. A fine, dark golden crust will form. Serve immediately to enjoy the hot and cold contrasts or refrigerate and serve cold.

**To measure sieved brown sugar, press sugar through sieve, letting it fall lightly into measuring cup.*

Note: Since the custard should be very cold when placed under the broiler, it is best to make it the day before you plan to serve it.

BREAKFAST & BRUNCH

Chocolate Waffles with Raspberry Syrup (page 324)

BREAKFAST BASICS

Start your day off right with a great breakfast. Included here are the basics to get you going—eggs, cereal, pancakes and waffles. They're all simple and easy to make, but tasty enough to capture your attention.

Pictured here is Three-Egg Omelet; *see page 288 for recipe.*

THREE-EGG OMELET

This omelet can be served plain or filled with one or more of the suggested fillings.

1 tablespoon butter or margarine
3 eggs, lightly beaten
Salt and freshly ground pepper to taste
Fillings (see below)

1. Melt butter in 10-inch skillet over medium heat.

2. Add eggs; lift cooked edges with spatula to allow uncooked eggs to flow under cooked portion. Season with salt and pepper. Shake pan to loosen omelet. Cook until set. Place desired fillings on ½ of omelet. Fold in half. Turn out onto plate.

Makes 1 serving

Filling Suggestions:
Shredded cheese
Chopped ham
Shredded crabmeat
Cooked small shrimp
Shredded cooked chicken
Cooked chopped bell pepper
Cooked sliced mushrooms
Chopped tomatoes
Cooked chopped onion
Cooked chopped asparagus, broccoli or other vegetables
Avocado slices

BERRY CRÊPES WITH ORANGE SAUCE

1 cup fresh blueberries
1 cup sliced strawberries
1 tablespoon sugar
3 packages (3 ounces each) cream cheese, softened
¼ cup honey
¾ cup orange juice
8 (6½-inch) Crêpes (page 289)

1. Combine blueberries, strawberries and sugar in small bowl; set aside.

2. To prepare sauce, beat cream cheese and honey until light; slowly beat in orange juice.

3. Spoon about ½ cup of berry filling in center of 1 crêpe. Spoon about 1 tablespoon sauce over berries. Roll up; place on serving plate. Repeat with remaining crêpes.

4. Pour remaining sauce over crêpes.

Makes 4 servings

CRÊPES

3/4 cup all-purpose flour
3 eggs
1 cup milk
3 tablespoons butter or margarine, melted
1/2 teaspoon salt
About 2 tablespoons vegetable oil

1. Combine all ingredients except oil in blender or food processor container. Cover; process until combined. Cover and refrigerate at least 1 hour.

2. Brush 7-inch skillet with oil. Place over medium heat until hot. Add 3 tablespoons crêpe batter, tilting skillet to cover bottom evenly.

3. Cook until golden brown on bottom; turn over. Cook until browned on underside.

4. Stack crêpes between waxed paper squares to prevent sticking together. Repeat with remaining batter, oiling skillet occasionally.

Makes 16 crêpes

Tip: *Stacked crêpes can be placed in plastic bag and refrigerated 2 to 3 days or frozen up to 1 month. Thaw before using.*

SAUSAGE GRAVY

Serve over hot biscuits for a Southern-style breakfast.

1/4 pound spicy bulk sausage
1/4 cup all-purpose flour
2 cups milk
1/2 teaspoon salt
1/4 teaspoon freshly ground pepper

1. Cook sausage in medium saucepan over medium heat until browned, stirring to crumble.

2. Drain off all fat except about 2 tablespoons. Stir in flour. Cook, stirring constantly, until thickened and bubbly.

3. Gradually whisk in milk, salt and pepper. Cook, stirring constantly, until thickened and bubbly, about 5 minutes.

Makes about 4 servings

WAFFLES

Tightly wrap and freeze leftover waffles. They can go straight from the freezer to the toaster to make a quick hot breakfast!

2¼ cups all-purpose flour
2 tablespoons sugar
1 tablespoon baking powder
½ teaspoon salt
2 eggs, beaten
¼ cup vegetable oil
2 cups milk

1. Preheat waffle iron; grease lightly.

2. Sift flour, sugar, baking powder and salt into large bowl. Combine eggs, oil and milk in medium bowl. Stir liquid ingredients into dry ingredients until moistened.

3. For each waffle, pour about ¾ cup of batter into waffle iron. Close lid and bake until steaming stops.* *Makes about 6 round waffles*

*Check the manufacturer's directions for recommended amount of batter and baking time.

STRAWBERRY SAUCE

Enjoy the fresh sweet taste of strawberries in the morning by serving this sauce with yogurt, hot cereal, pancakes or waffles.

1 pint strawberries, hulled
2 to 3 tablespoons sugar
1 tablespoon strawberry- or orange-flavored liqueur (optional)

Combine strawberries, sugar and liqueur in blender or food processor container. Cover; process until strawberries are puréed.

Makes 1½ cups

For crispier waffles, use less batter and let them cook for a few seconds longer after the steaming has stopped.

Waffles with Strawberry Sauce

PUFF PANCAKE WITH SUMMER BERRIES

2 eggs
1/2 cup all-purpose flour
1/2 cup milk
2 tablespoons butter or margarine, melted
1 tablespoon sugar
1/4 teaspoon salt
Summer Berries (recipe follows)

1. Preheat oven to 425°F. Grease 10-inch ovenproof skillet.

2. With electric mixer, beat eggs. Add flour, milk, butter, sugar and salt; beat until smooth.

3. Pour batter into prepared skillet. Bake 15 minutes.

4. *Reduce oven temperature to 350°F.* Continue baking 10 to 15 minutes or until puffed and golden brown.

5. Serve pancake in skillet with Summer Berries. *Makes 6 servings*

Summer Berries

2 cups blueberries
1 cup sliced strawberries
1 cup raspberries
Sugar to taste
Cream (optional)

Combine blueberries, strawberries and raspberries in medium bowl. Gently toss with sugar. Let stand 5 minutes. Top with cream if desired.

BAKING POWDER BISCUITS

2 cups all-purpose flour
1 tablespoon baking powder
1/2 teaspoon salt
1/4 cup butter or margarine
3 tablespoons shortening
About 3/4 cup milk

1. Preheat oven to 450°F. Grease baking sheet.

2. Sift flour, baking powder and salt into medium bowl. Using pastry blender or 2 knives, cut in butter and shortening until mixture resembles coarse crumbs. Stir in enough milk to make soft dough.

3. Turn out onto lightly floured surface. Knead dough lightly. Roll out ½ inch thick. Cut biscuit rounds with 2-inch cutter. Place on greased baking sheet.

4. Bake 8 to 10 minutes or until browned. *Makes 16 biscuits*

Drop Biscuits: Make dough as above, increasing milk to about 1 cup or enough to make stiff batter. Drop by tablespoonfuls onto greased baking sheet. Bake 5 to 8 minutes or until browned.

Makes about 28 biscuits

CREAMY OATMEAL

Even when made with low-fat milk, this cooking method gives a rich, creamy flavor.

1⅓ cups old-fashioned rolled oats
3 cups milk
½ cup raisins
4 teaspoons sugar
⅛ teaspoon salt

1. Combine oats, milk, raisins, sugar and salt in medium saucepan over medium heat.

2. Bring to a boil, stirring occasionally. Reduce heat and simmer 5 minutes. Cover; remove from heat. Let stand 5 minutes.

Makes 4 servings

For a quick, make-ahead breakfast, freeze oatmeal in individual portions. It can be reheated quickly in the microwave, saving the fuss of measuring, cooking and cleaning up.

SUNRISE PANCAKES

Drizzle rich Vanilla Cream Syrup over these light, fluffy pancakes for a breakfast or brunch treat.

Vanilla Cream Syrup (recipe follows)
1 cup all-purpose flour
2 tablespoons sugar
1 teaspoon baking powder
½ teaspoon baking soda
½ teaspoon salt
2 eggs, slightly beaten
½ cup plain yogurt
½ cup water
2 tablespoons butter or margarine, melted

1. Prepare Vanilla Cream Syrup; set aside.

2. Combine flour, sugar, baking powder, baking soda and salt in large bowl.

3. Combine eggs, yogurt and water in medium bowl. Whisk in butter. Pour liquid ingredients, all at once, into dry ingredients; stir until moistened.

4. Preheat griddle or large skillet over medium heat; grease lightly. Pour about ¼ cup batter onto hot griddle for each pancake; spread batter out to make 5-inch circles. Cook until tops of pancakes are bubbly and appear dry; turn and cook until browned, about 2 minutes.

Makes about 8 pancakes

Vanilla Cream Syrup

½ cup sugar
½ cup light corn syrup
½ cup whipping cream
1 teaspoon vanilla
1 nectarine, diced

Combine sugar, corn syrup and cream in 1-quart pan. Cook, stirring constantly, over medium heat until sugar is dissolved. Simmer 2 minutes or until syrup thickens slightly. Remove from heat. Stir in vanilla and nectarine. *Makes 1 cup*

Sunrise Pancakes

SCRAMBLED EGGS

For great scrambled eggs, be sure to cook them slowly over medium heat. Do not overcook or they will become tough.

1 tablespoon butter or margarine
6 eggs, lightly beaten
1/2 teaspoon salt
1/4 teaspoon freshly ground pepper

1. Melt butter in 10-inch skillet over medium heat.

2. Season eggs with salt and pepper. Add eggs to skillet; cook, stirring gently and lifting to allow uncooked eggs to flow under cooked portion. Do not overcook; eggs should be soft with no liquid remaining.

Makes 4 servings

Scrambled Egg Options

Add one or more of the following to the beaten egg mixture and cook as above:

Chopped fresh herbs
Diced green chilies
Cooked chopped onions
Chopped sun-dried tomatoes
Cooked chopped vegetables
Shredded cheese
Crumbled cooked bacon or cooked sausage
Chopped smoked salmon
Chopped ham or Canadian bacon

BUTTERMILK PANCAKES

2 cups all-purpose flour
1 tablespoon sugar
1 1/2 teaspoons baking powder
1/2 teaspoon baking soda
1/2 teaspoon salt
1 egg, beaten
1 1/2 cups buttermilk
1/4 cup vegetable oil

1. Sift flour, sugar, baking powder, baking soda and salt into large bowl.

2. Combine egg, buttermilk and oil in medium bowl. Stir liquid ingredients into dry ingredients until moistened.

3. Preheat griddle or large skillet over medium heat; grease lightly. Pour about 1/2 cup batter onto hot griddle for each pancake. Cook until tops of pancakes are bubbly and appear dry; turn and cook until browned, about 2 minutes. *Makes about 12 (5-inch) pancakes*

Silver Dollar Pancakes: Use 1 tablespoon batter for each pancake. Cook as above. Makes about 40 pancakes.

Buttermilk Substitution

If you don't have buttermilk on hand, try this easy substitution:

Place 1 tablespoon vinegar in measuring cup. Add milk to measure 1 1/2 cups. Stir well; let stand 5 minutes.

COUNTRY BREAKFAST SAUSAGE

Sausage is surprisingly easy to make and is leaner than the commercial variety. Feel free to adjust the seasonings to your personal taste.

1 pound ground pork
1 teaspoon ground cumin
1/2 teaspoon dried leaf thyme
1/2 teaspoon dried leaf sage
1 teaspoon salt
1/2 teaspoon freshly ground pepper
1/8 teaspoon ground red (cayenne) pepper (optional)

1. Combine all ingredients in medium bowl; mix well. Cover and refrigerate overnight for flavors to blend.

2. Shape into 6 patties. Cook in lightly greased skillet over medium heat about 15 minutes or until browned on both sides and centers are no longer pink, turning occasionally. *Makes 6 servings*

QUICK BREAKFASTS

No time for breakfast? There's no excuse with these terrific, quick-as-a-flash recipes. Make up one of the creamy Bagel Toppers or the Breakfast in a Glass and you can be off and running in the morning.

Pictured here is Pita in the Morning; *see page 300 for recipe.*

PITA IN THE MORNING

1 teaspoon butter or margarine
2 eggs, lightly beaten
¼ teaspoon salt
Dash pepper
1 whole-wheat pita bread, cut in half
¼ cup sprouts
2 tablespoons shredded Cheddar cheese
2 tablespoons chopped tomato
Avocado slices (optional)

1. Melt butter at HIGH (100%) 30 seconds in microwave-safe 1-quart casserole.

2. Season eggs with salt and pepper. Add eggs to casserole. Microwave at HIGH 1½ to 2½ minutes, stirring once. Do not overcook; eggs should be soft with no liquid remaining.

3. Open pita to make pockets. Arrange sprouts in pockets. Divide cheese and eggs evenly between pockets. Top with tomato and avocado slices.

Makes 1 sandwich

SUNRISE BURRITO

2 ounces bulk sausage
¼ cup chopped onion
2 eggs
1 tablespoon water
2 tablespoons canned chopped green chilies
1 (10-inch) flour tortilla

1. Combine sausage and onion in microwave-safe 1-quart casserole. Microwave at HIGH (100%) 1½ to 2½ minutes or until sausage is brown and onion is tender, stirring once to break up meat.

2. Beat eggs with water in small bowl. Stir in chilies.

3. Drain fat from casserole. Add egg mixture to sausage and onion; mix well. Microwave at HIGH 1½ to 2½ minutes, stirring once. Do not overcook; eggs should be soft with no liquid remaining.

4. Microwave tortilla at HIGH about 15 seconds. Fill with scrambled egg mixture.

Makes 1 burrito

DANISH BAGEL

1 raisin or blueberry bagel, halved
½ cup ricotta cheese
8 teaspoons Cinnamon Sugar (recipe follows), divided
1 peach, thinly sliced

1. Preheat broiler.

2. Spread bagel halves with ricotta. Sprinkle each bagel with 2 teaspoons Cinnamon Sugar. Arrange peach slices over cheese. Sprinkle with remaining Cinnamon Sugar.

3. Place bagel halves on baking sheet. Broil 6 inches from heat, about 4 minutes, until sugar is bubbly and mixture is hot. Serve warm.
Makes 2 servings

Cinnamon Sugar: Combine ½ cup sugar with 1 tablespoon ground cinnamon. Store in shaker-top jar.

MICROWAVED OATS CEREAL

1¾ cups water
⅓ cup old-fashioned rolled oats
⅓ cup oat bran
1 tablespoon brown sugar
¼ teaspoon ground cinnamon
⅛ teaspoon salt

1. Combine all ingredients in large microwave-safe bowl (cereal expands rapidly when it cooks). Cover with plastic wrap; vent.

2. Microwave on HIGH (100%) about 6 minutes or until thickened. Stir well. Let stand 2 minutes before serving. *Makes 2 servings*

Add some excitement to your oatmeal by stirring in peanut butter, mashed bananas or molasses. (Or maybe all three!)

BAGEL TOPPERS

All of these versatile spreads and toppers can be made ahead of time and kept on hand for a quick breakfast anytime.

Orange-Cream Bagel Spread

1 package (8 ounces) cream cheese, softened
3 tablespoons orange marmalade

Combine cream cheese and marmalade in small bowl.
Makes about 1 cup

Chocolate-Cream Bagel Spread

1 package (8 ounces) cream cheese, softened
3 ounces white chocolate, melted
2 tablespoons mini chocolate chips

Combine cream cheese and white chocolate in small bowl. Stir in chocolate chips. *Makes about 1¼ cups*

Crab Bagel Spread

4 ounces cream cheese, softened
2 ounces crabmeat, shredded
4 teaspoons lemon juice
2 tablespoons chopped green onion tops
1 tablespoon milk

Combine all ingredients in medium bowl. *Makes about ¾ cup*

Peanut Butter Topper

2 tablespoons creamy peanut butter
1 tablespoon raisins
1 small banana, thinly sliced
1 tablespoon sunflower kernels

Spread bagel with peanut butter. Top with raisins, banana slices and sunflower kernels. *Makes 1 to 2 servings*

Crab Bagel Spread and Peanut Butter Topper

BREAKFAST IN A GLASS

Cool and refreshing, these shakes, smoothies and coolers are a great way to start the day. Just mix everything together in a blender, pour it into a glass and you are off and running!

Peachy Banana Shake

1 cup milk
1/2 cup vanilla ice cream
1 ripe banana, cut into chunks
1 peach, sliced
1 teaspoon vanilla extract

Place all ingredients in blender container. Cover; process until smooth.
Makes about 2 cups

Berry-Banana Breakfast Smoothie

1 carton (8 ounces) berry-flavored yogurt
1 ripe banana, cut into chunks
1/2 cup milk

Place all ingredients in blender container. Cover; process until smooth.
Makes about 2 cups

Peanut Butter-Banana Shake

1 ripe banana, cut into chunks
2 tablespoons peanut butter
1/2 cup vanilla ice cream
1 cup milk

Place all ingredients in blender container. Cover; process until smooth.
Makes about 2 cups

Mocha Cooler

1 cup milk
1 tablespoon instant coffee granules
1 tablespoon chocolate syrup
1/4 cup vanilla or coffee ice cream

Place all ingredients in blender container. Cover; process until smooth.
Makes about 1 1/2 cups

Rise 'n' Shine Shake

- **1 cup milk**
- **1 cup strawberries, hulled**
- **1 kiwifruit, peeled and quartered**
- **1/4 cup vanilla or strawberry frozen yogurt**
- **1 to 2 tablespoons sugar**

Place all ingredients in blender container. Cover; process until smooth.

Makes about 1 1/2 cups

Raspberry Lemon Smoothie

- **1 cup frozen raspberries**
- **1 carton (8 ounces) lemon-flavored yogurt**
- **1/2 cup milk**
- **1 teaspoon vanilla**

Place all ingredients in blender container. Cover; process until smooth.

Makes about 1 1/2 cups

Mango Yogurt Drink

- **1/2 cup plain yogurt**
- **1 ripe mango, peeled, seeded and sliced**
- **1/4 cup orange juice**
- **1 teaspoon honey**
- **2 ice cubes**
- **Milk (optional)**

Place all ingredients in blender container. Cover; process until smooth. Add milk to obtain preferred consistency. *Makes about 1 1/2 cups*

Tip: *The skin of most mangos tinges with more red or yellow as the fruit ripens. Mangos are ready to eat when they yield to gentle pressure.*

A Nutritious Breakfast

Nutritionists suggest you include foods from three of the four food groups for a healthy breakfast. The four food groups are: milk and dairy products, fruits and vegetables, breads and cereals and meat and protein foods (including eggs and dried peas and beans).

EGG ENTRÉES

No breakfast or brunch would be complete without eggs, and this delightful chapter presents them in all their glory. From classic dishes such as quiches and omelets to unique creations like Chilies Rellenos Casserole, there's a recipe here to fit every menu.

Pictured here are Egg Blossoms; see page 308 for recipe, with Papaya-Kiwifruit Salad with Orange Dressing; see page 340 for recipe.

EGG BLOSSOMS

Egg Blossoms will add a bright and cheery note to your morning meal.

4 sheets filo pastry
2 tablespoons butter, melted
4 teaspoons grated Parmesan cheese
4 eggs
4 teaspoons minced green onion
Salt and freshly ground pepper
Tomato Sauce (recipe follows)

1. Preheat oven to 350°F. Grease 4 (2½-inch) muffin cups.

2. Brush 1 sheet of filo with butter. Top with another sheet; brush with butter. Cut stack into 6 (4-inch) squares. Repeat with remaining 2 sheets. Stack 3 squares together, rotating so corners do not overlap. Press into greased muffin cup. Repeat with remaining squares.

3. Sprinkle 1 teaspoon cheese into each filo-lined cup. Break 1 egg into each cup. Sprinkle onion over eggs. Season with salt and pepper. Bake 15 to 20 minutes or until pastry is golden and eggs are set. Serve with Tomato Sauce. *Makes 4 servings*

Tomato Sauce

1 can (16 ounces) whole tomatoes, undrained, chopped
1 clove garlic, minced
½ cup chopped onion
1 tablespoon white wine vinegar
¼ teaspoon dried leaf oregano
½ teaspoon salt

Combine tomatoes, garlic, onion, vinegar, oregano and salt in medium saucepan. Cook, stirring occasionally, over medium heat until onion is tender, about 20 minutes. Serve warm.

CHILIES RELLENOS CASSEROLE

For a weekend brunch, bake this in individual baking dishes, then lavish with your choice of garnishes.

3 eggs, separated
3/4 cup milk
3/4 cup all-purpose flour
1/2 teaspoon salt
1 tablespoon butter or margarine
1/2 cup chopped onion
2 cans (7 ounces each) whole green chilies, drained
8 slices (1 ounce each) Monterey Jack cheese, cut into halves
Garnishes: Sour cream, sliced green onions, pitted ripe olive slices, guacamole and salsa

1. Preheat oven to 350°F.

2. Combine egg yolks, milk, flour and salt in blender or food processor container. Cover; process until smooth. Pour into bowl and let stand.

3. Melt butter in small skillet over medium heat. Add onion; cook until tender.

4. Pat chilies dry with paper towels. Slit each chili lengthwise and carefully remove seeds. Place 2 halves of cheese and 1 tablespoon onion in each chili; reshape chilies to cover cheese.

5. Place chilies in single layer in greased 13×9-inch baking dish.

6. In small clean bowl, beat egg whites until soft peaks form; fold into yolk mixture. Pour over chilies.

7. Bake 20 to 25 minutes or until topping is puffed and knife inserted in center comes out clean. Broil 4 inches below heat 30 seconds or until topping is golden brown. Serve with desired garnishes.

Makes 4 servings

MUSHROOM & ONION EGG BAKE

1 tablespoon vegetable oil
4 green onions, chopped
4 ounces mushrooms, sliced
1 cup low-fat cottage cheese
1 cup sour cream
6 eggs
2 tablespoons all-purpose flour
1/4 teaspoon salt
1/8 teaspoon freshly ground pepper
Dash hot pepper sauce

1. Preheat oven to 350°F. Grease shallow 1-quart baking dish.

2. Heat oil in medium skillet over medium heat. Add onions and mushrooms; cook until tender. Set aside.

3. In blender or food processor, process cottage cheese until almost smooth. Add sour cream, eggs, flour, salt, pepper and hot pepper sauce; process until combined. Stir in onions and mushrooms. Pour into greased dish. Bake about 40 minutes or until knife inserted near center comes out clean.

Makes about 6 servings

STUFFED TOMATOES & CREAMED SPINACH

4 medium tomatoes
1/4 cup grated Parmesan cheese
4 eggs
4 teaspoons minced green onion
Salt and freshly ground pepper to taste
Creamed Spinach (page 312)

1. Preheat oven to 375°F.

2. Cut thin slice off blossom end of each tomato; remove seeds and pulp, being careful not to pierce side of tomato. Place tomato shells in shallow baking dish.

3. Sprinkle 1 tablespoon Parmesan cheese inside each tomato. Break an egg into each tomato. Top with onion, salt and pepper. Bake 15 to 20 minutes or until eggs are set. Serve with Creamed Spinach.

Makes 4 servings

Mushroom & Onion Egg Bake with Country Breakfast Sausage (page 297)

Creamed Spinach

1 package (10 ounces) frozen chopped spinach, thawed
2 tablespoons butter or margarine
2 tablespoons all-purpose flour
1 cup milk
1/4 teaspoon salt
Dash freshly ground pepper
1 tablespoon grated Parmesan cheese (optional)

1. Press spinach to remove all moisture; set aside. Melt butter in medium saucepan over medium heat. Stir in flour; cook until bubbly.

2. Slowly stir in milk. Cook until thickened. Add spinach; continue cooking over low heat, stirring constantly, about 5 minutes or until spinach is tender. Season with salt, pepper and cheese.

EASY CRAB-ASPARAGUS PIE

4 ounces crabmeat, shredded
12 ounces fresh asparagus, cooked
1/2 cup chopped onion, cooked
1 cup (4 ounces) shredded Monterey Jack cheese
1/4 cup grated Parmesan cheese
Freshly ground pepper
3/4 cup all-purpose flour
3/4 teaspoon baking powder
1/2 teaspoon salt
2 tablespoons butter or margarine, chilled
1 1/2 cups milk
4 eggs

1. Preheat oven to 350°F. Lightly grease 10-inch quiche dish or pie plate.

2. Layer crabmeat, asparagus and onion in prepared pie plate. Top with cheeses. Season with pepper.

3. Combine flour, baking powder and salt in large bowl. With pastry blender or 2 knives, cut in butter. Add milk and eggs; stir until blended. Pour over vegetables and cheeses.

4. Bake about 30 minutes or until filling is puffed and knife inserted near center comes out clean. Serve hot. *Makes 6 servings*

SPANISH POTATO OMELET

Cut this cook-ahead omelet into thin wedges to serve as an appetizer. It is sturdy enough to pick up with your fingers and is traditionally served at room temperature.

1/4 cup olive oil
1/4 cup vegetable oil
1 pound thin-skinned red or white potatoes, cut into 1/8-inch slices
1/2 teaspoon salt, divided
1 small onion, cut in half lengthwise, thinly sliced crosswise
1/4 cup chopped green bell pepper
1/4 cup chopped red bell pepper
3 eggs

1. Heat oils in large skillet over medium-high heat. Add potatoes to hot oil. Turn with spatula several times to coat all slices with oil.

2. Sprinkle with 1/4 teaspoon salt. Cook 6 to 9 minutes or until potatoes become translucent, turning occasionally. Add onion and peppers. Reduce heat to medium.

3. Cook 10 minutes or until potatoes are tender, turning occasionally. Drain mixture in colander placed in large bowl; reserve oil. Let potato mixture stand until cool.

4. Beat eggs with remaining 1/4 teaspoon salt in large bowl. Gently stir in potato mixture; lightly press into bowl until mixture is covered with eggs. Let stand 15 minutes.

5. Heat 2 teaspoons reserved oil in 6-inch skillet over medium-high heat. Spread potato mixture in pan to form solid layer. Cook until egg on bottom and side of pan is set but top still looks moist.

6. Cover pan with plate. Flip omelet onto plate, then slide omelet back into pan uncooked side down. Continue to cook until bottom is lightly browned.

7. Slide omelet onto serving plate. Let stand 30 minutes before serving. Cut into 8 wedges to serve. *Makes 8 servings*

ARTICHOKE FRITTATA

A frittata is an Italian omelet with the filling mixed in with the eggs instead of folded inside.

1 can (14 ounces) artichoke hearts, drained and rinsed
Olive oil
1/2 cup minced green onions
5 eggs
1/2 cup (2 ounces) shredded Swiss cheese
2 tablespoons grated Parmesan cheese
1 tablespoon minced fresh savory *or* 1 teaspoon dried leaf savory
1 tablespoon minced fresh parsley
1 teaspoon salt
Freshly ground pepper to taste

1. Chop artichoke hearts; set aside.

2. Heat 1 tablespoon olive oil in 10-inch skillet over medium heat. Add green onions; cook until tender. Remove with slotted spoon; set aside.

3. Beat eggs in medium bowl until light. Stir in artichokes, green onions, cheeses, herbs, salt and pepper.

4. Heat 1 1/2 teaspoons olive oil in same skillet over medium heat. Pour egg mixture into skillet.

5. Cook 4 to 5 minutes or until bottom is lightly browned. Place large plate over skillet. Invert frittata onto plate. Return frittata, uncooked side down, to skillet. Cook about 4 minutes more or until center is just set. Cut into 6 wedges to serve. *Makes 6 servings*

Cooking Eggs

Remember when cooking eggs that too high a temperature will cause them to be tough and rubbery. Use either low or medium heat.

Artichoke Frittata with Greek Three Pepper Salad (page 335)

SCRAMBLED EGGS WITH TAMALES

1 can (15 ounces) tamales
8 eggs
2 tablespoons milk
1/2 teaspoon salt
2 tablespoons butter or margarine
1 large tomato, chopped
2 tablespoons minced onion
2 tablespoons diced green chilies
1 cup (4 ounces) shredded Monterey Jack cheese

1. Preheat oven to 350°F.

2. Drain tamales, reserving 1/2 of sauce from can. Remove paper wrappings from tamales; place tamales in single layer in 10×6-inch baking dish. Cover with reserved sauce. Bake 10 minutes or until heated through.

3. Whisk eggs, milk and salt in medium bowl. Set aside.

4. Melt butter in large skillet over medium heat. Add tomato, onion and chilies. Cook 2 minutes or until vegetables are heated through. Add egg mixture. Cook, stirring gently, until eggs are soft set.

5. Remove tamales from oven. Spoon eggs over tamales; sprinkle with cheese. Broil 4 inches below heat 30 seconds or just until cheese melts.

Makes 4 to 6 servings

FRESH STRAWBERRY BANANA OMELETS

A fruit-filled omelet can be a refreshing change of pace.

1 cup sliced strawberries
1 banana, sliced
4 teaspoons sugar
1/4 teaspoon grated lemon peel
1 tablespoon lemon juice
4 eggs
1/4 cup water
1/4 teaspoon salt
2 tablespoons butter or margarine, divided

1. Combine strawberries, banana, sugar, lemon peel and juice in medium bowl; mix lightly. Cover; let stand 15 minutes at room temperature.

2. Combine eggs, water and salt in small bowl. Melt 1 tablespoon butter in 8-inch omelet pan or skillet over medium heat.

3. Add ½ egg mixture (about ½ cup). Lift cooked edges with spatula to allow uncooked eggs to flow under cooked portion. Shake pan to loosen omelet.

4. Cook until almost set; add ½ cup fruit filling. Fold in half. Turn out onto plate. Keep warm. Repeat with remaining egg mixture. Top with remaining egg filling. *Makes 2 servings*

SPINACH CHEESE STRATA

This is a perfect make-ahead meal because it must be refrigerated for at least 6 hours. So make it up the day before, refrigerate overnight and just pop it in the oven about an hour before brunch.

6 slices whole wheat bread
2 tablespoons butter or margarine, softened
1 cup (4 ounces) shredded Cheddar cheese
½ cup (2 ounces) shredded Monterey Jack cheese
1¼ cups milk
6 eggs, lightly beaten
1 package (10 ounces) frozen spinach, thawed and well drained
¼ teaspoon salt
⅛ teaspoon pepper

1. Spread bread with butter. Arrange buttered slices in single layer in greased 13×9-inch baking dish. Sprinkle with cheeses.

2. Combine milk, eggs, spinach, salt and pepper in large bowl; stir well. Pour over bread and cheese.

3. Cover; refrigerate at least 6 hours or overnight.

4. Bake, uncovered, at 350°F about 1 hour or until puffy and lightly golden. *Makes 4 to 6 servings*

BREADS & COFFEECAKES

Syrup-drenched French toast, crispy waffles, and muffins and coffeecakes fresh from the oven—you'll love the variety of fantastic flavors when making these exceptional treats for your next breakfast or brunch.

Pictured here is French Raisin Toast; see page 320 for recipe.

FRENCH RAISIN TOAST

2 tablespoons sugar
1 teaspoon ground cinnamon
4 eggs, lightly beaten
½ cup milk
8 slices raisin bread
4 tablespoons butter or margarine, divided
Powdered sugar

1. Combine sugar and cinnamon in wide shallow bowl. Beat in eggs and milk. Add bread; let stand to coat, then turn to coat other side.

2. Heat 2 tablespoons of butter in large skillet over medium-low heat. Add bread slices; cook until brown. Turn and cook other side. Remove and keep warm. Repeat with remaining butter and bread. Sprinkle with powdered sugar. *Makes 4 servings*

HAM & SWISS CHEESE BISCUITS

This classy combination is terrific as a breakfast biscuit and any leftovers make great snacks.

2 cups all-purpose flour
2 teaspoons baking powder
½ teaspoon baking soda
½ cup butter or margarine, chilled, cut into pieces
½ cup (2 ounces) shredded Swiss cheese
2 ounces ham, minced
About ⅔ cup buttermilk

1. Preheat oven to 450°F. Grease baking sheet.

2. Sift flour, baking powder and baking soda into medium bowl. Using pastry blender or 2 knives, cut in butter until mixture resembles coarse crumbs. Stir in cheese, ham and enough buttermilk to make soft dough.

3. Turn out dough onto lightly floured surface; knead lightly. Roll out dough ½ inch thick. Cut biscuit rounds with 2-inch cutter. Place on greased baking sheet.

4. Bake about 10 minutes or until browned. *Makes about 18 biscuits*

PEAR BREAD PUDDING

4 eggs, beaten
3/4 cup sugar
3 cups milk
1 tablespoon vanilla extract
8 slices egg bread, crusts removed
3 to 4 tablespoons butter or margarine, softened
1 can (16 ounces) sliced pears, drained, sliced *or* 1 cup sliced cooked pears
Cream or Vanilla Sauce (recipe follows)

1. Grease 9×9-inch baking dish.

2. Combine eggs and sugar in large bowl. Gradually stir in milk and vanilla; set aside.

3. Lightly spread both sides of bread with butter. Arrange layer of bread slices in dish; top with another layer of bread slices. Arrange pear slices on bread. Pour egg mixture over bread and pears; let stand 30 minutes.

4. Preheat oven to 350°F. Place dish in larger pan, then fill larger pan with enough hot water to come halfway up sides of dish.

5. Bake about 55 minutes or until mixture is puffed and knife inserted near center comes out clean. Serve warm with cream or Vanilla Sauce.

Makes 10 servings

Vanilla Sauce

1 cup sugar
3 tablespoons all-purpose flour
3 tablespoons cornstarch
4 1/2 cups milk
4 egg yolks, beaten
2 tablespoons butter or margarine
1 tablespoon vanilla extract

1. Combine sugar, flour and cornstarch in large saucepan.

2. Gradually whisk in milk. Cook over medium heat, stirring constantly, until mixture comes to a boil, 10 to 15 minutes. Remove from heat.

3. Stir 1 cup of hot mixture into egg yolks. Stir egg yolk mixture into hot mixture; return to heat. Cook, stirring constantly, until mixture is bubbly. Continue cooking, stirring constantly, 2 minutes. Pour into heatproof bowl; stir in butter and cool. Stir in vanilla. *Makes about 5 cups*

BLUEBERRY LATTICE COFFEECAKE

1 package (1/4 ounce) active dry yeast
1 teaspoon sugar
1/4 cup warm water (110°F)
1 egg, beaten
1/2 cup butter or margarine, softened
1/3 cup milk
3 cups all-purpose flour
1/4 cup sugar
1/2 teaspoon salt
2 packages (8 ounces each) cream cheese, softened
2 egg yolks
2/3 cup sugar
1 teaspoon vanilla extract or lemon extract
1 tablespoon grated lemon peel (optional)
1 cup fresh or frozen blueberries

1. Dissolve yeast and 1 teaspoon sugar in warm water in large bowl. Let stand 10 minutes.

2. Beat in 1 egg, butter and milk. Beat in flour, 1/4 cup sugar and salt to make soft dough. Knead on lightly floured surface about 10 minutes or until smooth and satiny, adding more flour as necessary to prevent sticking. Cover and let rest while making filling.

3. Combine cream cheese, 2 egg yolks, 2/3 cup sugar, vanilla and lemon peel in medium bowl. Beat until combined; set aside.

4. Grease 13×9-inch pan. Divide dough into thirds; set 1/3 aside. Roll out remaining 2/3 of dough to 13×9-inch rectangle. Place in greased pan and press dough 1/2 inch up sides to contain filling.

5. Spoon filling into dough-lined pan. Arrange blueberries over filling, pressing blueberries lightly into filling. Roll out remaining dough to 10-inch square. Cut dough into 1-inch strips. Arrange strips diagonally across pan in lattice pattern over filling, sealing strips to edges.

6. Cover with plastic wrap and refrigerate at least 2 hours or overnight.

7. Preheat oven to 350°F. Bake, uncovered, about 40 minutes or until lightly browned and filling is set. Serve warm or at room temperature.

Makes 1 coffeecake (15 servings)

Top: Pear Bread Pudding (page 321)
Bottom: Blueberry Lattice Coffeecake

CHOCOLATE WAFFLES

A fruity topping like Raspberry Syrup is the perfect complement to the delicate chocolate flavor of these waffles.

2 cups all-purpose flour
1/4 cup unsweetened cocoa powder
2 tablespoons sugar
1 tablespoon baking powder
1/2 teaspoon salt
2 cups milk
2 eggs, beaten
1/4 cup vegetable oil
1 teaspoon vanilla extract
Raspberry Syrup (recipe follows)

1. Preheat waffle iron; grease lightly.

2. Sift flour, cocoa, sugar, baking powder and salt into large bowl. Combine milk, eggs, oil and vanilla in small bowl. Stir liquid ingredients into dry ingredients until moistened.

3. For each waffle, pour about 3/4 cup batter into waffle iron. Close lid and bake until steaming stops.* Serve with Raspberry Syrup.

Makes about 6 waffles

*Check manufacturer's directions for recommended amount of batter and baking time.

Raspberry Syrup

1 cup water
1 cup sugar
1 package (10 ounces) frozen raspberries in syrup

1. Combine water and sugar in large saucepan. Cook over medium heat, stirring constantly, until sugar has dissolved. Continue cooking until mixture thickens slightly, about 10 minutes.

2. Stir in frozen raspberries; cook, stirring, until berries are thawed. Bring to a boil; continue cooking until syrup thickens slightly, about 5 to 10 minutes. Serve warm.

Makes about 1 1/3 cups

APPLE-ALMOND COFFEECAKES

You can prepare this coffeecake the night before, top it with the apples just before baking and have the aroma of fresh coffeecake filling the house when your guests arrive.

1 package (1/4 ounce) active dry yeast
1 teaspoon sugar
1/4 cup warm water (110°F)
3 eggs, divided
1/2 cup butter or margarine, softened
1/3 cup milk
3 cups all-purpose flour
1 cup sugar, divided
1/2 teaspoon salt
2 packages (7 ounces each) almond paste
3 small apples

1. Dissolve yeast and 1 teaspoon sugar in warm water in large bowl. Let stand 10 minutes.

2. Beat in 1 egg, butter and milk. Beat in flour, 1/4 cup sugar and salt to make soft dough. Knead on lightly floured surface about 10 minutes or until smooth and satiny, adding flour as necessary to prevent sticking. Cover and let rest while making filling.

3. Cut almond paste into small pieces. Combine almond paste, remaining 2 eggs and 1/2 cup sugar in blender or food processor container. Cover; process until combined. Set aside.

4. Grease two 9-inch round cake pans. Divide dough in half. Roll out 1/2 of dough to 9-inch circle. Place in greased pan and press dough 1/2 inch up side to contain filling. Repeat with remaining dough.

5. Divide almond filling equally between pans. Cover with plastic wrap and refrigerate at least 2 hours or overnight.

6. Preheat oven to 350°F. Core apples and cut into thin slices; do not peel. Arrange apple slices over almond filling. Sprinkle each coffeecake with 2 tablespoons sugar. Bake about 40 minutes or until filling is set. Serve warm or at room temperature.

Makes 2 coffeecakes (8 to 10 servings each)

APRICOT RING

FILLING

1 cup dried apricots, chopped
1 cup apple juice
3/4 cup sugar or to taste

DOUGH

1 package (1/4 ounce) active dry yeast
4 tablespoons sugar, divided
1 cup warm water (110°F)
About 4 cups all-purpose flour, divided
1 teaspoon salt
2 eggs, beaten
1/4 cup butter or margarine, softened
1 egg white, lightly beaten
2 tablespoons sliced almonds

1. To make filling, combine apricots and apple juice in small saucepan over medium heat. Cover and cook, stirring occasionally, about 12 minutes or until apricots are tender and juice is absorbed. Stir in sugar to taste. Cook, stirring constantly, about 3 minutes or until mixture is thick paste. Cool.

2. To make dough, dissolve yeast and 1 tablespoon sugar in warm water in large bowl of electric mixer. Let stand 10 minutes. Add remaining 3 tablespoons sugar, 1 cup flour and salt.

3. Beat with electric mixer 2 minutes. Add eggs and butter. Beat 1 minute. Stir in enough of remaining 3 cups flour to make soft dough.

4. Knead dough on lightly floured surface about 10 minutes or until smooth, adding flour as necessary to prevent sticking. Cover and let rest 20 minutes.

5. Grease large baking sheet. On lightly floured surface, roll dough to 18×11-inch rectangle. Spread filling over dough. Roll up jellyroll-style, starting at long side. Seal edge; form into ring on greased baking sheet, sealing ends.

6. Cut ring at 1-inch intervals about two-thirds of the way through, using kitchen scissors or sharp knife. Turn each slice outward to form a petal as you cut.

7. Cover with damp cloth and let rise in warm place until doubled in bulk, about 45 minutes.

8. Preheat oven to 350°F. Brush with egg white and sprinkle with almonds. Bake about 30 minutes or until browned.

Makes 1 large coffeecake (15 to 18 servings)

PET
PASTEURIZED MILK
GRADE "A"
LABORATORY
CONTROLLED
HALF PINT
LIQUID
100
PURE
SWEE

MUFFIN SURPRISE

These muffins need no butter or jam, that's the surprise inside! They are perfect for a buffet.

1½ cups all-purpose flour
2½ teaspoons baking powder
¼ teaspoon salt
1 cup oat bran
½ cup packed light brown sugar
1 cup milk
⅓ cup vegetable oil
2 eggs, lightly beaten
1 teaspoon vanilla extract
1 package (3 ounces) cream cheese
¾ cup apricot-pineapple jam

1. Preheat oven to 425°F. Grease 12 (2½-inch) muffin cups.

2. Sift flour, baking powder and salt into large bowl. Stir in oat bran and brown sugar; set aside. In small bowl, combine milk, oil, eggs and vanilla. Stir milk mixture into dry ingredients just until moistened.

3. Cut cream cheese into 12 equal pieces. Spoon about ½ of batter into prepared muffin cups, filling about ⅓ full. Spoon about 1 tablespoon jam on top of batter. Top with 1 piece of cream cheese. Spoon remaining batter over jam and cheese, filling each muffin cup ⅔ full. Bake about 14 to 16 minutes or until browned. *Makes 12 muffins*

Honey Butter

For a sweet spread that is terrific on everything from muffins to toast, combine equal amounts of softened butter or margarine and honey, then add a little vanilla extract. You'll want to keep a batch of this on hand to sweeten all your breakfasts.

***Top:** Spicy Sweet Potato Muffins (page 330)*
***Bottom:** Muffin Surprise*

SPICY SWEET POTATO MUFFINS

The unusual addition of sweet potatoes makes this a very moist and tasty muffin.

2 tablespoons packed brown sugar
1 teaspoon ground cinnamon
1½ cups all-purpose flour
2 teaspoons baking powder
1 teaspoon ground cinnamon
½ teaspoon salt
½ teaspoon baking soda
½ teaspoon ground allspice
⅓ cup packed brown sugar
1 cup mashed cooked or canned sweet potatoes
¾ cup buttermilk
¼ cup vegetable oil
1 egg, beaten

1. Preheat oven to 425°F. Grease 12 (2½-inch) muffin cups.

2. Combine 2 tablespoons brown sugar and cinnamon in small bowl; set aside.

3. Sift flour, baking powder, cinnamon, salt, baking soda and allspice into large bowl. Stir in ⅓ cup brown sugar.

4. In medium bowl, combine sweet potato, buttermilk, oil and egg. Stir buttermilk mixture into dry ingredients just until combined. Spoon batter into prepared muffin cups, filling each ⅔ full. Sprinkle each muffin with ½ teaspoon of cinnamon mixture. Bake about 14 to 16 minutes or until toothpick inserted in center comes out clean. *Makes 12 muffins*

RAISIN OAT SCONES

These scones are also perfect with a cup of afternoon tea.

2 cups all-purpose flour
2 teaspoons baking powder
½ teaspoon baking soda
¼ teaspoon salt
1 cup rolled oats
½ cup butter or margarine, chilled, cut into pieces
1 cup raisins
About 1 cup buttermilk

1. Preheat oven to 425°F. Grease baking sheet.

2. Sift flour, baking powder, baking soda and salt into medium bowl. Stir in oats. Using pastry blender or 2 knives, cut in butter until mixture resembles coarse crumbs. Add raisins. Stir in enough buttermilk to make soft dough.

3. Turn out dough onto lightly floured surface; knead until smooth. Roll out dough to 12 × 10-inch rectangle. Cut into 2-inch squares.

4. Arrange scones on prepared baking sheet. Bake about 15 minutes or until browned. *Makes 30 scones*

CARAMEL-TOPPED MEGA MUFFINS

6 tablespoons butter or margarine
6 tablespoons packed brown sugar
1/4 cup corn syrup
1 cup raisin and bran cereal
3/4 cup milk
1/4 cup unprocessed wheat bran
3/4 cup molasses
1/4 cup vegetable oil
1 egg, beaten
2 cups all-purpose flour
1 tablespoon baking powder
2 teaspoons ground allspice or cinnamon
1/2 teaspoon baking soda
1/2 teaspoon salt
1/2 cup raisins (optional)

1. Preheat oven to 400°F. Grease 6 large (4-inch) muffin cups.

2. Combine butter, brown sugar and corn syrup in small saucepan over medium heat. Cook, stirring constantly, until sugar has dissolved. Bring to a boil without stirring. Pour about 2 tablespoons of mixture into each prepared muffin cup; set aside.

3. Combine cereal, milk and wheat bran in medium bowl. Let stand about 10 minutes to soften. Stir in molasses, oil and egg. Sift flour, baking powder, allspice, baking soda and salt into large bowl. Stir liquid ingredients into dry ingredients just until combined. Stir in raisins.

4. Spoon batter over topping, using about 1/2 cup for each muffin. Bake about 25 minutes or until toothpick inserted in center comes out clean. Immediately turn out on cooling rack. *Makes 6 large muffins*

SPECIAL BRUNCHES

When planning that next special get-together, check out these scrumptious dishes suitable for all kinds of brunches. Everything from crêpes and quiches to beverages is included here. You're sure to find one (or more) perfect for the occasion.

Pictured here is Shrimp-Spinach Crêpe Stack; see page 334 for recipe and Orange Juice & Champagne; see page 334 for recipe.

SHRIMP-SPINACH CRÊPE STACK

1 recipe Creamed Spinach (page 312)
1 tablespoon vegetable oil
½ medium onion, chopped
1 clove garlic, minced
8 ounces fresh mushrooms, sliced
8 ounces small cooked shrimp
2 tablespoons lemon juice
¼ teaspoon dried leaf tarragon
½ teaspoon salt
⅛ teaspoon freshly ground pepper
6 (6½-inch) Crêpes (page 289)
1 cup (4 ounces) shredded Swiss cheese

1. Prepare Creamed Spinach; set aside.

2. Heat oil in medium skillet over medium heat; add onion and garlic. Cook, stirring occasionally, until onion is tender. Add mushrooms; cook until mushrooms are tender.

3. Continue cooking until moisture has evaporated. Stir in Creamed Spinach, shrimp, lemon juice, tarragon, salt and pepper.

4. Preheat oven to 375°F. Place 1 crêpe in lightly greased shallow baking dish. Spread ¾ cup shrimp filling over crêpe. Repeat layers with remaining crêpes and filling, ending with crêpe. Sprinkle top with cheese. Bake about 30 minutes or until filling is heated through. Cut into wedges to serve. *Makes 4 servings*

Rolled Shrimp-Spinach Crêpes: Use 8 (6½-inch) crêpes. Prepare filling as above. Spoon about ⅓ cup of filling on each crêpe. Roll to enclose filling. Place in lightly greased 13×9-inch baking dish. Repeat with remaining crêpes and filling. Sprinkle with cheese. Bake about 15 minutes or until filling is heated through. *Makes 4 servings*

ORANGE JUICE & CHAMPAGNE

6 teaspoons orange-flavored liqueur
1 quart orange juice, chilled
1 bottle (750 ml) champagne, chilled

Pour 1 teaspoon liqueur into each of 6 wine glasses. Fill each two-thirds full with orange juice. Fill glasses with champagne.

Makes 6 servings

HAM & CHEESE QUESADILLAS

½ cup (2 ounces) shredded Monterey Jack cheese
½ cup (2 ounces) shredded Cheddar cheese
4 (10-inch) flour tortillas
4 ounces ham, finely chopped
¼ cup chopped canned green chilies
Salsa (optional)

1. Combine cheeses; divide equally between 2 tortillas. Place ham and green chilies over cheese. Top each with another tortilla.

2. Heat large skillet over medium heat. Add 1 quesadilla; cook until cheese starts to melt and bottom is browned, about 2 minutes. Turn over and cook other side until browned. Remove and keep warm while cooking remaining quesadilla. Cut each quesadilla into 8 wedges. Serve with salsa, if desired.

Makes 2 servings

GREEK THREE PEPPER SALAD

½ cup olive oil
2 tablespoons lemon juice
1 tablespoon water
2 teaspoons white wine vinegar
1 tablespoon chopped fresh parsley
¾ teaspoon minced fresh oregano *or* ¼ teaspoon dried leaf oregano
½ teaspoon sugar
1 red bell pepper, thinly sliced
1 green bell pepper, thinly sliced
1 yellow or orange bell pepper, thinly sliced
½ red onion, thinly sliced
½ cup Greek-style olives
2 ounces feta cheese, crumbled
Salt and pepper to taste

1. Pour oil into small bowl. Add lemon juice, water, vinegar, parsley, oregano and sugar; whisk until thickened.

2. Combine peppers, onion and olives in large bowl. Add dressing. Toss to combine, cover and let stand at room temperature 1 hour. Drain off excess dressing. Add cheese to pepper mixture; toss. Season with salt and pepper.

Makes 6 servings

CHICKEN WITH MUSHROOM SAUCE

MUSHROOM SAUCE

3 tablespoons butter or margarine
8 ounces fresh mushrooms, sliced
3 tablespoons all-purpose flour
1½ cups chicken broth
1 tablespoon minced chives
1 tablespoon minced parsley
1 teaspoon Dijon-style mustard
¼ teaspoon salt
⅛ teaspoon freshly ground pepper
½ cup sour cream

CHICKEN

1 tablespoon vegetable oil
4 boneless skinless chicken breast halves
4 slices ham
4 slices Monterey Jack cheese
2 English muffins, split and toasted
½ red bell pepper, cut into thin strips

1. For Mushroom Sauce, melt butter in medium saucepan over medium heat. Add mushrooms; cook until tender. Remove with slotted spoon; set aside. Stir flour into pan; cook until bubbly. Slowly whisk in broth.

2. Add mushrooms, chives, parsley, mustard, salt and pepper. Cook, stirring constantly, until thickened. Stir in sour cream; heat until hot. *Do not boil.* Keep warm on very low heat.

3. For Chicken, heat oil in large skillet over medium heat. Add chicken; cook, turning occasionally, about 8 minutes or until chicken is browned and no longer pink in center.

4. Reduce heat to low; place ham, then cheese on chicken. Cover and cook 1 to 2 minutes or just until cheese melts. Place chicken on English muffins. Spoon sauce over chicken and top with pepper strips.

Makes 4 servings

> *A combination of melons (honeydew, watermelon, cantaloupe or any of the regional varieties) cut into different shapes, make a charming accompaniment to many brunch dishes. For a distinctive touch, top each serving with a splash of champagne.*

Chicken with Mushroom Sauce

BROCCOLI-SALMON QUICHE

1 (9-inch) Pastry Shell (page 340)
1 tablespoon vegetable oil
1½ cups chopped broccoli
⅓ cup chopped onion
⅓ cup chopped red bell pepper
½ cup (2 ounces) shredded Swiss cheese
1 cup flaked canned or cooked salmon (about 5 ounces)
3 eggs, beaten
1¼ cups milk
1 teaspoon dried leaf tarragon
¼ teaspoon salt
⅛ teaspoon freshly ground pepper

1. Preheat oven to 425°F.

2. Place piece of foil inside pastry shell; partially fill with uncooked beans or rice. Bake 10 minutes. Remove foil and beans; continue baking 5 minutes or until lightly browned. Let cool.

3. *Reduce oven temperature to 375°F.*

4. Heat oil in medium skillet over medium heat. Add broccoli, onion and bell pepper; cook and stir 3 to 4 minutes or until crisp-tender. Set aside to cool.

5. Sprinkle cheese over bottom of pastry shell. Arrange salmon and vegetables over cheese.

6. Combine eggs, milk, tarragon, salt and pepper in medium bowl. Pour over salmon and vegetables.

7. Bake 35 to 40 minutes or until filling is puffed and knife inserted in center comes out clean. Let stand 10 minutes before cutting.

Makes 6 servings

Broccoli-Salmon Quiche

Pastry Shell

1½ cups all-purpose flour
¼ teaspoon salt
¼ cup butter or margarine, chilled
¼ cup shortening
4 to 5 tablespoons cold water

1. Combine flour and salt in large bowl. With pastry blender or 2 knives, cut in butter and shortening until mixture resembles cornmeal.

2. Add water, 1 tablespoon at a time; stir just until mixture holds together. Knead lightly with your hands to form ball. Wrap in plastic wrap and refrigerate 30 minutes.

3. Roll out dough on lightly floured surface to 12-inch circle. Gently press into 9-inch quiche dish or pie pan. Trim edges and flute.

PAPAYA-KIWIFRUIT SALAD WITH ORANGE DRESSING

Enjoy the tropical sweet-tart combination of papaya and kiwifruit in this easy-to-make salad.

1 papaya
4 kiwifruit
6 tablespoons frozen orange juice concentrate, thawed
3 tablespoons honey
1 cup sour cream
1 tablespoon grated orange peel
1 tablespoon grated lime peel

1. Peel and remove seeds from papaya. Slice lengthwise into thin slices.

2. Peel kiwifruit and cut crosswise into thin slices. Arrange papaya and kiwifruit on 4 salad plates.

3. Combine orange juice concentrate and honey in small bowl. Stir in sour cream. Spoon dressing over salads; sprinkle with peels.

Makes 4 servings

SAUSAGE & APPLE QUICHE

Shredded apple adds a terrific flavor twist to this fabulous quiche.

1 (9-inch) Pastry Shell (page 340)
1/2 pound bulk spicy pork sausage
1/2 cup chopped onion
3/4 cup shredded, peeled tart apple
1 tablespoon lemon juice
1 tablespoon sugar
1/8 teaspoon crushed red pepper flakes
1 cup (2 ounces) shredded Cheddar cheese
3 eggs
1 1/2 cups half-and-half
1/4 teaspoon salt
Ground black pepper

1. Preheat oven to 425°F.

2. Place piece of foil inside pastry shell; partially fill with uncooked beans or rice. Bake 10 minutes. Remove foil and beans; continue baking pastry 5 minutes or until lightly browned. Let cool.

3. *Reduce oven temperature to 375°F.*

4. Crumble sausage into large skillet; add onion. Cook over medium heat until meat is browned and onion is tender. Spoon off and discard pan drippings.

5. Add apple, lemon juice, sugar and chili pepper to skillet. Cook on medium-high, stirring constantly, 4 minutes or until apple is just tender and all liquid is evaporated. Let cool.

6. Spoon sausage mixture into pastry shell; top with cheese. Whisk eggs, half-and-half, salt and dash of black pepper in medium bowl. Pour over sausage mixture.

7. Bake 35 to 45 minutes or until filling is puffed and knife inserted in center comes out clean. Let stand 10 minutes before cutting.

Makes 6 servings

STRAWBERRY-PEACH COOLER

1 cup sliced strawberries
1 cup chopped peaches
2 tablespoons sugar
1 bottle (750 ml) white wine, chilled
1 bottle (1 quart) sparkling water, chilled
Mint sprigs
Ice

1. Combine strawberries and peaches in small bowl. Sprinkle with sugar; stir gently. Let stand at room temperature 30 minutes.

2. Pour fruit into punch bowl. Gently pour in wine and water. Add mint sprigs and ice. *Makes about 2 quarts*

Non-Alcoholic Cooler: Use only 1 tablespoon sugar. Substitute 1 quart apple juice for wine.

SPARKLING APPLE PUNCH

2 bottles (750ml each) sparkling apple cider, chilled
1½ quarts papaya or apricot nectar, chilled
Ice
1 or 2 papayas, peeled and chopped
Orange slices, quartered

Combine apple cider, papaya nectar and ice in punch bowl. Add papaya and orange slices. *Makes about 4 quarts*

Papaya

Papaya is a tropical fruit with a flavor similar to melon. It is available year-round. You can tell the fruit is ripe when at least half the skin has turned yellow.

Left: Sparkling Apple Punch
Right: Strawberry-Peach Cooler

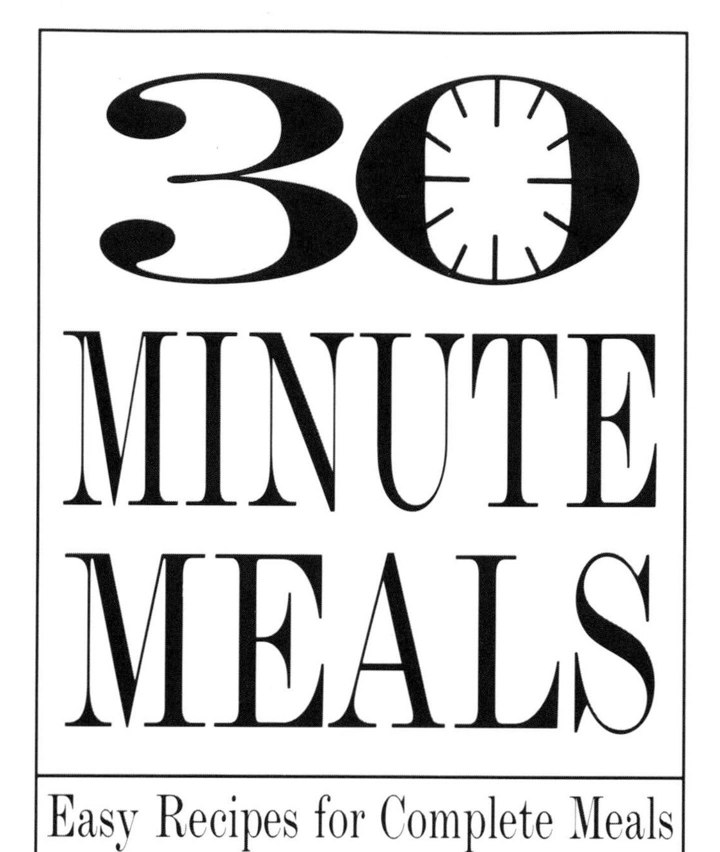

Oriental Beef Kabobs (page 362)

Turkey Cordon Bleu

Calico Vegetable Sauté

Peachy Strawberry Shortcake

GAME PLAN

- ▲ Whip cream and combine fruit for dessert.
- ▲ Cut zucchini and cherry tomatoes.
- ▲ Prepare Turkey Cordon Bleu.
- ▲ While turkey is cooking, cook Calico Vegetable Sauté.
- ▲ Just before serving, assemble Peachy Strawberry Shortcake.

Clockwise from top left: Peachy Strawberry Shortcake, Turkey Cordon Bleu, Calico Vegetable Sauté

Turkey Cordon Bleu

4 turkey cutlets
½ teaspoon dried oregano leaves, crushed
1 tablespoon vegetable oil
1 tablespoon butter or margarine
Pepper
4 ham slices
4 provolone cheese slices

1. Place turkey between sheets of plastic wrap; pound to ¼-inch thickness. Remove plastic wrap. Sprinkle turkey with oregano.

2. Heat oil and butter in large skillet over medium heat.

3. Add turkey; cook 8 minutes or until no longer pink in center, turning after 4 minutes. Season with pepper to taste.

4. Top each cutlet with ham and cheese; cover. Continue cooking 3 to 5 minutes or until cheese is melted. Garnish as desired.

Makes 4 servings

Calico Vegetable Sauté

1 tablespoon vegetable oil
2 medium zucchini, halved lengthwise, sliced crosswise
1 pint cherry tomatoes, halved
1 teaspoon dried basil leaves, crushed
Salt and pepper

1. Heat oil in medium skillet; add zucchini. Cook 3 minutes, stirring occasionally.

2. Add tomatoes and basil. Season with salt and pepper to taste. Continue cooking 2 minutes or until thoroughly heated, stirring occasionally.

Makes 4 servings

Peachy Strawberry Shortcake

1 (10-ounce) package frozen strawberries with sugar, thawed
1 (8- to 10-ounce) package frozen peach slices, thawed
½ pint (1 cup) whipping cream
1 (9-inch) yellow cake layer

1. Drain strawberries, reserving juice. Combine strawberries and peaches; cover. Refrigerate.

2. Beat whipping cream at high speed with electric mixer until stiff peaks form; cover. Refrigerate.

3. When ready to serve, cut cake into wedges; drizzle with small amount of reserved strawberry juice. Top with fruit mixture and whipped cream. Refrigerate leftovers.

Makes 4 to 6 servings

Mini Turkey Loaves

Vegetable Stir-Fry

Creamy Mashed Potatoes

Apple pie

GAME PLAN

- ▲ Preheat oven to 425°F.
- ▲ Boil water for potatoes.
- ▲ Prepare Mini Turkey Loaves.
- ▲ While turkey is baking, slice vegetables for stir-fry. Peel and cut potatoes.
- ▲ Cook potatoes.
- ▲ While potatoes are cooking, finish Vegetable Stir-Fry.
- ▲ Finish Creamy Mashed Potatoes.

Mini Turkey Loaves

1 pound ground turkey
1 small apple, chopped
½ small onion, chopped
½ cup uncooked rolled oats
2 teaspoons Dijon-style mustard
1 teaspoon dried rosemary leaves, crushed
1 teaspoon salt
Dash of pepper

1. Preheat oven to 425°F. Grease twelve muffin cups.

2. Combine all ingredients. Press into prepared muffin cups.

3. Bake 20 minutes or until lightly browned and no longer pink in center. Garnish as desired. Serve with cranberry sauce, if desired.

Makes 4 servings

Vegetable Stir-Fry

1 tablespoon vegetable oil
3 or 4 carrots, diagonally sliced
2 zucchini, diagonally sliced
3 tablespoons orange juice
Salt and pepper

1. Heat oil in medium skillet or wok over medium heat. Add carrots; stir-fry 3 minutes.

2. Add zucchini and orange juice; stir-fry 4 minutes or until vegetables are crisp-tender. Season with salt and pepper to taste.

Makes 4 servings

For better nutrition, do not peel carrots before slicing for this quick stir-fry. Since valuable nutrients lie in the protective outer peel, it is best to just thoroughly scrub the carrots with a vegetable brush before using.

Creamy Mashed Potatoes

2 pounds potatoes, peeled, cut into 1-inch pieces
Salt
2 tablespoons butter or margarine
⅓ to ½ cup milk
Dash of pepper
Dash of ground nutmeg

1. Cook potatoes in lightly salted boiling water 10 minutes or until tender; drain.

2. Add butter. Mash potatoes, adding enough milk for a good consistency. Season with pepper and nutmeg.

Makes 4 servings

Top to bottom: Creamy Mashed Potatoes, Mini Turkey Loaves with Vegetable Stir-Fry

Citrus Chicken

Poppy Seed Noodles

Garden Vegetable Medley

Blueberry pie

GAME PLAN

- ▲ Boil water for noodles and for vegetables.
- ▲ Slice carrots.
- ▲ Cook chicken breasts.
- ▲ While chicken is cooking, mince garlic, section grapefruit and cook noodles, green beans and carrots.
- ▲ Finish Citrus Chicken, Poppy Seed Noodles and Garden Vegetable Medley.

Clockwise on plate from top right: Citrus Chicken, Garden Vegetable Medley, Poppy Seed Noodles

Citrus Chicken

1 tablespoon vegetable oil
4 boneless, skinless chicken breast halves (about 1 pound)
1 cup orange juice
4 teaspoons sugar
1 clove garlic, minced
1 teaspoon dried rosemary leaves, crushed
2 teaspoons cornstarch
1/4 cup dry white wine
Salt and pepper
2 pink grapefruit, sectioned

1. Heat oil in large skillet over medium heat. Add chicken; cook 8 minutes or until browned on both sides and no longer pink in center, turning after 4 minutes. Remove chicken from skillet; keep warm.

2. Add orange juice, sugar, garlic and rosemary to skillet; bring to a boil.

3. Combine cornstarch and winc. Add to skillet; cook, stirring constantly, until sauce is clear and thickened. Season with salt and pepper to taste.

4. Add grapefruit; heat thoroughly, stirring occasionally. Serve over chicken.

Makes 4 servings

Poppy Seed Noodles

8 ounces uncooked noodles
1 tablespoon butter or margarine
1 teaspoon poppy seeds

1. Cook noodles in lightly salted boiling water according to package directions; drain. Place in serving bowl.

2. Add butter and poppy seeds; toss lightly.

Makes 4 servings

Garden Vegetable Medley

1 pound fresh green beans
4 large carrots, diagonally sliced
2 tablespoons butter or margarine
1/4 teaspoon dill weed (optional)
Salt and pepper

1. Place 1 to 2 inches of water and steamer basket in large saucepan; bring water to a boil.

2. Add green beans and carrots; cover. Steam 10 minutes or until vegetables are crisp-tender.

3. Place vegetables in serving bowl. Add butter and dill weed; mix lightly. Season with salt and pepper to taste.

Makes 4 servings

Broiled Chicken Salad

Tortillas

Cherry Sundaes

GAME PLAN

- ▲ Preheat broiler.
- ▲ Prepare Broiled Chicken Salad.
- ▲ Just before serving, prepare Cherry Sundaes.

Broiled Chicken Salad

4 boneless, skinless chicken breast halves (about 1 pound)
1 (15-ounce) can black beans, drained, rinsed
2 green onions, chopped
Bottled oil and vinegar dressing
1 (10-ounce) package frozen whole kernel corn, thawed, drained
2 tablespoons chopped pimento
2 tablespoons chopped cilantro
2 large tomatoes, cut into wedges

1. Preheat broiler. Position oven rack about 4 inches from heat source.

2. Place chicken on rack of broiler pan. Broil 8 minutes or until browned on both sides and no longer pink in center, turning after 4 minutes. Set aside.

3. Combine beans, onions and a small amount of dressing in medium bowl; mix lightly. Set aside.

4. Combine corn, pimento and chopped cilantro in separate bowl; mix lightly. Set aside.

5. Diagonally cut each chicken piece into thick slices; arrange on salad plates.

6. Arrange tomato wedges and spoonfuls of bean and corn mixtures around chicken. Garnish as desired.

7. Drizzle a small amount of dressing over chicken. Serve with additional dressing.

Makes 4 servings

Cherry Sundaes

1 quart ice cream, any flavor
1 cup cherry pie filling
¾ cup chocolate sauce, warmed

1. Scoop ice cream into individual dessert dishes.

2. Top with pie filling and chocolate sauce. Serve with cookies, if desired.

Makes 4 servings

> To heat chocolate sauce in the microwave oven, pour sauce into 1-cup glass measuring cup. Microwave on HIGH 1 to 2 minutes or until thoroughly heated, stirring after each minute.

Top to bottom: Cherry Sundae, Broiled Chicken Salad

Monterey Chicken Sandwiches

Corn-on-the-Cob with Chili Butter

Raspberry Dessert Pizza

GAME PLAN

- ▲ Preheat oven to 450°.
- ▲ Cook chicken.
- ▲ While chicken is cooking, slice onion and split rolls for sandwiches.
- ▲ Bake crust for Raspberry Dessert Pizza.
- ▲ While crust is baking, boil water for corn.
- ▲ Finish dessert.
- ▲ Cook corn.
- ▲ While corn is cooking, finish Monterey Chicken Sandwiches.
- ▲ Finish Corn-on-the-Cob with Chili Butter.

Left to right: Monterey Chicken Sandwich, Corn-on-the-Cob with Chili Butter

Monterey Chicken Sandwiches

1 tablespoon vegetable oil
1 tablespoon butter or margarine
4 boneless, skinless chicken breast halves (about 1 pound)
1 teaspoon dried thyme leaves, crushed
Salt and pepper
1 large red onion, thinly sliced
4 Kaiser rolls, split
Radicchio or lettuce leaves

1. Heat oil and butter in large skillet over medium heat. Add chicken; sprinkle with thyme. Cook 8 minutes or until browned on both sides and no longer pink in center, turning after 4 minutes. Season with salt and pepper to taste. Remove from skillet; keep warm.

2. Add onion to skillet; cook until tender.

3. Fill rolls with radicchio leaves, chicken and onions. Serve with mango chutney and olives, if desired.

Makes 4 sandwiches

Corn-on-the-Cob with Chili Butter

4 ears of corn
1/4 cup butter or margarine, softened
1 tablespoon snipped fresh chives
1 teaspoon chili powder
Salt and pepper

1. Bring large pan of water to a boil. Add corn; boil 5 minutes.

2. Meanwhile, combine butter, chives and chili powder.

3. Remove corn from water; spread with butter mixture. Season with salt and pepper to taste.

Makes 4 servings

Raspberry Dessert Pizza

1 (9-inch) refrigerated pie crust
1/3 cup white chocolate chips
1 cup raspberry or blueberry pie filling

1. Preheat oven to 450°F.

2. Unfold pie crust; place on baking sheet. Bake 6 to 8 minutes or until golden brown.

3. Remove crust from oven; sprinkle with chips. Continue baking 1 minute or until chips are softened.

4. Spread chocolate with spatula to cover crust; top with pie filling. Cool before serving. Refrigerate leftovers.

Makes 6 to 8 servings

Refrigerate leftover pie filling. Use as a topping for ice cream or cake slices.

Roast Beef in Onion Rolls

Potato Salad Plus

Brownie S'Mores

GAME PLAN

▲ Prepare Potato Salad Plus.

▲ Prepare Roast Beef in Onion Rolls.

▲ Just before serving, prepare Brownie S'Mores.

Clockwise from top right: Potato Salad Plus, Roast Beef in Onion Roll, Brownie S'Mores

Roast Beef in Onion Rolls

Horseradish Sauce (recipe follows)
2 onion rolls, split
½ pound sliced roast beef
4 tomato slices
Watercress or lettuce leaves

1. Prepare Horseradish Sauce; spread on rolls.

2. Fill rolls with beef, tomatoes and watercress. Serve with dill pickles and olives, if desired.
Makes 2 sandwiches

Horseradish Sauce

2 tablespoons mayonnaise
2 tablespoons sour cream
1 or 2 teaspoons prepared horseradish
1 teaspoon Dijon-style mustard

Combine ingredients; mix until well blended.

Potato Salad Plus

½ pound deli creamy potato salad
1 small celery stalk, chopped
2 tablespoons chopped onion
2 tablespoons chopped red pepper (optional)
⅛ teaspoon black pepper

Combine all ingredients; mix lightly. *Makes 2 servings*

Brownie S'Mores

2 (about 3-inch) unfrosted brownie squares
6 small chocolate-mint candies
⅓ to ½ cup marshmallow creme
Chopped nuts

1. Place brownies on microwave-safe plate. Arrange three candies on each brownie. Microwave on HIGH 10 to 15 seconds or just until chocolate candy begins to soften.

2. Top each brownie with marshmallow creme. Microwave on HIGH 10 to 15 seconds or just until marshmallow creme begins to soften. Sprinkle with nuts.
Makes 2 servings

Variation: Substitute other flavors of chocolate candy for mint candies.

Glazed Ham with Sweet Potatoes

Buttered Brussels Sprouts

Whole-wheat dinner rolls

Pumpkin pie

GAME PLAN

- ▲ Preheat broiler.
- ▲ Boil water for Brussels sprouts.
- ▲ Trim Brussels sprouts; cook.
- ▲ While Brussels sprouts are cooking, prepare Glazed Ham with Sweet Potatoes.
- ▲ Finish Buttered Brussels Sprouts.

Glazed Ham with Sweet Potatoes

1 (1¼-pound) slice ham steak
1 (16-ounce) can sliced peaches, drained
1 (16-ounce) can sweet potatoes, drained
Maple syrup
2 tablespoons apricot jam
1 teaspoon Dijon-style mustard

1. Preheat broiler. Position oven rack about 4 inches from heat source.

2. Place ham in shallow pan. Surround with peaches and sweet potatoes; drizzle peaches and sweet potatoes with small amount of maple syrup.

3. Broil 5 minutes or until lightly browned.

4. Meanwhile, heat combined jam and mustard in microwave or in saucepan on rangetop until jam is melted; stir until well blended.

5. Turn ham, peaches and sweet potatoes over; brush ham with jam mixture. Drizzle peaches and sweet potatoes with additional maple syrup. Continue broiling 5 minutes or until thoroughly heated.

Makes 4 servings

Buttered Brussels Sprouts

1 pound Brussels sprouts
2 tablespoons butter or margarine

1. Trim ends of Brussels sprouts.

2. Bring about 2 inches of lightly salted water to a boil in medium saucepan.

3. Add Brussels sprouts; return to a boil. Reduce heat; cover. Simmer 10 minutes or until crisp-tender; drain.

4. Spoon Brussel sprouts into serving bowl. Add butter; toss lightly to coat.

Makes 4 servings

Sweet potatoes and yams are often considered to be one and the same. Although similar in size and shape, these two vegetables come from different plant species, each with its own color, flavor and texture characteristics. For example, yams have a slightly higher moisture content and a slightly sweeter flavor than sweet potatoes. Since these differences are only subtle, both vegetables can usually be used interchangeably in recipes.

Top to bottom: Buttered Brussels Sprouts, Glazed Ham with Sweet Potatoes

Steamed Brats

German Sauerkraut

Pumpernickel bread

Raspberry Fluff

GAME PLAN

- ▲ Tear cake into pieces and whip cream for dessert.
- ▲ Prepare German Sauerkraut.
- ▲ While sauerkraut is cooking, prepare Steamed Brats.
- ▲ Just before serving, assemble Raspberry Fluff.

Left to right on plate: Steamed Brats, German Sauerkraut

Steamed Brats

8 fully cooked bratwurst
½ cup beer or water

1. Pierce bratwurst with fork.

2. Place bratwurst and beer in medium skillet. Bring to a boil. Reduce heat to medium; cover. Simmer 5 minutes.

3. Remove lid; continue simmering until beer is evaporated. Cook until bratwurst is browned, turning occasionally. Serve with mustard, if desired.

Makes 4 servings

German Sauerkraut

1 (32-ounce) jar sauerkraut, drained
2 Golden Delicious apples, quartered, sliced
1 cup apple juice
1 bay leaf
8 juniper berries (optional)

1. Combine all ingredients in large saucepan. Bring to a boil.

2. Reduce heat to medium. Simmer 15 minutes or until apples are tender and liquid is almost evaporated, stirring occasionally.

3. Remove bay leaf and juniper berries before serving.

Makes 4 servings

Raspberry Fluff

½ angel food cake loaf
½ pint (1 cup) whipping cream
1 (10-ounce) package frozen raspberries, thawed, drained

1. Tear cake into small pieces; cover. Set aside.

2. Beat whipping cream at high speed with electric mixer until stiff peaks form; cover. Refrigerate.

3. When ready to serve, combine cake and raspberries in medium bowl; mix lightly. Fold in whipped cream. Spoon into individual dessert dishes. Garnish as desired. Refrigerate leftovers.

Makes 4 to 6 servings

Variation: Substitute 1½ to 2 cups fresh raspberries for frozen raspberries.

Place frozen raspberries in refrigerator several hours before preparing the meal *or* place in refrigerator overnight to thaw.

Oriental Beef Kabobs

Green Rice

Pear Dessert Crisp

GAME PLAN

- ▲ Preheat broiler.
- ▲ Prepare Green Rice.
- ▲ While rice is cooking, prepare Oriental Beef Kabobs.
- ▲ While kabobs are broiling, prepare and assemble dessert.
- ▲ When kabobs are done, finish Pear Dessert Crisp.

Oriental Beef Kabobs

1 tablespoon olive oil
1 tablespoon soy sauce
1 tablespoon seasoned rice vinegar
4 purchased beef kabobs

1. Preheat broiler. Position oven rack about 4 inches from heat source.

2. Whisk together oil, soy sauce and vinegar; brush on kabobs.

3. Arrange kabobs on rack of broiler pan. Broil 10 minutes or to desired doneness, turning after 5 minutes.

Makes 4 servings

Green Rice

2 cups chicken broth
1 cup uncooked rice
¼ cup chopped fresh parsley
¼ cup chopped green onions with tops
1 tablespoon butter or margarine

1. Combine broth and rice in medium saucepan. Bring to a boil; stir.

2. Reduce heat to low; cover. Simmer, without stirring, 15 minutes or until rice is tender and liquid is absorbed. *(Do not remove lid during cooking.)*

3. Remove saucepan from heat; stir in parsley, onions and butter. Cover; keep warm until ready to serve.

Makes 4 servings

To chop fresh parsley the no-mess way, place parsley sprigs in 1-cup measuring cup; snip with kitchen scissors until finely chopped.

Pear Dessert Crisp

1 (29-ounce) can pear halves, drained
½ cup uncooked rolled oats
2 tablespoons sugar
2 tablespoons butter or margarine, cut into pieces

1. Preheat broiler.

2. Arrange pears, cut side up, in 9-inch baking dish.

3. Combine oats and sugar. Cut in butter until mixture resembles coarse crumbs. Spoon about 1 tablespoon oat mixture into each pear half.

4. Broil 1½ minutes or until topping begins to brown. **(Caution: Topping browns quickly.)** Refrigerate leftovers.

Makes 6 servings

Oriental Beef Kabobs with Green Rice

Pork Chops with Glazed Apples

Nutty Vegetable Duo

Whole-grain rolls

Raspberry sherbet with cookies

GAME PLAN

- ▲ Prepare Pork Chops with Glazed Apples.
- ▲ While pork chops are cooking, prepare Nutty Vegetable Duo.

Left to right on plate: Pork Chops with Glazed Apples, Nutty Vegetable Duo

Pork Chops with Glazed Apples

1 tablespoon vegetable oil
4 boneless pork chops, 1/4 inch thick
1/2 teaspoon ground sage
Salt and pepper
2 large Granny Smith apples, thinly sliced
2 tablespoons sugar
1/2 teaspoon ground cinnamon

1. Heat oil in large skillet over medium heat. Add pork chops; sprinkle with sage.

2. Cook 8 minutes or until no longer pink in center, turning after 4 minutes. Season with salt and pepper to taste. Remove pork chops from skillet; keep warm.

3. Add apples, sugar and cinnamon to skillet. Reduce heat to low; cover. Cook 5 minutes, stirring occasionally. Serve over pork chops. *Makes 4 servings*

Nutty Vegetable Duo

1 (10-ounce) package frozen green beans
1/2 (16-ounce) package frozen small whole onions
1/4 cup toasted slivered almonds
2 tablespoons butter or margarine
Salt and pepper

1. Combine beans and onions in medium saucepan; cook according to package directions. Drain.

2. Return vegetables to saucepan. Add almonds and butter; stir over low heat until butter is melted and mixture is thoroughly heated. Season with salt and pepper to taste.
Makes 4 servings

To toast almonds in the conventional oven, spread almonds evenly in shallow baking pan. Bake at 350°F, 8 to 10 minutes or until lightly toasted, stirring occasionally.

To toast almonds in the microwave oven, spread almonds evenly in microwave-safe pie plate. Microwave on HIGH 3 to 5 minutes or until lightly toasted, stirring after each minute. For extra flavor, add 1 tablespoon butter or margarine to toasted almonds and continue microwaving 30 seconds; stir to coat. Let stand 5 minutes.

Beefy Rice Salad Sandwiches

Chocolate Pudding Parfaits

GAME PLAN

- ▲ Prepare Chocolate Pudding Parfaits.
- ▲ Prepare Beefy Rice Salad Sandwiches.

Beefy Rice Salad Sandwiches

¾ pound lean ground beef
½ small onion, chopped
½ teaspoon dried thyme leaves, crushed
1½ cups cooked rice
½ red pepper, chopped
½ avocado, peeled, pitted and chopped
¼ cup chopped fresh parsley
3 tablespoons olive oil
3 tablespoons seasoned rice vinegar
Salt and black pepper
3 pita bread rounds, cut in half
Lettuce leaves
Tomato slices

1. Brown meat with onion over medium-high heat. Stir in thyme.

2. Combine rice, red pepper, avocado and parsley in medium bowl. Add meat mixture; mix lightly.

3. Whisk together oil and vinegar. Pour over meat mixture; toss lightly. Season with salt and black pepper to taste.

4. Fill pita halves with lettuce, tomatoes and meat mixture.

Makes 6 sandwiches

Chocolate Pudding Parfaits

2 ounces semisweet chocolate, chopped
2 ounces white chocolate, chopped
½ cup sugar
2 tablespoons flour
1 tablespoon cornstarch
2¼ cups milk
2 egg yolks, beaten
2 teaspoons vanilla, divided

1. Place semisweet chocolate and white chocolate in separate heatproof bowls; set aside.

2. Combine sugar, flour and cornstarch in medium saucepan. Gradually whisk in milk. Cook, stirring constantly, over medium heat until mixture comes to a boil. Boil 2 minutes, stirring constantly.

3. Remove saucepan from heat. Stir small amount of hot mixture into beaten egg yolks; return to hot mixture in pan. Cook, stirring constantly, 2 minutes or until thickened.

4. Spoon half of the egg mixture over each of the two chocolates in bowls; stir until chocolates are completely melted. Add 1 teaspoon of the vanilla to each bowl; stir until blended.

5. Alternate layers of puddings in parfait glasses; cover. Refrigerate until ready to serve.

Makes 3 to 4 servings

Top to bottom: Chocolate Pudding Parfait, Beefy Rice Salad Sandwiches

Pepper Steak Sandwiches

Garden Pasta Salad

Fruity Dessert Cups

GAME PLAN

- ▲ Prepare fruit mixture for Fruity Dessert Cups.
- ▲ Boil water for pasta; cut vegetables for pasta salad and for sandwiches.
- ▲ Cook pasta.
- ▲ While pasta is cooking, finish Pepper Steak Sandwiches.
- ▲ While steak is cooking, finish Garden Pasta Salad.
- ▲ Just before serving, finish dessert.

Clockwise from top left: Fruity Dessert Cup, Pepper Steak Sandwich, Garden Pasta Salad

Pepper Steak Sandwiches

1½ teaspoons vegetable oil
1 pound sirloin tip steak
½ teaspoon dried oregano leaves, crushed
1 large onion, thinly sliced
1 clove garlic, minced
1 green pepper, cut into strips
1 red pepper, cut into strips
Salt and black pepper
4 (6-inch) French bread rolls, split
½ cup (2 ounces) shredded Monterey Jack cheese

1. Heat oil in large nonstick skillet over medium-high heat. Add steak. Sprinkle with oregano. Cook 3 to 4 minutes or until steak is browned on both sides, turning after 2 minutes.

2. Add onion and garlic to steak in skillet. Continue cooking 3 minutes.

3. Add green and red peppers; cook until peppers are tender and steak is medium-rare, stirring occasionally.

4. Remove steak from skillet; slice thinly. Season with salt and black pepper to taste.

5. Return steak slices to skillet; mix lightly with vegetables. Fill rolls with steak mixture and cheese.

Makes 4 sandwiches

Garden Pasta Salad

1 (9-ounce) package fresh tri-color rotini or shell macaroni
1 pint cherry tomatoes, halved
1 zucchini, chopped
¼ to ⅓ cup bottled Italian dressing
¼ cup chopped fresh parsley
⅛ teaspoon pepper

1. Cook pasta in lightly salted boiling water according to package directions (about 5 minutes); drain.

2. Place pasta, tomatoes and zucchini in serving bowl.

3. Add enough dressing to moisten; toss lightly. Add parsley and pepper; toss lightly. Serve warm.

Makes 4 servings

Variation: Substitute dried tri-color shell macaroni or rotini for fresh pasta.

Fruity Dessert Cups

1 (8-ounce) can pineapple chunks, drained
1¼ cups red grapes (about ½ pound)
2 kiwifruit, peeled, sliced
4 scoops vanilla ice cream
¼ cup orange-flavored liqueur (optional)

1. Combine pineapple, grapes and kiwifruit; cover. Refrigerate.

2. When ready to serve, spoon fruit mixture into individual dessert dishes. Top with ice cream; drizzle with liqueur.

Makes 4 servings

Thai Tea

Scallop Stir-Fry

Tropical Fruit Compote

Fortune cookies

GAME PLAN

- ▲ Boil water for noodles and for tea.
- ▲ Cut vegetables and scallops for stir-fry.
- ▲ Steep tea.
- ▲ While tea is steeping, prepare fruit mixture for fruit compote.
- ▲ Remove tea bags; cool tea.
- ▲ While tea is cooling, finish Scallop Stir-Fry.
- ▲ Finish Thai Tea.
- ▲ Just before serving, finish Tropical Fruit Compote.

Scallop Stir-Fry

Thai Tea

4 tea bags
4 cups boiling water
½ cup sweetened condensed milk
Ice cubes

1. Place tea bags in teapot or other heatproof container. Add boiling water; steep 4 minutes. Remove tea bags. Cool tea slightly.

2. Spoon 2 tablespoons sweetened condensed milk into each of four tall glasses. Add ice cubes. Fill with tea. Stir to combine.

Makes 4 servings

Scallop Stir-Fry

6 ounces uncooked ramen noodles
1 tablespoon olive oil
1 pound asparagus, cut into 1-inch pieces
1 red pepper, cut into thin rings
3 green onions, chopped
1 large clove garlic, minced
1 pound sea scallops, halved crosswise
2 tablespoons soy sauce
1 teaspoon hot pepper sauce
1 teaspoon sesame oil
Juice of ½ lime

1. Cook noodles in lightly salted boiling water according to package directions.

2. Meanwhile, heat olive oil in wok or large skillet over high heat. Add asparagus, red pepper, onions and garlic. Stir-fry 2 minutes.

3. Add scallops; stir-fry until scallops turn opaque.

4. Stir in soy sauce, hot pepper sauce, sesame oil and lime juice. Add noodles; heat thoroughly, stirring occasionally.

Makes 4 servings

Variation: Substitute vermicelli for ramen noodles.

Tropical Fruit Compote

1 banana
Lemon juice
2 kiwifruit, peeled, sliced
1 (8-ounce) can pineapple tidbits, drained
1 papaya, cut into chunks
Shredded coconut (optional)

1. Cut banana into chunks. Place in medium bowl; toss with enough lemon juice to coat to prevent browning.

2. Add kiwifruit, pineapple and papaya; mix lightly. Cover; refrigerate.

3. When ready to serve, spoon fruit mixture into individual dessert dishes; sprinkle with coconut. *Makes 4 servings*

Poached Salmon with Basil Mayonnaise

Pea-Pod Medley

Couscous

Strawberries Elegante

GAME PLAN

- ▲ Prepare strawberry-sugar mixture for Strawberries Elegante.
- ▲ Cut vegetables for Basil Mayonnaise and for Pea-Pod Medley.
- ▲ Cook couscous.
- ▲ While couscous is cooking, finish Poached Salmon with Basil Mayonnaise.
- ▲ While salmon is cooking, finish Pea-Pod Medley.
- ▲ Just before serving, finish dessert.

Poached Salmon with Basil Mayonnaise

Basil Mayonnaise (recipe follows)
1 bay leaf
4 peppercorns
4 salmon steaks, 1 to 1½ inches thick

1. Prepare Basil Mayonnaise; cover. Set aside.

2. Add bay leaf, peppercorns and enough water to medium skillet to fill to 1-inch depth. Bring to a boil. Add salmon.

3. Reduce heat; cover. Simmer 5 minutes or until salmon flakes easily when tested with fork.

4. Remove salmon from poaching liquid; serve with Basil Mayonnaise.

Makes 4 servings

Basil Mayonnaise

½ cup mayonnaise
½ cup sour cream or plain yogurt
1 green onion, cut into 1-inch pieces
2 tablespoons fresh parsley
2 tablespoons fresh basil
Salt and pepper

Combine mayonnaise, sour cream, onion, parsley and basil in food processor or blender container; process until well blended. Season with salt and pepper to taste.

Pea-Pod Medley

2 tablespoons vegetable oil
½ pound snow peas, trimmed
¼ pound mushrooms, sliced
1 yellow or red pepper, cut into strips
Salt and black pepper

1. Heat oil over medium-high heat in large skillet or wok. Add snow peas, mushrooms and yellow pepper.

2. Stir-fry 4 minutes or until vegetables are crisp-tender. Season with salt and black pepper to taste.

Makes 4 servings

Strawberries Elegante

1 pint strawberries, halved
2 tablespoons sugar
6 tablespoons half-and-half
2 tablespoons orange-flavored liqueur
1 tablespoon anise-flavored liqueur
⅛ teaspoon pepper
4 scoops vanilla ice cream

1. Combine strawberries and sugar in medium bowl; cover. Refrigerate.

2. When ready to serve, stir half-and-half, liqueurs and pepper into strawberry mixture. Serve over ice cream.

Makes 4 servings

Strawberries in Cream: Omit liqueurs and pepper. Increase half-and-half to ½ cup. Add ½ teaspoon orange extract, if desired.

Left to right: Pea-Pod Medley, Poached Salmon with Basil Mayonnaise

Baked Halibut with Roasted Pepper Sauce

Lemony Steamed Broccoli

Oven-Baked Potatoes

Peach yogurt with peach slices

GAME PLAN

- ▲ Preheat oven to 425°F.
- ▲ Prepare Baked Halibut with Roasted Pepper Sauce.
- ▲ Boil water for broccoli.
- ▲ While fish is baking, prepare Oven-Baked Potatoes. Bake potatoes with fish during last 10 minutes of fish baking time.
- ▲ While potatoes are baking, prepare Lemony Steamed Broccoli.

Clockwise from top: Lemony Steamed Broccoli, Baked Halibut with Roasted Pepper Sauce, Oven-Baked Potatoes

Baked Halibut with Roasted Pepper Sauce

Roasted Pepper Sauce (recipe follows)
1 medium onion, thinly sliced
1 large clove garlic, minced
1 (1½-pound) halibut fillet, skinned

1. Preheat oven to 425°F. Grease shallow baking dish.

2. Prepare Roasted Pepper Sauce; set aside.

3. Cover bottom of prepared baking dish with onion and garlic. Top with fish. Pour sauce over fish.

4. Bake 20 minutes or until fish flakes easily when tested with fork. Garnish as desired.
Makes 4 to 6 servings

Roasted Pepper Sauce

1 (7-ounce) can chopped green chilies, drained
1 (7-ounce) jar roasted red peppers, drained
⅔ cup chicken broth

Combine ingredients in food processor or blender container; process until puréed.

Lemony Steamed Broccoli

1 pound broccoli
1 tablespoon butter or margarine
2 teaspoons lemon juice
Salt and pepper

1. Break broccoli into flowerets. Discard large stems. Trim smaller stems; cut stems into thin slices.

2. Place 2 to 3 inches of water and steamer basket in large saucepan; bring water to a boil.

3. Add broccoli; cover. Steam 6 minutes or until crisp-tender.

4. Place broccoli in serving bowl. Add butter and lemon juice; toss lightly to coat. Season with salt and pepper to taste. *Makes 4 servings*

Oven-Baked Potatoes

2 large baking potatoes (about 10 ounces each)
2 tablespoons butter or margarine, melted
2 tablespoons vegetable oil
Salt and pepper

1. Preheat oven to 425°F.

2. Scrub potatoes; do not peel. Thinly slice potatoes crosswise. Pat potato slices dry with paper towels.

3. Place potatoes in medium bowl. Add butter and oil; toss lightly to coat. Place on nonstick baking sheet.

4. Bake 10 minutes or until tender and lightly browned, stirring lightly after 5 minutes. Season with salt and pepper to taste. *Makes 4 servings*

Vegetable-Shrimp Stir-Fry

Oh-So-Easy Rice

Berried Cantaloupe with Honey Dressing

GAME PLAN

- ▲ Prepare Oh-So-Easy Rice.
- ▲ While bringing broth to a boil, prepare Honey Dressing and cantaloupe shells.
- ▲ While rice is simmering, prepare Vegetable-Shrimp Stir-Fry.
- ▲ Just before serving, finish dessert.

Vegetable-Shrimp Stir-Fry

1 tablespoon olive oil
6 ounces snow peas, trimmed
6 green onions, cut into 1-inch pieces
1 red pepper, cut into ½-inch strips
1 pound peeled, deveined bay shrimp
¼ pound large mushrooms, quartered
2 tablespoons soy sauce
1 tablespoon seasoned rice vinegar
1 teaspoon sesame oil

1. Heat oil in large skillet or wok over medium-high heat. Add snow peas, onions and red pepper; stir-fry 2 minutes.

2. Add shrimp; stir-fry 2 minutes or until shrimp turn pink.

3. Add mushrooms; stir-fry until tender and most of liquid evaporates.

4. Add remaining ingredients; heat thoroughly, stirring constantly.

Makes 4 servings

Note: If using small mushrooms, leave whole.

Oh-So-Easy Rice

2 cups chicken broth
1 cup uncooked rice
1 tablespoon butter or margarine

1. Combine broth and rice in medium saucepan. Bring to a boil; stir.

2. Reduce heat to low; cover. Simmer 15 minutes or until rice is tender and liquid is absorbed. *(Do not remove lid during cooking.)*

3. Remove saucepan from heat; stir in butter. Cover; keep warm until ready to serve.

Makes 4 servings

Berried Cantaloupe with Honey Dressing

Honey Dressing (recipe follows)
2 small cantaloupes
2 cups raspberries

1. Prepare Honey Dressing; cover. Refrigerate.

2. Cut cantaloupes in half; remove seeds. Cover; refrigerate.

3. When ready to serve, place cantaloupe halves in individual bowls; fill centers with raspberries. Drizzle with dressing. *Makes 4 servings*

Honey Dressing

1 cup plain yogurt
2 tablespoons honey
2 teaspoons grated orange peel

Combine all ingredients; mix until well blended.

Top to bottom: Berried Cantaloupe with Honey Dressing, Vegetable-Shrimp Stir-Fry with Oh-So-Easy Rice

Mediterranean Tuna Salad

Bread sticks

Brownie Sundaes

GAME PLAN

- ▲ Prepare Mediterranean Tuna Salad.
- ▲ Just before serving, prepare Brownie Sundaes.

Mediterranean Tuna Salad

Mediterranean Tuna Salad

¼ pound fresh green beans
1 (12-ounce) can tuna, drained, separated into chunks
2 tablespoons capers (optional)
1 (15-ounce) can Great Northern beans, drained, rinsed
1 large tomato, chopped
12 ripe Greek olives
Snipped fresh chives (optional)
Bottled Italian dressing

1. Cook green beans in lightly salted boiling water 5 minutes or until crisp-tender; drain. Rinse with cold water; drain again.

2. Place tuna in center of serving platter; sprinkle with capers.

3. Arrange beans, tomatoes and olives around tuna; surround with green beans. Sprinkle with chives, if desired. Serve with dressing.

Makes 4 servings

Brownie Sundaes

1 cup marshmallow creme
3 to 4 teaspoons milk
4 brownies
4 scoops ice cream, any flavor

1. Combine marshmallow creme and 3 teaspoons milk in small saucepan. Stir over medium-low heat until marshmallow creme is melted and mixture is smooth. (Add additional milk if necessary for good pouring consistency.) Keep warm.

2. Place brownies in individual dessert dishes. Top with ice cream and marshmallow sauce.

Makes 4 servings

If using a 7-ounce jar of marshmallow creme, mix one (3-ounce) package softened cream cheese with the remaining marshmallow creme for a quick fruit dip.

Salmon, Fettuccine & Cabbage

Sourdough rolls

Make-It-Easy Lemon Tarts

GAME PLAN

- ▲ Preheat oven to 450°F.
- ▲ Boil water for fettuccine.
- ▲ Shred cabbage and flake salmon.
- ▲ Prepare and bake tart shells for Make-It-Easy Lemon Tarts.
- ▲ While tart shells are baking, prepare pie filling for dessert.
- ▲ Finish Salmon, Fettuccine & Cabbage.
- ▲ Just before serving, finish dessert.

Salmon, Fettuccine & Cabbage

1 (9-ounce) package fresh fettuccine
1/4 cup plus 2 tablespoons seasoned rice vinegar
2 tablespoons vegetable oil
1/2 small head of cabbage, shredded (about 7 cups)
1/2 teaspoon fennel seeds
1 (15 1/2-ounce) can salmon, drained, flaked, bones removed
Salt and pepper

1. Cook fettuccine in lightly salted boiling water according to package directions (about 5 minutes); drain.

2. Heat vinegar and oil in large skillet over medium-high heat. Add cabbage; cook 3 minutes or until crisp-tender, stirring occasionally.

3. Stir in fennel seeds. Add fettuccine; toss lightly to coat. Add salmon; mix lightly.

4. Heat thoroughly, stirring occasionally. Season with salt and pepper to taste. Garnish as desired.

Makes 4 servings

Variation: Substitute dried fettuccine for fresh fettuccine.

Make-It-Easy Lemon Tarts

1 (9-inch) refrigerated pie crust
1 package (4-serving size) lemon instant pudding and pie filling (plus ingredients to prepare mix)

1. Preheat oven to 450°F.

2. Cut four (4 1/2-inch) circles from pie crust. Line muffin cups with pastry circles. Prick bottoms and sides with fork.

3. Bake 8 minutes or until lightly browned. Cool.

4. Meanwhile, prepare pie filling according to package directions. Let stand 5 minutes or until thickened; cover. Refrigerate.

5. Just before serving, spoon pie filling into tart shells.

Makes 4 servings

Variation: Substitute your favorite flavor canned pie filling for prepared pie filling.

Salmon, Fettuccine & Cabbage

Garlic Shrimp & Vegetables

Spinach Fettuccine

Cheesy Lahvosh

Honey-Glazed Pineapple Slices

GAME PLAN

- ▲ Preheat oven to 375°F and boil water for fettuccine.
- ▲ Chop vegetables and mince garlic for Garlic Shrimp & Vegetables.
- ▲ Prepare Cheesy Lahvosh and cook fettuccine.
- ▲ While lahvosh is baking and fettuccine is cooking, finish stir-fry.
- ▲ Finish Spinach Fettuccine.
- ▲ Just before serving, prepare Honey-Glazed Pineapple Slices.

Top to bottom: Garlic Shrimp & Vegetables with Spinach Fettuccine, Cheesy Lahvosh

Garlic Shrimp & Vegetables

2 tablespoons butter or margarine
1 tablespoon olive oil
1 bunch green onions, chopped
1 red pepper, chopped
1 pound peeled, deveined large shrimp
2 cloves garlic, minced
Juice of 1 lime
Salt and black pepper

1. Heat butter and oil in medium skillet or wok over medium heat. Add onions and red pepper. Stir-fry 2 minutes or until vegetables are crisp-tender.

2. Add shrimp and garlic; stir-fry 2 minutes or until shrimp turn pink.

3. Stir in lime juice. Season with salt and black pepper to taste. Garnish as desired.

Makes 4 servings

Spinach Fettuccine

1 (9-ounce) package fresh spinach fettuccine
1 tablespoon butter or margarine
1 teaspoon dried basil leaves, crushed (optional)
Salt and pepper

1. Cook fettuccine in lightly salted boiling water according to package directions (about 5 minutes); drain.

2. Combine fettuccine, butter and basil in serving bowl; toss lightly to coat. Season with salt and pepper to taste.

Makes 4 servings

Variation: Substitute dried spinach fettuccine for fresh fettuccine.

Cheesy Lahvosh

12 small lahvosh (3 inches in diameter)
3 tablespoons butter or margarine, melted
¼ cup (1 ounce) grated Parmesan cheese

1. Preheat oven to 375°F.

2. Brush lahvosh with butter. Sprinkle with cheese. Place on ungreased baking sheet.

3. Bake 5 minutes or until cheese begins to melt.

Makes 4 servings

Variation: Substitute 3 pita bread rounds, quartered, for lahvosh.

Honey-Glazed Pineapple Slices

1 (16-ounce) can pineapple slices, drained
¼ to ⅓ cup honey
Toasted shredded coconut (optional)

1. Preheat broiler. Position oven rack about 4 inches from heat source.

2. Place pineapple slices on rack of broiler pan. Drizzle honey over pineapple slices.

3. Broil 5 minutes or until honey starts to bubble. Sprinkle with coconut, if desired. Serve warm.

Makes 4 servings

HURRY-UP HAMBURGER

Beef and Mushroom Filled Gougere (page 396)

Wonton Soup

2 green onions
¼ lb. extra-lean ground beef
¼ cup finely chopped celery
1 tablespoon finely chopped fresh parsley
¼ teaspoon salt
Dash of pepper
12 to 18 wonton skins
6 cups chicken broth
½ cup spinach or bok choy leaves, halved lengthwise, shredded
¼ cup shredded carrot

Reserve one green onion top for garnish; chop remaining green onions. Combine chopped green onions, ground beef, celery, parsley, salt and pepper in small bowl; mix lightly.

Place approximately 1½ tablespoonfuls ground beef mixture in center of each wonton square. Lightly dampen edges of square with water. Bring together corners; pinch to seal. Set aside.

Bring broth to boil in large saucepan; reduce heat to medium. Add ½ of wontons; simmer 4 minutes. Remove cooked wontons with slotted spoon; keep warm. Repeat with remaining wontons.

Cut reserved green onion top into thin diagonal slices. Add to hot broth with spinach and carrot. Place wontons in soup bowls. Top with broth mixture. *Makes 6 servings*

Beef and Pistachio Pâté

6 ounces sliced beef bacon
½ cup finely chopped onion
3 cloves garlic, minced
2 tablespoons butter or margarine
2 pounds lean ground beef
½ cup fresh bread crumbs
⅓ cup shelled pistachio nuts
¼ cup snipped parsley
2 tablespoons brandy
1 egg, beaten
1½ teaspoons salt
¾ teaspoon dried thyme, crushed
½ teaspoon pepper
⅛ teaspoon ground nutmeg

Line bottom and sides of 9×5-inch pan with bacon; reserve 4 slices. Cook and stir onion and garlic in butter in medium skillet over medium-high heat 3 minutes; cool. Combine ground beef, onion mixture, bread crumbs, nuts, parsley, brandy, egg, salt, thyme, pepper and nutmeg in large bowl; mix lightly but thoroughly. Press mixture firmly into bacon-lined pan; cover with reserved bacon. Set pan in 11¾×7½-inch baking dish on lowest rack of oven. Pour 1 quart boiling water into dish. Bake at 350°F 1½ hours. Remove pan from water. Fit another pan directly on top of pâté; add 3 pounds of weight (canned goods) and let rest 3 hours in cool place. Refrigerate, covered, 24 hours. Remove top bacon; invert and slice.

Makes 8 to 10 appetizer servings

Recipe courtesy of **National Live Stock & Meat Board**

Goat Cheese Tarts

6 ounces lean ground beef
1 large onion, chopped
¼ cup chopped mushrooms
¼ cup sun-dried tomatoes, finely chopped
2 tablespoons sour cream
1 tablespoon chopped fresh basil or 1 teaspoon dried leaf basil
½ teaspoon Worcestershire sauce
Pastry for single-crust 9-inch pie
4 ounces goat cheese or feta cheese
Pitted ripe olives, halved or quartered

Preheat oven to 425°F.

Brown ground beef in medium skillet. Drain. Add onions and mushrooms; cook until tender. Stir in tomatoes, sour cream, basil and Worcestershire sauce; set aside.

Roll out pastry to ⅛-inch thickness. Cut into 2-inch rounds. Press rounds into mini muffin cups. Fill with ground beef mixture; top with cheese and olives.

Bake 10 minutes or until pastry is golden brown.

Makes about 30 appetizers

Wonton Soup

Nutty Cheese-Beef Crudites

Preparation time: 10 minutes

½ pound ground beef
¼ cup chopped walnuts
3 ounces Neufchatel cheese, softened
3 tablespoons finely chopped green onions with tops
¼ teaspoon salt
Dash of pepper
24 vegetable pieces (zucchini, cucumber or jicama slices; red, green or yellow bell pepper, cut into 1½ inch squares; or pea pods, blanched and split)
1 tablespoon sliced green onions with tops

Place walnuts in 1-cup microwave-safe glass measure. Microwave at High 4 to 5 minutes or until lightly browned, stirring after 2 minutes. Break up ground beef with a fork; place in microwave-safe sieve or colander. Place sieve in microwave-safe bowl. Microwave at High 2½ minutes. Pour off drippings and place beef in same bowl. Stir in Neufchatel cheese, chopped green onions, walnuts, salt and pepper. Microwave at High 2 to 2½ minutes. Top or fill desired vegetable pieces with one rounded teaspoon of meat mixture. Garnish each appetizer with sliced green onion.

Microwave cooking time: 8½ to 10 minutes *24 appetizers*

Recipe courtesy of **National Live Stock & Meat Board**

Eggplant Appetizer

1 medium eggplant (about 1 pound)
¼ lb. lean ground beef
¼ cup finely chopped onion
1 large garlic clove, minced
1 large tomato, chopped
1 small green bell pepper, finely chopped
¼ cup diced green olives
2 tablespoons olive oil
1 teaspoon white wine vinegar
1 tablespoon chopped fresh oregano or 1 teaspoon dried leaf oregano
Salt and freshly ground black pepper

Preheat oven to 350°F.

Pierce eggplant with fork; place in shallow baking pan.

Bake 1 hour or until skin is wrinkled and eggplant is soft. Set aside until cool enough to handle.

Meanwhile, brown ground beef in medium skillet. Drain. Add onion and garlic; cook until tender.

Peel eggplant; cut into small cubes. Combine eggplant, ground beef mixture, tomatoes, green peppers and olives in medium bowl. Whisk together oil, vinegar and oregano in small bowl. Add to eggplant mixture; mix lightly. Season with salt and pepper to taste.

Serve with toasted pita wedges as an appetizer or serve on lettuce leaves as a first course.

Makes about 8 servings

Meatballs in Spicy Red Pepper Sauce

Preparation time: 45 minutes
Cooking time: 12 to 15 minutes

1 pound ground beef
1 red bell pepper
3 tablespoons dry bread crumbs
1 egg, beaten
2 tablespoons chopped parsley
2 cloves garlic, minced
¾ teaspoon salt
¼ teaspoon ground red pepper
1 tablespoon olive oil
1 small onion, finely chopped
2 cloves garlic, minced
½ cup ready-to-serve beef broth
1 teaspoon cornstarch
½ cup dry white wine
1 tablespoon tomato paste
½ teaspoon dried thyme leaves

Place red bell pepper on rack in broiler pan so surface of pepper is 3 to 5 inches from heat source. Broil 10 to 15 minutes or until skin blisters, turning occasionally. Place pepper in paper bag; close and let stand 15 to 20 minutes to loosen skin. Meanwhile, combine ground beef, bread crumbs, egg, parsley, garlic, salt and ground red pepper, mixing lightly but thoroughly. Shape meat mixture into 35 meatballs, using about 1 teaspoon for each. Place on rack in open roasting pan; reserve. Remove loosened skin and seeds from pepper; cut into ¼-inch pieces. Heat oil in large skillet over medium-high heat. Add onion and garlic; cook and stir 2 to 3 minutes. Combine broth and cornstarch. Add broth mixture, wine, tomato paste, thyme and red pepper pieces to pan. Cook over low heat 10 to 12 minutes or until slightly thickened, stirring occasionally. Meanwhile, bake meatballs in 325°F oven 10 minutes. Remove meatballs; drain on paper towels. Stir meatballs into sauce; serve hot. *Makes 4 servings*

Recipe courtesy of **National Live Stock & Meat Board**

Beef & Corn Gumbo

½ lb. ground beef
¾ lb. fresh okra or 1 (10-ounce) package frozen okra, thawed
1 small onion, chopped
1 garlic clove, minced
5 cups chicken broth
4 medium tomatoes, chopped
1 cup whole-kernel corn, fresh or frozen
3 parsley sprigs
1 bay leaf
1½ teaspoons chopped fresh thyme or ½ teaspoon dried leaf thyme
⅛ teaspoon ground red pepper (optional)
Salt and freshly ground pepper
Chopped fresh parsley
Lemon wedges

Brown ground beef in medium skillet. Drain. Add okra, onions and garlic; cook 10 minutes.

Stir in broth, tomatoes, corn, parsley sprigs, bay leaf, thyme and ground red pepper. Season with salt and pepper to taste.

Bring to boil. Reduce heat to low; cover. Simmer 20 minutes or until vegetables are tender, stirring occasionally. Discard parsley sprigs and bay leaf. Ladle into bowls. Sprinkle with chopped parsley. Serve with lemon wedges.

Makes about 6 servings

Variation: Increase ground beef to 1 lb. for a main-dish soup.

Easy Beef Tortilla Pizzas

1 pound ground beef
1 medium onion, chopped
1 teaspoon dried oregano, crushed
1 teaspoon salt
4 large flour tortillas (10-inch diameter)
4 teaspoons olive oil
1 medium tomato, seeded, chopped
Greek or Mexican Toppings (recipes follow)

Cook and stir ground beef and onion in large skillet over medium-high heat until beef loses pink color. Pour off drippings. Sprinkle oregano and salt over beef, stirring to combine. Place tortillas on 2 large baking sheets. Lightly brush surface of each tortilla with oil. Bake in preheated 400°F oven 3 minutes. Divide beef mixture evenly over tops of tortillas; divide tomato and desired topping over beef mixture. Bake at 400°F 12 to 14 minutes, rearranging baking sheets halfway through cooking time.

Makes 4 servings

Greek Topping:
Combine 1 teaspoon dried basil, crushed, ½ teaspoon lemon pepper, 4 ounces crumbled Feta cheese and ¼ cup grated Parmesan cheese in small bowl.

Mexican Topping:
Combine 1 teaspoon dried cilantro, crushed, ½ teaspoon crushed dried red chilies, 1 cup (4 ounces) shredded Monterey Jack or Cheddar cheese and ⅓ cup sliced ripe olives in small bowl.

Recipe courtesy of **National Live Stock & Meat Board**

Zucchini Lasagna

1½ pounds ground beef
¾ pound sweet Italian sausage, casing removed
3 tablespoons FILIPPO BERIO® Olive Oil
1½ cups coarsely chopped mushrooms
1 large onion, chopped
1 large clove garlic, minced
1 can (14½ ounces) tomatoes, chopped, undrained
1 jar (15 ounces) marinara sauce
1 teaspoon salt
1 teaspoon dried basil, crushed
½ teaspoon Italian herb seasoning
1 container (24 ounces) ricotta cheese
1 package (8 ounces) mozzarella cheese, cubed, divided
¼ cup chopped Italian parsley
2 eggs, beaten
6 unpeeled zucchini, cut lengthwise into thin slices about 8 inches long

Cook beef and sausage in hot oil in large skillet over medium-high heat until meats are no longer pink. Add mushrooms, onion and garlic. Cook several minutes, stirring frequently. Add tomatoes, marinara sauce, salt, basil and Italian seasoning. Combine ricotta, ¾ of the mozzarella, the parsley and eggs in medium bowl. Spoon 1 cup of the sauce onto bottom of 13×9-inch baking dish. Top with ⅓ of the zucchini, ⅓ of the cheese mixture and then 1 cup of the sauce. Repeat layers, ending with sauce. Cover with foil. Bake at 350°F 45 minutes. Sprinkle with remaining mozzarella. Bake, uncovered, 10 minutes more or until cheese melts. Let stand 10 minutes before cutting. Heat remaining sauce and serve with lasagna.

Makes 8 servings

Easy Beef Tortilla Pizzas

Two-Way Burgers

Prepare Grilled Burgers and choose one of two different burger recipes— California Burgers or English Burgers.

*Grilled Burgers

Preparation time: 10 minutes
Cooking time: 10 to 12 minutes

1 pound ground beef
¼ cup minced onion
¼ teaspoon pepper

Combine ground beef, onion and pepper, mixing lightly but thoroughly. Divide beef mixture into 4 equal portions and form into patties 4 inches in diameter. Broil patties on grid over medium coals, turning once. Broil 10 minutes for rare; 12 minutes for medium. Prepare recipe desired and assemble as directed. *4 beef patties*

California Burgers

Preparation time: 15 minutes

1 recipe Grilled Burgers*
¼ cup plain yogurt
1 teaspoon Dijon-style mustard
4 whole wheat hamburger buns, split
12 large spinach leaves, stems removed
4 thin slices red onion
4 large mushrooms, sliced
1 small avocado, peeled, seeded and cut into 12 wedges

Combine yogurt and mustard. On bottom half of each bun, layer an equal amount of spinach leaves, onions and mushrooms; top each with a Grilled Burger. Arrange 3 avocado wedges on each patty; top with an equal amount of yogurt mixture. Close each sandwich with bun top. *4 servings*

English Burgers

Preparation time: 15 minutes

1 recipe Grilled Burgers*
¼ cup each horseradish sauce and chopped tomato
2 tablespoons crumbled crisply cooked bacon
4 English muffins, split, lightly toasted

Combine horseradish sauce, tomato and bacon. Place a Grilled Burger on each muffin half. Spoon an equal amount of horseradish sauce mixture over each patty. Cover with remaining muffin half. *4 servings*

Note: One tablespoon canned real bacon bits may be substituted for cooked bacon.

Recipe courtesy of **National Live Stock & Meat Board**

Scandinavian Burgers

1 pound lean ground beef
¾ cup shredded zucchini
⅓ cup shredded carrot
2 tablespoons finely minced onion
1 tablespoon fresh chopped dill or 1 teaspoon dried dill weed
½ teaspoon salt
Dash of freshly ground pepper
1 egg, beaten
¼ cup beer

Preheat grill.

Combine ground beef, zucchini, carrots, onions and seasonings in medium bowl; mix lightly. Stir in egg and beer. Shape into four patties.

Grill 8 minutes or to desired doneness, turning once. Serve on whole-wheat buns or rye rolls, if desired. *Makes 4 servings*

Two-Way Burgers

Beef & Broccoli

1 pound lean ground beef
4 tablespoons soy sauce, divided
2 tablespoons dry sherry
1 tablespoon all-purpose flour
1 tablespoon sugar
1 tablespoon seasoned rice vinegar
2 teaspoons grated gingerroot or 1 teaspoon ground ginger
1 pound fresh broccoli, stems sliced, tops broken in flowerets (about 6 cups)
1 medium onion, sliced crosswise, separated into rings
Dash of hot pepper sauce
Salt and freshly ground pepper
Hot cooked rice

Crumble ground beef into large microwave-safe bowl. Stir together soy sauce, sherry, flour, sugar, vinegar and gingerroot in 2-cup glass measure. Add to ground beef; mix well. Cover; chill 30 minutes.

Microwave marinated ground beef mixture, uncovered, on HIGH 6 minutes or until ground beef is no longer pink, stirring twice during cooking. Drain; keep meat warm.

Combine broccoli and onions in microwave-safe casserole dish. Cover with plastic wrap; vent. Microwave on HIGH 5 to 6 minutes or until crisp-tender. Add to meat with hot pepper sauce; mix lightly. Season with salt and pepper to taste. Serve with rice.

Makes 4 servings

Variation: Stir in 1 medium tomato, chopped, just before serving.

Recipe courtesy of **Rice Council**

Festive Chili con Carne

1 pound ground beef or pork
1 medium onion, chopped
1 medium green bell pepper, chopped
1 clove garlic, minced
2 to 4 teaspoons chili powder
1 teaspoon salt
½ teaspoon dried oregano, crumbled
1 can (16 ounces) whole tomatoes, undrained
1 can (8 ounces) tomato sauce
1 can (15 ounces) red kidney beans, drained
1 tablespoon red wine vinegar
Tortilla chips or crackers

1. Crumble meat into microwave-safe plastic colander.* Place colander in 2-quart microwave-safe casserole. Microwave, uncovered, at High power until meat is no longer pink, 4 to 6 minutes; stir with fork to break up meat every 2 minutes during cooking.

2. Discard meat drippings from casserole. Transfer meat from colander to casserole; break up into small pieces with back of spoon. Stir in onion, green pepper and garlic. Microwave, uncovered, at High power until onion and pepper are tender, 4 to 5 minutes.

3. Add chili powder, salt and oregano to casserole; mix well. Drain tomato liquid into casserole. Chop tomatoes in can with scissors or knife; add to casserole. Add tomato sauce and beans; mix well. Microwave, covered with lid, at High power 5 minutes.

4. Add vinegar to chili; stir to mix well. Microwave, uncovered, at Medium (50%) power 20 to 25 minutes until slightly thickened and to allow flavors to blend; stir twice during cooking. Serve with chips or crackers.

Makes 4 servings

*For microwave-safe colander, use dishwasher-safe plastic colander with no metal parts.

Beef & Broccoli

Here's proof that a healthy diet can have lots of flavor! Each serving of these delicious lean ground beef recipes is surprisingly under 475 calories . . . a real treat for the dieter who is looking for a delicious alternative to chicken or fish.

Beef and Mushroom Filled Gougere

½ lb. extra-lean (90% lean) ground beef
½ cup chopped fresh mushrooms
1 small onion, chopped
1 garlic clove, minced
1½ teaspoons chopped fresh thyme or ½ teaspoon dried leaf thyme, crushed
Salt and freshly ground pepper
¼ cup butter or margarine
¾ cup cold water
¾ cup all-purpose flour
½ teaspoon salt
3 eggs
¾ cup (3 ounces) shredded part-skim mozzarella cheese

Preheat oven to 425°F.

Brown ground beef in medium skillet. Drain. Add mushrooms, onions, garlic and thyme; cook until vegetables are tender. Season with salt and pepper to taste. Set aside.

Bring butter and water to boil in heavy medium saucepan. Add flour and ½ teaspoon salt, all at once. Beat with wooden spoon until mixture is smooth and forms a ball. Remove from heat. Add eggs, one at a time, beating well after each addition.

Thinly spread dough onto bottom and up sides of greased 10-inch round baking dish; fill with ground beef mixture. Bake 25 minutes or until puffed and golden brown. Sprinkle with cheese; continue baking 5 minutes. Serve hot. *Makes 6 servings*

Nutrient data per serving: 309 calories, 19 g fat, 166 mg cholesterol, 382 mg sodium, 23 mg iron.

Corn & Zucchini Medley

¾ lb. extra-lean (90% lean) ground beef
1 (10-ounce) package frozen whole kernel corn, thawed
2 small zucchini (approx. ½ lb.), chopped
1 large tomato, chopped
½ cup chopped onion
1 tablespoon chopped fresh basil or 1 teaspoon dried leaf basil
1½ teaspoons chopped fresh thyme or ½ teaspoon dried leaf thyme
Salt and freshly ground pepper

Brown ground beef in large skillet. Drain. Reduce heat to medium-low. Stir in corn, zucchini, tomatoes, onions, basil and thyme; cover. Cook 10 minutes or until zucchini is tender. Season with salt and pepper to taste. *Makes 4 servings*

Nutrient data per serving: 297 calories, 14 g fat, 71 mg cholesterol, 67 mg sodium, 3 mg iron.

Beef and Mushroom Filled Gougere

Thai Beef Salad with Cucumber Dressing

Cool cooked ramen noodles in a bowl of iced water; drain well just before serving.

Cucumber Dressing (recipe follows)
1 lb. extra-lean (90% lean) ground beef
½ red pepper, cut in thin strips
6 mushrooms, quartered
2 green onions, diagonally cut into 1-inch pieces
1 garlic clove, minced
1 tablespoon seasoned rice vinegar
1 teaspoon soy sauce
Salt and freshly ground pepper
Lettuce leaves
3 ounces ramen noodles, cooked
12 cherry tomatoes, halved
Mint sprigs

Prepare Cucumber Dressing; set aside.

Brown ground beef in medium skillet. Drain. Add red peppers, mushrooms, onions and garlic; cook until tender. Stir in vinegar and soy sauce; season with salt and pepper to taste.

Arrange lettuce leaves on four luncheon-size plates. Top with noodles and ground beef mixture. Garnish with cherry tomatoes and mint sprigs. Serve with dressing.

Makes 4 servings

Cucumber Dressing

1 medium cucumber, coarsely chopped
½ cup coarsely chopped onion
½ cup loosely packed cilantro leaves
1 garlic clove, minced
1 tablespoon diced jalapeño or green chili pepper
½ cup seasoned rice vinegar

Place cucumbers, onions, cilantro, garlic and peppers in food processor container; process 1 minute. Spoon mixture into small bowl; stir in vinegar.

Nutrient data per serving: 367 calories, 21 g fat, 98 mg cholesterol, 313 mg sodium, 4.3 mg iron.

Spinach-Potato Bake

1 lb. extra-lean (90% lean) ground beef
½ cup fresh mushroom slices
1 small onion, chopped
2 garlic cloves, minced
1 (10-ounce) package frozen chopped spinach, thawed, well drained
½ teaspoon grated nutmeg
1 lb. russet potatoes, peeled, cooked, mashed
¼ cup light sour cream
¼ cup skim milk
Salt and freshly ground pepper
½ cup (2 ounces) shredded Cheddar cheese

Preheat oven to 400°F. Spray deep 9-inch casserole dish with nonstick cooking spray.

Brown ground beef in large skillet. Drain. Add mushrooms, onions and garlic; cook until tender. Stir in spinach and nutmeg; cover. Heat thoroughly, stirring occasionally.

Combine potatoes, sour cream and milk. Add to ground beef mixture; season with salt and pepper to taste. Spoon into prepared casserole dish; sprinkle with cheese.

Bake 15 to 20 minutes or until slightly puffed and cheese is melted.

Makes 6 servings

Nutrient data per serving: 341 calories, 17 g fat, 77 mg cholesterol, 166 mg sodium, 3.1 mg iron.

Thai Beef Salad with Cucumber Dressing

Stuffed Mushrooms with Tomato Sauce and Pasta

Tomato Sauce (recipe follows)
1 lb. extra-lean (90% lean) ground beef
¼ cup finely chopped onion
¼ cup finely chopped green or red pepper
1 large garlic clove, minced
2 tablespoons finely chopped parsley
2 teaspoons finely chopped fresh basil or 1 teaspoon dried leaf basil, crushed
1 teaspoon finely chopped fresh oregano or ½ teaspoon dried leaf oregano, crushed
½ teaspoon salt
Dash of freshly ground pepper
12 very large mushrooms
¼ cup (1 ounce) grated Parmesan cheese
4½ cups cooked spaghetti

Prepare Tomato Sauce; set aside.

Preheat oven to 350°F.

Combine ground beef, onions, green peppers, garlic, parsley, basil, oregano, salt and pepper in medium bowl; mix lightly. Remove stems from mushrooms; finely chop stems. Add to ground beef mixture. Stuff into mushroom caps, rounding tops.

Pour Tomato Sauce into shallow casserole dish large enough to hold mushrooms in single layer. Place mushrooms, stuffing side up, in sauce; cover.

Bake 20 minutes; remove cover. Sprinkle with Parmesan cheese. Continue baking, uncovered, 15 minutes. Serve with spaghetti. Garnish with additional fresh basil leaves, if desired.

Makes 6 servings

Tomato Sauce

2 (14½-ounce) cans tomatoes, chopped, undrained
Dash of hot pepper sauce
1 teaspoon finely chopped fresh marjoram or ½ teaspoon dried leaf marjoram, crushed
1 teaspoon fennel seeds, crushed
Salt and freshly ground pepper

Combine all ingredients except salt and pepper in medium saucepan. Bring to boil. Reduce heat; simmer 5 minutes. Season with salt and pepper to taste.

Nutrient data per serving: 409 calories, 15 g fat, 664 mg cholesterol, 556 mg sodium, 4.8 mg iron.

Roasted Bell Pepper Quesadillas

½ lb. extra-lean (90% lean) ground beef
¼ cup chopped onion
Salt and freshly ground black pepper
1 cup (4 ounces) shredded provolone cheese
8 (6-inch) extra-thin corn tortillas
½ cup roasted bell pepper strips
¼ cup chopped cilantro

Brown ground beef in medium skillet. Drain. Add onions; cook until tender. Season with salt and pepper to taste.

Sprinkle 2 tablespoons cheese onto each of four tortillas; cover with ground beef mixture, pepper strips, cilantro and remaining cheese. Top with remaining tortillas.

Cook, in batches, in nonstick skillet over medium heat about 4 minutes or until cheese is melted, carefully turning after 2 minutes.

Makes 4 servings

Nutrient data per serving: 387 calories, 19.3 g fat, 68 mg cholesterol, 339 mg sodium, 3 mg iron.

Stuffed Mushrooms with Tomato Sauce and Pasta

Beef with Snow Peas & Baby Corn

¾ lb. extra-lean (90% lean) ground beef
1 garlic clove, minced
1 teaspoon vegetable oil
6 ounces snow peas, halved lengthwise
1 red pepper, cut into strips
1 (15-ounce) can baby corn, drained, rinsed
1 tablespoon soy sauce
1 teaspoon sesame oil
Salt and freshly ground pepper
2 cups cooked rice

Brown ground beef in wok or large skillet. Drain. Add garlic; cook until tender. Set aside. Wipe out wok with paper towel.

Heat vegetable oil in wok over medium-high heat. Add snow peas and red peppers; stir-fry 2 to 3 minutes or until vegetables are crisp-tender. Stir in ground beef mixture, baby corn, soy sauce and sesame oil. Season with salt and pepper to taste. Serve over rice.
Makes 4 servings

Nutrient data per serving: 461 calories, 17 g fat, 71 mg cholesterol, 625 mg sodium, 5 mg iron.

Greek Pasta Salad

½ lb. extra-lean (90% lean) ground beef
⅓ cup chopped fresh mint or 2 tablespoons dried leaf mint
1 garlic clove, minced
1¾ cups (approx. 6 ounces) small shell macaroni, cooked
10 cherry tomatoes, quartered
2 ounces feta cheese, crumbled
½ red pepper, chopped
½ red onion, cut into rings
¼ cup reduced-calorie Italian dressing
2 tablespoons lemon juice
Salt and freshly ground black pepper
Lettuce leaves

Brown ground beef in medium skillet. Drain. Add mint and garlic; cook 2 minutes, stirring constantly.

Spoon ground beef mixture into large bowl. Stir in pasta, tomatoes, cheese, red peppers and onions. Add dressing and lemon juice; toss lightly. Season with salt and pepper to taste. Serve on lettuce-covered salad plates. *Makes 4 servings*

Note: Salad can be made up to 4 hours in advance.

Nutrient data per serving: 342 calories, 15 g fat, 892 mg cholesterol, 330 mg sodium, 3.2 mg iron.

Beef Fried Rice

¾ lb. extra-lean (90% lean) ground beef
6 green onions, chopped
3 large celery stalks, chopped
8 ounces bean sprouts
½ cup chopped fresh mushrooms
½ cup finely chopped red pepper
1 teaspoon grated gingerroot
3 cups cooked rice
2 tablespoons soy sauce
Salt and freshly ground black pepper

Brown ground beef in large skillet. Drain. Stir in onions, celery, bean sprouts, mushrooms, red peppers and gingerroot. Cook over medium-high heat 5 minutes or until vegetables are crisp-tender, stirring frequently. Stir in rice and soy sauce. Season with salt and black pepper to taste. Heat thoroughly, stirring occasionally. *Makes 4 servings*

Variation: Substitute low-sodium soy sauce for soy sauce.

Nutrient data per serving: 425 calories, 14 g fat, 71 mg cholesterol, 609 mg sodium, 4.9 mg iron.

Beef with Snow Peas & Baby Corn

Asparagus-Mushroom Stir-Fry

¾ pound extra-lean (90% lean) ground beef
4 green onions, chopped
1 garlic clove, minced
2 teaspoons grated fresh gingerroot
1 teaspoon vegetable oil
1 pound asparagus spears, diagonally cut into 1-inch pieces
1 cup quartered fresh mushrooms
1 tablespoon soy sauce
Salt and freshly ground pepper
4 ounces ramen noodles, cooked, drained

Brown ground beef in wok or large skillet. Drain. Add onions, garlic and gingerroot; cook 1 minute. Set aside.

Wipe out wok with paper towel. Add oil to wok; heat over medium-high heat. Add asparagus and mushrooms; stir-fry 2 or 3 minutes or until asparagus is crisp-tender.

Add ground beef mixture to vegetables in wok; stir until heated thoroughly. Stir in soy sauce; season with salt and pepper to taste. Add noodles; toss lightly.

Makes 4 servings

Nutrient data per serving: 294 calories, 17 g fat, 71 mg cholesterol, 426 mg sodium, 3.3 mg iron.

Cantaloupe & Beef Salad

1 lb. extra-lean (90% lean) ground beef
3 tablespoons chopped fresh mint or 1 tablespoon dried leaf mint
1 garlic clove, minced
Salt and freshly ground pepper
4 cups cantaloupe balls
1 cup cubed jicama
½ cup creamy reduced-calorie Italian dressing
8 cups torn lettuce leaves

Brown ground beef in medium skillet. Drain. Add mint and garlic; cook 2 minutes, stirring constantly. Season with salt and pepper to taste.

Combine ground beef mixture, cantaloupe and jicama in serving bowl; stir in dressing. Add lettuce; toss lightly.

Makes 4 servings

Nutrient data per serving: 402 calories, 22 g fat, 97 mg cholesterol, 345 mg sodium, 4.8 mg iron.

Taco Salad

1 lb. extra-lean (90% lean) ground beef
1 small onion, finely chopped
1 garlic clove, minced
2 teaspoons chili powder
1 teaspoon ground cumin
½ teaspoon salt
Dash of freshly ground black pepper
1 large head iceberg lettuce, torn into bite-size pieces (approx. 10 cups)
2 large tomatoes
1 medium avocado, peeled, sliced
2 cups salsa

Brown ground beef in medium skillet. Drain. Add onions and garlic; cook until tender. Stir in seasonings.

Combine lettuce, tomatoes and avocado in large serving bowl; toss lightly. Top with ground beef mixture. Serve with salsa.

Makes 4 servings

Nutrient data per serving: 453 calories, 30 g fat, 95 mg cholesterol, 826 mg sodium, 5.9 mg iron.

Artichoke Casserole

- **¾ lb. extra-lean (90% lean) ground beef**
- **½ cup fresh mushroom slices**
- **¼ cup chopped onion**
- **1 garlic clove, minced**
- **1 (14-ounce) can artichoke hearts, drained, rinsed, chopped**
- **½ cup dry bread crumbs**
- **¼ cup (1 ounce) grated Parmesan cheese**
- **2 tablespoons chopped fresh rosemary or 1 teaspoon dried leaf rosemary**
- **1½ teaspoons chopped fresh marjoram or ½ teaspoon dried leaf marjoram**
- **Salt and freshly ground pepper**
- **3 egg whites**

Preheat oven to 400°F. Spray 1-quart casserole with nonstick cooking spray.

Brown ground beef in medium skillet. Drain. Add mushrooms, onions and garlic; cook until tender.

Combine ground beef, artichokes, crumbs, cheese, rosemary and marjoram; mix lightly. Season with salt and pepper to taste.

Beat egg whites until stiff peaks form; fold into ground beef mixture. Spoon into prepared casserole.

Bake 20 minutes or until lightly browned around edges.

Makes 4 servings

Nutrient data per serving: 364 calories, 17 g fat, 76 mg cholesterol, 375 mg sodium, 4.4 mg iron.

Calzones

- **½ lb. extra-lean (90% lean) ground beef**
- **2 green peppers, thinly sliced**
- **½ cup fresh mushroom slices**
- **1 medium onion, thinly sliced**
- **1 garlic clove, minced**
- **1 tablespoon chopped fresh oregano or 1 teaspoon dried leaf oregano**
- **1 tablespoon chopped fresh basil or 2 teaspoons dried leaf basil**
- **Dash of hot pepper flakes (optional)**
- **Salt and freshly ground black pepper**
- **1 loaf frozen whole-wheat bread dough, thawed**
- **4 ounces feta cheese, crumbled**
- **⅓ cup (1½ ounces) grated Parmesan cheese**

Brown ground beef in medium skillet. Drain. Add peppers, mushrooms, onions and garlic; cook until vegetables are tender and all liquid has evaporated. Stir in oregano, basil and pepper flakes; season with salt and pepper to taste. Set aside.

Preheat oven to 400°F.

Divide dough into six equal pieces. For each calzone, roll out one piece of dough on lightly floured surface to 8-inch circle. Spoon ground beef mixture onto center of dough; top with cheeses. Lightly dampen edges of dough with water. Bring edges together over filling; press edges together with fork to seal. Place on nonstick baking sheet.

Bake 15 minutes or until golden brown.

Makes 6 servings

Nutrient data per serving: 360 calories, 14 g fat, 53 mg cholesterol, 730 mg sodium, 3.4 mg iron.

Tortellini with Creamed Mushroom Sauce (page 416)

Appetizers

An antipasto should make a light and tempting start to the meal. Beyond that there are no set rules. It can be one simple dish, such as Frittata, Bagna Cauda, or any of the dishes included in this chapter. Or, it can consist of an assortment of delicatessen meats, marinated vegetables and salads, and fresh fruits, artfully displayed in colorful array on a platter. We have on our platter clockwise from marinated mushrooms: mortadella, smoked bacon, genoa salami overlapping with capicola, tongue; Center of platter: marinated artichoke hearts and olives, roasted red peppers, prosciutto and melon.

Antipasto

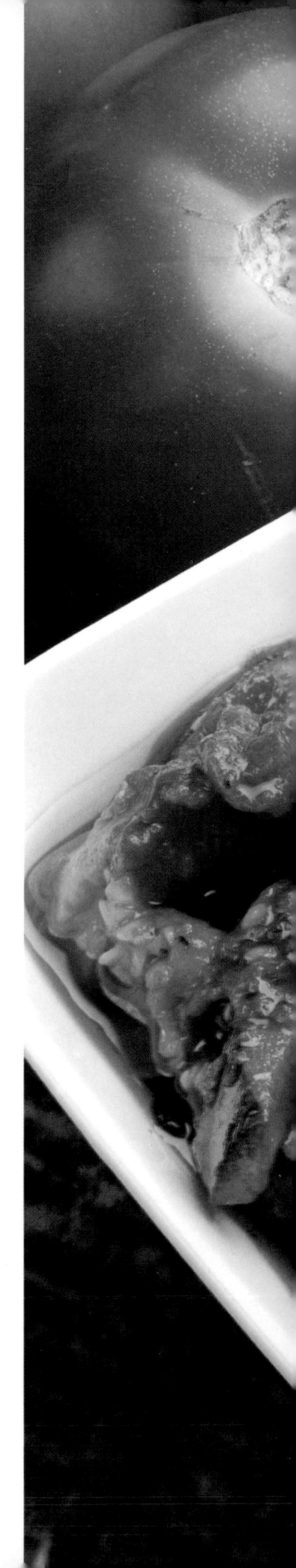

Eggplant Appetizer

3 large ripe tomatoes
3 medium cloves garlic
2 pounds (900 g) eggplant (2 medium)
1 cup (250 mL) olive oil
¾ teaspoon (4 mL) dried basil, crumbled
½ teaspoon (2 mL) dried oregano, crumbled
½ cup (125 mL) water
1 tablespoon (15 mL) tomato paste
1½ teaspoons (7 mL) salt
¼ teaspoon (1 mL) pepper

1. Place tomatoes in large saucepan with boiling water to cover, 60 seconds to loosen skins. Immediately drain tomatoes and rinse under cold running water. Peel, seed and chop tomatoes; reserve. Mince garlic; reserve.

2. Rinse eggplant; cut lengthwise into ½-inch- (1.5 cm) thick slices. Cut slices crosswise in half; then cut lengthwise into ½-inch- (1.5 cm) wide sticks.

3. Heat oil in large skillet over medium-high heat. Add half the eggplant to skillet; cook and stir 5 minutes. Remove eggplant with slotted spoon, draining well, to plate or bowl. Add remaining eggplant to oil remaining in skillet; cook and stir 5 minutes. Remove eggplant with slotted spoon to plate or bowl.

4. If there is no oil remaining in skillet, press eggplant with back of spoon to extract at least 2 tablespoons (30 mL) oil and place oil in skillet. Add reserved garlic, the basil and oregano to skillet; sauté over medium heat 30 seconds. Stir in reserved tomatoes, the water, tomato paste, salt and pepper. Simmer uncovered, stirring occasionally, 5 minutes. Stir eggplant into sauce. Cook and stir over low heat until thick, about 5 minutes longer. Serve hot or at room temperature.

Makes about 6 cups (1.5 L); 10 to 12 servings.

Frittata

¼ cup (60 mL) olive oil
5 small yellow onions, thinly sliced
1 can (14½ ounces or 415 g) whole peeled tomatoes, drained and chopped
¼ pound (115 g) smoked ham, chopped
¼ cup (60 mL) grated Parmesan cheese
2 tablespoons (30 mL) minced fresh parsley
½ teaspoon (2 mL) dried marjoram, crumbled
¼ teaspoon (1 mL) dried basil, crumbled
¼ teaspoon (1 mL) salt
Large pinch pepper
6 large eggs
2 tablespoons (30 mL) butter

1. Heat oil in medium skillet over medium-high heat. Add onions; cook, stirring frequently, until onions are

golden brown, 6 to 8 minutes. Drain chopped tomatoes and stir into onions; cook over medium heat, stirring constantly, 5 minutes. Remove tomatoes and onions from skillet to large bowl with slotted spoon; discard drippings. Let tomato-onion mixture cool to room temperature.

2. Add ham, cheese, parsley, marjoram, basil, salt and pepper to cooled tomato-onion mixture; mix lightly. Whisk eggs in small bowl; stir into ham mixture.

3. Heat broiler. Heat butter over medium heat in 10-inch (25 cm) heavy skillet with flameproof handle; when foam subsides, reduce heat to very low.

4. Add egg mixture to skillet; spread in even layer. Cook without stirring over very low heat until all but top ¼-inch (0.5 cm) of egg mixture is set, 8 to 10 minutes; shake pan gently to test. Place skillet under broiler, about 4 inches (10 cm) from heat; cook just until top of egg mixture is set, 1 to 2 minutes. Do not let top brown or frittata will be dry. Frittata can be served hot, room temperature or cold.

Makes 6 to 8 appetizer or 3 to 4 luncheon servings.

Crostini

12 slices firm white bread
5 tablespoons (75 mL) butter
2 tablespoons (30 mL) all-purpose flour
½ cup (125 mL) milk
3 ounces (85 g) fresh mushrooms (about 9 medium), finely chopped
6 tablespoons (90 mL) grated Parmesan cheese
2 teaspoons (10 mL) anchovy paste
¼ teaspoon (1 mL) salt
⅛ teaspoon (0.5 mL) pepper
Green and ripe olive halves; red and green bell pepper strips; rolled anchovy fillets

1. Heat oven to 350°F (180°C). Cut circles out of bread slices with 2-inch (5 cm) round cutter. Melt 3 tablespoons (45 mL) of the butter in a small saucepan. Brush both sides of bread circles lightly with butter. Bake bread circles on ungreased baking sheet, turning circles over once, until golden, 5 to 6 minutes per side. Cool on wire rack. Do not turn oven off; increase setting to 425°F (220°C).

2. Melt remaining 2 tablespoons (30 mL) butter in small saucepan. Stir in flour; cook and stir over medium heat until bubbly. Whisk in milk; cook, stirring constantly, until sauce thickens and bubbles for 1 minute. Sauce will be very thick. Stir sauce into mushrooms in large bowl; stir in 3 tablespoons (45 mL) of the cheese, the anchovy paste, salt and pepper.

3. Spread a heaping teaspoon of mushroom mixture on top of each toast round; place on ungreased baking sheet. Sprinkle remaining 3 tablespoons (45 mL) cheese over crostini, dividing evenly. Decorate with olive halves, pepper strips, or rolled anchovy fillets. Bake until tops are light brown, 5 to 7 minutes. Serve hot.

Makes 2 to 2½ dozen crostini; 8 to 10 servings.

Soups

Minestrone

- 3 medium carrots
- 3 stalks celery
- 2 medium onions
- 1 large potato
- ¼ pound (115 g) green beans
- 2 medium zucchini
- ½ pound (225 g) cabbage
- 1 medium clove garlic
- ⅓ cup (80 mL) olive oil
- 3 tablespoons (45 mL) butter
- 3½ cups (825 mL) beef broth
- 1½ cups (375 mL) water
- 1 can (28 ounces or 790 g) Italian plum tomatoes
- ½ teaspoon (2 mL) each salt and dried basil, crumbled
- ¼ teaspoon (1 mL) each pepper and dried rosemary, crumbled
- 1 bay leaf
- 1 can (1 pound or 450 g) cannellini beans

1. Pare carrots; chop coarsely. Chop celery coarsely. Chop onions. Pare potato; cut into ¾-inch (2 cm) cubes. Trim green beans; cut into 1-inch (2.5 cm) pieces. Trim zucchini; cut into ½-inch (1.5 cm) cubes. Coarsely shred cabbage. Mince garlic.

2. Heat oil and butter in 5-quart (5 L) Dutch oven over medium heat. Add onions; sauté stirring occasionally, until soft and golden but not brown, 6 to 8 minutes. Stir in carrots and potato; sauté 5 minutes. Stir in celery and green beans; sauté 5 minutes. Stir in zucchini; sauté 3 min-

utes. Stir in cabbage and garlic; cook 1 minute.

3. Add broth, water and liquid from tomatoes to pan. Chop tomatoes coarsely; add to pan. Stir in salt, basil, rosemary, pepper and bay leaf. Heat to boiling; reduce heat to low. Simmer covered, stirring occasionally, 1½ hours.

4. Rinse and drain cannellini beans; add beans to soup. Cook uncovered over

medium-low heat, stirring occasionally, until soup is thick, 30 to 40 minutes longer. Remove bay leaf.

Makes about 12 cups (3 L); 8 to 10 servings.

Note: Soup can be served with grated Parmesan cheese to sprinkle, if desired.

Clam Soup

1 dozen hard-shell clams
3 cups (750 mL) plus 3 tablespoons (45 mL) water
1 large yellow onion, sliced
1 stalk celery, chopped
1 cup (250 mL) dry white wine
3 sprigs parsley
¼ teaspoon (1 mL) dried thyme
1 pound (450 g) red snapper, cod or striped bass fillets, skinned
6 ounces (170 g) fresh mushrooms, thinly sliced
5 green onions, thinly sliced
2 tablespoons (30 mL) olive oil
½ teaspoon (2 mL) salt
⅛ teaspoon (0.5 mL) pepper
⅛ to ¼ (0.5 to 1 mL) teaspoon hot red pepper sauce
1 tablespoon (15 mL) cornstarch
½ cup (125 mL) whipping cream

1. Scrub clams with stiff brush under cold running water. Soak clams in large basin of cold water 30 minutes. Lift out clams; discard water. Repeat soaking 2 more times.

2. Combine clams and 2 tablespoons (30 mL) of the water in large saucepan. Cook covered over medium heat just until clams open, 5 to 10 minutes. Check frequently and

remove clams as they open so they don't overcook. Discard any clams that fail to open. Strain clam broth through triple thickness of dampened cheesecloth; reserve. Rinse clams; reserve.

3. To make court bouillon: Combine yellow onion, celery, 3 cups (750 mL) of the water, the wine, parsley and thyme in medium noncorrosive saucepan. Heat to simmering. Simmer 30 minutes. Do not boil. Strain bouillon; discard solids. Combine fish fillets with bouillon in saucepan. Cook over low heat just until fish is opaque, about 5 minutes. Remove fish with slotted spoon to plate; reserve. Reserve bouillon.

4. Sauté mushrooms and green onions in oil in small noncorrosive Dutch oven over medium heat until mushrooms are tender, 4 to 5 minutes. Stir in reserved bouillon, reserved clam broth, the salt, pepper and pepper sauce. Mix cornstarch and remaining 1 tablespoon (15 mL) water in cup until smooth; stir into soup. Simmer over low heat, stirring frequently, 5 minutes. Remove from heat.

5. Flake reserved fish with fork; add to soup. Stir cream into soup. Remove half the clams from their shells and discard shells; add clams to soup. Add remaining clams, still in their shells, to soup. Heat over medium-low heat just until soup is hot; do not boil. Serve at once.

Makes about 7 cups (1.75 L); 4 to 6 servings.

Bean & Pasta Soup

1¼ cups (310 mL) dried navy (pea) beans
6 cups (1.5 L) cold water
3 strips bacon, finely chopped
1 large onion, finely chopped
1 large stalk celery, chopped
¾ pound (340 g) smoked pork rib or neck bones
2 medium cloves garlic, minced
½ teaspoon (2 mL) each dried thyme and marjoram, crumbled
¼ teaspoon (1 mL) pepper
¾ cup (180 mL) uncooked small pasta
2 tablespoons (30 mL) minced fresh parsley
Pinch salt
1 cup (250 mL) beef broth, if needed

1. Rinse and sort beans. Combine beans and 6 cups (1.5 L) water in large saucepan. Heat over high heat to boiling; boil uncovered 2 minutes. Remove from heat; let beans soak covered 1 hour. Do not drain.

2. Cook bacon in medium skillet over medium-high heat 2 minutes. Add onion and celery; sauté, stirring frequently, until vegetables are light brown, about 6 minutes. Remove bacon and vegetables with slotted spoon to plate; discard drippings. Rinse pork bones to remove excess salt; add bones to beans and soaking water in saucepan. Add sautéed bacon and vegetables. Stir garlic, thyme, marjoram and pepper into bean mixture. Heat over high heat to boiling; reduce heat to low. Simmer covered, stirring occasionally, until beans are tender, about 1 hour. Remove from heat.

3. Remove bones from soup to plate; reserve. Remove about half the beans from soup with slotted spoon; puree these beans with 2 tablespoons (30 mL) soup liquid in blender or food processor. Stir puree into soup remaining in saucepan.

4. Heat soup to boiling. Stir in pasta; cook uncovered over medium heat, stirring occasionally, until pasta is tender, 8 to 12 minutes.

5. While pasta is cooking, remove meat from reserved bones; discard bones. Chop meat fine. Stir meat and parsley into soup just before serving. Taste soup; add salt if needed. Soup will thicken on standing; if necessary, stir in as much of the beef broth as needed to thin.

Makes about 6 cups (1.5 L); 6 servings.

Note: Soup can be served with grated Parmesan cheese to sprinkle if desired.

ED. WÜSTHOF DREIZACKWERK
TRIDENT SOLINGEN GERMANY INOX

Pasta & Sauces

Tortellini with Creamed Mushroom Sauce

2 cups (500 mL) plus 1 tablespoon (15 mL) all-purpose flour
½ teaspoon (2 mL) salt
4 large eggs
1 tablespoon (15 mL) milk
1 teaspoon (5 mL) olive oil
1 small cooked chicken breast, skinned, boned, and minced
2 ounces (60 g) fresh spinach, cleaned, cooked, squeezed very dry and minced
2 ounces (60 g) prosciutto, minced
⅓ cup (80 mL) plus 5 tablespoons (75 mL) grated Parmesan cheese
2 cups (500 mL) whipping cream
Pinch pepper
½ pound (225 g) fresh mushrooms, thinly sliced
3 tablespoons (45 mL) butter
Boiling salted water
3 tablespoons (45 mL) chopped fresh parsley

1. Mix flour and ¼ teaspoon (1 mL) of the salt on board; make well in center. Whisk 3 of the eggs, the milk and oil in small bowl; gradually pour into well in flour while mixing with fingertips or a fork to form firm dough. Knead dough until smooth and elastic, about 5 minutes. Reserve dough, at room temperature, wrapped in plastic while making filling.

2. Combine chicken, spinach, prosciutto and the remaining egg in medium bowl; mix well. Add 2 tablespoons (30 mL) of the Parmesan cheese, 1 tablespoon (15 mL) of the cream, the remaining ¼ teaspoon (1 mL) salt and the pepper to spinach mixture; mix well.

3. Knead pasta dough briefly on lightly floured surface; divide dough in thirds. Roll out, cut and fill a third of dough at a time as follows; keep unused pieces and any scraps wrapped in plastic to prevent drying. Let dough rest 1 minute; then roll out on lightly floured surface until 1/16-inch (2 mm) or less thick. Cut out dough circles with 2-inch (5 cm) round cutter. Cover rolled dough with clean kitchen towel to prevent drying while you work. Place ½ teaspoon (2 mL) spinach filling in center of a dough circle; brush edge of circle lightly with water. Fold circle in half to enclose filling; pinch outside edges together firmly to seal. Brush end of half-circle with water; wrap around finger, overlap ends, and pinch to seal. Place tortellini on clean kitchen towel. Repeat process until all filling has been used; dough scraps can be rerolled, cut, and filled if needed. Let tortellini dry on towel for 30 minutes before cooking.

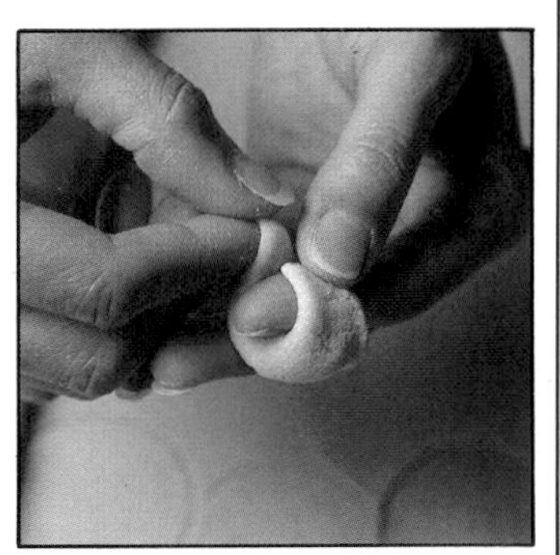

4. Sauté mushrooms in butter in 3-quart (3 L) saucepan over medium heat 3 minutes. Stir in remaining cream. Heat to boiling; reduce heat to low. Simmer uncovered 3 minutes. Stir in ⅓ cup (80 mL) of the cheese; cook and stir 1 minute. Remove from heat.

5. Cook tortellini, a third at a time, in large pot of boiling salted water just until al dente, 2 to 3 minutes. Drain well; add to sauce. When all tortellini have been cooked, heat in sauce over medium heat to simmering. Reduce heat to low; simmer 2 minutes. Serve sprinkled with parsley and remaining cheese.

Makes 6 to 8 servings.

Fettuccine Alfredo

¾ pound (340 g) uncooked fettuccine
Boiling salted water
6 tablespoons (90 mL) unsalted butter
⅔ cup (160 mL) whipping cream
½ teaspoon (2 mL) salt
Large pinch ground white pepper
Large pinch ground nutmeg
1 cup (250 mL) freshly grated Parmesan cheese (about 3 ounces or 85 g)
2 tablespoons (30 mL) chopped fresh parsley

1. Cook fettuccine in large pot of boiling salted water just until al dente, 6 to 8 minutes; drain well. Return to dry pot.

2. While fettuccine is cooking, place butter and cream in 10-inch (25 cm) heavy skillet over medium-low heat. Cook, stirring constantly, until blended and mixture bubbles for 2 minutes. Stir in salt, pepper and nutmeg. Remove from heat. Gradually stir in Parmesan cheese until thoroughly blended and fairly smooth. Return skillet briefly to heat if necessary to completely blend cheese, but don't let sauce bubble or cheese will become lumpy and tough.

3. Pour sauce over fettuccine in pot. Place over low heat. Stir and toss with 2 forks until sauce is slightly thickened and fettuccine evenly coated, 2 to 3 minutes. Sprinkle with parsley. Serve immediately.

Makes 4 servings.

Fettuccine Carbonara

4 ounces (115 g) pancetta (Italian bacon) or lean American bacon, cut into ½-inch-(1.5 cm) wide strips
3 cloves garlic, cut into halves
¼ cup (60 mL) dry white wine
⅓ cup (80 mL) whipping cream
½ pound (225 g) uncooked fettuccine or spaghetti
Boiling salted water
1 large egg
1 large egg yolk
⅔ cup (160 mL) freshly grated Parmesan cheese (about 2 ounces or 60 g)
Large pinch ground white pepper

1. Cook and stir pancetta and garlic in 10-inch (25 cm) noncorrosive skillet over medium-low heat until pancetta is light brown, about 4 minutes. Discard garlic and all but 2 tablespoons (30 mL) of the drippings.

2. Add wine to skillet; cook over medium heat until wine is almost completely evaporated, about 3 minutes. Stir in cream; cook and stir 2 minutes. Remove from heat.

3. Cook fettuccine in large saucepan of boiling salted water just until al dente, 6 to 8 minutes; drain well. Return to dry saucepan.

4. Whisk egg and egg yolk in small bowl; whisk in ⅓ cup (80 mL) of the cheese and the pepper. Pour bacon-cream mixture over fettuccine in saucepan; toss to coat. Heat over medium-low heat just until hot. Stir in egg-cheese mixture. Toss to coat evenly. Immediately remove from heat. Serve with remaining cheese.

Makes 4 servings.

Spaghetti with Seafood Sauce

¼ cup (60 mL) cold water
1 tablespoon (15 mL) cornstarch
2 small green onions
2 medium cloves garlic
8 small fresh oysters
¼ pound (115 g) fresh scallops*
1 pound (450 g) fresh medium shrimp in shells
¼ cup (60 mL) butter
10 ounces (285 g) uncooked spaghetti
Boiling salted water
½ cup (125 mL) dry white wine
1¼ cups (310 mL) whipping cream
2 teaspoons (10 mL) fresh lemon juice
½ teaspoon (2 mL) salt
⅛ teaspoon (0.5 mL) pepper
2 tablespoons (30 mL) chopped fresh parsley
Lemon wedges

Note: *Occasionally, in some coastal areas, fresh scallops are available with the roe or coral attached. These are the orangish-pink-colored, crescent-shaped pieces shown in the photo, above right. If coral is present, separate it from the scallops and cook along with scallops in recipe.

1. Mix ¼ cup (60 mL) cold water and the cornstarch in cup until smooth; reserve. Trim and slice green onions. Mince garlic. Reserve.

2. Scrub oysters thoroughly with stiff brush under cold running water. Shuck oysters over bowl to catch liquor; reserve shells for garnish, if desired. Strain oyster liquor through triple thickness of dampened cheesecloth; reserve.

3. Rinse scallops under cold running water; drain and pat dry. Cut scallops into 1-inch (2.5 cm) pieces.

4. Shell shrimp under cold running water. Cut a shallow

slit down the back of shrimp; pull out and discard intestinal vein. Pat shrimp dry.

5. Heat butter in large noncorrosive skillet over medium heat. When foam subsides, add oysters; sauté just until edges begin to curl, 1 to 2 minutes. Remove oysters with slotted spoon to plate. Add scallops and shrimp to pan; sauté just until opaque, 2 to 3 minutes. Remove scallops and shrimp with slotted spoon to separate plate. Reserve drippings in pan.

6. Cook spaghetti in large kettle of boiling salted water just until al dente, 8 to 12 minutes; drain well.

7. While spaghetti is cooking, sauté reserved garlic in drippings remaining in skillet over medium heat 30 seconds. Stir in wine; then stir in reserved oyster liquor and the cream. Heat to boiling. Cook over medium heat, stirring and scraping brown bits from bottom of pan, 5 minutes. Stir in reserved cornstarch mixture; simmer over low heat, stirring constantly, 3 minutes. Stir in lemon juice, salt and pepper. Stir in shrimp and scallops; cook just until heated through. Pour sauce over spaghetti in heated serving bowl. Top with reserved green onions, the parsley and oysters; toss. Garnish with reserved shells, if desired. Serve with lemon wedges.

Makes 3 to 4 servings.

Pesto

¼ cup (60 mL) plus 1 tablespoon (15 mL) olive oil
2 tablespoons (30 mL) pine nuts (pignolias)
1 cup (250 mL) tightly packed, rinsed, drained, stemmed fresh basil leaves (do not use dried basil)
2 medium cloves garlic
¼ teaspoon (1 mL) salt
¼ cup (60 mL) freshly grated Parmesan cheese
1½ tablespoons (22 mL) freshly grated Romano cheese

Serving Suggestions: Toss pesto with hot cooked buttered fettuccine or linguine; this recipe will dress ½ to ¾ pound (225 to 340 g) pasta. Stir small amount of pesto into broth-based vegetable or meat soups. Whisk small amount of pesto into vinaigrette for tossed salads. Mix pesto with softened butter to be used on steamed vegetables, poached fish or omelets.

1. Heat 1 tablespoon (15 mL) of the oil in small saucepan or skillet over medium-low heat. Add pine nuts; sauté, stirring

and shaking pan constantly until nuts are light brown, 30 to 45 seconds. Transfer nuts immediately to paper towel-lined plate to drain.

2. Combine pine nuts, basil leaves, garlic, salt and remaining ¼ cup (60 mL) oil in food processor or blender container. Process until mixture is evenly blended and pieces are very finely chopped.

3. Transfer basil mixture to small bowl. Stir in Parmesan and Romano cheeses. Pesto can be refrigerated, covered with thin layer of olive oil, up to 1 week; or pesto can be frozen for several months. Thaw and bring to room temperature before using.

Makes about ¾ cup (180 mL) pesto.

Summer Spaghetti

1 pound (450 g) firm, ripe fresh plum tomatoes
1 medium onion
6 pitted green olives
2 medium cloves garlic
⅓ cup (80 mL) chopped fresh parsley
2 tablespoons (30 mL) finely shredded fresh basil or ¾ teaspoon (4 mL) dried basil, crumbled
2 teaspoons (10 mL) drained capers
½ teaspoon (2 mL) paprika
¼ teaspoon (1 mL) dried oregano, crumbled
1 tablespoon (15 mL) red wine vinegar
½ cup (125 mL) olive oil
1 pound (450 g) uncooked spaghetti
Boiling salted water

1. Chop tomatoes coarsely. Chop onion and olives. Mince garlic. Combine tomatoes, onion, olives, garlic, parsley,

basil, capers, paprika and oregano in medium bowl; toss well. Drizzle vinegar over tomato mixture. Then pour oil over tomato mixture. Stir until thoroughly mixed. Refrigerate covered at least 6 hours or overnight.

2. Just before serving, cook spaghetti in large kettle of boiling salted water just until al dente, 8 to 12 minutes; drain well. Immediately toss hot pasta with cold marinated tomato sauce. Serve at once.

Makes 4 to 6 servings.

Note: In this dish, the contact of the very cold sauce with the hot spaghetti releases a unique and delicious flavor. The resulting tepid pasta salad makes a refreshing lunch or light supper for a hot summer day. Or, you may serve the versatile sauce as a relish with grilled meats, as a dressing for mixed greens, or stirred into cooled cooked rice.

Pasta with Oil & Garlic

½ pound (225 g) uncooked pasta such as plain or spinach fettuccine, spaghetti or linguine
Boiling salted water
⅓ cup (80 mL) olive oil
3 medium cloves garlic, minced
¼ cup (60 mL) chopped fresh parsley
½ teaspoon (2 mL) salt
⅛ teaspoon (0.5 mL) pepper
½ cup (125 mL) freshly grated Parmesan cheese (about 1½ ounces or 45 g)

1. Cook pasta in large kettle of boiling salted water just until al dente, 6 to 12 minutes; drain well. Keep warm.

2. Heat oil in 10-inch (25 cm) skillet over low heat. Add garlic to skillet; cook gently until light gold, 2 to 3 minutes. Do not brown garlic or it will become bitter. Remove pan from heat. Stir in parsley, salt and pepper.

3. Add hot pasta to skillet. Toss to coat evenly. Serve immediately with cheese to sprinkle.

Makes 3 to 4 servings.

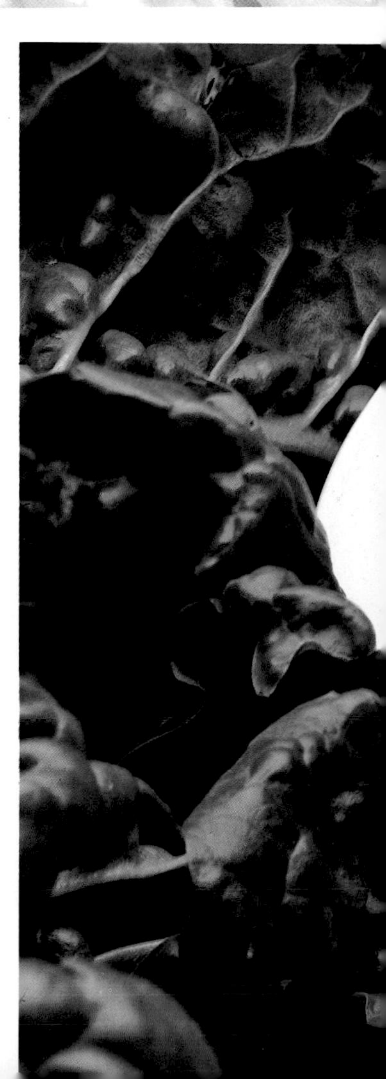

Spaghetti Marinara

8 fresh oysters
½ pound (225 g) fresh scallops (see note for Seafood Sauce, page 420)
6 flat anchovy fillets
⅓ cup (80 mL) chopped onion
2 tablespoons (30 mL) olive oil
1 large clove garlic, minced
½ cup (125 mL) dry white wine
10 ounces (285 g) uncooked spaghetti
Boiling salted water
5 large ripe fresh tomatoes, seeded and chopped
1 tablespoon (15 mL) tomato paste
¾ teaspoon (4 mL) dried basil, crumbled
¾ teaspoon (4 mL) salt
½ teaspoon (2 mL) dried oregano, crumbled
⅛ teaspoon (0.5 mL) pepper
1 pound (450 g) fresh medium shrimp, shelled and deveined
3 tablespoons (45 mL) chopped fresh parsley

1. Scrub oysters; shuck over bowl; discard shells. Strain oyster liquor; reserve. Cut scallops into ¾-inch (2 cm) pieces. Drain and mince anchovies.

2. Sauté onion in oil in 3-quart (3 L) noncorrosive saucepan over medium-high heat until soft, about 4 minutes. Add garlic; cook 30 seconds. Add wine; cook until wine is completely evaporated, 4 to 5 minutes. Remove from heat.

3. Cook spaghetti in large kettle of boiling salted water just until al dente, 8 to 12 minutes; drain well.

4. While spaghetti is cooking, stir tomatoes, oyster liquor, anchovies, tomato paste, basil, salt, oregano and pepper into onion mixture. Heat to boiling; reduce heat to medium. Cook uncovered, stirring occasionally, until sauce is very thick, about 20 minutes. Stir in shrimp, scallops and oysters. Cook covered, stirring occasionally, just until shrimp are cooked through, 2 to 3 minutes. Stir in parsley. Toss sauce with spaghetti; serve immediately

Makes 3 to 4 servings.

Tomato Sauces

Neapolitan Sauce

1 can (28 ounces or 790 g) Italian plum tomatoes
2 tablespoons (30 mL) butter
1 tablespoon (15 mL) olive oil
1 teaspoon (5 mL) dried basil, crumbled
½ teaspoon (2 mL) salt
⅛ teaspoon (0.5 mL) pepper
3 tablespoons (45 mL) chopped fresh parsley
½ pound (225 g) spaghetti, cooked
½ cup (125 mL) freshly grated Parmesan cheese, if desired

1. Press tomatoes and their liquid through sieve into bowl; discard seeds.

2. Heat butter and oil in 2-quart (2 L) noncorrosive saucepan over medium heat. Stir in sieved tomatoes, basil, salt and pepper. Heat to boiling; reduce heat to medium-low. Cook uncovered, stirring frequently, until sauce is reduced and measures 2 cups (500 mL), 30 to 40 minutes. Stir in parsley. Toss with spaghetti. Serve immediately with Parmesan cheese to sprinkle.

Makes 2 to 3 servings.

Pizzaiola Sauce

1 can (28 ounces or 790 g) Italian plum tomatoes
2 cloves garlic
1 tablespoon (15 mL) olive oil
¾ teaspoon (4 mL) dried marjoram, crumbled
½ teaspoon (2 mL) salt
⅛ teaspoon (0.5 mL) pepper
2 tablespoons (30 mL) minced fresh parsley
½ pound (225 g) spaghetti, cooked
½ cup (125 mL) freshly grated Parmesan cheese, if desired

1. Press tomatoes and their liquid through sieve into bowl; discard seeds. Cut garlic in half.

2. Heat oil in 2-quart (2 L) noncorrosive saucepan over medium heat. Add garlic; cook and stir until garlic is golden but not brown, 2 to 3 minutes. Remove and discard garlic. Add sieved tomatoes to oil; stir in marjoram, salt and pepper. Heat to boiling; reduce heat to medium-low. Cook uncovered, stirring frequently, until sauce is reduced and measures 2 cups (500 mL), 30 to 40 minutes. Stir in parsley. Toss with spaghetti. Serve immediately with Parmesan cheese to sprinkle.

Makes 2 to 3 servings.

Gnocchi, Polenta & Rice

Gnocchi Verdi

2 packages (10 ounces or 285 g each) frozen spinach
1 cup (250 mL) ricotta cheese
2 large eggs
⅔ cup (160 mL) freshly grated Parmesan cheese (about 2 ounces or 60 g)
1 cup (250 mL) plus 3 tablespoons (45 mL) all-purpose flour
½ teaspoon (2 mL) salt
⅛ teaspoon (0.5 mL) pepper
⅛ teaspoon (0.5 mL) ground nutmeg
Boiling salted water
3 tablespoons (45 mL) butter

1. Cook spinach according to package directions. Drain well; let cool. Squeeze spinach very dry. Chop spinach very fine; place in medium bowl. Stir in ricotta cheese. Add eggs; mix well. Add ⅓ cup (80 mL) of the Parmesan cheese, 3 tablespoons (45 mL) of the flour, the salt, pepper and nutmeg; stir to mix very well. Refrigerate covered 1 hour.

2. Spread remaining 1 cup (250 mL) flour in shallow baking pan. Press a heaping table-

spoonful of spinach mixture between spoon and hand to form oval gnocchi; place on flour. Repeat until all spinach mixture is used.

3. Roll gnocchi lightly in flour to coat evenly; discard excess flour. Slip 8 to 12 gnocchi into large kettle of boiling salted water; reduce heat to medium. Cook uncovered until gnocchi are slightly puffed and medium-firm to the touch, about 5 minutes. Remove gnocchi with slotted spoon to paper towel-lined plate; then transfer immediately to greased flameproof shallow baking dish. Reheat water to

boiling. Continue cooking and draining gnocchi in batches until all have been cooked. Arrange gnocchi so that they are in single layer in baking dish.

4. Heat broiler. Melt butter in small saucepan. Spoon butter over gnocchi; sprinkle with remaining ⅓ cup (80 mL) Parmesan cheese. Broil gnocchi, 5 inches (13 cm) from heat source, until cheese topping is light brown, 2 to 3 minutes. Serve at once.

Makes about 24 gnocchi; 4 to 6 servings.

Gnocchi alla Romana

Vegetable oil
3 cups (750 mL) milk
1½ teaspoons (7 mL) salt
Large pinch ground nutmeg
Large pinch pepper
1 cup (250 mL) plus 2 tablespoons (30 mL) semolina
2 large egg yolks, lightly beaten
1 cup (250 mL) freshly grated Parmesan cheese (about 3 ounces or 85 g)
6 tablespoons (90 mL) butter

1. Line bottom of 15½ × 10½ × 1-inch (39 × 26.5 × 2.5 cm) baking pan with aluminum foil. Generously oil the foil.

2. Heat milk, salt, nutmeg and pepper in heavy 3-quart (3 L) saucepan over medium-high heat just to simmering. Do not boil; reduce heat to medium-low. Begin whisking or stirring milk briskly and add semolina in thin steady stream, taking care not to let lumps form. Cook, stirring frequently, until thick enough for spoon to stand upright and unsupported in center of mixture, 5 to 10 minutes. Reduce heat to low; continue cooking, stirring constantly, until very thick, about 5 minutes longer. Remove from heat.

3. Add egg yolks, ¾ cup (180 mL) of the cheese and 2 tablespoons (30 mL) of the butter to semolina mixture; stir until butter is melted and mixture is smooth.

4. Transfer mixture to prepared pan. Pat out with spatula to ⅜-inch (1 cm) thickness. Refrigerate uncovered until cold, at least 1 hour.

5. Heat oven to 425°F (220°C). Turn mixture out of pan onto flat surface; peel off foil. Cut

gnocchi out of mixture with 2-inch (5 cm) round cutter. Arrange gnocchi overlapping in 10-inch (25 cm) shallow flameproof baking dish. Melt remaining 4 tablespoons (60 mL) butter in small saucepan. Drizzle melted butter over gnocchi; sprinkle with remaining ¼ cup (60 mL) cheese. Bake until tops of gnocchi are crisp and golden, 20 to 25 minutes. Place under broiler about 4 inches (10 cm) from heat, until light brown, 1 to 2 minutes. Serve at once.

Makes 4 to 6 servings.

Polenta

6 cups (1.5 L) water
2 teaspoons (10 mL) salt
2 cups (500 mL) yellow cornmeal
¼ cup (60 mL) plus 2 teaspoons (10 mL) vegetable oil

Note: Polenta, an important component of Northern Italian cooking, is the basis of countless dishes. The basic preparation presented here can be served in two forms. Hot, freshly made polenta, prepared through step 1, can be mixed with ⅓ cup (80 mL) each butter and grated Parmesan cheese and served as a first course; or it can be poured onto a large platter and topped with Bolognese Sauce (see Index for recipe) or other hearty meat sauces. Fried polenta, prepared through step 4, is appropriate as an appetizer or as an accompaniment for roasted or sauteed meats.

1. Heat 6 cups (1.5 L) water and the salt in heavy 4-quart (4 L) Dutch oven or saucepan to boiling. Begin whisking water vigorously and add cornmeal in very thin but

steady stream, taking care not to let lumps form. Reduce heat to low. Continue cooking polenta uncovered, stirring frequently, until very thick, 40 to 60 minutes. Polenta is ready when thick enough for spoon to stand upright and unsupported in center of mixture. Polenta can be served at this point (see Note at left).

2. For fried polenta, coat inside of 11 × 7 × 2-inch (28 × 18 × 5 cm) baking pan with 2 teaspoons (10 mL) of the oil.

Transfer polenta mixture to baking pan; spread in smooth, even layer. Let stand uncovered at room temperature until completely cooled and very firm, at least 6 hours.

3. Unmold polenta onto cutting board. Cut polenta crosswise into 1¼-inch- (3 cm) wide strips. Cut strips crosswise into 2-to 3-inch-(5 to 8 cm) long pieces.

4. Heat remaining ¼ cup (60 mL) oil in large heavy skillet over medium-high heat until hot; reduce heat to medium. Fry half the polenta pieces at a time, turning as needed, until golden on all sides, 4 to 5 minutes.

Makes 6 to 8 servings.

Vegetable Risotto

½ pound (225 g) eggplant (about 1 small)
1¾ teaspoons (9 mL) salt
1 small zucchini
1 small red bell pepper
1 small green bell pepper
¼ pound (115 g) fresh mushrooms
4 tablespoons (60 mL) butter
½ cup (125 mL) fresh or frozen peas
1 large onion
2 tablespoons (30 mL) olive oil
2 cups (500 mL) uncooked rice
2 cups (500 mL) chicken broth
1¾ cups (430 mL) hot water
⅛ teaspoon (0.5 mL) black pepper
⅔ cup (160 mL) grated Parmesan cheese (about 2 ounces or 60 g)

1. Cut eggplant crosswise into ½-inch- (1.5 cm) thick slices. Sprinkle both sides with 1 teaspoon (5 mL) of the salt. Let stand in colander in sink for 1 hour to drain.

2. Thinly slice zucchini. Core, seed and dice red and green bell peppers. Trim mushrooms; wipe clean with damp kitchen towel and thinly slice.

3. Heat 2 tablespoons (30 mL) of the butter in 4-quart (4 L) saucepan over medium-high heat. Add mushrooms; sauté 3 minutes. Transfer mushrooms to medium bowl. Rinse and drain eggplant; press dry between paper towels. Cut eggplant into ½-inch (1.5 cm) cubes. Add eggplant, zucchini, bell peppers and peas to mushrooms in bowl.

4. Chop onion. Heat remaining 2 tablespoons (30 mL) butter and the oil in the 4-quart (4 L) saucepan over medium heat. Add onion; sauté until onion is soft, about 5 minutes. Stir in rice; cook and stir 2 minutes.

5. Stir broth, 1¾ cups (430 mL) hot water, remaining ¾ teaspoon (4 mL) salt and the black pepper into rice mixture. Heat over high heat to boiling; reduce heat to low. Simmer covered, stirring occasionally, 8 minutes. Add vegetables; stir well. Cook uncovered, stirring

frequently, until rice is tender and all liquid is absorbed, about 10 minutes longer. Remove from heat; stir in cheese.

6. Pack rice mixture into greased 3-quart (3 L) bowl. Let stand 3 minutes. Cover bowl with serving plate; invert and lift off bowl. Serve risotto at once.

Makes 8 to 10 servings.

Rice & Peas

2 pounds (900 g) fresh peas in pods*
1 medium onion
1 stalk celery
2¼ to 3 cups (560 to 750 mL) chicken broth**
¼ cup (60 mL) butter
¾ cup (180 mL) uncooked rice
½ cup (125 mL) dry white wine
½ teaspoon (2 mL) salt
Large pinch pepper
¼ cup (60 mL) grated Parmesan cheese

Notes: *One package (10 ounces or 285 g) frozen peas, thawed, can be substituted for fresh, if desired; add to rice mixture in step 3 after rice has simmered for 6 minutes.

**This dish traditionally has the consistency of a thick soup and is eaten with a spoon; for this consistency, use the larger amount of broth. If you prefer thicker consistency, use the smaller amount of broth.

1. Shell peas; discard pods. Chop onion and celery. Heat broth in small saucepan over medium heat to simmering; keep hot over low heat.

2. Heat butter in 2½-quart (2.5 L) noncorrosive saucepan over medium heat. When foam subsides, add onion and celery; sauté until onion is soft, about 5 minutes. Stir in rice; cook and stir 2 minutes.

3. Stir hot broth into rice mixture in saucepan; stir in wine, salt and pepper. Add peas. Heat over high heat to boiling; reduce heat to low. Simmer covered, stirring occasionally, until rice is tender but firm to the bite, about 12 minutes. Remove from heat.

4. Stir cheese into cooked rice mixture. Serve at once.

Makes 6 servings.

W.A. -N.T.: 45c
MELBOURNE — Tel.: 347 6297
230 Faraday St., Carlton
G.P.O. Sydney for
as a Newspaper
più

Rice Croquettes

1 cup (250 mL) chicken broth
2 tablespoons (30 mL) butter
1 small onion, chopped
½ cup (125 mL) uncooked rice
¼ cup (60 mL) dry white wine
¼ teaspoon (1 mL) salt
Pinch pepper
Pinch saffron threads
¼ cup (60 mL) grated Parmesan cheese
1 large egg
1½ ounces (45 g) mozzarella cheese, cut into ½-inch (1.5 cm) cubes
Vegetable oil
½ cup (125 mL) fine dry unseasoned breadcrumbs

1. Heat broth in small saucepan over medium heat to simmering; keep hot over low heat.

2. Heat butter in heavy 1½-quart (1.5 L) saucepan over medium heat; when foam subsides add onion. Sauté until onion is soft, 3 to 4 minutes. Stir in rice; cook and stir 2 minutes.

3. Stir half the hot broth, the wine, salt and pepper into rice mixture; reduce heat to medium-low. Cook uncovered, stirring frequently, until liquid is absorbed, 5 to 8 minutes. Meanwhile, crush saffron in mortar with pestle to a powder; stir into remaining broth. Add saffron-flavored broth to rice mixture. Continue cooking uncovered, stirring frequently, until rice is tender and broth is absorbed, about 5 minutes longer. Remove from heat; stir in Parmesan cheese. Let stand at room temperature until completely cool, about 45 minutes.

4. Lightly beat egg in small bowl; stir into cooled rice mixture.

5. To form croquettes: Place scant tablespoonful (scant 15 mL) of rice mixture in palm of hand; top with 1 cheese cube. Cover cheese with second tablespoonful (15 mL) of rice; press between palms to form ball, making sure that cheese is completely covered with rice mixture. Place croquettes on waxed paper.

6. Heat 2 inches (5 cm) oil in medium saucepan to 350°F (180°C). Heat oven to 200°F (95°C). Spread breadcrumbs in shallow bowl. Roll croquettes in crumbs to coat evenly; press between palms. Transfer 3 or 4 croquettes with wire skimmer to oil; fry until brown, about 3 minutes. Remove croquettes with skimmer to paper towel-lined plate; place in oven. Repeat until all croquettes have been fried; leave in oven 5 minutes before serving to be sure cheese has melted.

Makes about 10 croquettes.

Risotto Milanese

3½ to 4 cups (875 mL to 1 L) chicken broth
7 tablespoons (105 mL) butter
1 large onion, chopped
1½ cups (375 mL) uncooked rice
½ cup (125 mL) dry white wine
½ teaspoon (2 mL) salt
Pinch pepper
¼ teaspoon (1 mL) saffron threads
¼ cup (60 mL) grated Parmesan cheese

1. Heat broth in small saucepan over medium heat to simmering; keep hot over low heat.

2. Heat 6 tablespoons (90 mL) of the butter in heavy 10-inch (25 cm) skillet or 2½-quart (2.5 L) saucepan over medium

heat. When foam subsides, add onion; sauté until onion is soft, about 5 minutes. Stir in rice; cook and stir 2 minutes. Stir in wine, salt and pepper. Cook uncovered over medium-high heat, stirring occasionally, until wine is evaporated, 3 to 5 minutes.

3. Measure ½ cup (125 mL) of the hot broth; stir into rice. Adjust heat during this step between medium and low to maintain simmer. Cook uncovered, stirring frequently, until broth is absorbed. Repeat this process of adding ½ cup

(125 mL) broth and cooking until absorbed until a total of 2 cups (500 mL) broth has been added. Meanwhile, crush saffron in mortar with pestle to a powder; stir in ½ cup (125 mL) of the remaining broth to dissolve saffron. Add saffron-flavored broth to rice and cook until absorbed. Continue adding remaining broth, ½ cup (125 mL) at a time, and cooking, until rice is tender but firm to the bite and mixture has slightly creamy consistency. Not all the broth may be required. Total cooking time will be about 20 minutes.

4. Remove risotto from heat. Stir in remaining 1 tablespoon (15 mL) butter and the cheese. Serve at once.

Makes 6 to 8 servings.

Note: Risotto Milanese is the traditional accompaniment to Osso Buco (page 442). It is also an appropriate first course for or accompaniment to roasted meat or poultry dishes.

Fish & Shellfish

Fried Smelts

Herbed Butter

½ cup (125 mL) butter
1 tablespoon (15 mL) minced fresh parsley
1 green onion, minced
1 clove garlic, minced
Pinch each salt and pepper

Fried Smelts

3 to 4 dozen fresh smelts*
¾ cup (180 mL) all-purpose flour
1½ teaspoons (7 mL) salt
¼ teaspoon (1 mL) pepper
2 large eggs
¼ cup (60 mL) milk
2½ cups (625 mL) soft fresh breadcrumbs
¼ cup (60 mL) butter
¼ cup (60 mL) vegetable oil
Lemon wedges

Note: *In Italy, this preparation is commonly done with fresh sardines. Try this dish with scaled fresh sardines if they are available in your area.

1. For Herbed Butter: Beat butter in small bowl until smooth and creamy. Stir in parsley, green onion, garlic, salt and pepper. Let stand covered at room temperature 30 minutes to blend flavors.

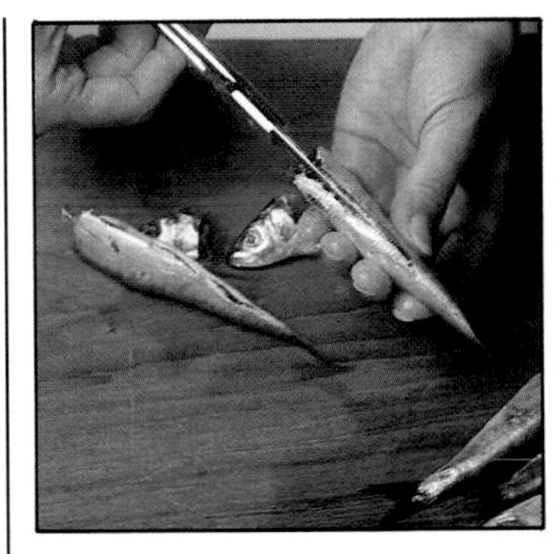

2. For Fried Smelts: Cut off heads of smelts with knife; discard. Cut undersides of smelts open with scissors; clean insides of smelts.

3. Spread smelts open. Cut through backbones at tail end with scissors as shown. Starting at tail end, gently pull backbones out; discard. Rinse smelts under gently running cold water. Drain smelts; pat dry with paper towels.

4. Mix flour, salt and pepper in shallow dish or on waxed paper. Beat eggs and milk in second dish. Place breadcrumbs in third dish.

5. Dip smelts in flour mixture to coat both sides evenly. Dip smelts in egg mixture, then in bread crumbs to coat evenly; place in single layer on tray.

6. Heat ¼ cup (60 mL) butter and oil in large skillet over medium heat. Add as many smelts as will fit in single layer without crowding. Cook uncovered, turning once, until deep golden brown and cooked through, about 2 minutes per side. Repeat until all smelts are cooked. Serve with lemon wedges and Herbed Butter.

Makes 4 entree servings or 8 first course servings.

Fritto Misto

1 cup (250 mL) all-purpose flour
½ teaspoon (2 mL) salt
⅛ teaspoon (0.5 mL) white pepper
Large pinch cayenne pepper
1 cup (250 mL) warm water
1 tablespoon (15 mL) olive oil
1 pound (450 g) squid
1 pound (450 g) large shrimp, shelled and deveined
½ pound (225 g) fresh scallops cut into 1-inch (2.5 cm) pieces
½ pound (225 g) firm white fish fillets, such as haddock or flounder, cut into 2 × 1-inch (5 × 2.5 cm) pieces
Vegetable oil
2 large egg whites, at room temperature
Lemon wedges
Tartar Sauce (recipe below)

1. Combine flour, salt, white pepper and cayenne pepper in medium bowl; stir to mix well. Combine 1 cup (250 mL) warm water and the olive oil; stir into flour mixture. Whisk until smooth. Let batter stand covered, at room temperature, 1 hour.

2. Meanwhile, clean and slice squid following directions for Marinated Calamari (see Index for recipe). Pat squid and all other seafood thoroughly dry with paper towels.

3. Heat 1½ inches (4 cm) vegetable oil in large saucepan to 375°F (190°C). While oil is heating, beat egg whites in small mixer bowl until stiff but not dry peaks form; fold into batter until smooth. Heat oven to 200°F (95°C).

4. Dip a few pieces of seafood into batter to coat well; let excess batter drip off. Fry in oil, turning once or twice, until golden, 1½ to 2 minutes. (***Caution:*** Squid will pop and spatter during frying; stand at arm's length from pan.) Remove from oil with slotted spoon. Drain on paper towel-lined rack; keep warm in oven. Repeat until all seafood has been fried. Serve at once with lemon wedges and Tartar Sauce.

Makes 6 servings.

Tartar Sauce

2 large egg yolks, at room temperature*
1 tablespoon (15 mL) fresh lemon juice
1 teaspoon (5 mL) white wine vinegar
1 teaspoon (5 mL) Dijon-style mustard
½ teaspoon (2 mL) salt
Pinch white pepper
1 cup (250 mL) vegetable oil, at room temperature
1 green onion
1 tablespoon (15 mL) drained capers
1 small sweet gherkin
2 tablespoons (30 mL) chopped fresh parsley

Note: *Mayonnaise can be made in blender or food processor, if desired. Substitute 1 whole egg for the egg yolks and follow manufacturer's instructions for mixing mayonnaise.

1. To make mayonnaise, bowl must be at room temperature; if bowl is cold, fill with hot water, then empty bowl and dry thoroughly. Combine egg yolks, lemon juice, vinegar,

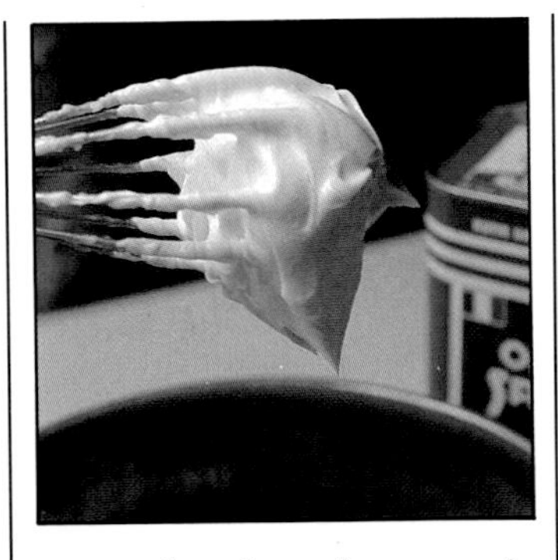

mustard, salt and pepper in medium bowl; whisk until smooth. Add half the oil, drop by drop, whisking continuously, to thoroughly incorporate oil. Whisking continuously, add remaining oil in slow steady stream.

2. Trim and thinly slice green onion. Mince capers and gherkin. Fold green onion, capers, gherkin and parsley into mayonnaise. Refrigerate covered until ready to serve. Serve with Fritto Misto (recipe above), Fried Calamari (see Index for recipe) or other fried fish dishes.

Makes about 1⅓ cups (330 mL).

Fish with Zucchini

2 small zucchini
1 can (14½ ounces or 415 g) whole peeled tomatoes
1 pound (450 g) skinned red snapper, cod or striped bass fillets
¼ cup (60 mL) plus 1 tablespoon (15 mL) butter
2 tablespoons (30 mL) olive oil
1 tablespoon (15 mL) chopped fresh basil or ¾ teaspoon (4 mL) dried basil, crumbled
½ teaspoon (2 mL) salt
1 sprig fresh rosemary or ¼ teaspoon (1 mL) dried rosemary, crumbled
⅛ teaspoon (0.5 mL) pepper
2 tablespoons (30 mL) fine dry unseasoned breadcrumbs
2 teaspoons (10 mL) lemon juice

1. Heat oven to 400°F (200°C). Cut zucchini crosswise into ¼-inch- (0.5 cm) thick slices. Press tomatoes and their liquid through sieve into bowl; discard seeds. Pat fish dry.

2. Heat ¼ cup (60 mL) of the butter in 12-inch (30 cm) noncorrosive skillet over medium-high heat; when foam subsides, reduce heat to medium. Add fish fillets; cook, turning once, until fish is light brown, 1 to 2 minutes per side. Remove fish with slotted spatula to greased shallow baking dish.

3. Add oil to butter remaining in skillet; increase heat to medium-high. Add zucchini; cook and stir until light brown, about 3 minutes. Stir in half the basil, the salt, rosemary and pepper; cook 30 seconds. Stir in sieved tomatoes. Heat to boiling; reduce heat to medium. Cook uncovered, stirring frequently, until sauce is slightly thickened, about 5 minutes. (Remove and discard rosemary at this point if using fresh).

4. Spoon zucchini-tomato mixture over fish in baking dish. Sprinkle with breadcrumbs and remaining basil. Drizzle lemon juice over crumbs; dot with remaining 1 tablespoon (15 mL) butter. Bake uncovered just until fish is cooked through and topping is light brown, 10 to 15 minutes.

Makes 2 to 3 servings.

Fish Milanese

⅓ cup (80 mL) plus 2 tablespoons (30 mL) olive oil
2 tablespoons (30 mL) lemon juice
½ teaspoon (2 mL) salt
Pinch pepper
1 small onion, finely chopped
1 pound (450 g) flounder or haddock fillets (4 to 8 pieces)
2 large eggs
1 tablespoon (15 mL) milk
¾ cup (180 mL) fine dry unseasoned breadcrumbs
½ cup (125 mL) all-purpose flour
¼ cup (60 mL) plus 2 tablespoons (30 mL) butter
1 small clove garlic, minced
1 tablespoon (15 mL) chopped fresh parsley
Lemon wedges

1. Whisk ⅓ cup (80 mL) of the oil, the lemon juice, salt and pepper in small bowl; stir in onion. Transfer marinade to noncorrosive baking dish.

2. Rinse fish; pat dry with paper towels. Place fish in marinade in baking dish; spoon marinade over fish to coat thoroughly. Refrigerate covered, turning fish over occasionally, 1 hour.

3. Whisk eggs and milk in shallow bowl. Spread breadcrumbs on plate. Spread flour on waxed paper or on plate. Remove fish from marinade; pat dry with paper towels. Discard marinade.

4. Dip fish to coat both sides evenly, first in flour, then in eggs, then in breadcrumbs. Press crumb coating firmly onto fish. Place on waxed paper; refrigerate 15 minutes.

5. Heat 2 tablespoons (30 mL) of the butter and remaining 2 tablespoons (30 mL) oil in large skillet over medium heat. When foam subsides, add fish. Cook, turning once, until fish is golden brown and cooked through, 2 to 3 minutes per side. Remove to plate.

6. Melt remaining ¼ cup (60 mL) butter in medium skillet over medium heat. Add garlic. Cook until butter turns light brown, 1 to 2 minutes; stir in parsley. Pour browned butter over fish. Serve at once with lemon wedges.

Makes 3 to 4 servings.

Marinated Calamari

1 pound (450 g) fresh or thawed frozen squid
⅓ cup (80 mL) olive oil
¼ cup (60 mL) fresh lemon juice
1 small clove garlic, minced
1 tablespoon (15 mL) chopped fresh parsley
1 tablespoon (15 mL) chopped fresh basil or ½ teaspoon (2 mL) dried basil, crumbled
¼ teaspoon (0.5 mL) salt
Pinch white pepper

1. To clean squid, work in sink. Hold body of squid firmly in one hand; grasp head firmly with other hand; pull head, twisting gently from side to side. Head and contents of body should come away in one piece. Cut tentacles off head; reserve. Discard head and contents of body.

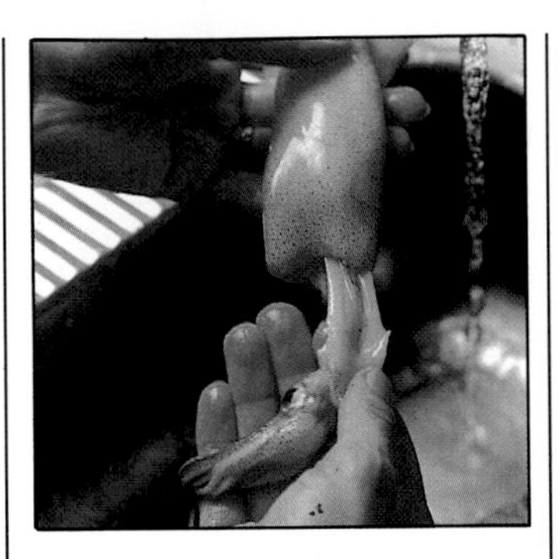

Grasp tip of pointed, thin, clear cartilage protruding from body; pull out and discard.

2. Rinse squid under cold running water. Peel off and discard spotted outer membrane. Pull off side fins; reserve. Rinse inside of squid bodies thoroughly under running water to remove any grit or extraneous matter. Cut squid

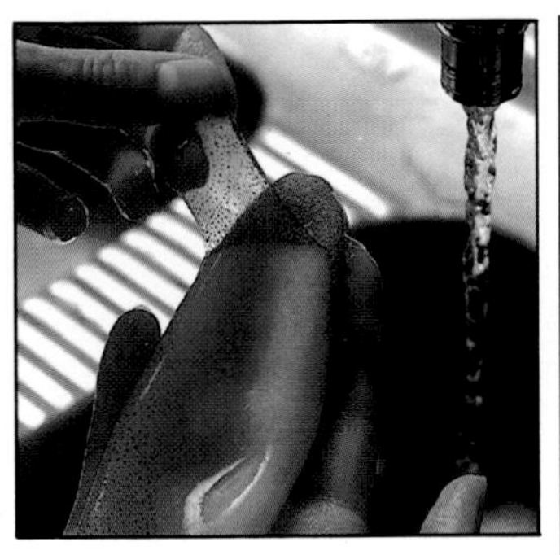

bodies crosswise into ¼-inch (0.5 cm) rings. Cut reserved fins into thin slices. Body rings, fins and reserved tentacles are all edible parts.

3. Drop squid pieces into large saucepan of boiling water; reduce heat to medium. Cook uncovered until squid is tender, about 15 minutes.

4. Meanwhile, mix oil and lemon juice in medium bowl. Remove squid from water with skimmer or slotted spoon, draining well. Add to oil mixture; stir to coat. Refrigerate covered, stirring occasionally, 12 to 24 hours.

5. Stir remaining ingredients into squid mixture. Refrigerate covered 2 to 4 hours. Serve in the marinade.

Makes 2 to 3 servings.

Fried Calamari

1 pound (450 g) fresh or thawed frozen squid
1 large egg
1 tablespoon (15 mL) milk
¾ cup (180 mL) fine dry unseasoned breadcrumbs
Vegetable oil
Tartar Sauce, if desired (page 436)
Lemon wedges

1. Clean and slice squid following directions for Marinated Calamari (see above). Pat squid pieces thoroughly dry with paper towels.

2. Beat egg with milk in small bowl. Add squid pieces; stir to

coat well. Remove a few squid pieces from egg mixture and place in single layer on breadcrumbs. Turn pieces over to coat evenly with crumbs. Place coated squid in shallow bowl or on plate. Repeat process to coat all squid. Let stand 10 to 15 minutes before frying.

3. To deep-fry squid, heat 1½ inches (4 cm) oil in large saucepan to 350°F (180°C). (***Caution:*** Squid will pop and spatter during frying; stand at arm's length from pan.) Fry 8 to 10 pieces of squid at a time in hot oil until light brown, 45 to 60 seconds. Remove with slotted spoon to paper towel-lined rack.

4. Squid can be shallow-fried, if desired; this method uses less oil but requires slightly more hand-work. Heat about 3/16 inch (0.5 cm) oil in large skillet over medium-high heat

until hot; reduce heat to medium. (***Caution:*** Squid will pop and spatter during frying; stand at arm's length from pan.) Add as many pieces of squid as will fit in single layer without crowding. Cook, turning once with 2 forks, until light brown on both sides, 1 to 1½ minutes. Remove with slotted spoon to paper towel-lined rack. Repeat until all squid have been fried.

5. Serve hot with Tartar Sauce and lemon wedges.

Makes 2 to 3 servings.

Meat & Poultry

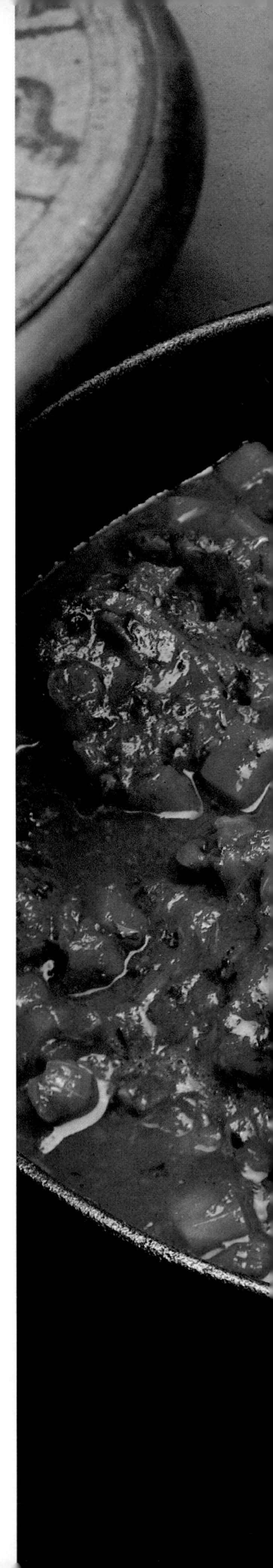

Osso Buco

8 pieces veal shank, cut 2 to 2½ inches (5 to 6.5 cm) thick (about 6½ pounds or 2925 g)
5 tablespoons (75 mL) butter
2 medium carrots, pared and diced
2 stalks celery, chopped
2 medium onions, chopped
1 medium clove garlic, minced
¾ cup (180 mL) all-purpose flour
2 tablespoons (30 mL) olive oil
1 cup (250 mL) dry white wine
1 can (14½ ounces or 415 g) whole peeled tomatoes
1½ cups (375 mL) beef broth
1 teaspoon (5 mL) dried basil, crumbled
½ teaspoon (2 mL) dried rosemary, crumbled
¼ teaspoon (1 mL) dried thyme, crumbled
1 bay leaf
¼ teaspoon (1 mL) salt
⅛ teaspoon (0.5 mL) pepper
1 medium clove garlic, minced
3 tablespoons (45 mL) minced fresh parsley
1 teaspoon (5 mL) grated lemon peel

1. Tie any loose veal shanks around circumference with kitchen twine.

2. Heat 3 tablespoons (45 mL) of the butter in large skillet over medium heat. When foam subsides, add carrots, celery and onions; sauté just until onions begin to color, 7 to 8 minutes. Add 1 clove garlic; cook 30 seconds. Transfer mix-

ture to wide shallow noncorrosive Dutch oven.

3. Roll veal shanks in flour to coat lightly. Heat oil and remaining 2 tablespoons (30 mL) butter in large skillet over medium heat; add shanks. Cook, turning occasionally, until shanks are brown on all

sides; remove shanks to paper towel-lined tray.

4. Add wine to skillet. Cook over medium heat, scraping up brown bits that cling to bottom and sides of pan, 1 minute. Remove from heat. Press tomatoes and their liquid through sieve into skillet. Stir in broth, basil, rosemary,

thyme, bay leaf, salt and pepper.

5. Arrange veal shanks upright on top of vegetables in Dutch oven. Pour in tomato-wine mixture. Heat to boiling on high heat; reduce heat to very low. Simmer covered,

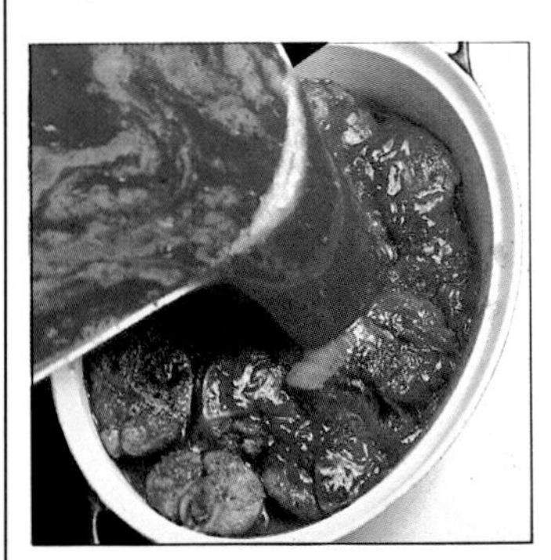

basting shanks with cooking liquid occasionally, until veal is very tender, 1½ to 2 hours. Remove shanks from Dutch oven to deep serving dish. Cook and stir sauce over high heat, until slightly thickened; pour over shanks. Mix 1 clove garlic, parsley, and lemon peel. Sprinkle over shanks.

Makes 8 servings.

Veal Florentine

6 ounces (170 g) fresh spinach
Warm salted water
6 tablespoons (90 mL) butter
1 can (14½ ounces or 415 g) whole peeled tomatoes
2 cloves garlic, minced
¼ cup (60 mL) dry white wine
¼ cup (60 mL) water
1 tablespoon (15 mL) tomato paste
½ teaspoon (2 mL) sugar
¾ teaspoon (4 mL) salt
¼ teaspoon (1 mL) pepper
¼ cup (60 mL) all-purpose flour
4 veal cutlets, cut ⅜-inch (1 cm) thick, about 4 ounces (115 g) each
1 tablespoon (15 mL) olive oil
4 slices mozzarella cheese (1 ounce or 30 g each)

1. Rinse spinach in large basin of warm salted water to remove sand; drain. Trim stems. Stack leaves; cut crosswise into coarse shreds. Place spinach with water that clings to leaves in medium saucepan over medium heat. Steam covered, stirring occasionally, until tender, about 4 minutes. Add 2 tablespoons (30 mL) of the butter; cook and stir uncovered until butter is absorbed. Remove spinach from pan. Reserve.

2. Press tomatoes and their liquid through sieve into bowl; discard seeds. Heat 2 tablespoons (30 mL) of the remaining butter in medium saucepan over medium heat. Add garlic; sauté 30 seconds. Add sieved tomatoes, the wine, ¼ cup (60 mL) water, the tomato paste, sugar, ½ teaspoon (2 mL) of the salt and ⅛ teaspoon (0.5 mL) of the pepper to pan. Heat to boiling; reduce heat to low. Simmer uncovered, stirring occasionally, 10 minutes. Remove from heat.

3. Mix flour and remaining ¼ teaspoon (1 mL) salt and ⅛ teaspoon (0.5 mL) pepper in small bag. Pound veal cutlets until

¼-inch (0.5 cm) or less thick. Pat dry with paper toweling. Shake one piece of veal at a time in seasoned flour in bag to coat evenly. Heat oil and remaining 2 tablespoons (30 mL) butter in large noncorrosive skillet over medium heat. Add veal to skillet; cook, turning once, until light brown, 2 to 3 minutes per side. Remove from heat. Spoon off excess fat. Top veal with reserved spinach, dividing evenly; top each with 1 slice of cheese.

4. Pour tomato sauce into skillet around veal; do not let sauce cover cheese. Lift edges of veal to let sauce flow under. Cook uncovered over medium heat until sauce is bubbly; reduce heat to very low. Barely simmer covered 8 minutes. Serve at once.

Makes 4 servings.

Chicken Marsala

2 tablespoons (30 mL) unsalted butter
1 tablespoon (15 mL) vegetable oil
4 skinned boned chicken breast halves (about 1¼ pounds or 565 g)
4 slices mozzarella cheese (1 ounce or 30 g each)
12 capers, drained
4 flat anchovy fillets, drained
1 tablespoon (15 mL) chopped fresh parsley
1 clove garlic, minced
3 tablespoons (45 mL) marsala
⅔ cup (160 mL) whipping cream
Pinch salt
Pinch pepper

1. Heat butter and oil in 10-inch (25 cm) skillet over medium-high heat. When foam subsides, add chicken; reduce heat to medium. Cook uncovered, turning once, until chicken is deep golden brown on both sides and cooked through, 5 to 6 minutes per side. Remove chicken from skillet to board. Top each chicken piece with one cheese slice, 3 capers and 1 anchovy fillet.

2. Return chicken to skillet. Sprinkle with parsley. Cook covered over low heat just until cheese is semi-melted, about 3 minutes. Remove chicken from pan to heated serving platter. Keep warm.

3. Add garlic to drippings in skillet; sauté over medium heat 30 seconds. Stir in marsala; cook, stirring and scraping up brown bits which cling to bottom and sides of skillet, 45 seconds. Stir in cream. Cook uncovered, stirring constantly, until sauce is slightly thickened, about 3 minutes. Stir in salt and pepper. Spoon sauce over chicken. (Serve with buttered new potatoes and green vegetable, if desired.)

Makes 4 servings.

Chicken Cacciatore

1 broiler-fryer chicken, 3 to 3½ pounds (1350 to 1600 g), cut up into 8 pieces
1 tablespoon (15 mL) olive oil
4 ounces (115 g) fresh mushrooms, finely chopped
1 medium onion, chopped
1 medium clove garlic, minced
½ cup (125 mL) dry white wine
1½ tablespoons (22 mL) white wine vinegar
½ cup (125 mL) chicken broth
1 teaspoon (5 mL) dried basil, crumbled
½ teaspoon (2 mL) dried marjoram, crumbled
½ teaspoon (2 mL) salt
⅛ teaspoon (0.5 mL) pepper
1 can (14½ ounces or 415 g) whole peeled tomatoes
8 Italian- or Greek-style black olives
1 tablespoon (15 mL) chopped fresh parsley

1. Rinse chicken; drain and pat dry. Heat oil in large noncorrosive skillet over medium heat. Add as many chicken pieces as will fit in single layer without crowding. Cook, turning once, until chicken is brown, about 8 minutes per side; remove chicken to flameproof casserole or Dutch oven. Repeat until all chicken has been browned.

2. Add mushrooms and onion to drippings remaining in skillet. Sauté over medium heat until onion is soft, about 5 mintues. Add garlic; sauté 30 seconds. Add wine and vinegar to skillet; cook over medium-high heat until liquid is almost completely evaporated, about 5 minutes. Stir in chicken broth, basil, marjoram, salt and pepper. Remove from heat.

3. Press tomatoes and their liquid through sieve into bowl; discard seeds. Stir sieved tomatoes into onion mixture in skillet. Heat to boiling; boil uncovered 2 minutes.

4. Pour tomato-onion mixture over chicken. Heat to boiling; reduce heat to low. Simmer covered until chicken is tender, about 25 minutes. Remove chicken pieces to serving dish; keep warm.

5. Heat tomato-onion mixture to boiling; boil uncovered over medium-high heat 5 minutes. Cut olives in half, remove and discard pits. Add olives and parsley to sauce; cook 1 minute longer. Pour sauce over chicken and serve.

Makes 4 servings.

Veal Casserole

¼ pound (115 g) sliced pancetta*
1 fennel bulb
½ pound (225 g) fresh medium mushrooms
3 small onions
6 veal loin chops, ¾-inch (2 cm) thick, or 2½ pounds (1125 g) veal shoulder steaks, ¾-inch (2 cm) thick
3 medium cloves garlic
3 tablespoons (45 mL) butter
1 tablespoon (15 mL) olive oil
1 cup (250 mL) chicken broth
¾ cup (180 mL) dry white wine
1 tablespoon (15 mL) tomato paste
1 teaspoon (5 mL) salt
⅛ teaspoon (0.5 mL) pepper
1½ tablespoons (22 mL) all-purpose flour
1½ tablespoons (22 mL) cold water

Note: *Pancetta, an unsmoked, cured bacon, is available in Italian delicatessens. If necessary, use American bacon.

1. Cut pancetta into 1-inch (2.5 cm) pieces. Trim bottom end of fennel bulb and cut off stalks; discard. Cut fennel bulb lengthwise in half, then slice crosswise. Clean and trim mushrooms; cut into quarters. Quarter onions. Trim any fat or gristle from veal. Mince garlic.

2. Heat oven to 325°F (160°C). Heat butter and oil in large skillet over medium heat. Add veal in single layer; cook until deep brown, about 4 minutes per side. Remove veal to large shallow casserole.

3. Add pancetta to drippings in skillet. Sauté over medium heat 3 minutes. Add onions, fennel, mushrooms and garlic; sauté until onions are light brown, about 5 minutes. Add broth, wine, tomato paste, salt and pepper. Heat to boiling, stirring and scraping up brown bits which cling to bottom and sides of skillet.

4. Pour vegetable-broth mixture over veal in casserole. Bake covered until veal is tender, 30 to 45 minutes. Remove veal from casserole to deep, heatproof serving dish; keep warm. Transfer vegetable-broth mixture back to skillet. Mix flour and water in cup until smooth. Stir into vegetable mixture; cook, stirring constantly, over medium heat until sauce thickens and bubbles for 1 mintue. Pour vegetable sauce over veal. Serve at once.

Makes 4 to 6 servings.

Salads & Vegetables

Calamari & Vegetable Salad

1 can (2 ounces or 60 g) flat anchovy fillets
1 tablespoon (15 mL) chopped fresh parsley
3 tablespoons (45 mL) olive oil
2 small cloves garlic
1 large ripe avocado
1 tablespoon (15 mL) white wine vinegar
1 large green bell pepper
2 large ripe tomatoes
8 Italian- or Greek-style black olives
2 teaspoons (10 mL) chopped fresh basil or ¾ teaspoon (4 mL) dried basil, crumbled
1 teaspoon (5 mL) dried oregano, crumbled
¼ teaspoon (1 mL) salt
⅛ teaspoon (0.5 mL) pepper
1 small cucumber
½ small head iceberg lettuce
Fried Calamari (page 440)

1. Drain anchovies and discard liquid. Combine anchovies, parsley and 1 tablespoon (15 mL) of the olive oil in small bowl. Crush 1 of the garlic cloves through a press into bowl; stir to mix. Reserve mixture at room temperature until you assemble salad.

2. Pare and pit avocado. Cut lengthwise into ½-inch- (1.5 cm) wide slices; cut slices crosswise in thirds. Toss avocado with vinegar in large bowl.

3. Core and seed bell pepper; cut into thin slices and add to avocado in bowl. Cut each tomato into 6 wedges; add to bowl. Add olives, basil, oregano, salt and pepper to bowl. Crush remaining garlic clove; add to bowl.

4. Cut cucumber crosswise into thin slices. Add to avocado mixture in bowl. Drizzle remaining 2 tablespoons (30 mL) oil over mixture; toss gently to mix.

5. Break lettuce into small pieces; place in bottom of salad bowl. Spoon avocado mixture in even layer over lettuce. Refrigerate covered until serving time.

6. Prepare Fried Calamari.

7. Just before serving, arrange Fried Calamari in a border on top of salad. Arrange reserved anchovies in center of salad; drizzle anchovy marinade over salad.

Makes 4 to 6 servings.

Radicchio & Fennel Salad

11 Italian- or Greek-style black olives
¼ cup (60 mL) olive oil
1 tablespoon (15 mL) fresh lemon juice
1 flat anchovy fillet or ½ teaspoon (2 mL) anchovy paste
¼ teaspoon (1 mL) salt
Large pinch pepper
Large pinch sugar
1 fresh fennel bulb
1 head radicchio*

Note: *Radicchio, a tart red chicory, is available in some Italian and specialty food shops. If not available, 2 heads of Belgian endive can be used; although it does not provide the dramatic red color, it will give a similar texture and its slightly bitter flavor will interplay well with the robust dressing and the sweet anise-bite of the fennel.

1. For dressing: Pit 3 of the olives; discard pits. Place pitted olives, the oil, lemon juice and anchovy in blender or food processor; process 5 seconds. Add salt, pepper and sugar; process until olives are finely chopped, about 5 seconds longer. Reserve.

2. Cut off and discard fennel stalks. Cut off and discard root end at base of fennel bulb and any discolored parts of bulb. Cut fennel bulb lengthwise into 8 wedges; separate segments of each wedge.

3. Separate radicchio leaves; rinse thoroughly in large basin of water. Drain well.

4. Arrange radicchio leaves, fennel and remaining olives on serving plate. Spoon dressing over salad. Serve immediately.

Makes 3 to 4 servings.

Vegetable Salad

3½ tablespoons (52 mL) white wine vinegar
1½ teaspoons (7 mL) minced fresh basil or ½ teaspoon (2 mL) dried basil, crumbled
½ teaspoon (2 mL) salt
⅛ teaspoon (0.5 mL) pepper
Pinch sugar
6 tablespoons (90 mL) olive oil
2 medium ripe tomatoes
⅓ cup (80 mL) green olives
⅓ cup (80 mL) Italian- or Greek-style black olives
1 head leaf or red leaf lettuce
1 small head curly endive
2 heads Belgian endive

1. For dressing: Whisk vinegar, basil, salt, pepper and sugar in small bowl. Whisking continuously, add oil in slow steady stream; whisk until oil is thoroughly blended. Cut tomatoes into quarters.

2. Combine tomatoes and green and black olives in medium bowl. Add dressing; mix lightly. Let stand uncovered at room temperature, stirring occasionally, 30 minutes.

3. Meanwhile, rinse leaf lettuce and curly endive; drain well. Core Belgian endive and separate into leaves; rinse and drain well. Refrigerate greens until ready to assemble salad.

4. Arrange greens, petal-fashion, in large shallow serving bowl. Transfer tomatoes and olives with slotted spoon to center of greens. Spoon remaining dressing over greens. Serve at once or refrigerate covered up to 30 minutes.

Makes 6 servings.

Cauliflower Neapolitan

6 pitted or stuffed green olives
½ small onion
1 stalk celery
½ head cauliflower (about ¾ pound or 340 g)
2 tablespoons (30 mL) fresh lemon juice
¼ teaspoon (1 mL) salt
Pinch pepper
⅓ cup (80 mL) olive oil
2 tablespoons (30 mL) chopped fresh parsley
½ teaspoon (2 mL) drained capers

1. Slice olives. Thinly slice onion. Chop celery. Reserve.

2. Rinse, core and cut cauliflower into 1-inch (2.5 cm) flowerets; place in large saucepan of boiling water. Cook uncovered for 5 minutes after water returns to boiling. Drain cauliflower; rinse under cold running water until cauliflower is completely cooled. Drain well; pat dry.

3. Whisk lemon juice, salt and pepper in medium bowl. Whisking continuously, add oil in slow steady stream; whisk until oil is thoroughly blended. Add reserved olives, onion and celery, the parsley and capers; stir to mix well. Stir in cauliflower. Serve at once or refrigerate covered up to 3 hours.

Makes about 2½ cups (625 mL); about 4 servings.

Tomato & Salami Salad

1 tablespoon (15 mL) fresh lemon juice
1 tablespoon (15 mL) chopped fresh parsley
1 tablespoon (15 mL) chopped fresh basil or 1 teaspoon (5 mL) dried basil, crumbled
1 medium clove garlic, minced
½ teaspoon (2 mL) grated lemon peel
¼ teaspoon (1 mL) salt
⅛ teaspoon (0.5 mL) pepper
⅓ cup (80 mL) olive oil
4 ounces (115 g) hard salami, thinly sliced
3 large ripe tomatoes

1. For dressing: Whisk lemon juice, parsley, basil, garlic, lemon peel, salt and pepper in small bowl. Whisking continuously, add oil in slow steady stream; whisk until oil is thoroughly blended.

2. Spread salami slices out in large shallow bowl or casserole. Pour dressing over slices. Lift slices with fork to allow dressing to flow underneath. Let stand covered at room temperature, turning slices over once, 1 hour.

3. Cut tomatoes into ¼-inch (0.5 cm) thick slices. Top each tomato slice with a salami slice and arrange overlapping on large platter. Drizzle any dressing remaining in bowl over slices.

Makes 6 to 8 servings.

Stuffed Tomatoes

4 large or 5 medium firm, ripe tomatoes
Salt
5 ounces (140 g) fresh spinach
⅓ cup (80 mL) uncooked long-grain rice
1 tablespoon (15 mL) plus 2 teaspoons (10 mL) olive oil
1 tablespoon (15 mL) pine nuts (pignolias)
1 small clove garlic
¼ teaspoon (1 mL) dried basil, crumbled
¼ teaspoon (1 mL) salt
Pinch pepper
⅓ cup (80 mL) grated Parmesan cheese
2 teaspoons (10 mL) butter

1. Cut ½-inch (1.5 cm) slice off top of each tomato and discard. Cut out core of each tomato; scoop out and discard seeds and liquid. Sprinkle insides of tomatoes lightly with salt. Let tomatoes drain, inverted, on paper towel-lined wire rack, while proceeding with recipe.

2. Rinse spinach thoroughly in large basin of lukewarm water; drain. Pinch off and discard stems. Place spinach with water that clings to leaves in

large saucepan over medium heat. Steam covered until spinach is tender, about 5 minutes; drain. Reserve.

3. Cook rice according to package directions until tender. Transfer to medium bowl. Reserve.

4. Heat 2 teaspoons (10 mL) of the oil in small skillet over medium-low heat; add pine nuts. Sauté until nuts are light brown, 30 to 45 seconds. Transfer nuts immediately to paper towel-lined plate to drain.

5. Heat oven to 350°F (180°C). Squeeze reserved spinach gently to remove excess moisture but do not squeeze very dry. Process spinach in blender or food processor until coarsely chopped. Add pine nuts; process 5 seconds.

6. Mince garlic; add to reserved rice. Add spinach mixture, basil, ¼ teaspoon (1 mL) salt, the pepper and remaining 1 tablespoon (15 mL) oil; stir to mix. Stir in cheese.

7. Spoon rice mixture into tomatoes, mounding slightly. Dot tops of rice filling with butter. Place tomatoes in greased shallow casserole. Bake just until tomatoes are tender but not soft, 15 to 20 minutes.

Makes 4 to 5 servings.

Fried Eggplant & Mozzarella

1 medium eggplant (about 1 pound or 450 g)
2 teaspoons (10 mL) salt
6 ounces (170 g) mozzarella cheese, in one piece
½ teaspoon (2 mL) active dry yeast
1½ cups (375 mL) very warm water (105°F to 115°F or 40°C to 46°C)
2 cups (500 mL) all-purpose flour
⅛ teaspoon (0.5 mL) pepper
4½ tablespoons (67 mL) olive oil
1½ teaspoons (7 mL) minced fresh basil or ½ teaspoon (2 mL) dried basil, crumbled
Vegetable oil
1 large egg white
Lemon wedges

1. Rinse eggplant; cut crosswise into ¼-inch- (0.5 cm) thick slices. Sprinkle slices with salt; stand slices on edge in colander. Let stand and drain in sink or over bowl 1 hour. Cut cheese into ⅛-inch- (0.5 cm) thick slices; trim roughly to

diameter of eggplant slices. Reserve, wrapped in plastic.

2. Sprinkle yeast over the very warm water in medium bowl; stir until dissolved. Whisk in 1½ cups (375 mL) of the flour and the pepper until smooth. Reserve batter at room temperature 30 minutes.

3. Meanwhile, rinse eggplant and drain well; press slices between paper towels to extract moisture. Heat 1½ tablespoons (22 mL) of the olive oil in 12-inch (30 cm) skillet over

medium-high heat; add as many eggplant slices as will fit in single layer. Cook, turning once, until slices are light brown, about 2 minutes per side; remove to paper towel-lined wire rack. Repeat, using remaining olive oil, until all eggplant slices are browned. Sprinkle cheese slices with basil. Place each cheese slice between 2 eggplant slices; press firmly together and dip in remaining flour to coat lightly.

4. Heat 1½ inches (4 cm) vegetable oil in large saucepan to

350°F (180°C). Beat egg white in small mixer bowl until stiff but not dry peaks form; fold into yeast batter. Dip one eggplant sandwich at a time into batter and gently shake off excess; place in hot oil. Fry 3 to 4 sandwiches at a time, turning once, until light brown, 1 to 2 minutes per side. Transfer to paper towel-lined rack to drain. Serve hot with lemon wedges.

Makes 4 to 6 servings.

Chinese Cooking Class

Kung Pao Chicken (page 487)

Appetizers

Stuffed Mushrooms

MUSHROOMS
- **24 fresh large mushrooms (about 1 pound)**
- **6 ounces boneless lean pork**
- **¼ cup whole water chestnuts (¼ of 8-ounce can)**
- **3 green onions**
- **½ small red or green bell pepper**
- **1 small stalk celery**
- **1 teaspoon cornstarch**
- **1 teaspoon minced fresh ginger**
- **2 teaspoons dry sherry**
- **1 teaspoon soy sauce**
- **½ teaspoon hoisin sauce**
- **1 egg white**
- **Vegetable oil for frying**
- **Batter (recipe follows)**
- **½ cup all-purpose flour**

BATTER
- **½ cup cornstarch**
- **½ cup all-purpose flour**
- **1½ teaspoons baking powder**
- **¾ teaspoon salt**
- **⅓ cup milk**
- **⅓ cup water**

1. Clean mushrooms by wiping with a damp paper towel. Remove stems; chop stems finely and transfer to large bowl.

2. Finely chop pork, water chestnuts, onions, red pepper and celery with cleaver or food processor. Add to chopped mushroom stems. Add cornstarch, ginger, sherry, soy sauce, hoisin sauce and egg white; mix well.

3. Spoon pork mixture into mushroom caps, mounding in center. Heat oil in wok or large skillet over high heat to 375°F.

4. For Batter, combine cornstarch, flour, baking powder and salt in medium bowl. Stir in milk and water; blend well.

5. Dip mushrooms in flour, then in batter, coating completely. Cook 6 to 8 mushrooms at a time until golden, about 5 minutes. Drain on paper towels. *Makes 2 dozen*

3

Pot Stickers

2 cups all-purpose flour
¾ cup plus 2 tablespoons boiling water
½ cup very finely chopped napa cabbage
8 ounces lean ground pork
2 tablespoons finely chopped water chestnuts
1 green onion, finely chopped
1½ teaspoons soy sauce
1½ teaspoons dry sherry
½ teaspoon minced fresh ginger
1½ teaspoons cornstarch
½ teaspoon sesame oil
¼ teaspoon sugar
2 tablespoons vegetable oil, divided
⅔ cup chicken broth, divided
Soy sauce, vinegar and chili oil

1. Place flour in large bowl and make a well in center. Pour in boiling water; stir with wooden spoon until dough begins to hold together. Knead dough until smooth and satiny on lightly floured surface, about 5 minutes. Cover and let rest 30 minutes.

2. For filling, squeeze cabbage to remove as much moisture as possible; place in large bowl. Add pork, water chestnuts, onion, soy sauce, sherry, ginger, cornstarch, sesame oil and sugar; mix well.

3. Divide dough into 2 equal portions; cover 1 portion with plastic wrap or a clean towel while you work with the other portion. Roll out dough to ⅛-inch thickness on lightly floured work surface. Cut out 3-inch circles with round cookie cutter or clean can. Place 1 rounded teaspoon filling in center of each dough circle.

4. To shape each pot sticker, lightly moisten edges of dough circle with water; fold in half. Starting at one end, pinch curled edges together making 4 pleats along edge. Set dumpling down firmly seam-side up. Cover finished pot stickers while you make remaining dumplings. (Cook dumplings immediately, refrigerate for up to 4 hours or freeze in resealable plastic bag.)

5. To cook pot stickers, heat 1 tablespoon of the vegetable oil in large nonstick skillet over medium heat. Set ½ of pot stickers in pan seam-side up. (If cooking frozen dumplings, do not thaw.) Cook until bottoms are golden brown, 5 to 6 minutes. Pour in ⅓ cup of the chicken broth. Cover tightly, reduce heat and cook until all liquid is absorbed, about 10 minutes (15 minutes if frozen). Repeat with remaining vegetable oil, pot stickers and chicken broth.

6. Place pot stickers browned-side up on serving platter. Serve with soy sauce, vinegar and chili oil for dipping.

Makes 32 pot stickers

2

Hors d'Oeuvre Rolls

½ cup Chinese-style thin egg noodles, broken into 1-inch pieces
2 tablespoons butter or margarine
4 ounces boneless lean pork, finely chopped
6 medium fresh mushrooms, finely chopped
6 green onions, finely chopped
8 ounces shelled, deveined shrimp, cooked and finely chopped
1 hard-cooked egg, finely chopped
1½ tablespoons dry sherry
½ teaspoon salt
⅛ teaspoon pepper
2 sheets commercial puff pastry dough or 40 wonton wrappers
1 egg beaten
Vegetable oil for frying
Prepared sweet and sour sauce, optional

1. Cook noodles according to package directions until tender but still firm, 2 to 3 minutes. Drain and rinse under cold running water and drain again. Chop noodles finely.

2. Heat butter in wok or large skillet over medium-high heat. Add pork and stir-fry until browned, about 5 minutes. Add mushrooms and onions; stir-fry 2 minutes. Remove from heat and add shrimp, hard-cooked egg, cooked noodles, sherry, salt and pepper; mix well.

3. If using puff pastry, roll and trim each sheet into a 15×12-inch rectangle. Cut each rectangle into 20 (3-inch) squares.

4. Place 1 tablespoon pork mixture across center of each pastry square or wonton wrapper. Brush edges lightly with beaten egg. Roll up tightly around filling and pinch edges slightly to seal.

3

4

5. Heat oil in wok or large skillet to 375°F. Cook 6 to 8 rolls at a time until golden and crisp, 3 to 5 minutes. Drain on paper towels. Serve with sweet and sour sauce, if desired.

Makes 40 rolls

1

2

3

Spring Rolls

1 pound medium shrimp, shelled, deveined
1 pound boneless lean pork
4 ounces fresh mushrooms
8 green onions
1 red bell pepper
½ head bok choy or napa cabbage (about 8 ounces)
1 can (8 ounces) water chestnuts, drained
3 tablespoons dry sherry
1½ tablespoons soy sauce
2 teaspoons minced fresh ginger
1 teaspoon sugar
½ teaspoon salt
¼ cup water
1½ tablespoons cornstarch
24 spring roll or egg roll wrappers
Vegetable oil for frying

1. Finely chop shrimp, pork, mushrooms, onions, red pepper, cabbage and water chestnuts.

2. Transfer all chopped ingredients to large bowl. Add sherry, soy sauce ginger, sugar and salt; mix well. Blend water and cornstarch in small cup; mix well.

3. Place about ¼ cup pork mixture evenly across one corner of each wrapper. Brush cornstarch mixture evenly over all edges of wrappers. Carefully roll wrappers around filling, folding in corners to seal.

4. Heat oil in wok or large skillet over high heat to 375°F. Cook 3 or 4 rolls at a time until golden, 3 to 5 minutes. Drain on paper towels.

Makes 2 dozen

Fried Wontons

1 ounce dried mushrooms
1 pound boneless lean pork
4 ounces fresh spinach
1½ tablespoons dry sherry
4 teaspoons soy sauce, divided
¼ teaspoon pepper
48 wonton wrappers (about 1 pound)
1 can (6 ounces) pineapple juice
½ cup distilled white vinegar
1 tablespoon catsup
½ cup sugar
1½ tablespoons cornstarch
¼ cup water
½ cup Chinese mixed pickled vegetables
Vegetable oil for frying

1. Place mushrooms in bowl and cover with hot water. Let stand 30 minutes. Drain and squeeze out excess water. Cut off and discard stems.

2. Finely chop pork, spinach and mushrooms with cleaver or food processor; transfer to large bowl. Add sherry, 2 teaspoons of the soy sauce and the pepper; mix well.

3. For wontons, work with about 12 wrappers at a time keeping remaining wrappers covered with plastic wrap. Spoon 1 rounded teaspoon pork mixture onto center of each wonton wrapper. Gather edges around filling, pressing firmly at top to seal.

4. Combine pineapple juice, vinegar, catsup, sugar and remaining 2 teaspoons soy sauce in small saucepan. Bring to a boil. Blend cornstarch and water in small cup; stir into pineapple mixture. Reduce heat; cook and stir until thickened, about 3 minutes. Stir in Chinese mixed pickled vegetables; keep warm.

5. Heat oil in wok or large skillet over medium-high heat to 375°F. Cook 8 to 10 wontons at a time until golden and crisp, 2 to 3 minutes. Drain on paper towels. To serve, pour pineapple mixture over wontons.

Makes 4 dozen

3

3

5

3

4

5

Chicken and Banana Squares

- 2 whole boneless, skinless chicken breasts, cooked
- 2 ripe medium bananas
- 6 slices white sandwich bread, trimmed and quartered
- 4 eggs
- ½ cup milk
- ½ cup all-purpose flour
- 4 cups soft bread crumbs (10 to 12 bread slices)
- Vegetable oil for frying

1. Cut chicken breasts into 8 pieces, then cut each of those pieces into thirds, yielding 24 pieces total.

2. Cut each banana lengthwise into quarters. Cut each quarter into thirds, yielding 24 pieces total.

3. Beat eggs and milk in medium bowl until blended. Brush one side of the 24 bread pieces with egg mixture. Place 1 piece of chicken and 1 piece of banana on each egg-glazed bread piece.

4. Place flour in one bowl and soft bread crumbs in another. Coat each chicken-banana square lightly with flour, dip in egg mixture, then coat with bread crumbs. Dip in egg mixture again and coat with crumbs.

5. Heat oil in wok or large skillet over high heat to 375°F. Cook 4 to 6 squares at a time until golden, 2 to 3 minutes. Drain on paper towels.

Makes 2 dozen

Shrimp Toast

12 large shrimp, shelled and deveined, leaving tails intact
1 egg
2½ tablespoons cornstarch
¼ teaspoon salt
Pinch pepper
3 slices white sandwich bread, crusts removed and quartered
1 hard-cooked egg yolk, cut into ½-inch pieces
1 slice cooked ham, cut into ½-inch pieces
1 green onion, finely chopped
Vegetable oil for frying

1. Cut down back of shrimp; press gently to flatten. Beat the 1 egg, cornstarch, salt and pepper in large bowl until blended. Add shrimp to egg mixture; toss to coat well.

2. Place 1 shrimp cut-side down on each bread piece. Press shrimp gently into bread. Brush or rub small amount of egg mixture over each shrimp.

3. Place 1 piece each of egg yolk and ham and a scant ¼ teaspoon onion on top of each shrimp.

4. Heat oil in wok or large skillet over medium-high heat to 375°F. Cook 3 or 4 shrimp-bread pieces at a time until golden, 1 to 2 minutes on each side. Drain on paper towels.

Makes 1 dozen

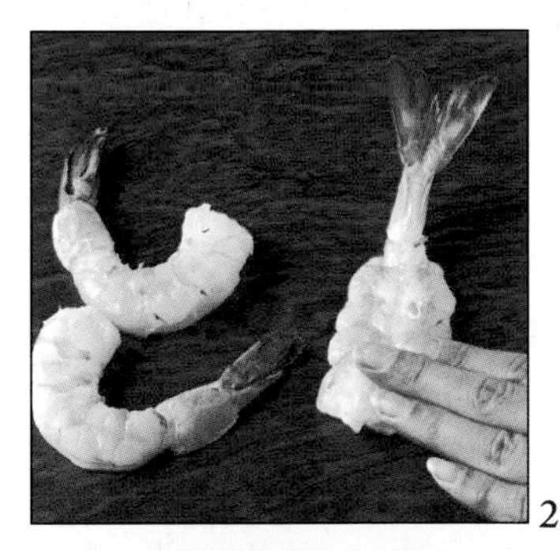
2

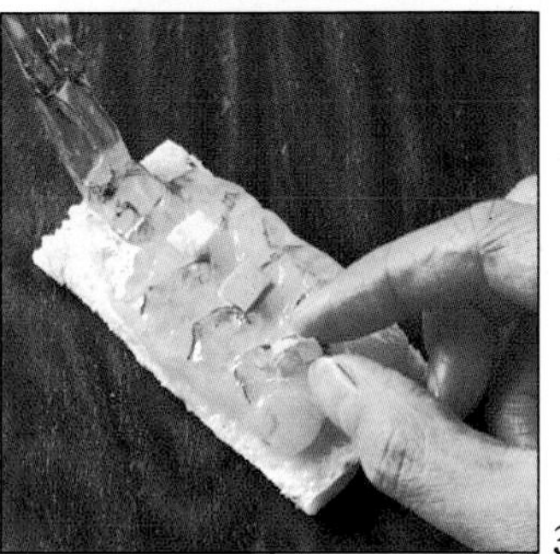
3

4

Meats

Satay Beef

- 1 pound beef tenderloin, trimmed
- 5 tablespoons water, divided
- 1 teaspoon cornstarch
- 3½ teaspoons soy sauce, divided
- 1 to 2 teaspoons sesame oil
- 2 tablespoons vegetable oil
- 1 medium yellow onion, coarsely chopped
- 1 clove garlic, crushed
- 1 tablespoon dry sherry
- 1 tablespoon satay sauce
- 1 teaspoon curry powder
- ½ teaspoon sugar

1. Cut beef across the grain into thin slices. Flatten each slice by pressing with fingers.

2. Combine 3 tablespoons of the water, the cornstarch, 1½ teaspoons of the soy sauce and the sesame oil in medium bowl. Add beef; mix to coat well. Let stand 20 minutes.

3. Heat vegetable oil in wok or large skillet over high heat. Add ½ of beef, spreading out slices so they do not overlap. Cook slices on each side just until light brown, 2 to 3 minutes. Remove and set aside. Repeat with remaining meat.

4. Add onion and garlic to wok; stir-fry until onion is soft, about 3 minutes.

5. Combine remaining 2 tablespoons water, 2 teaspoons soy sauce, the sherry, satay sauce, curry powder and sugar in small cup. Add to wok; cook and stir until liquid boils. Return beef to wok; cook and stir until heated through.

Makes 4 servings

1

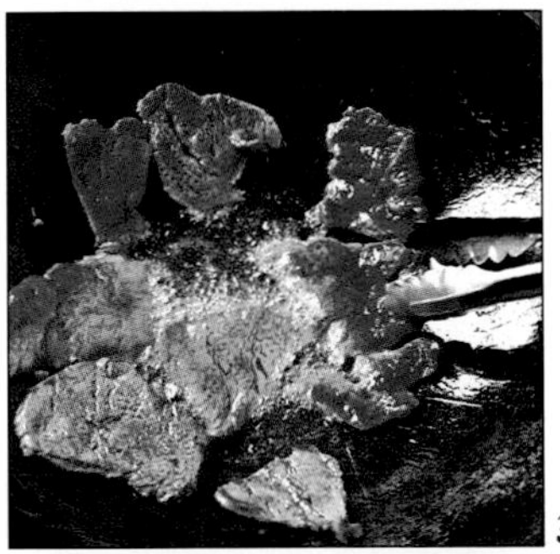

3

5

2

Beef with Noodles

- **8 ounces Chinese-style thin egg noodles, cooked and drained**
- **½ cup water**
- **3 teaspoons soy sauce, divided**
- **¼ teaspoon salt**
- **2 teaspoons instant chicken bouillon granules**
- **1 pound beef rump steak, trimmed**
- **6 tablespoons vegetable oil, divided**
- **6 green onions, diagonally sliced**
- **1 piece fresh ginger (about 1 inch square), pared and thinly sliced**
- **2 cloves garlic, crushed**

1. Place a clean towel over wire cooling racks. Spread cooked noodles evenly over towel. Let dry about 3 hours.

2. Combine water, 2 teaspoons of the soy sauce, the salt and bouillon granules in small bowl. Cut beef across the grain into thin slices about 2-inches long.

3. Heat 4 tablespoons of the oil in wok or large skillet over high heat. Add noodles and stir-fry 3 minutes. Pour water mixture over noodles; toss until noodles are completely coated, about 2 minutes. Transfer noodles to serving plate; keep warm.

4. Heat remaining 2 tablespoons oil in wok over high heat. Add beef, onions, ginger, garlic and remaining 1 teaspoon soy sauce. Stir-fry until beef is cooked through, about 5 minutes. Spoon meat mixture over noodles.

Makes 4 servings

3

4

Beef with Black Bean Sauce

- 1½ pounds beef rump steak, trimmed
- 2½ tablespoons soy sauce
- 1½ tablespoons dry sherry
- 3 teaspoons cornstarch, divided
- 1 egg white
- ⅔ cup water, divided
- 1½ tablespoons fermented, salted black beans
- ¼ teaspoon sugar
- 4 tablespoons vegetable oil, divided
- 4 green onions, cut into 1-inch pieces
- 1 red bell pepper, thinly sliced
- ½ cup sliced bamboo shoots (½ of 8-ounce can)
- 1 teaspoon curry powder

1. Cut beef across the grain into thin slices 2 inches long. Combine soy sauce, sherry, 1 teaspoon of the cornstarch and the egg white in medium bowl; beat lightly. Add beef; stir to coat well. Let stand 30 minutes, stirring occasionally.

2. Combine ⅓ cup of the water and the beans in small bowl. Let stand 15 minutes. Drain beans, reserving 1 teaspoon of the water. Combine beans, reserved water and the sugar on a small plate. Mash well with fork.

3. Heat 2 tablespoons of the oil in wok or large skillet over high heat. Add onions, red pepper, bamboo shoots and curry powder; stir-fry until vegetables are crisp-tender, 2 minutes. Remove and set aside.

4. Combine remaining ⅓ cup water and 2 teaspoons cornstarch in small cup. Heat remaining 2 tablespoons oil in wok over high heat. Add beef and marinade; stir-fry until beef is brown, about 5 minutes. Add vegetables and mashed beans; mix well. Stir in cornstarch mixture. Cook and stir until liquid boils and thickens.

Makes 4 servings

1

2

4

Beef with Cashews

1 pound beef rump steak, trimmed
4 tablespoons vegetable oil, divided
½ cup water
4 teaspoons cornstarch
4 teaspoons soy sauce
1 teaspoon sesame oil
1 teaspoon oyster sauce
1 teaspoon Chinese chili sauce
8 green onions, cut into 1-inch pieces
2 cloves garlic, crushed
1 piece fresh ginger (about 1-inch square), pared and finely chopped
⅔ cup unsalted, roasted cashews (about 3 ounces)

1. Cut beef across the grain into thin slices about 2 inches long. Heat 2 tablespoons of the vegetable oil in wok or large skillet over high heat. Stir-fry ½ of beef until brown, 3 to 5 minutes. Remove and set aside. Repeat with remaining beef.

2. Combine water, cornstarch, soy sauce, sesame oil, oyster sauce and chili sauce in small bowl; mix well.

3. Heat remaining 2 tablespoons vegetable oil in wok over high heat. Add onions, garlic, ginger and cashews. Stir-fry 1 minute. Add meat and cornstarch mixture. Cook and stir until liquid boils and thickens. *Makes 4 servings*

1

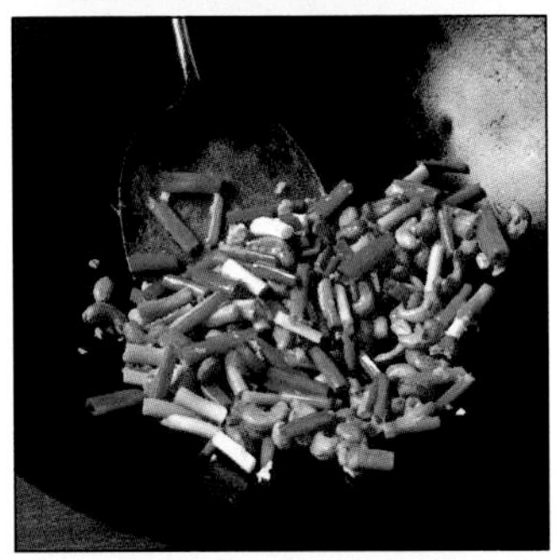
3

3

1

3

4

Sherried Beef and Spinach

1 pound beef tenderloin, trimmed
3 tablespoons dry sherry
1½ tablespoons soy sauce
1 teaspoon sugar
½ teaspoon sesame oil
1 pound fresh spinach, trimmed
3 tablespoons vegetable oil, divided
1 piece fresh ginger (about 2×1-inch), pared and thinly sliced
2 tablespoons water
½ teaspoon cornstarch
1 teaspoon instant chicken bouillon granules

1. Cut beef across the grain into thin slices. Cut each slice in half. Flatten slightly by pressing with fingers.

2. Combine sherry, soy sauce, sugar and sesame oil in medium bowl. Add beef; mix to coat well. Cover; refrigerate 2 hours, stirring occasionally.

3. Cut spinach leaves into large pieces. If spinach has thick stems, cut them into ½-inch diagonal slices.

4. Heat 2 tablespoons of the vegetable oil in wok or large skillet over high heat. Add ginger and spinach stems and stir-fry 2 minutes. Remove and set aside.

5. Add remaining 1 tablespoon vegetable oil to wok. Drain meat, reserving marinade. Add ½ of beef to wok spreading out slices so they do not overlap. Cook slices on each side just until light brown, 2 to 3 minutes. Remove and set aside. Repeat with remaining beef.

6. Blend water, cornstarch and bouillon granules into reserved marinade; add to wok. Cook until liquid boils, 1 to 2 minutes. Add spinach leaves, stems and ginger. Stir-fry until spinach is wilted, about 3 minutes. Add beef; stir-fry until heated through, about 1 minute more.

Makes 4 servings

Beef with Peppers

- 1 ounce dried mushrooms
- 1 pound beef tenderloin, trimmed
- 2½ tablespoons vegetable oil
- 1 clove garlic, crushed
- ¼ teaspoon Chinese five-spice powder
- 2 small yellow onions, cut into wedges
- 1 green bell pepper, thinly sliced
- 1 red bell pepper, thinly sliced
- ¼ cup water
- 1 tablespoon soy sauce
- 1 teaspoon cornstarch
- 1 teaspoon instant beef bouillon granules
- 1 teaspoon sesame oil

1. Place mushrooms in bowl and cover with hot water. Let stand 30 minutes. Drain and squeeze out excess water. Remove and discard stems; slice caps into thin strips.

2. Cut beef into thin slices 1-inch long.

3. Heat vegetable oil in wok or large skillet over high heat. Add garlic and five-spice powder; stir-fry 15 seconds. Add beef and stir-fry until brown, about 5 minutes. Add onions; stir-fry 2 minutes. Add mushrooms and peppers; stir-fry until peppers are crisp-tender, about 2 minutes.

4. Combine remaining ingredients in small bowl. Stir into wok. Cook and stir until liquid boils and thickens.

Makes 4 servings

2

3

4

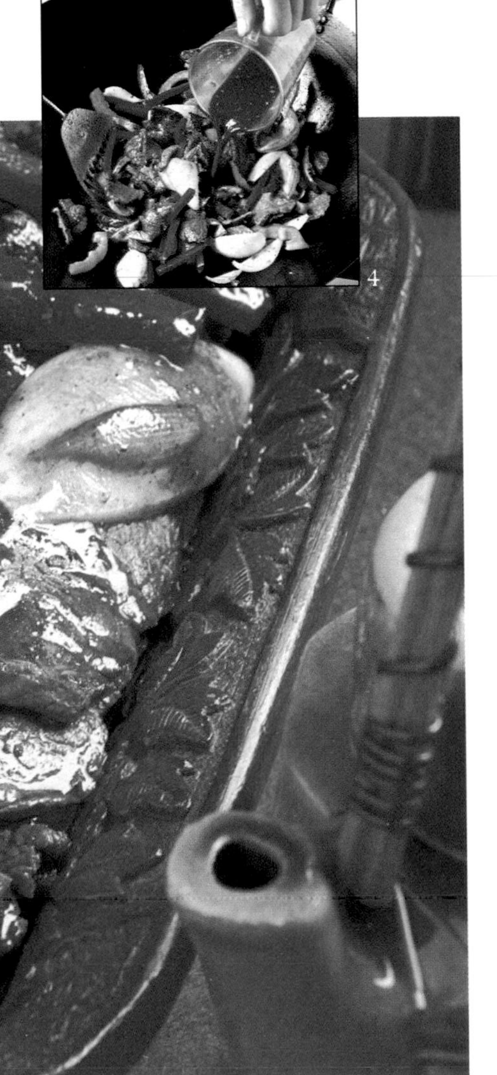

Curried Beef

1 pound beef tenderloin
3½ tablespoons vegetable oil, divided
2 medium potatoes, cut into ½-inch cubes
2 yellow onions, cut into wedges and separated
4 teaspoons curry powder, divided
⅓ cup water
1 tablespoon cornstarch
2 tablespoons satay sauce
1½ tablespoons soy sauce
1½ tablespoons dry sherry
1 tablespoon Chinese chili sauce
1 teaspoon instant chicken bouillon granules
Steamed Rice (page 510), optional

1. Cut beef across the grain into thin slices. Heat 2½ tablespoons of the oil in wok or large skillet over high heat. Add potatoes and stir-fry until crisp-tender, about 5 minutes. Add onions and 2 teaspoons of the curry powder; stir-fry 2 minutes. Remove and set aside.

2. Heat remaining 1 tablespoon oil in wok over high heat. Add beef slices and stir-fry until light brown, 3 to 4 minutes. Return potato mixture to wok.

3. Combine remaining 2 teaspoons curry powder and remaining ingredients in small cup. Pour into wok; cook and stir until liquid boils. Reduce heat and simmer 3 minutes. Serve with Steamed Rice, if desired.

Makes 4 servings

1

3

Mongolian Lamb

SESAME SAUCE
- **1 tablespoon sesame seeds**
- **¼ cup soy sauce**
- **1 tablespoon dry sherry**
- **1 tablespoon red wine vinegar**
- **1½ teaspoons sugar**
- **1 clove garlic, minced**
- **1 green onion, minced**
- **½ teaspoon sesame oil**

LAMB
- **1 pound boneless lean lamb (leg or shoulder)**
- **2 small leeks, cut into 2-inch slivers**
- **4 green onions, cut into 2-inch slivers**
- **2 medium carrots, shredded**
- **1 medium zucchini, shredded**
- **1 red pepper, cut into matchstick pieces**
- **1 green bell pepper, cut into matchstick pieces**
- **½ small head napa cabbage, thinly sliced**
- **1 cup bean sprouts**
- **4 tablespoons vegetable oil, divided**
- **4 slices pared fresh ginger, divided**
- **Chili oil, optional**

1. For sauce, place sesame seeds in small frying pan. Shake over medium heat until seeds begin to pop and turn golden, about 2 minutes. Let cool. Crush seeds with mortar and pestle (or place on cutting board and crush with a rolling pin; scrape up sesame paste with knife) and transfer to small serving bowl. Add remaining sauce ingredients; mix well.

2. For lamb, slice meat across the grain into strips ¼ inch thick and 2 inches long.

3. Arrange meat and vegetables on large platter. Have Sesame Sauce, vegetable oil, ginger and chili oil near cooking area.

4. At serving time, heat electric griddle or wok to 350°F. Cook one serving at a time. For each serving, heat 1 tablespoon vegetable oil; add 1 slice ginger and cook 30 seconds; discard. Add ½ cup meat strips, stir-fry until lightly browned, about 1 minute. Add 2 cups assorted vegetables; stir-fry 1 minute. Drizzle with 2 tablespoons Sesame Sauce; stir-fry 30 seconds. Season with a few drops chili oil, if desired. Repeat for remaining servings.

Makes 4 servings

1

2

3

Braised Lion's Head

MEATBALLS
1 pound lean ground pork
4 ounces shrimp, shelled, deveined and finely chopped
¼ cup sliced water chestnuts, finely chopped
1 teaspoon minced fresh ginger
1 green onion, finely chopped
1 tablespoon soy sauce
1 tablespoon dry sherry
½ teaspoon salt
½ teaspoon sugar
1 tablespoon cornstarch
1 egg, lightly beaten
2 tablespoons vegetable oil

SAUCE
1½ cups chicken broth
2 tablespoons soy sauce
½ teaspoon sugar
1 head napa cabbage (1½ to 2 pounds)
2 tablespoons cornstarch
3 tablespoons cold water
1 teaspoon sesame oil

1. For meatballs, combine all meatball ingredients except oil in large bowl; mix well. Divide mixture into 8 portions. Shape each portion into a ball.

2. Heat vegetable oil in wok or large nonstick skillet over medium-high heat. Brown meatballs, shaking or stirring occasionally so meatballs keep their shape, 6 to 8 minutes.

3. Transfer meatballs to 5-quart stockpot; discard drippings. Add chicken broth, soy sauce and sugar. Bring to a boil; reduce heat, cover and simmer 30 minutes.

4. While meatballs are cooking, core cabbage; cut base of leaves into 2-inch squares. Cut leafy tops in half. Place cabbage over meatballs. Cover and simmer 10 minutes more.

5. Using slotted spoon, transfer cabbage and meatballs to serving platter. Blend cornstarch and water in small cup. Stirring constantly, slowly add cornstarch mixture to pan juices; cook until slightly thickened. Stir in sesame oil. To serve, pour sauce over meatballs and cabbage.

Makes 4 to 6 servings

2

4

Sweet and Sour Pork

- ¼ cup soy sauce
- 1½ tablespoons dry sherry
- 2 teaspoons sugar
- 1 egg yolk
- 2 pounds boneless lean pork, cut into 1-inch pieces
- 10 tablespoons cornstarch, divided
- 3 cups plus 3 tablespoons vegetable oil, divided
- 1 can (20 ounces) pineapple chunks in syrup
- ¼ cup distilled white vinegar
- 3 tablespoons tomato sauce
- 1 cup water
- 1 large yellow onion, thinly sliced
- 8 green onions, diagonally cut into 1-inch pieces
- 1 red or green bell pepper, chopped
- 4 ounces fresh mushrooms, cut into quarters
- 2 stalks celery, diagonally cut into ½-inch slices
- 1 medium cucumber, seeded and cut into ¼-inch wide pieces

1. For marinade, combine soy sauce, sherry, sugar and egg yolk in large bowl. Add pork; mix to coat well. Cover and refrigerate 1 hour, stirring occasionally.

2. Drain pork, reserving marinade. Place 8 tablespoons of the cornstarch into large bowl. Add pork pieces; toss to coat well. Heat 3 cups of the oil in wok or large skillet over high heat to 375°F. Add ½ of pork pieces until brown, about 5 minutes. Drain on paper towels. Repeat with remaining pork.

3. Drain pineapple, reserving syrup. Combine the syrup, reserved soy sauce marinade, vinegar and tomato sauce in small bowl. Blend remaining 2 tablespoons cornstarch and the water in another small bowl.

4. Heat remaining 3 tablespoons oil in wok over high heat. Add all vegetables and stir-fry 3 minutes. Add pineapple syrup mixture and cornstarch mixture; cook and stir until sauce boils and thickens. Add pork and pineapple; stir-fry until heated through. *Makes 4 servings*

2

4

Spiced Pork

- 3 tablespoons soy sauce, divided
- 2 tablespoons cornstarch
- 2 tablespoons dry sherry
- 1 teaspoon minced fresh ginger
- ½ teaspoon Chinese five-spice powder
- ⅛ teaspoon pepper
- 2 pounds boneless lean pork, cut into large pieces
- Vegetable oil for frying
- ¼ cup water
- 1 teaspoon instant chicken bouillon granules
- Chinese mixed pickled vegetables, optional

1. Combine 2 tablespoons of the soy sauce, the cornstarch, the sherry, ginger, five-spice powder and pepper in large bowl. Add pork, one piece at a time, turning to coat well. Cover and refrigerate 1 hour, stirring occasionally.

2. Heat oil in wok or large skillet to 375°F. Cook ½ of pork until brown and cooked through, 3 to 5 minutes. Drain on paper towels. Repeat with remaining pork. Cut pork into ¼- to ½-inch wide slices. Transfer to serving dish; keep warm.

3. Combine water, bouillon granules and remaining 1 tablespoon soy sauce in small saucepan. Bring to a boil. Pour mixture over sliced pork. Garnish with Chinese mixed pickle vegetables, if desired. *Makes 4 servings*

2

2

3

Mu Shu Pork

8 teaspoons soy sauce, divided
5 teaspoons dry sherry, divided
4 teaspoons cornstarch, divided
8 ounces boneless lean pork, cut into matchstick pieces
3 dried mushrooms
2 dried wood ears
7 teaspoons vegetable oil, divided
2 eggs, lightly beaten
1 tablespoon water
½ teaspoon sugar
1 teaspoon sesame oil
1 teaspoon minced fresh ginger
½ cup sliced bamboo shoots (½ of 8-ounce can), cut into matchstick pieces
1 small carrot, shredded
½ cup chicken broth
2 cups bean sprouts (about 4 ounces)
2 green onions, cut into 1½-inch slivers
½ cup hoisin sauce
16 Mandarin Pancakes (recipe follows)

1. For marinade, combine 2 teaspoons of the soy sauce, 2 teaspoons of the sherry and 1 teaspoon of the cornstarch in large bowl. Add pork and stir to coat. Let stand 30 minutes.

2. Place dried mushrooms and wood ears in small bowl and cover with hot water. Let stand 30 minutes. Drain and squeeze out excess water. Cut off and discard mushroom stems; cut caps into thin slices. Pinch out hard nobs from center of wood ears and discard; cut wood ears into thin strips.

3. Heat ½ teaspoon vegetable oil in small nonstick skillet over medium-high heat. Add ½ of eggs and tilt skillet to cover bottom. Cook just until egg is set. Loosen edges, turn omelet over and cook other side 5 seconds. Remove from skillet and repeat with another ½ teaspoon oil and remaining egg. When omelets are cool, cut in half. Stack halves and cut crosswise into ⅛-inch wide strips.

4. For sauce, combine remaining 6 teaspoons soy sauce, 3 teaspoons sherry and 3 teaspoons cornstarch in small bowl. Add the water, sugar and sesame oil; mix well.

5. Heat remaining 6 teaspoons vegetable oil in wok or large skillet over high heat. Add ginger and stir once. Add pork and stir-fry until meat is no longer pink, about 2 minutes. Add mushrooms, wood ears, bamboo shoots, carrot and chicken broth. Stir and toss 2 minutes. Add bean sprouts and onions; stir-fry 1 minute.

6. Stir cornstarch mixture; pour into wok and cook, stirring constantly, until sauce bubbles and thickens. Stir in omelet strips.

7. To serve, spread about 2 teaspoons hoisin sauce on each pancake. Spoon about 3 tablespoons pork mixture down center. Fold in bottom and roll up. *Makes 8 servings*

2

3

Mandarin Pancakes

2 cups all-purpose flour
¾ cup boiling water
2 tablespoons sesame oil

1. Place flour in bowl and make a well in center. Pour in boiling water; stir with wooden spoon until dough looks like lumpy meal. Press into a ball. Knead dough until smooth and satiny on lightly floured work surface, about 5 minutes. Cover with clean towel and let rest 30 minutes.

2. Roll dough into 10-inch long log. Cut into 10 equal pieces; keep covered.

3. Cut each piece of dough in half. Roll each half into a ball; flatten slightly. Roll each piece into a 3-inch circle on lightly floured work surface. Brush top of each with a small amount of sesame oil. Stack dough circles together, oil-side in. Roll the pair together into a 6- to 7-inch circle. Repeat for remaining pieces of dough. (Keep uncooked pancakes covered while you roll out remaining dough.)

4. Heat nonstick skillet over medium-low heat. Cook pancakes, 1 pair at a time, turning every 30 seconds, until cakes are flecked with brown and feel dry, 2 to 3 minutes. (Be careful not to overcook; cakes become brittle.)

5. Remove from pan and separate into 2 pancakes while still hot. Stack on plate and keep covered while you cook remaining pancakes. Serve at once, refrigerate or freeze in resealable plastic bag. To reheat, wrap pancakes in clean towel (thaw completely, if using frozen). Steam over simmering water 5 minutes. Fold pancakes into quarters and arrange in serving basket.

Makes 20 pancakes

2

3

4

Two-Onion Pork Shreds

- ½ teaspoon Szechuan peppercorns
- 4 teaspoons soy sauce, divided
- 4 teaspoons dry sherry, divided
- 7½ teaspoons vegetable oil, divided
- 1 teaspoon cornstarch
- 8 ounces boneless lean pork
- 2 teaspoons red wine vinegar
- ½ teaspoon sugar
- 2 cloves garlic, crushed
- ½ small yellow onion, cut into ¼-inch slices
- 8 green onions, cut into 2-inch pieces
- ½ teaspoon sesame oil

1. For marinade, place peppercorns in small skillet. Shake over medium-low heat, shaking skillet often, until fragrant, about 2 minutes. Let cool. Crush peppercorns with mortar and pestle (or place between paper towels and crush with a hammer).* Transfer to medium bowl. Add 2 teaspoons of the soy sauce, 2 teaspoons of the sherry, 1½ teaspoons of the vegetable oil and the cornstarch; mix well.

2. Cut pork into ⅛-inch thick slices, then cut into 2×½-inch pieces. Add to marinade and stir to coat well. Let stand 30 minutes.

3. Combine remaining 2 teaspoons soy sauce, 2 teaspoons sherry, the vinegar and sugar in small bowl; mix well.

4. Heat remaining 6 teaspoons vegetable oil in wok or large skillet over high heat. Add garlic and stir once. Add pork and stir-fry until meat is no longer pink, about 2 minutes. Add yellow onion and stir-fry 1 minute; add green onion and stir-fry 30 seconds. Add soy-vinegar mixture and cook 30 seconds. Stir in sesame oil. *Makes 2 to 3 servings*

***Note:** Szechuan peppercorns are deceptively potent. Wear rubber or plastic gloves when crushing them and do not touch your eyes or lips when handling.

Honey-Glazed Spareribs

1 side pork spareribs (about 2 pounds)
¼ cup plus 1 tablespoon soy sauce, divided
3 tablespoons hoisin sauce
3 tablespoons dry sherry, divided
1 tablespoon sugar
1 teaspoon minced fresh ginger
2 cloves garlic, minced
¼ teaspoon Chinese five-spice powder
2 tablespoons honey
1 tablespoon cider vinegar
Green onion curls for garnish

1. Have your butcher cut ribs in half lengthwise so that each piece is 2 to 3 inches long. Cut between bones to make 6-inch pieces. Trim excess fat. Place ribs in heavy plastic bag.

2. For marinade, combine ¼ cup of the soy sauce, the hoisin sauce, 2 tablespoons of the sherry, the sugar, ginger, garlic and five-spice powder in small bowl; mix well. Pour marinade over ribs. Seal bag tightly and place in large bowl. Refrigerate 8 hours or overnight, turning bag occasionally.

3. Foil-line a large baking pan. Place rack in pan and place ribs on rack (reserve marinade). Bake in preheated 350°F oven 30 minutes. Turn ribs over, brush with marinade and bake until ribs are tender when pierced with fork, about 40 minutes more.

4. For glaze, combine honey, vinegar, remaining 1 tablespoon soy sauce and 1 tablespoon sherry in small bowl; mix well. Brush ½ of mixture over ribs; place under broiler 4 to 6 inches from heat source and broil until ribs are glazed, 2 to 3 minutes. Turn ribs over, brush with remaining honey mixture and broil until glazed. Cut into serving-size pieces. Garnish with green onion curls, if desired.

Makes about 4 servings

1

3

4

Poultry

Lemon Chicken

CHICKEN

4 whole chicken breasts
½ cup cornstarch
½ teaspoon salt
⅛ teaspoon pepper
¼ cup water
4 egg yolks, lightly beaten
Vegetable oil for frying
4 green onions, sliced

LEMON SAUCE

1½ cups water
½ cup lemon juice
3½ tablespoons brown sugar
3 tablespoons cornstarch
3 tablespoons honey
2 teaspoons instant chicken bouillon granules
1 teaspoon minced fresh ginger

1. Remove skin from chicken and discard. Cut chicken breasts in half. Remove and discard bones. Pound with mallet or rolling pin to flatten slightly.

2. Combine cornstarch, salt and pepper in small bowl. Gradually blend in water and egg yolks.

3. Heat oil in wok or large skillet over high heat to 375°F. Dip chicken breasts, one at a time, into cornstarch-egg yolk mixture. Cook chicken breasts, two at a time, until golden, about 5 minutes. Drain on paper towels. Keep warm while cooking remaining chicken.

4. Cut each breast into three or four pieces and arrange on serving plate. Sprinkle with onions.

5. For sauce, combine all sauce ingredients in medium saucepan; mix well. Cook over medium heat, stirring constantly, until sauce boils and thickens, about 5 minutes. Pour over chicken. *Makes 4 to 6 servings*

1
3
4

Beggar's Chicken

1 broiler/fryer chicken (3 to 4 pounds)
6½ tablespoons soy sauce, divided
2½ tablespoons vegetable oil
2½ tablespoons dry sherry
1 teaspoon sugar
¼ teaspoon Chinese five-spice powder
4 green onions, finely chopped
1 piece (about 1-inch square) fresh ginger, pared and thinly sliced
4 cups all-purpose flour
3 cups salt (about 2 pounds)
1½ to 2 cups water

1. Rinse chicken and pat dry with paper towels. Place chicken on large piece of greased extra-wide heavy-duty aluminum foil. Rub or brush with 2½ tablespoons of the soy sauce. Rub or brush completely with oil. Pull skin at the neck end under chicken and secure with small skewer. Tuck wing tips under chicken.

2. Combine remaining 4 tablespoons soy sauce, the sherry, sugar, five-spice powder, onions and ginger in small bowl. Pour mixture into cavity of chicken, tipping chicken up slightly so mixture does not run out. Secure tail end of chicken with small skewers. Wrap foil around chicken, sealing securely.

3. Combine flour and salt in large bowl. Gradually mix in enough water to make a firm dough. Roll out dough on lightly floured work surface until about ¼-inch thick. Dough should be large enough to completely cover chicken.

4. Place foil-wrapped chicken onto center of dough. Fold dough around chicken, pressing edges together to seal tightly. Place dough-wrapped chicken in well-greased 13×9×2-inch baking dish.

5. Bake chicken in preheated 450°F oven 1 hour. Reduce oven temperature to 300°F. Bake 2½ hours more.

6. Remove chicken from oven. Using mallet or hammer, break pastry. Remove chicken and place on serving plate (discard pastry). Carefully remove foil and skewers.

Makes 4 servings

1

4

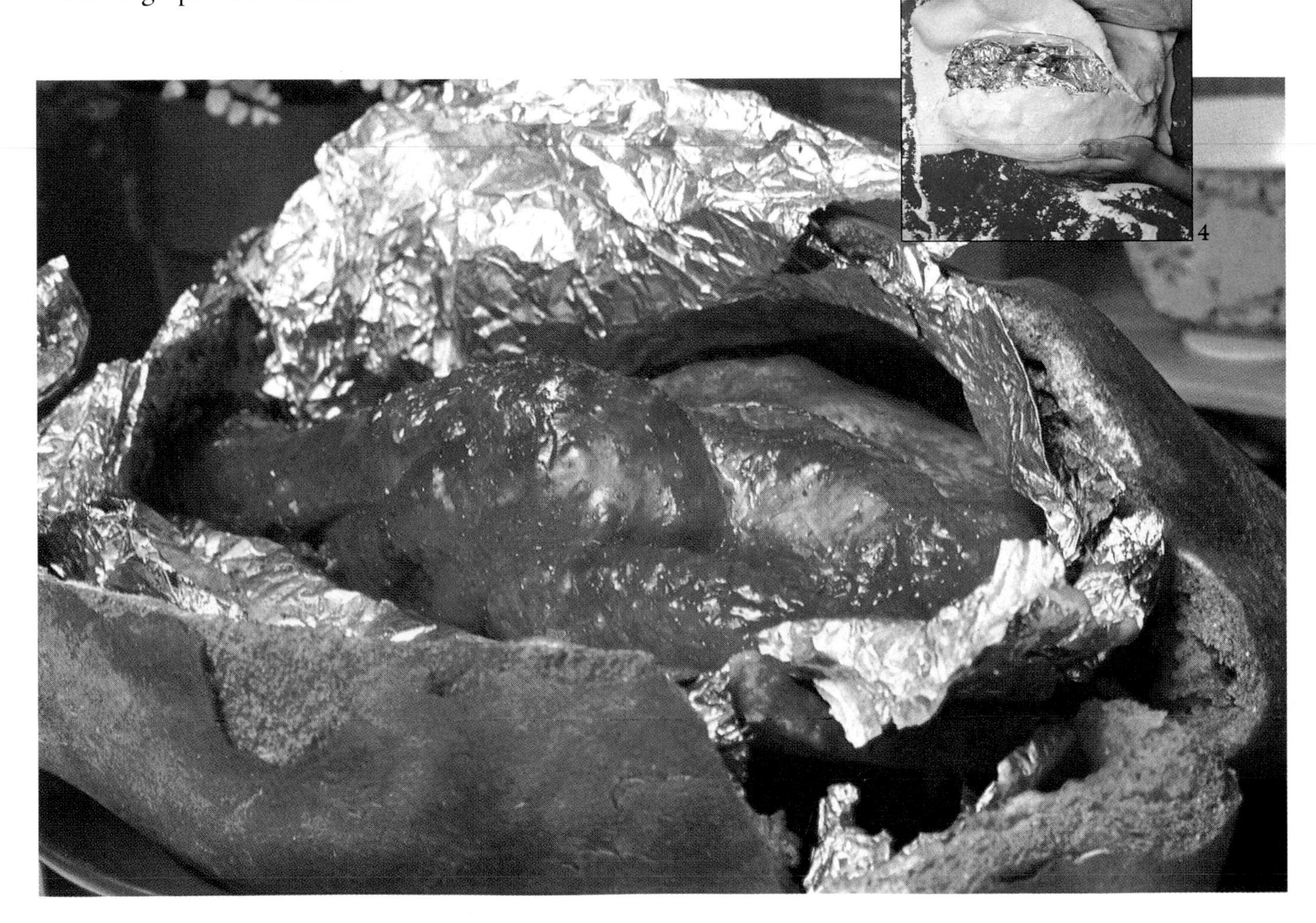

Tea Smoked Chicken

1 teaspoon Szechuan peppercorns
2 tablespoons dry sherry
2 tablespoons soy sauce
½ teaspoon granulated sugar
6 thin slices pared fresh ginger
2 green onions, cut into 2-inch pieces
1 teaspoon salt
1 broiler/fryer chicken (3 to 4 pounds)
⅓ cup black tea leaves
3 tablespoons brown sugar
⅓ cup long-grain rice
1 strip dried tangerine peel (about 2 inches long) or 1 teaspoon grated orange peel
Mandarin Pancakes (page 478)
Prepared plum sauce or hoisin sauce
4 green onions, cut into 2-inch slivers

1. For marinade, crush peppercorns with mortar and pestle (or place between paper towels and crush with a hammer). Combine crushed peppercorns, sherry, soy sauce, granulated sugar, ginger, onion pieces and salt. Rub chicken inside and out with marinade.* Cover and refrigerate 8 hours or overnight.

2. Place chicken breast-side up on rack in large stockpot. Pour in 1½-inches water. Cover, bring to a boil, and steam until meat near thigh bone is no longer pink, about 45 to 50 minutes. Let stand until cool enough to handle. Lift chicken from rack and drain juices from cavity.

3. Line a large wok and its lid with foil. (Do not use an electric wok with nonstick finish.) For smoking, place tea leaves, brown sugar, rice and tangerine peel in bottom of foil-lined wok; mix well. Set rack on top of mixture in wok. Place chicken breast-side up on rack. Cover wok with foil-lined lid.

4. Cook over high heat 2 minutes. Turn off heat and leave covered 5 minutes. Repeat 2 more times. After final smoking, let stand, covered, to allow smoke to subside, about 30 minutes. Discard smoking mixture.

5. Slice chicken from bones and arrange on serving platter. Serve 1 or 2 chicken slices in Mandarin Pancake; top with plum sauce and slivered onions. *Makes 6 to 8 servings*

***Note:** Szechuan peppercorns are deceptively potent. Wear rubber or plastic gloves when rubbing chicken with marinade and do not touch your eyes or lips when handling peppercorns or marinade.

1

3

Combination Chop Suey

2 whole chicken breasts, cooked
½ head bok choy or napa cabbage (about 8 ounces)
1 cup water
2 teaspoons cornstarch
1 teaspoon chicken bouillon granules
4 teaspoons soy sauce
3 tablespoons vegetable oil
8 ounces boneless lean pork, finely chopped
4 ounces fresh green beans, trimmed and cut into ½-inch pieces
3 stalks celery, diagonally cut into ½-inch pieces
2 yellow onions, chopped
1 large carrot, finely chopped
8 ounces medium shrimp, shelled and deveined
1 can (8 ounces) sliced bamboo shoots, drained

1. Remove skin and bones from cooked chicken. Coarsely chop chicken. Finely chop cabbage with cleaver or large knife.

2. Combine water, cornstarch, boullion and soy sauce in small bowl; set aside.

3. Heat oil in wok or large skillet over high heat. Add pork and stir-fry until brown, about 5 minutes. Remove and set aside.

4. Add cabbage, beans, celery, onions and carrot to wok. Stir-fry until vegetables are crisp-tender, about 3 minutes. Stir soy sauce mixture and pour over vegetables in wok. Cook and stir until liquid boils and thickens, about 3 minutes. Add chicken, shrimp, pork and bamboo shoots. Cook and stir until shrimp turn pink and are cooked through, about 3 minutes more.

Makes 4 to 6 servings

4

4

Kung Pao Chicken

- 5 teaspoons soy sauce, divided
- 5 teaspoons dry sherry, divided
- 3½ teaspoons cornstarch, divided
- ¼ teaspoon salt
- 3 boneless, skinless chicken breast halves, cut into bite-size pieces
- 1 tablespoon red wine vinegar
- 2 tablespoons chicken broth or water
- 1½ teaspoons sugar
- 3 tablespoons vegetable oil, divided
- ⅓ cup salted peanuts
- 6 to 8 small dried hot chili peppers
- 1½ teaspoons minced fresh ginger
- 2 green onions, cut into 1½-inch pieces

1. For marinade, combine 2 teaspoons of the soy sauce, 2 teaspoons of the sherry, 2 teaspoons of the cornstarch and the salt in large bowl; mix well. Add chicken; stir to coat well. Let stand 30 minutes.

2. Combine remaining 3 teaspoons soy sauce, 3 teaspoons sherry, the vinegar, chicken broth, sugar and remaining 1½ teaspoons cornstarch in small bowl; mix well and set aside.

3. Heat 1 tablespoon of the oil in wok or large skillet over medium heat. Add peanuts and cook until golden. Remove and set aside.

4. Heat remaining 2 tablespoons oil in wok over medium heat. Add chili peppers and stir-fry until peppers just begin to char, about 1 minute. Increase heat to high. Add chicken and stir-fry 2 minutes. Add ginger; stir-fry until chicken is cooked through, about 1 minute more. Add onions and peanuts to wok. Stir cornstarch mixture and add to wok; cook and stir until sauce boils and thickens.

Makes 3 servings

Hoisin Chicken

- 1 broiler/fryer chicken (3 to 4 pounds)
- ½ cup plus 1 tablespoon cornstarch, divided
- Vegetable oil for frying
- 2 teaspoons grated fresh ginger
- 2 medium yellow onions, chopped
- 8 ounces fresh broccoli, cut into 1-inch pieces
- 1 red or green bell pepper, chopped
- 2 cans (4 ounces each) whole button mushrooms, drained
- 1 cup water
- 3 tablespoons dry sherry
- 3 tablespoons cider vinegar
- 3 tablespoons hoisin sauce
- 4 teaspoons soy sauce
- 2 teaspoons instant chicken bouillon granules

1. Rinse chicken and cut into small serving-size pieces. Place ½ cup of the cornstarch in large bowl. Add chicken pieces and toss to coat well.

2. Heat oil in wok or large skillet over high heat to 375°F. Add chicken pieces, one at a time (cook only about ⅓ of the chicken pieces at a time), and cook until golden and cooked through, about 5 minutes. Drain on paper towels. Repeat with remaining chicken.

3. Remove all but 2 tablespoons oil from wok. Add ginger and stir-fry 1 minute. Add onions; stir-fry 1 minute. Add broccoli, red pepper and mushrooms; stir-fry 2 minutes.

4. Combine remaining ingredients and remaining 1 tablespoon cornstarch in small bowl. Add to wok. Cook and stir until sauce boils and turns translucent. Return chicken to wok. Cook and stir until chicken is heated through, about 2 minutes.

Makes 6 servings

3

4

4

Chinese Chicken Salad

- 2 whole chicken breasts
- 4 cups water
- 1 tablespoon dry sherry
- 2 slices pared fresh ginger
- 2 whole green onions
- 1/4 cup prepared Chinese plum sauce
- 2 tablespoons distilled white vinegar
- 1 tablespoon vegetable oil
- 1 tablespoon sesame oil
- 1 1/2 teaspoons soy sauce
- 1 1/2 tablespoons sugar
- 1 teaspoon dry mustard
- 3 tablespoons slivered almonds
- 2 tablespoons sesame seeds
- 4 cups shredded iceberg lettuce
- 1 small carrot, shredded
- 1 1/2 cups bean sprouts (about 3 ounces)
- 3 green onions, cut into 1 1/2-inch slivers
- 1/4 cup cilantro leaves (Chinese parsley)
- Bean threads or Vermicelli (page 515), cooked and drained

1. Combine chicken, water, sherry, ginger and whole green onions in 3-quart saucepan. Bring to a boil; reduce heat, cover and simmer 20 minutes. Remove from heat. Let stand until chicken is cool.

2. Strain stock and refrigerate or freeze for another use. Remove and discard skin and bones from chicken. Pull meat into long shreds.

3. For dressing, combine plum sauce, vinegar, vegetable and sesame oils, soy sauce, sugar and mustard in small bowl; mix well.

4. Place almonds in small dry skillet. Shake over medium heat until golden and fragrant, about 3 minutes. Transfer to large salad bowl. Toast sesame seeds in same skillet until seeds are golden and begin to pop, about 2 minutes. Add sesame seeds to almonds.

5. Add lettuce, carrot, bean sprouts, green onion slivers, cilantro and cooked chicken. Toss to coat evenly. Add bean threads and toss to mix well. *Makes 6 to 8 servings*

2

3

4

Fish & Seafood

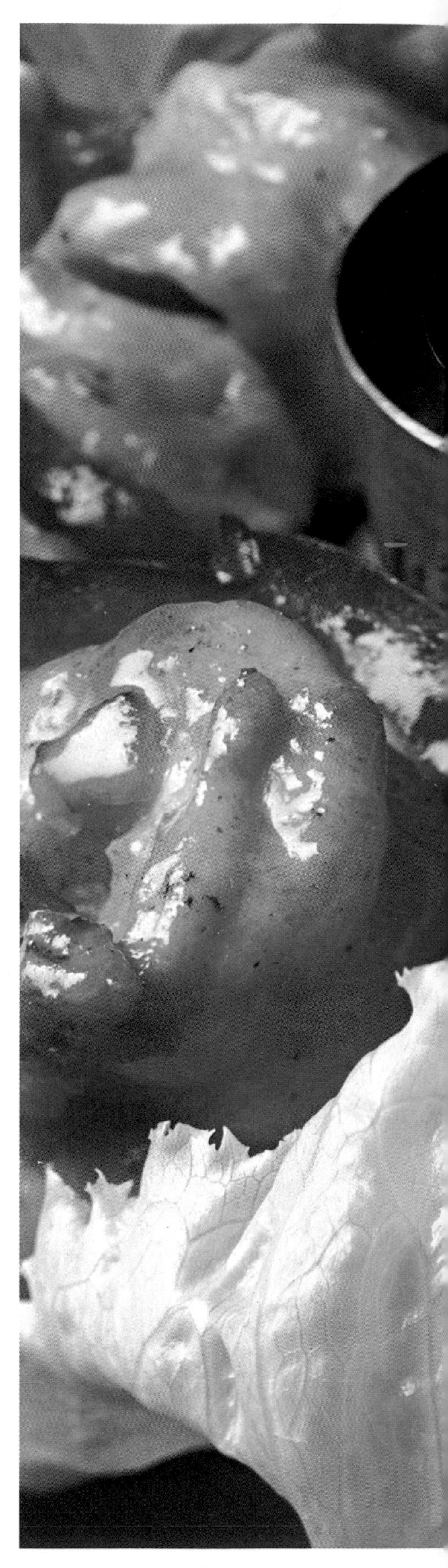

Barbecued Shrimp

- 1 pound large shrimp, shelled and deveined
- 1 egg white
- 2 teaspoons cornstarch
- 1 teaspoon salt
- 1 cup vegetable oil
- 1 cup finely chopped yellow onions
- 1 teaspoon curry powder
- ¼ teaspoon sugar
- ¼ teaspoon Chinese chili powder
- ¼ cup whipping or heavy cream
- 2 tablespoons American-style barbecue sauce or satay sauce
- 1 small red bell pepper, thinly sliced
- ½ cup brandy, optional

1. Rinse shrimp and pat dry with paper towels. Combine egg white, cornstarch and salt in medium bowl. Add shrimp and stir to coat well. Cover and refrigerate 1 hour.

2. Heat oil in wok or large skillet over medium-high heat to 375°F. Add shrimp, one at a time (cook only about ½ of shrimp at a time), and cook until golden, about 2 minutes. Drain on paper towels.

3. Remove all but 2 tablespoons oil from wok. Add onions, curry powder, sugar and chili powder; stir-fry 2 minutes. Add shrimp; stir-fry 1 minute. Add cream and barbecue sauce; cook and stir 1 minute. Stir in red pepper and remove from heat.

4. Arrange shrimp on serving platter and spoon sauce over shrimp. If desired, heat brandy in small saucepan and pour into small metal bowl on serving platter. Carefully ignite brandy with long wooden match. Hold shrimp over flame for a few seconds. *Makes 2 to 4 servings*

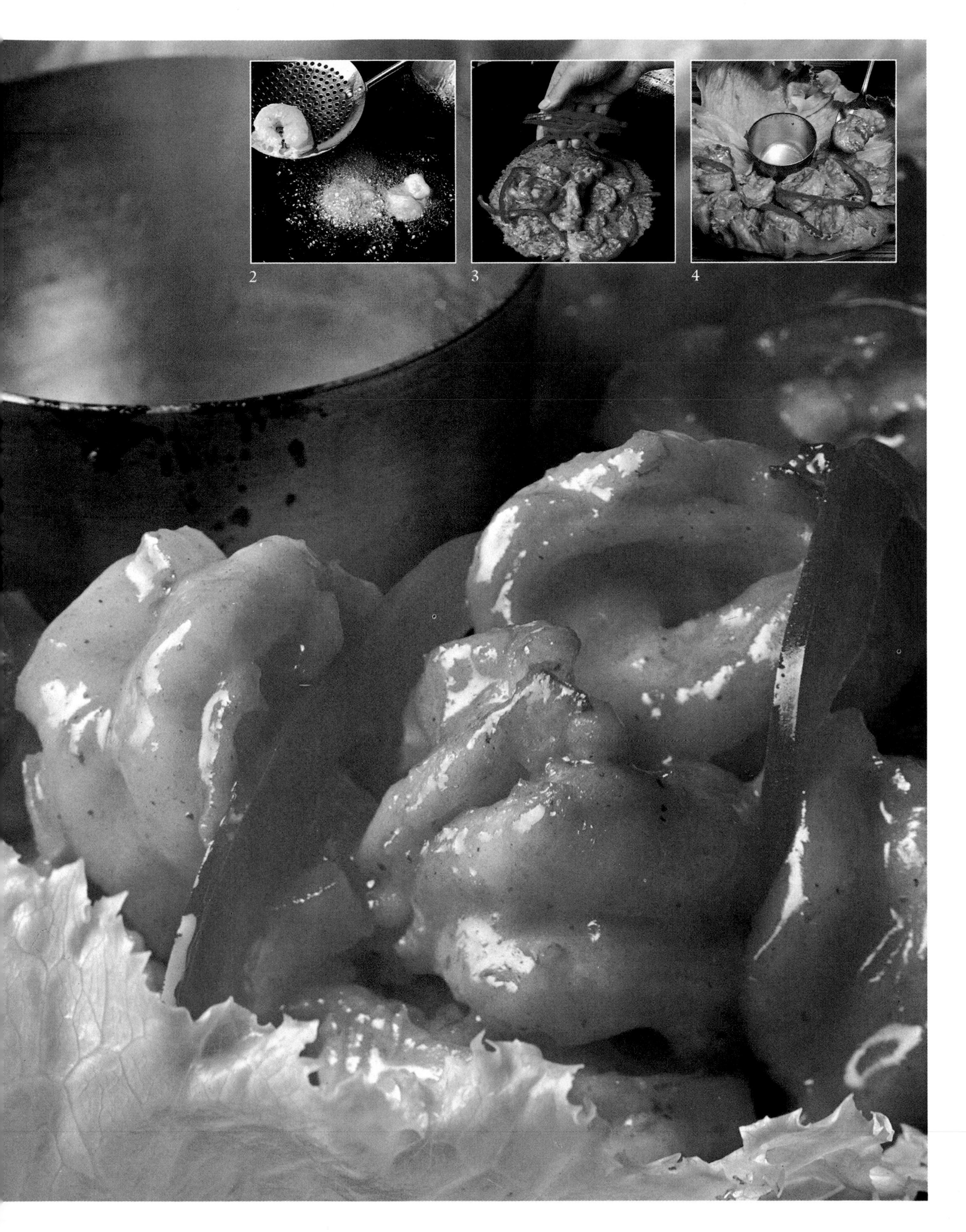
2
3
4

Braised Shrimp with Vegetables

1 tablespoon vegetable oil
1 pound large shrimp, shelled and deveined
8 ounces fresh broccoli, cut into small pieces
2 cans (4 ounces each) whole button mushrooms, drained
1 can (8 ounces) bamboo shoots, thinly sliced
½ cup chicken broth
1 teaspoon cornstarch
1 teaspoon oyster sauce
¼ teaspoon sugar
½ teaspoon minced fresh ginger
⅛ teaspoon pepper

1. Heat oil in wok or large skillet over high heat. Add shrimp and stir-fry until shrimp turn pink, about 3 minutes.

2. Add broccoli to wok; stir-fry 1 minute. Add mushrooms and bamboo shoots; stir-fry 1 minute more.

3. Combine remaining ingredients in small bowl; mix well. Pour over shrimp-vegetable mixture. Cook and stir until sauce boils and thickens, about 2 minutes more.

Makes 4 servings

1 1 2 3

Butterfly Shrimp

1½ pounds large shrimp, shelled and deveined, leaving tails intact
3 egg yolks
1½ teaspoons cornstarch
½ teaspoon salt
⅛ teaspoon pepper
2 slices bacon, cut into 1½×¼-inch strips
Vegetable oil for frying

1. Cut deep slit down back of each shrimp. Flatten cut side slightly with fingers.

2. Beat egg yolks, cornstarch, salt and pepper with fork in medium bowl. Dip each shrimp into egg mixture. Place a bacon strip on cut side of each shrimp.

3. Heat oil in wok or large skillet over medium-high heat to 400°F. Cook shrimp, a few at a time, until golden, 2 to 3 minutes. Drain on paper towels.

Makes 4 to 6 main dish or 8 to 10 appetizer servings

Shrimp Omelets

3

- 3 to 5 tablespoons vegetable oil, divided
- 8 fresh medium mushrooms, finely chopped
- 1 cup water
- 4 teaspoons cornstarch
- 1 teaspoon sugar
- 2 teaspoons soy sauce
- 2 teaspoons instant chicken bouillon granules
- 8 eggs
- ½ teaspoon salt
- ⅛ teaspoon pepper
- 8 ounces bean sprouts
- 8 ounces shrimp, shelled, deveined and finely chopped
- 4 green onions, finely chopped
- 1 stalk celery, finely chopped
- 2 green onions, thinly sliced

1. Heat 1 tablespoon of the oil in small skillet. Add mushrooms and cook 1 minute. Remove and set aside.

2. Combine water, cornstarch, sugar, soy sauce and bouillon granules in small saucepan. Cook over medium heat until mixture boils and thickens, about 5 minutes. Keep warm.

3. Combine eggs, salt and pepper in large bowl. Beat until frothy. Add sprouts, shrimp, chopped onions, celery and mushrooms; mix well.

4. For each omelet, heat ½ tablespoon oil in 7-inch omelet pan or skillet. Pour ½ cup egg mixture into pan. Cook until light brown, 2 to 3 minutes on each side. Stack omelets on serving plate. Pour warm soy sauce mixture over omelets. Garnish with sliced onions.

Makes 4 servings

3

4

Crab-Stuffed Shrimp

SAUCE
- 2 tablespoons vegetable oil
- 1 small yellow onion, finely chopped
- 1 teaspoon curry powder
- 1½ tablespoons dry sherry
- 1 tablespoon satay sauce
- 1 teaspoon sugar
- 2 teaspoons soy sauce
- ¼ cup cream or milk

SHRIMP
- 2 egg whites
- 4 teaspoons cornstarch
- 1 tablespoon dry sherry
- 1 tablespoon soy sauce
- 2 cans (6½ ounces each) crab meat, drained and flaked
- 8 green onions, finely chopped
- 2 stalks celery, finely chopped
- 1½ pounds large shrimp, shelled and deveined
- ½ cup all-purpose flour
- 3 eggs
- 3 tablespoons milk
- 2 to 3 cups soft bread crumbs (8 to 10 bread slices)
- Vegetable oil for frying

1. For sauce, heat 2 tablespoons oil in small saucepan over medium heat. Add onion and cook until onion is transparent, about 3 minutes. Add curry powder; cook and stir 1 minute. Add sherry, satay sauce, sugar and soy sauce; cook and stir 2 minutes. Stir in cream; bring to a boil. Boil 2 minutes. Keep warm.

2. For shrimp, blend egg whites, cornstarch, sherry and soy sauce in medium bowl. Add crab meat, onions and celery; mix well.

3. Cut deep slit into but not through back of each shrimp. Flatten shrimp by pounding gently with mallet or rolling pin. Spoon crab mixture onto each shrimp and press with back of spoon or small spatula.

4. Coat each shrimp lightly with flour. Beat eggs and milk with fork in shallow bowl until blended. Place each shrimp stuffed-side up in egg mixture, then spoon mixture over shrimp to cover completely. Coat each shrimp completely with bread crumbs, pressing crumbs lightly onto shrimp. Place shrimp in single layer on cookie sheets or plates. Refrigerate 30 minutes.

5. Heat oil in wok or large skillet over high heat to 375°F. Cook 4 or 5 shrimp at a time until golden, about 3 minutes. Drain on paper towels. Serve with warm sauce.

Makes 4 servings

3

Crab Claws

1 cup prepared sweet and sour sauce
½ cup Chinese mixed pickled vegetables
10 thick crab claws (about 1½ to 2 pounds)
1½ pounds shrimp, shelled and deveined
6 green onions
2 stalks celery
2 teaspoons minced fresh ginger
2 teaspoons soy sauce
2 teaspoons oyster sauce
1 cup cornstarch, divided
½ cup all-purpose flour
½ teaspoon baking powder
½ teaspoon salt
⅔ cup water
Vegetable oil for frying

2

4

1. Combine sweet and sour sauce with Chinese mixed pickled vegetables in small saucepan. Heat over medium heat until sauce is melted. Reduce heat; keep warm.

2. Carefully remove the shell from the meat end of each claw using kitchen shears or nut cracker. If necessary, tap claw gently with a mallet or rolling pin to break shell (do not hit heavily or crab meat will be damaged). Leave shell on one part of pincher for holding crab meat.

3. Finely chop shrimp, onions and celery together using cleaver or food processor. Add ginger, soy sauce and oyster sauce; mix well. Divide into 10 equal portions (about ⅓ cup for each portion).

4. Flatten one portion in palm of hand. Place meat end of crab claw on top of flattened shrimp mixture. Carefully press shrimp mixture all around crab meat, leaving shell on pincher uncovered.

5. Place ½ cup of the cornstarch into small bowl. Carefully coat each shrimp-wrapped claw. Combine remaining ½ cup cornstarch, the flour, baking powder and salt in large bowl. Using whisk, blend in water; beat until smooth.

6. Heat oil in wok or large skillet over high heat to 375°F. Carefully dip each crab claw into batter, coating completely. Cook claws, a few at a time, until golden an cooked through, 3 to 5 minutes. Drain on paper towels. Serve with sweet and sour sauce mixture.

Makes 5 servings

Seafood Combination

Fried noodles (see page 513)
4 tablespoons vegetable oil, divided
8 green onions, diagonally cut into thin slices
3 stalks celery, diagonally cut into thin slices
1 can (8 ounces) water chestnuts, drained and cut into halves
1 can (8 ounces) bamboo shoots, thinly sliced
8 ounces fresh or thawed frozen sea scallops, cut into quarters
8 ounces fresh or thawed frozen shrimp, shelled and deveined
8 ounces fresh or thawed frozen fish fillets, skinned and cut into 1½-inch square pieces
8 ounces cleaned, ready-to-cook squid, optional
½ cup water
1 tablespoon soy sauce
2 teaspoons dry sherry
2 teaspoons cornstarch
1 teaspoon instant chicken bouillon granules

1. Prepare Fried Noodles; set aside.

2. Heat 2 tablespoons of the oil in wok or large skillet over high heat. Add onions, celery, water chestnuts and bamboo shoots; stir-fry until crisp-tender, about 2 minutes. Remove and set aside.

3. Heat remaining 2 tablespoons oil in wok over high heat. Add scallops, shrimp, fish pieces and squid; stir-fry until all fish turns opaque and is cooked through, about 3 minutes.

4. Combine water, soy sauce, sherry, cornstarch and bouillon granules in small bowl. Add to wok. Cook and stir until liquid boils. Return vegetables to wok; cook and stir 2 minutes more. Serve with Fried Noodles.

Makes 6 servings

2

4

Scallops with Vegetables

1 ounce dried mushrooms
2 tablespoons vegetable oil
2 yellow onions, cut into wedges and separated
3 stalks celery, diagonally cut into ½-inch pieces
8 ounces fresh green beans, trimmed and diagonally cut into 1-inch pieces
2 teaspoons minced fresh ginger
1 clove garlic, minced
1 cup water
2½ tablespoons dry sherry
4 teaspoons soy sauce
4 teaspoons cornstarch
2 teaspoons instant chicken bouillon granules
1 pound fresh of thawed frozen sea scallops, trimmed and cut into quarters
6 green onions, diagonally cut into thin slices
1 can (15 ounces) baby corn, drained

1. Place mushrooms in bowl and cover with hot water. Let stand 30 minutes. Drain and squeeze out excess water. Cut off and discard stems; cut caps into thin slices.

2. Heat oil in wok or large skillet over high heat. Add yellow onions, celery, green beans, ginger and garlic; stir-fry 3 minutes.

3. Combine water, sherry, soy sauce, cornstarch and bouillon granules in medium cup. Add to wok. Cook and stir until sauce boils.

4. Add scallops, mushrooms, green onions and baby corn. Cook and stir until scallops turn opaque, about 4 minutes. *Makes 4 to 6 servings*

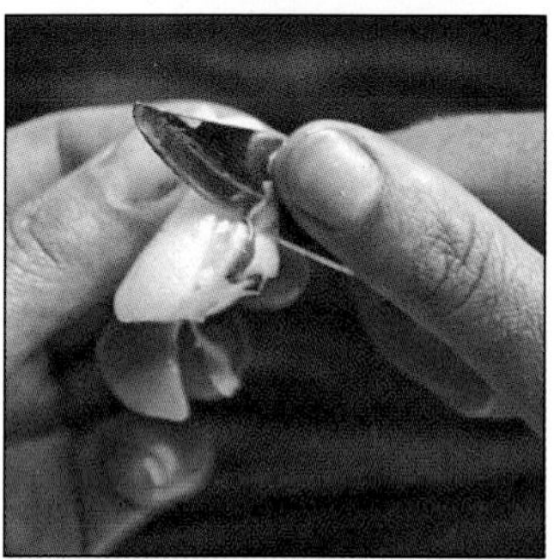

3

Ginger Chili Fish

2

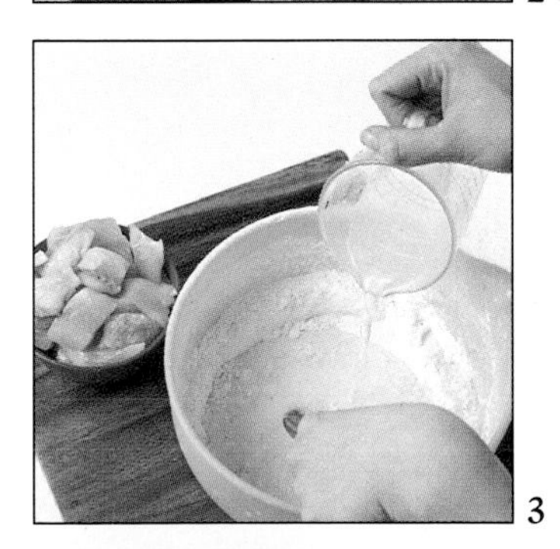

3

4

SAUCE
- **1 can (8 ounces) tomato sauce**
- **2 tablespoons dry sherry**
- **1 tablespoon minced fresh ginger**
- **1 tablespoon Chinese chili sauce**
- **1 tablespoon water**
- **1 tablespoon soy sauce**
- **2 teaspoons sugar**
- **3 cloves garlic, crushed**

FISH
- **1 pound fresh or thawed frozen fish fillets**
- **1 cup all-purpose flour**
- **⅓ cup cornstarch**
- **¾ cup water**
- **1 egg white**
- **½ teaspoon salt**
- **Vegetable oil for frying**

1. For sauce, combine all sauce ingredients in medium saucepan. Bring to a boil; cook and stir 2 minutes. Remove from heat.

2. For fish, remove skin from fillets. (To do this easily, rub some salt on your fingers and grasp skin at tail-end of fish.With a sharp knife held at an angle, separate fish from skin using sawing motion.) Cut fillets into 1-inch pieces.

3. Combine flour, cornstarch, water, egg white and salt. Beat with whisk until smooth.

4. Heat oil in wok or large saucepan over high heat to 375°F. Dip fish pieces, a few at a time, in batter; drain slightly then add to wok and cook until golden, about 5 minutes. Drain on paper towels.

5. Remove oil from wok. Place fish and sauce in wok. Cook over medium heat, tossing lightly, until fish is heated through and coated with sauce, about 2 minutes.

Makes 4 servings

Crispy Fish with Lemon Sauce

LEMON SAUCE
- **1 cup water**
- **1 piece lemon rind (about 1-inch square)**
- **⅓ cup fresh lemon juice**
- **3 tablespoons brown sugar**
- **1 piece fresh ginger (about 1-inch square) pared and thinly sliced**
- **1 teaspoon instant chicken bouillon granules**
- **1½ tablespoons cornstarch**
- **2 tablespoons water**

FISH
- **¾ cup all-purpose flour, divided**
- **2 whole fish (about 12 ounces each), cleaned and scaled**
- **6 tablespoons water**
- **1½ teaspoons vegetable oil**
- **Vegetable oil for frying**
- **1 egg white**
- **4 green onions, thinly sliced**

1. For sauce, combine 1 cup water, lemon rind and juice, sugar, ginger and bouillon in medium saucepan. Bring to a boil. Reduce heat and simmer, uncovered, 5 minutes. Remove from heat, strain sauce and return to saucepan.

2. Blend cornstarch and the 2 tablespoons water in small cup; stir into saucepan. Cook and stir until sauce boils and thickens. Simmer 5 minutes, stirring often. Keep warm.

3. For fish, place ¼ cup of the flour in shallow bowl. Coat fish on both sides with flour. Combine remaining ½ cup flour, the water and 1½ teaspoons vegetable oil in large bowl. Beat with whisk until smooth.

4. Heat vegetable oil in wok or large skillet over high heat to 375°F. Beat egg whites with electric mixer in large bowl until stiff peaks form. Fold whites into batter.

5. Dip one of the whole fish into batter, letting excess drain off. Carefully add fish to wok and cook until golden and cooked through, 8 to 10 minutes. Turn fish over once during cooking. Drain on paper towels. Repeat with second fish.

6. Place fish on serving plate. Stir onions into Lemon Sauce and pour over fish. *Makes 2 servings*

3

5

Vegetables

Chinese Vegetables

- 1 pound fresh broccoli
- ¾ cup water
- 1 tablespoon instant chicken bouillon granules
- 2 tablespoons vegetable oil
- 2 medium yellow onions, cut into wedges and separated
- 1 tablespoon minced fresh ginger
- 8 ounces fresh spinach, coarsely chopped
- 8 ounces fresh snow peas or 1 package (6 ounces) thawed frozen snow peas, trimmed and strings removed
- 4 stalks celery, diagonally cut into ½-inch pieces
- 8 green onions, diagonally cut into thin slices

1. Cut broccoli tops into florets. Cut stalks into 2×¼-inch thin strips. Combine water and bouillon granules in small cup; mix well.

2. Heat oil in wok or large skillet over high heat. Add broccoli stalks, yellow onions and ginger; stir-fry 1 minute. Add all remaining vegetables; toss lightly.

3. Add water mixture. Toss until vegetables well coated. Bring to a boil, cover and cook until vegetables are crisp-tender, 2 to 3 minutes.

Makes 4 to 6 servings

NOTE: Sliced carrots, zucchini, green beans or green bell peppers may be used in addition to, or in place of, the listed vegetables.

1
2
2
3

Zucchini Shanghai Style

- 4 dried mushrooms
- ½ cup chicken broth
- 2 tablespoons catsup
- 2 teaspoons soy sauce
- 1 teaspoon dry sherry
- ¼ teaspoon sugar
- ⅛ teaspoon salt
- 1 teaspoon red wine vinegar
- 2 tablespoons vegetable oil, divided
- 1 teaspoon minced fresh ginger
- 1 clove garlic, minced
- 1 green onion, minced
- 1 large tomato, peeled, seeded and chopped
- 4 tablespoons water, divided
- 1 teaspoon cornstarch
- 1 pound zucchini, diagonally cut into 1-inch pieces
- ½ small yellow onion, cut into wedges and separated

1. Place mushrooms in bowl and cover with hot water. Let stand 30 minutes. Drain, reserving ¼ cup liquid. Squeeze out excess water. Cut off and discard stems; cut caps into thin slices.

2. Combine the reserved ¼ cup mushroom liquid, the chicken broth, catsup, soy sauce, sherry, sugar, salt and vinegar in small bowl.

3. Heat 1 tablespoon of the oil in 2-quart saucepan over medium-high heat. Add ginger and garlic and stir-fry 10 seconds. Add mushrooms, green onion and tomato. Stir-fry 1 minute. Add chicken broth mixture and bring to a boil; reduce heat and simmer, uncovered, 10 minutes.

4. Blend 1 tablespoon of the water and the cornstarch in small cup. Heat remaining 1 tablespoon oil in wok or large skillet over medium-high heat. Add zucchini and yellow onion and stir-fry 30 seconds. Add remaining 2 tablespoons water, cover and cook, stirring occasionally, until vegetables are crisp-tender, 3 to 4 minutes.

5. Pour tomato sauce into wok. Stir cornstarch mixture and add to wok. Cook and stir until sauce boils and thickens. *Makes 4 to 6 servings*

1

4

Quick Stir-Fried Vegetables

2 cups cauliflower florets (about ½ of small head)
3 cups broccoli florets (about 1 pound broccoli)
½ small jicama (about 8 ounces), pared
2 tablespoons vegetable oil
1 teaspoon minced fresh ginger
½ cup chicken broth, divided
¼ teaspoon salt
¼ teaspoon sugar
1 red bell pepper, cut into thin strips
1 teaspoon sesame oil

1. Cut a small x in stem end of each cauliflower floret. If florets are large, cut them into 2 or 3 slices. Cut a small x in stem end of broccoli florets. Cut jicama into thick slices, then cut into 2×¼-inch strips. Set all vegetables, oil and seasonings near cooking area.

2. Heat vegetable oil in wok or large skillet over high heat. Add ginger and stir-fry 10 seconds. Add cauliflower and broccoli; stir-fry 30 seconds to coat with oil.

3. Pour about ⅓ cup of the chicken broth around edges of wok. Add salt and sugar. Cover and cook until vegetables are partially tender, 3 to 4 minutes.

4. Add jicama, bell pepper and remaining chicken broth. Cover and cook 1 minute. Uncover and stir-fry until vegetables are crisp-tender and all liquid has evaporated. Stir in sesame oil. *Makes 4 to 6 servings*

Braised Choice Vegetables

8 dried mushrooms
1 can (15 ounces) peeled straw mushrooms
1 cup baby corn (½ of 15-ounce can)
½ cup sliced bamboo shoots (½ of 8-ounce can)
2 tablespoons oyster sauce
2 teaspoons soy sauce
2 tablespoons vegetable oil
1 clove garlic, minced
½ cup chicken broth
2 teaspoons cornstarch
1 tablespoon water

1. Place dried mushrooms in bowl and cover with hot water. Let stand 30 minutes. Drain, reserving ½ cup liquid. Squeeze out excess water. Cut off and discard stems. Leave mushrooms whole, or, if large, cut into halves.

2. Drain straw mushrooms, baby corn and bamboo shoots. If corn is large, diagonally cut each ear into small pieces. Rinse under cold running water and drain. Combine oyster sauce and soy sauce in small cup.

3. Heat oil in wok or large skillet over high heat. Add garlic and stir-fry 10 seconds. Add dried mushrooms; stir-fry 1 minute. Add chicken broth and reserved ½ cup mushroom liquid. Cover and simmer over medium heat until mushrooms are tender and about ½ the liquid has evaporated, about 5 minutes.

4. Add straw mushrooms, corn, bamboo shoots and soy sauce mixture. Simmer 3 minutes. Blend cornstarch and water in small cup. Stir into wok; cook and stir until sauce boils and thickens slightly.

Makes 4 to 6 servings

2

2

Eggplant Szechuan Style

- **1 pound Oriental eggplants or 1 domestic eggplant**
- **3 green onions**
- **1 tablespoon minced garlic**
- **2 teaspoons minced fresh ginger**
- **2 teaspoons hot bean sauce**
- **½ cup chicken broth**
- **1 tablespoon soy sauce**
- **1 tablespoon red wine vinegar**
- **1½ teaspoons sugar**
- **5 tablespoons vegetable oil, divided**
- **1 tablespoon water**
- **1 teaspoon cornstarch**
- **1 teaspoon sesame oil**

1. Cut unpeeled eggplant into ½-inch thick slices; cut slices into 2×½-inch strips.

2. Cut 1 of the green onions into thin slices; reserve for garnish. Cut remaining 2 green onions into thin slices. Combine onions, garlic, ginger and hot bean sauce in medium bowl. Combine chicken broth, soy sauce, vinegar and sugar in small bowl.

3. Heat 2 tablespoons of the vegetable oil in wok or large skillet over medium-high heat. Add ½ of eggplant and cook, stirring often, until soft and moist, about 5 minutes. Remove to a colander to drain. Repeat, using 2 more tablespoons vegetable oil and the remaining eggplant.

4. Heat remaining 1 tablespoon vegetable oil in wok over medium-high heat. Add onion-garlic mixture and stir-fry 30 seconds, Return eggplant to wok. Add chicken broth mixture. Bring to a boil and cook, stirring occasionally, until liquid is almost evaporated.

5. Blend water and cornstarch in small cup; add to wok. Cook and stir until sauce boils and thickens slightly. Stir in sesame oil. Garnish with reserved onion slices.

Makes 4 to 5 servings

1

2

3

Rice & Noodles

Fried Rice

- 3 cups water
- 1½ teaspoons salt
- 1½ cups long-grain rice
- 4 slices bacon, chopped
- 3 eggs
- ⅛ teaspoon pepper
- 3 tablespoons vegetable oil, divided
- 2 teaspoons minced fresh ginger
- 8 ounces cooked pork, cut into thin strips
- 8 ounces cooked shrimp, shelled, deveined and coarsely chopped
- 8 green onions, finely chopped
- 1 to 2 tablespoons soy sauce

1. Combine water and salt in 3-quart saucepan. Cover and bring to a boil. Stir in rice; reduce heat, cover and simmer until rice is tender, 15 to 20 minutes; drain.

2. Cook bacon in wok over medium heat, stirring often, until crisp; drain. Remove all but 1 tablespoon bacon drippings from wok.

3. Beat eggs and pepper with fork in small bowl. Pour ⅓ of egg mixture into wok. Tilt wok slightly so egg covers bottom. Cook over medium heat until eggs are set, 1 to 2 minutes. Remove from wok. Roll up omelet and cut into thin strips. Pour ½ tablespoon of the oil into wok. Add ½ of remaining egg mixture; tilt wok and cook until eggs are set. Remove, roll up and cut into thin strips. Repeat with another ½ tablespoon oil and remaining eggs.

4. Heat remaining 2 tablespoons oil in wok over medium-high heat. Add ginger and stir-fry 1 minute. Add rice; cook and stir 5 minutes. Stir in eggs, bacon, pork, shrimp, onions and soy sauce. Cook and stir until heated through.

Makes 6 to 8 servings

Steamed Rice

1 cup long-grain rice
2 cups water
1 teaspoon salt
1 tablespoon vegetable oil

1. Place rice in strainer and rinse under cold running water to remove excess starch. Combine rice, water, salt and oil in 3-quart saucepan.

2. Cook over medium-high heat until water boils. Reduce heat to low, cover and simmer until rice is tender, 15 to 20 minutes.

3. Remove from heat; let stand 5 minutes. Uncover and fluff rice lightly with fork. *Makes 3 cups*

1

2

Vegetarian Fried Rice

4 dried mushrooms
4 cups cooked long-grain rice
3 eggs
¾ teaspoon salt, divided
2½ tablespoons vegetable oil, divided
1 teaspoon minced fresh ginger
1 clove garlic, minced
3 green onions, thinly sliced
4 ounces bean curd, deep fried and cut into ¼-inch cubes
1 tablespoon soy sauce
¼ teaspoon sugar
1 cup bean sprouts, coarsely chopped
½ cup thawed frozen peas

1. Place mushrooms in small bowl and cover with hot water. Let stand 30 minutes. Drain, reserving liquid. Squeeze out excess water. Cut off and discard stems; dice caps.

2. Rub rice with wet hands so all the grains are separated.

3. Beat eggs with ¼ teaspoon of the salt in medium bowl. Heat ½ tablespoon oil in wok or large skillet over medium heat. Add eggs; cook and stir until soft curds form. Remove from heat and cut eggs into small pieces using a spoon. Remove and set aside.

4. Heat remaining 2 tablespoons oil in wok over high heat. Add ginger, garlic and onions; stir-fry 10 seconds. Add mushrooms, ¼ cup of the reserved mushroom soaking liquid, the bean curd, soy sauce and sugar. Cook until most of the liquid evaporates, about 4 minutes. Add bean sprouts and peas; cook 30 seconds.

5. Add rice and remaining ½ teaspoon salt. Stir and toss until heated through. Add a few drops mushroom soaking liquid if rice appears dry. Fold in eggs before serving.

Makes 4 servings

Bean Threads with Minced Pork

4 ounces bean threads or Chinese rice vermicelli
3 dried mushrooms
1 small red or green hot chili pepper
3 green onions
2 tablespoons minced fresh ginger
2 tablespoons hot bean sauce
1½ cups chicken broth
1 tablespoon soy sauce
1 tablespoon dry sherry
2 tablespoons vegetable oil
6 ounces lean ground pork
2 cilantro sprigs (Chinese parsley), for garnish

1. Place bean threads and dried mushrooms in separate bowls. Cover each with hot water. Let stand 30 minutes; drain. Cut bean threads into 4-inch pieces. Squeeze out excess water from mushrooms. Cut off and discard stems; cut caps into thin slices.

2. Cut chili pepper in half and scrape out seeds.* Finely mince chili pepper. Thinly slice 2 of the green onions. Cut remaining onion into 1½-inch slivers and reserve for garnish. Combine ginger and hot bean sauce in small bowl. Combine chicken broth, soy sauce and sherry in medium bowl.

3. Heat oil in wok or large skillet over high heat. Add pork and stir-fry until meat is no longer pink, about 2 minutes. Add chili pepper, sliced onions and ginger-bean sauce mixture. Stir-fry until meat absorbs color from bean sauce, about 1 minute.

4. Add chicken broth mixture, bean threads and mushrooms. Simmer, uncovered, until most of the liquid is absorbed, about 5 minutes. Garnish with onion slivers and cilantro sprigs. *Makes 4 servings*

***Note:** Wear rubber or plastic gloves when cutting chili peppers. Do not touch eyes or lips when handling.

1

2

Fried Noodles

8 ounces Chinese-style thin egg noodles
Salt
Vegetable oil for frying

1. Cook noodles according to package directions until tender but still firm, 2 to 3 minutes. Drain, rinse under cold running water and drain again.

2. Place several layers of paper towels over cookie sheets or jelly-roll pans. Spread noodles over paper towels and let dry 2 to 3 hours.

3. Heat oil in wok or large skillet over medium-high heat to 375°F. Using tongs or slotted spoon, lower a small portion of noodles into hot oil. Cook until golden, about 30 seconds. Drain on paper towels. Repeat with remaining noodles.

Makes 4 servings

1 2 3 3

Cold Stirred Noodles

DRESSING
- **6 tablespoons soy sauce**
- **2 tablespoons sesame oil**
- **¼ cup red wine vinegar**
- **2½ tablespoons sugar**
- **¼ to ½ teaspoon chili oil (or to taste)**

NOODLES
- **1 pound Chinese-style thin egg noodles**
- **1 tablespoon sesame oil**
- **2 small carrots, cut into 3-inch pieces and shredded**
- **3 cups bean sprouts**
- **½ large thin-skinned cucumber, cut into 3-inch pieces and shredded**
- **1 bunch radishes, shredded**
- **4 green onions, cut into 2-inch slivers**
- **1 cup matchstick strips cooked pork, optional**

1. Combine all dressing ingredients in small bowl; mix well.

2. Cut noodles into 6-inch pieces. Cook noodles according to package directions until tender but still firm, 2 to 3 minutes. Drain, rinse under cold running water and drain again. Toss noodles with sesame oil until well coated. Refrigerate until ready to serve.

3. Cook carrots in pot of boiling water 30 seconds; drain and rinse under cold running water. Cook bean sprouts in boiling water 30 seconds; drain and rinse under cold running water.

4. To serve, arrange noodles on large platter. Arrange all remaining vegetables and pork on top; sprinkle with onions. Pass dressing separately.

Makes 6 to 8 servings

1

2

Vermicelli

8 ounces Chinese rice vermicelli or bean threads
Vegetable oil for frying

1. Cut bundle of vermicelli in half. Gently pull each half apart into small bunches.

2. Heat oil in wok or large skillet over medium-high heat to 375°F. Using tongs or slotted spoon, lower a small bunch of vermicelli into hot oil. Cook until vermicelli rises to top, 3 to 5 seconds. Immediately remove and drain on paper towels. Repeat with remaining bunches.

Makes about 4 servings

1

2

2

Beef Chow Mein

- 1½ pounds beef rump steak
- 3½ tablespoons soy sauce, divided
- 3½ tablespoons dry sherry, divided
- 1 tablespoon satay sauce
- 12 ounces Chinese-style thin egg noodles
- 4 tablespoons vegetable oil, divided
- ¾ cup water
- 1 tablespoon cornstarch
- 2½ tablespoons oyster sauce
- 2 teaspoons instant chicken bouillon granules
- 2 yellow onions, cut into wedges and separated
- 3 stalks celery, diagonally cut into ½-inch pieces
- 4 ounces fresh mushrooms, sliced
- 1 red or green bell pepper, cut into thin strips
- 4 ounces bean sprouts

1. Cut meat across the grain into thin slices. Combine 1½ tablespoons of the soy sauce, 1 tablespoon of the sherry and the satay sauce in medium bowl. Add meat and stir to coat well. Cover and refrigerate 1 hour.

2. Cook noodles according to package directions until tender but still firm, 2 to 3 minutes. Drain, rinse under cold running water and drain again. Heat 1 tablespoon of the oil in wok or large skillet over high heat. Add noodles and 1 tablespoon of the soy sauce; stir-fry until lightly browned, about 2 minutes. Transfer to serving plate; keep warm.

3. Blend water, cornstarch, oyster sauce, bouillon, remaining 2½ tablespoons sherry and 1 tablespoon soy sauce in small bowl.

4. Heat 1 tablespoon of the oil in wok over high heat. Add onions and stir-fry 1 minute. Add celery, mushrooms, red pepper and sprouts; stir-fry 2 minutes. Remove and set aside.

5. Heat remaining 2 tablespoons oil in wok over high heat. Add beef and stir-fry until browned, about 5 minutes. Stir in water mixture; cover and cook 3 minutes. Return vegetables to wok. Cook and stir until heated through, 1 to 2 minutes more. Spoon mixture over noodles.

Makes 4 to 6 servings

1

4

Chicken Chow Mein

Fried Noodles (page 513)
2½ tablespoons dry sherry, divided
2 tablespoons soy sauce divided
3 teaspoons cornstarch, divided
2 whole boneless, skinless chicken breasts, cut into 1-inch pieces
8 ounces boneless lean pork, cut into 1-inch pieces
½ cup water
2 teaspoons instant chicken bouillon granules
2 tablespoons vegetable oil
1 piece fresh ginger (1 inch square), pared and finely chopped
1 clove garlic, crushed
8 ounces shelled, deveined shrimp
2 medium yellow onions, chopped
1 red or green bell pepper, thinly sliced
2 stalks celery, diagonally cut into 1-inch slices
8 green onions, chopped
4 ounces cabbage (¼ of small head), shredded

1. Prepare Fried Noodles; set aside.

2. Blend ½ tablespoon of the sherry, ½ tablespoon of the soy sauce and 1 teaspoon of the cornstarch in large bowl. Add chicken and pork; toss to coat well. Cover and refrigerate 1 hour.

3. Combine water, bouillon granules, remaining 2 teaspoons cornstarch, 2 tablespoons sherry and 1½ tablespoons soy sauce in small bowl; set aside. Heat oil in wok or large skillet over high heat. Add ginger and garlic and stir-fry 1 minute. Add chicken and pork; stir-fry until pork is no longer pink, about 5 minutes. Add shrimp; stir-fry until shrimp turn pink, about 3 minutes.

4. Add all vegetables to wok. Stir-fry until vegetables are crisp-tender, 3 to 5 minutes. Add bouillon-soy sauce mixture to wok. Cook and stir until sauce boils and thickens, then cook and stir 1 minute more.

5. Arrange Fried Noodles on serving plate; spoon chow mein over noodles. *Makes 6 servings*

4

Chocolate LOVER'S *Cookies & Brownies*

Double Chocolate Crispy Bars (page 553), Chocolate Macadamia Bars (page 554) and Naomi's Revel Bars (page 554)

Extra-Easy Cookies

Chocolate Sugar Drops (page 522), Chocolate-Coconut Cookies (page 522), Chocolate & Peanut-Butter Tweed Cookies (page 523)

CHOCOLATE-COCONUT COOKIES

For a festive touch, top these easy-to-make cookies with red candied cherries and add them to your holiday cookie tray.

2 squares (1 ounce each) unsweetened chocolate
½ cup butter or margarine, softened
1 cup packed light brown sugar
1 egg
1¼ cups all-purpose flour
¼ teaspoon baking powder
⅛ teaspoon baking soda
Dash salt
½ cup chopped walnuts or pecans
½ cup flaked coconut
Pecan halves or halved red candied cherries

Preheat oven to 350°F. Lightly grease cookie sheets or line with parchment paper. Melt chocolate in top of double boiler over hot, not boiling, water. Remove from heat; cool. Cream butter and sugar in large bowl until blended. Add egg and melted chocolate; beat until light. Combine flour, baking powder, baking soda and salt in small bowl. Stir into creamed mixture until blended. Mix in nuts and coconut. Drop dough by teaspoonfuls 2 inches apart onto prepared cookie sheets. Press a pecan or cherry half into center of each cookie. Bake 10 to 12 minutes or until firm. Remove to wire racks to cool.

Makes 4 dozen cookies

CHOCOLATE SUGAR DROPS

Sugar cookies have never been easier! The dough is rolled into balls and flattened with the bottom of a glass dipped into sugar. Be sure to dip the glass into sugar before flattening each cookie.

½ cup butter or margarine, softened
½ cup vegetable oil
½ cup powdered sugar
½ cup granulated sugar
1 egg
2 cups all-purpose flour
¼ cup unsweetened cocoa
½ teaspoon baking soda
½ teaspoon cream of tartar
¼ teaspoon salt
1 teaspoon vanilla
Granulated sugar

Cream butter, oil, powdered sugar, ½ cup granulated sugar and the egg in large bowl until light and fluffy. Combine the flour, cocoa, baking soda, cream of tartar and salt in small bowl. Add to creamed mixture with vanilla, stirring until dough is smooth. Cover; refrigerate 30 minutes or overnight, if desired.

Preheat oven to 350°F. Lightly grease cookie sheets or line with parchment paper. Shape dough into balls the size of marbles. Place 2 inches apart on prepared cookie sheets. Flatten each cookie to about ⅓-inch thickness with bottom of glass dipped into granulated sugar. Bake 10 minutes or until firm. Do not overbake. Remove to wire racks to cool.

Makes about 5 dozen cookies

CHOCOLATE & PEANUT-BUTTER TWEED COOKIES

The chopped chocolate and peanut butter chips in these cookies give them a tweedy texture and appearance.

- **1 cup butter or margarine, softened**
- **½ cup packed light brown sugar**
- **¼ cup granulated sugar**
- **1 egg**
- **¼ teaspoon baking soda**
- **2½ cups all-purpose flour**
- **½ cup *each* semisweet chocolate chips and peanut butter chips, chopped***

Cream butter and sugars in large bowl until smooth. Add egg and baking soda, beat until light. Stir in flour until dough is smooth. Blend in chopped chips. Divide dough into 4 parts. Shape each part into a roll, about 1½ inches in diameter. Wrap in plastic wrap; refrigerate until firm, at least 1 hour or up to 2 weeks. (For longer storage, freeze up to 6 weeks.)

Preheat oven to 375°F. Lightly grease cookie sheets or line with parchment paper. Cut rolls into ⅛-inch-thick slices; place 2 inches apart on prepared cookie sheets. Bake 10 to 12 minutes or until lightly browned. Remove to wire racks to cool.

Makes about 6 dozen cookies

*Chips can be chopped in a food processor.

HONEY-GINGER BOURBON BALLS

- **1 cup gingersnap cookie crumbs**
- **1¼ cups powdered sugar, divided**
- **1 cup finely chopped pecans or walnuts**
- **1 square (1 ounce) unsweetened chocolate**
- **1½ tablespoons honey**
- **¼ cup bourbon**

Combine crumbs, 1 cup of the sugar and the nuts in large bowl. Combine chocolate and honey in small bowl over hot water; stir until chocolate is melted. Blend in bourbon. Stir bourbon mixture into crumb mixture until well blended. Shape into 1-inch balls. Sprinkle remaining ¼ cup powdered sugar over balls. Refrigerate until firm.

Makes about 4 dozen balls

Note: These improve with aging. Store them in an airtight container in the refrigerator. They will keep several weeks, but are best after two to three days.

COCOA SNICKERDOODLES

Snickerdoodle is a nineteenth-century nonsense word for a quick-to-make confection. The dough is dropped into a mixture of cocoa, cinnamon and sugar, making the cookies crinkle when baked.

1 cup butter or margarine, softened
¾ cup packed brown sugar
¾ cup plus 2 tablespoons granulated sugar
2 eggs
2 cups uncooked rolled oats
1½ cups all-purpose flour
¼ cup plus 2 tablespoons unsweetened cocoa
1 teaspoon baking soda
2 tablespoons ground cinnamon

Preheat oven to 375°F. Lightly grease cookie sheets or line with parchment paper. Beat butter, brown sugar and the ¾ cup granulated sugar in large bowl until light and fluffy. Add eggs; mix well. Combine oats, flour, the ¼ cup cocoa and the baking soda in medium bowl. Stir into butter mixture until blended. Mix the 2 tablespoons granulated sugar, the cinnamon and the 2 tablespoons cocoa in small bowl. Drop dough by rounded teaspoonfuls into cinnamon mixture; toss to coat. Place 2 inches apart on prepared cookie sheets. Bake 8 to 10 minutes or until firm in center. Do not overbake. Remove to wire racks to cool.

Makes about 4½ dozen cookies

CHOCOLATE-PEANUT COOKIES

1 cup butter or margarine, softened
¾ cup granulated sugar
¾ cup packed light brown sugar
2 eggs
1 teaspoon vanilla
1 teaspoon baking soda
¼ teaspoon salt
2¼ cups all-purpose flour
2 cups chocolate-covered peanuts

Preheat oven to 375°F. Line cookie sheets with parchment paper or leave ungreased. Cream butter with sugars, eggs and vanilla in large bowl until light. Beat in baking soda and salt. Stir in flour to make stiff dough. Blend in chocolate-covered peanuts. Drop by rounded teaspoonfuls 2 inches apart onto cookie sheets. Bake 9 to 11 minutes or until just barely golden. Do not overbake. Remove to wire racks to cool.

Makes about 5 dozen cookies

Cocoa Snickerdoodles, Chocolate-Peanut Cookies

COWBOY COOKIES

Loaded with raisins, nuts and chocolate chips, these are a cookie-jar favorite that kids love!

- ½ cup butter or margarine, softened
- ½ cup packed light brown sugar
- ¼ cup granulated sugar
- 1 egg
- 1 teaspoon vanilla
- 1 cup all-purpose flour
- 2 tablespoons unsweetened cocoa
- ½ teaspoon baking powder
- ¼ teaspoon baking soda
- 1 cup uncooked rolled oats
- 1 cup (6 ounces) semisweet chocolate chips
- ½ cup raisins
- ½ cup chopped nuts

Preheat oven to 375°F. Lightly grease cookie sheets or line with parchment paper. Cream butter with sugars in large bowl until blended. Add egg and vanilla; beat until fluffy. Combine flour, cocoa, baking powder and baking soda in small bowl; stir into creamed mixture with oats, chocolate chips, raisins and nuts. Drop dough by teaspoonfuls 2 inches apart onto prepared cookie sheets. Bake 10 to 12 minutes or until lightly browned around edges. Remove to wire racks to cool.

Makes about 4 dozen cookies

BETH'S CHOCOLATE OATMEAL COOKIES

All butter or margarine may be used in place of the shortening in this recipe. The shortening, however, gives the cookies a more tender texture.

- 3 squares (1 ounce each) unsweetened chocolate
- ½ cup butter or margarine, softened
- ½ cup shortening
- 1½ cups sugar
- 2 eggs
- 2 teaspoons vanilla
- 1½ cups all-purpose flour
- 2 teaspoons baking powder
- ½ teaspoon salt
- 3 cups uncooked rolled oats
- 1 cup chopped walnuts

Preheat oven to 350°F. Lightly grease cookie sheets or line with parchment paper. Melt chocolate in top of double boiler over hot, not boiling, water. Remove from heat; cool. Cream butter, shortening and sugar in large bowl. Add eggs, beating well. Blend in melted chocolate and vanilla. Combine flour, baking powder and salt in small bowl. Add to creamed mixture; blend well. Mix in oats and nuts. Drop dough by rounded teaspoonfuls 2 inches apart onto prepared cookie sheets. Bake 10 to 12 minutes or until lightly browned. Remove to wire racks to cool.

Makes about 8 dozen cookies

Cowboy Cookies

NUTTY CLUSTERS

- 2 squares (1 ounce each) unsweetened chocolate
- ½ cup butter or margarine, softened
- 1 cup granulated sugar
- 1 egg
- ⅓ cup buttermilk
- 1 teaspoon vanilla
- 1¾ cups all-purpose flour
- ½ teaspoon baking soda
- 1 cup mixed salted nuts, coarsely chopped
- Chocolate Icing (recipe follows)

Preheat oven to 400°F. Line cookie sheets with parchment paper or leave ungreased. Melt chocolate in top of double boiler over hot, not boiling, water. Remove from heat; cool. Cream butter and granulated sugar in large bowl until smooth. Beat in egg, melted chocolate, buttermilk and vanilla until light. Stir in flour, baking soda and nuts. Drop dough by teaspoonfuls 2 inches apart onto cookie sheets. Bake 8 to 10 minutes or until almost no imprint remains when touched. Immediately remove cookies from cookie sheet to wire rack. While cookies bake, prepare Chocolate Icing. Frost cookies while still warm.

Makes about 4 dozen cookies

CHOCOLATE ICING

- 2 squares (1 ounce each) unsweetened chocolate
- 2 tablespoons butter or margarine
- 2 cups powdered sugar
- 2 to 3 tablespoons water

Melt chocolate and butter in small heavy saucepan over low heat, stirring until completely melted. Add powdered sugar and water, mixing until smooth.

OAT & DRIED-FRUIT BALLS

- 3 cups uncooked rolled oats
- 1 cup flaked coconut
- 1 cup chopped dried mixed fruit
- ¼ cup sunflower seeds or chopped walnuts
- 1 cup sugar
- ½ cup milk
- ½ cup butter or margarine
- 6 tablespoons unsweetened cocoa
- ¼ teaspoon salt
- 1 teaspoon vanilla

Combine oats, coconut, fruit and sunflower seeds in large bowl; set aside. Combine sugar, milk, butter, cocoa and salt in 2-quart saucepan until blended. Heat to boiling. Boil 3 minutes, stirring constantly; remove from heat. Stir in vanilla. Pour hot sugar syrup into oat mixture; stir until well blended. When cool enough to handle, shape rounded tablespoonfuls into balls; place on waxed paper until completely cooled and firm.

Makes about 5 dozen balls

Nutty Clusters

PEANUT-BUTTER CHOCOLATE STARS

1 cup peanut butter
1 cup packed light brown sugar
1 egg
48 milk chocolate candy stars or other solid milk chocolate candy

Preheat oven to 350°F. Line cookie sheets with parchment paper or leave ungreased. Combine peanut butter, sugar and egg in medium bowl until blended and smooth. Shape into 48 balls about 1½ inches in diameter. Place 2 inches apart on cookie sheets. Press a chocolate star onto the top of each cookie. Bake 10 to 12 minutes or until set. Remove to wire racks to cool.

Makes 4 dozen cookies

FUDGE COOKIES

Satisfying and rich with chocolate, these fudgy cookies are gilded with a good fudge frosting, too.

1 cup (6 ounces) semisweet chocolate chips
½ cup butter or margarine, softened
1 cup granulated sugar
2 eggs
1½ cups all-purpose flour
Dash salt
1½ cups coarsely chopped pecans or walnuts
Fudge Frosting (recipe follows)

Preheat oven to 375°F. Lightly grease cookie sheets or line with parchment paper. Melt chocolate chips in top of double boiler over hot, not boiling, water. Remove from heat; cool. Cream butter, granulated sugar and eggs in large bowl until smooth. Beat in melted chocolate. Gradually add flour and salt, mixing until smooth. Stir in nuts. Drop dough by rounded teaspoonfuls 2 inches apart onto prepared cookie sheets. Bake 10 to 12 minutes or until slightly firm. Cool 5 minutes on cookie sheet, then remove to wire racks. While cookies bake, prepare Fudge Frosting. Frost cookies while still warm. Cool until frosting is set.

Makes about 5 dozen cookies

FUDGE FROSTING
1 square (1 ounce) semisweet chocolate
3 tablespoons heavy cream
1 cup powdered sugar
1 teaspoon vanilla

Melt chocolate with cream in small heavy saucepan over medium heat, stirring until chocolate melts completely. Remove from heat; beat in powdered sugar and vanilla. Spread over cookies while frosting is still warm.

Fudge Cookies, Oat & Dried-Fruit Balls (page 528), Peanut-Butter Chocolate Stars

ICE CREAM COOKIES

These cookies are simple, buttery and chocolatey—perfect to serve alongside ice cream or to make into ice cream sandwiches.

2 squares (1 ounce each) unsweetened chocolate
1 cup butter, softened
1 cup powdered sugar
4 egg yolks
1 teaspoon vanilla
3 cups all-purpose flour
Powdered sugar

Melt chocolate in top of double boiler over hot, not boiling, water. Remove from heat; cool. Cream butter and 1 cup sugar in large bowl until blended. Add egg yolks, vanilla and melted chocolate; beat until light. Blend in flour to make stiff dough. Divide dough into 4 parts. Shape each part into a roll, about 1½ inches in diameter. Wrap in plastic wrap; refrigerate until firm, at least 30 minutes or up to 2 weeks. (For longer storage, freeze up to 6 weeks.)

Preheat oven to 350°F. Line cookie sheets with parchment paper or leave ungreased. Cut rolls into ⅛-inch-thick slices; place 2 inches apart on ungreased cookie sheets. Bake 8 to 10 minutes or just until set, but not browned. Remove to wire racks to cool. Dust with powdered sugar.

Makes about 8 dozen cookies

Ice Cream Cookie Sandwiches: Prepare and bake cookies as directed; cool completely. Spread desired amount of softened ice cream on bottoms of half the cookies. Top with remaining cookies, bottom sides down, forming sandwiches. Dust tops with powdered sugar; serve immediately. Makes about 4 dozen sandwich cookies.

Ice Cream Cookie Sandwiches

Monster Cookies

Top left: White Chocolate Biggies (page 536), bottom left: Peanut Butter Jumbos (page 537)

WHITE CHOCOLATE BIGGIES

These huge chocolate cookies are studded with white chocolate chips, pecans and raisins. They bake to about four inches in diameter.

1½ cups butter or margarine, softened
1 cup granulated sugar
¾ cup packed light brown sugar
2 teaspoons vanilla
2 eggs
2½ cups all-purpose flour
⅔ cup unsweetened cocoa
1 teaspoon baking soda
½ teaspoon salt
1 package (10 ounces) large white chocolate chips
¾ cup pecan halves, coarsely chopped
½ cup golden raisins

Preheat oven to 350°F. Lightly grease cookie sheets or line with parchment paper. Cream butter, sugars, vanilla and eggs in large bowl until light. Combine flour, cocoa, baking soda and salt in medium bowl; blend into creamed mixture until smooth. Stir in white chocolate chips, pecans and raisins. Scoop out about ⅓ cupful of dough for each cookie. Place on prepared cookie sheets, spacing about 4 inches apart. Press each cookie to flatten slightly. Bake 12 to 14 minutes or until firm in center. Cool 5 minutes on cookie sheet, then remove to wire racks to cool completely.

Makes about 2 dozen cookies

CHOCOLATE PLATTER COOKIES

1 cup unsalted butter, softened
1 cup packed light brown sugar
½ cup granulated sugar
2 eggs
2⅓ cups all-purpose flour
1 teaspoon baking soda
½ teaspoon salt
1 package (12 ounces) semisweet chocolate chunks
2 cups chopped pecans

Preheat oven to 375°F. Lightly grease cookie sheets or line with parchment paper. Cream butter with sugars until smooth. Add eggs; beat until fluffy. Combine flour, baking soda and salt in small bowl. Add to creamed mixture, mixing until dough is stiff. Stir in chocolate chunks and pecans. Scoop out about ⅓ cupful of dough for each cookie. Place on prepared cookie sheets, spacing 4 inches apart. Using back of fork, flatten each cookie to about ½ inch thick. Bake 15 minutes or until light golden. Remove to wire racks to cool.

Makes about 16 cookies

PEANUT BUTTER JUMBOS

- ½ cup butter or margarine, softened
- 1 cup packed brown sugar
- 1 cup granulated sugar
- 1½ cups peanut butter
- 3 eggs
- 2 teaspoons baking soda
- 1 teaspoon vanilla
- 4½ cups uncooked rolled oats
- 1 cup (6 ounces) semisweet chocolate chips
- 1 cup candy-coated chocolate pieces

Preheat oven to 350°F. Lightly grease cookie sheets or line with parchment paper. Cream butter, sugars, peanut butter and eggs in large bowl until light. Blend in baking soda, vanilla and oats until well mixed. Stir in chocolate chips and candy pieces. Scoop out about ⅓ cupful of dough for each cookie. Place on prepared cookie sheets, spacing about 4 inches apart. Press each cookie to flatten slightly. Bake 15 to 20 minutes or until firm in center. Remove to wire racks to cool.

Makes about 1½ dozen cookies

GIANT RAISIN-CHIP FRISBEES

Decorate frisbees with candles for a birthday party—kids love them!

- 1 cup butter or margarine, softened
- 1 cup packed brown sugar
- ½ cup granulated sugar
- 2 eggs
- 1 teaspoon vanilla
- 1½ cups all-purpose flour
- ¼ cup unsweetened cocoa
- 1 teaspoon baking soda
- 1 cup (6 ounces) semisweet chocolate chips
- ¾ cup raisins
- ¾ cup chopped walnuts

Preheat oven to 350°F. Line cookie sheets with parchment paper or lightly grease and dust with flour. Cream butter with sugars in large bowl. Add eggs and vanilla; beat until light. Combine flour, cocoa and baking soda in small bowl. Add to creamed mixture with chocolate chips, raisins and walnuts; stir until well blended. Scoop out about ½ cupful of dough for each cookie. Place on prepared cookie sheets, spacing about 5 inches apart. Using knife dipped in water, smooth balls of dough out to 3½ inches in diameter. Bake 10 to 12 minutes or until golden. Remove to wire racks to cool.

Makes about 16 cookies

TRACY'S PIZZA-PAN COOKIES

Cream cheese adds flavor and a chewy texture to these pizza-sized cookies.

- 1 cup butter or margarine, softened
- ¾ cup granulated sugar
- ¾ cup packed brown sugar
- 1 package (8 ounces) cream cheese, softened
- 1 teaspoon vanilla
- 2 eggs
- 2¼ cups all-purpose flour
- 1 teaspoon baking soda
- ¼ teaspoon salt
- 1 package (12 ounces) semisweet chocolate chips
- 1 cup chopped walnuts or pecans

Preheat oven to 375°F. Lightly grease two 12-inch pizza pans. Cream butter, sugars, cream cheese and vanilla in large bowl. Add eggs; beat until light. Combine flour, baking soda and salt in small bowl. Add to creamed mixture; blend well. Stir in chocolate chips and nuts. Divide dough in half; press each half evenly into a prepared pan. Bake 20 to 25 minutes or until lightly browned around edges. Cool completely in pans on wire racks. To serve, cut into slim wedges or break into pieces.

Makes two 12-inch cookies

SUPER-DUPER CHOCOLATE PECAN COOKIES

- ½ cup butter or margarine, softened
- ⅓ cup peanut butter
- ⅓ cup granulated sugar
- ⅓ cup packed light brown sugar
- 1 egg
- 1 teaspoon vanilla
- 1¼ cups all-purpose flour
- ½ teaspoon baking soda
- 1 package (12 ounces) semisweet chocolate chunks *or* 4 semisweet chocolate bars (3 ounces each), cut into squares
- 1 cup pecan halves, cut into pieces

Preheat oven to 350°F. Lightly grease two cookie sheets or line with parchment paper. Cream butter, peanut butter, sugars, egg and vanilla in large bowl until light. Blend in flour and baking soda. Scoop out about ⅓ cupfuls of dough to form 12 balls. Place on prepared cookie sheets, spacing about 4 inches apart. Press each cookie to flatten slightly. Press chocolate chunks and pecan pieces into cookies, dividing them equally. Bake 15 to 17 minutes or until firm in center. Remove to wire racks to cool.

Makes 1 dozen cookies

Tracy's Pizza-Pan Cookies

Brownies & Bars

Left: Pecan Caramel Brownies (page 543), right: Chocolate Peanut Bars (page 542)

CHOCOLATE PEANUT BARS

- ½ cup butter or margarine, softened
- ¼ cup granulated sugar
- 1 cup packed brown sugar, divided
- 2 eggs, separated
- 1 teaspoon vanilla
- 2 cups all-purpose flour
- 2 teaspoons baking powder
- ½ teaspoon baking soda
- ¼ teaspoon salt
- 2 to 4 tablespoons milk
- 1 cup (6 ounces) semisweet chocolate chips
- ¾ cup salted peanuts, coarsely chopped

Preheat oven to 350°F. Lightly grease a 13×9-inch pan. Cream butter, granulated sugar and ¼ cup of the brown sugar in large bowl. Beat in egg yolks and vanilla. Combine flour, baking powder, baking soda and salt in small bowl. Blend into creamed mixture. Stir in enough milk to make a smooth, light dough. Press on bottom of prepared pan. Sprinkle chocolate chips over the top; press them down lightly into dough. In clean, dry bowl, beat egg whites until stiff, but not dry. Gradually beat in remaining ¾ cup brown sugar. Spread mixture evenly over dough in pan; top with peanuts. Bake 25 to 30 minutes or until top is puffed, lightly browned and feels dry. Cut into 2×1-inch bars while still warm.

Makes about 5 dozen bars

PEANUT-BUTTER-CHIP BROWNIES

- ½ cup butter or margarine
- 4 squares (1 ounce each) semisweet chocolate
- ½ cup sugar
- 2 eggs
- 1 teaspoon vanilla
- ½ cup all-purpose flour
- 1 package (12 ounces) peanut butter chips
- 1 cup (6 ounces) milk chocolate chips

Preheat oven to 350°F. Butter an 8-inch square pan. Melt butter and semisweet chocolate in small heavy saucepan over low heat, stirring just until chocolate melts completely. Remove from heat; cool. Beat sugar and eggs in large bowl until light. Blend in vanilla and chocolate mixture. Stir in flour until blended; fold in peanut butter chips. Spread batter evenly in prepared pan. Bake 25 to 30 minutes or just until firm and dry in center. Remove from oven; sprinkle milk chocolate chips over the top. Place pan on wire rack. When chocolate chips have melted, spread them over brownies. Refrigerate until chocolate topping is set. Cut into 2-inch squares.

Makes 16 brownies

PECAN CARAMEL BROWNIES

Pecans, caramel and chocolate make an irresistible combination.

- 50 caramel candy cubes
- 2 tablespoons milk
- 1½ cups granulated sugar
- 1 cup butter or margarine, melted
- 4 eggs
- 2 teaspoons vanilla
- 1 cup all-purpose flour
- ⅔ cup unsweetened cocoa
- ½ teaspoon baking powder
- ¼ teaspoon salt
- 1 cup (6 ounces) semisweet chocolate chips
- ⅓ cup pecan halves
- Cocoa Glaze (recipe follows)

Preheat oven to 350°F. Butter a 13×9-inch pan. Unwrap caramels; melt with milk in small heavy saucepan over medium to low heat, stirring until caramels melt completely. Keep warm. Combine granulated sugar, butter, eggs, vanilla, flour, cocoa, baking powder and salt in large bowl. Beat with mixer at medium speed until smooth. Spread half of the batter in prepared pan. Bake 15 minutes. Carefully remove from oven; sprinkle with chocolate chips. Drizzle melted caramel mixture over the top, covering evenly. Spoon remaining batter over all. Return to oven; bake 20 minutes longer. Do not overbake. Meanwhile, toast pecan halves in another pan in same oven 3 to 5 minutes. Prepare Cocoa Glaze. Pour over warm brownies; arrange toasted pecans on top. Cool completely in pan on wire rack. Cut into 2-inch squares.

Makes about 2 dozen brownies

COCOA GLAZE

- 2 tablespoons butter or margarine
- 2 tablespoons unsweetened cocoa
- 2 tablespoons milk
- Dash salt
- 1 cup powdered sugar
- 1 teaspoon vanilla

Combine butter, cocoa, milk and salt in small heavy saucepan. Bring to a boil over medium heat, stirring constantly. Remove from heat; add powdered sugar and beat until smooth. Stir in vanilla.

BROWNIE FUDGE

This recipe makes a huge batch of fudge-topped brownies—ideal to serve a crowd.

- 4 squares (1 ounce each) unsweetened chocolate
- 1 cup butter or margarine
- 2 cups sugar
- 4 eggs
- 1 cup all-purpose flour
- 1 cup chopped walnuts
- 2 teaspoons vanilla
- Fudge Topping (recipe follows)

Preheat oven to 350°F. Butter a 13×9-inch pan. Melt chocolate and butter in small heavy saucepan over low heat, stirring until completely melted; cool. Beat sugar and eggs in large bowl until light and fluffy. Gradually whisk chocolate mixture into egg mixture. Stir in flour, walnuts and vanilla. Spread batter evenly in prepared pan. Bake 25 to 35 minutes or just until set. Do not overbake. Meanwhile, prepare Fudge Topping. Remove brownies from oven. Immediately pour topping evenly over hot brownies. Cool in pan on wire rack. Place in freezer until firm. Cut into 1-inch squares.

Makes about 9 dozen brownies

FUDGE TOPPING

- 4½ cups sugar
- ⅓ cup butter or margarine
- 1 can (12 ounces) evaporated milk
- 1 jar (7 ounces) marshmallow creme
- 1 package (12 ounces) semisweet chocolate chips
- 1 package (12 ounces) milk chocolate chips
- 2 teaspoons vanilla
- 2 cups walnuts, coarsely chopped

Combine sugar, butter and milk in large saucepan. Bring to a boil over medium heat; boil 5 minutes, stirring constantly. Remove from heat; add remaining ingredients *except* walnuts. Beat until smooth. Stir in walnuts.

Left: White Chocolate & Almond Brownies (page 546), right: Brownie Fudge

WHITE CHOCOLATE & ALMOND BROWNIES

Use a high-quality white chocolate when you make these brownies. The white chocolate sweetens them so sugar is not needed in the recipe.

12 ounces white chocolate, broken into pieces
1 cup unsalted butter
3 eggs
¾ cup all-purpose flour
1 teaspoon vanilla
½ cup slivered almonds

Preheat oven to 325°F. Grease and flour 9-inch square pan. Melt chocolate and butter in large saucepan over low heat, stirring constantly. (Do not be concerned if the white chocolate separates.) Remove from heat when chocolate is just melted. With electric mixer, beat in eggs until mixture is smooth. Beat in flour and vanilla. Spread batter evenly in prepared pan. Sprinkle almonds evenly over the top. Bake 30 to 35 minutes or just until set in center. Cool completely in pan on wire rack. Cut into 2-inch squares.

Makes about 16 brownies

FUDGY FUDGE BROWNIES

Rich, moist and chewy, these brownies are for real chocolate lovers!

½ cup butter or margarine
2 squares (1 ounce each) unsweetened chocolate
2 eggs
1 cup granulated sugar
½ cup all-purpose flour
1 teaspoon vanilla
Fudgy Frosting, optional (recipe follows)

Preheat oven to 325°F. Grease and flour an 8-inch square pan. Melt butter and chocolate in small heavy saucepan over low heat. Remove from heat; cool. Beat eggs in medium bowl until light and fluffy. Add granulated sugar, beating well. Blend in chocolate mixture. Stir in flour and vanilla. Spread batter evenly in prepared pan. Bake 30 minutes or until firm in center. Cool in pan on wire rack. Frost with Fudgy Frosting, if desired. Cut into 2-inch squares.

Makes 16 brownies

FUDGY FROSTING
2 squares (1 ounce each) unsweetened chocolate
½ cup heavy cream
1 cup granulated sugar
Dash salt
1 teaspoon vanilla
½ to ¾ cup powdered sugar

Melt chocolate with cream in small heavy saucepan over low heat, stirring until chocolate melts completely. Stir in granulated sugar and salt. Bring to a boil. Boil 1 minute. Remove from heat; stir in vanilla. Beat until smooth. Add enough powdered sugar to make frosting a soft spreading consistency. Beat until slightly cooled; spread over brownies.

HEAVENLY HASH BROWNIES

This version of heavenly hash uses a combination of chocolate, nuts and marshmallows. For best results, be sure to use fresh marshmallows.

- 1 cup butter or margarine
- ¼ cup unsweetened cocoa
- 4 eggs
- 1¼ cups granulated sugar
- 1½ cups all-purpose flour
- 2 cups chopped walnuts or pecans
- 2 teaspoons vanilla
- Creamy Cocoa Icing (recipe follows)
- 1 package (10 ounces) miniature marshmallows

Preheat oven to 350°F. Grease a 13×9-inch pan. Melt butter in 2-quart saucepan; stir in cocoa. Remove from heat; beat in eggs and granulated sugar. Blend in flour, nuts and vanilla. Spread batter evenly in prepared pan. Bake 20 to 25 minutes or until center feels dry. Do not overbake. Meanwhile, prepare Creamy Cocoa Icing. Remove brownies from oven. Immediately sprinkle marshmallows over hot brownies. Pour hot icing evenly over marshmallows. Cool in pan on wire rack. Cut into 2-inch squares.

Makes about 2 dozen brownies

CREAMY COCOA ICING

- 6 tablespoons butter or margarine
- ¾ cup undiluted evaporated milk
- 6 cups powdered sugar
- ¾ cup unsweetened cocoa

Combine butter, milk, powdered sugar and cocoa in 2-quart saucepan. Stir over low heat until smooth and creamy.

COCONUT-ALMOND MOUND BARS

- 2 cups graham cracker crumbs
- ½ cup butter or margarine, softened
- ¼ cup powdered sugar
- 2 cups flaked coconut
- 1 can (14 ounces) sweetened condensed milk
- ½ cup whole blanched almonds
- 1 cup (6 ounces) milk chocolate chips

Preheat oven to 350°F. Lightly grease a 13×9-inch pan. Combine crumbs, butter and powdered sugar in large bowl until blended and smooth. Press on bottom of prepared pan. Bake 10 to 12 minutes or just until golden. Combine coconut and milk in small bowl; spread evenly over baked crust. Arrange almonds evenly over coconut mixture. Bake 15 to 18 minutes or until almonds are toasted. Remove from oven; sprinkle chocolate chips over the top. Let stand a few minutes until chips melt, then spread evenly over bars. Cool completely in pan on wire rack. Cut into 2×1½-inch bars.

Makes about 3 dozen bars

RASPBERRY FUDGE BROWNIES

½ cup butter or margarine
3 squares (1 ounce each) bittersweet chocolate*
2 eggs
1 cup sugar
1 teaspoon vanilla
¾ cup all-purpose flour
¼ teaspoon baking powder
Dash salt
½ cup sliced or slivered almonds
½ cup raspberry preserves
1 cup (6 ounces) milk chocolate chips

Preheat oven to 350°F. Butter and flour an 8-inch square pan. Melt butter and bittersweet chocolate in small heavy saucepan over low heat. Remove from heat; cool. Beat the eggs, sugar and vanilla in large bowl until light. Beat in chocolate mixture. Stir in flour, baking powder and salt until just blended. Spread ¾ of the batter in prepared pan; sprinkle almonds over the top. Bake 10 minutes. Remove from oven; spread preserves over almonds. Carefully spoon remaining batter over preserves, smoothing top. Bake 25 to 30 minutes or just until top feels firm. Remove from oven; sprinkle chocolate chips over the top. Let stand a few minutes until chips melt, then spread evenly over brownies. Cool completely in pan on wire rack. When chocolate is set, cut into 2-inch squares.

Makes 16 brownies

*Bittersweet chocolate is available in specialty food stores. One square unsweetened chocolate plus 2 squares semisweet chocolate may be substituted.

HONEY BROWNIES

The rich chocolate taste of these cake-like brownies is enhanced by golden honey.

1 cup (6 ounces) semisweet chocolate chips
6 tablespoons butter or margarine
2 eggs
⅓ cup honey
1 teaspoon vanilla
½ cup all-purpose flour
½ teaspoon baking powder
Dash salt
1 cup chopped walnuts

Preheat oven to 350°F. Butter an 8-inch square pan. Melt chocolate and butter in medium-sized heavy saucepan over low heat. Remove from heat; cool slightly. Stir in eggs, honey and vanilla. Combine flour, baking powder and salt in small bowl. Stir into chocolate mixture with walnuts. Spread batter evenly in prepared pan. Bake 20 to 25 minutes or just until center feels springy. Cool in pan on wire rack. Cut into 2-inch squares.

Makes 16 brownies

Raspberry Fudge Brownies

ROCKY ROAD BROWNIES

½ cup butter or margarine
½ cup unsweetened cocoa
1 cup sugar
1 egg
½ cup all-purpose flour
¼ cup buttermilk
1 teaspoon vanilla
1 cup miniature marshmallows
1 cup coarsely chopped walnuts
1 cup (6 ounces) semisweet chocolate chips

Preheat oven to 350°F. Lightly grease an 8-inch square pan. Combine butter and cocoa in medium-sized heavy saucepan over low heat, stirring constantly until smooth. Remove from heat; stir in sugar, egg, flour, buttermilk and vanilla. Mix until smooth. Spread batter evenly in prepared pan. Bake 25 minutes or until center feels dry. (Do not overbake or brownies will be dry.) Remove from oven; sprinkle marshmallows, walnuts and chocolate chips over the top. Return to oven for 3 to 5 minutes or just until topping is warmed enough to meld together. Cool in pan on wire rack. Cut into 2-inch squares.

Makes 16 brownies

CHUNKY OATMEAL BARS

Large chocolate chunks are scattered throughout these buttery oatmeal bars. If you can't find chocolate chunks, cut chocolate candy bars into chunks.

¾ cup butter or margarine, softened
1 cup packed light brown sugar
2 teaspoons vanilla
1 cup all-purpose flour
2 tablespoons unsweetened cocoa
1½ teaspoons baking powder
¼ teaspoon salt
¼ cup water
2 cups uncooked rolled oats
1 package (12 ounces) semisweet chocolate chunks

Preheat oven to 375°F. Lightly grease a 9-inch square pan. Cream butter with sugar until smooth. Add vanilla, beating until light. Combine flour, cocoa, baking powder and salt in small bowl. Blend into creamed mixture with water. Stir in oats and chocolate chunks. Spread dough evenly in prepared pan. Bake 25 to 30 minutes or just until center feels firm. Cool in pan on wire rack. Cut into 2×1-inch bars.

Makes about 3 dozen bars

Rocky Road Brownies

DOUBLE CHOCOLATE CRISPY BARS

Both sides of these crispy bars are painted with chocolate—dark chocolate on one side, white chocolate on the other.

6 cups crispy rice cereal
½ cup peanut butter
⅓ cup butter or margarine
2 squares (1 ounce each) unsweetened chocolate
1 package (8 ounces) marshmallows
1 cup (6 ounces) semisweet chocolate chips *or* 6 ounces bittersweet chocolate, chopped
6 ounces white chocolate, chopped
2 teaspoons shortening, divided

Preheat oven to 350°F. Line a 13×9-inch pan with waxed paper. Spread cereal on cookie sheet; toast in oven 10 minutes or until crispy. Place in large bowl. Meanwhile, combine peanut butter, butter and unsweetened chocolate in large heavy saucepan. Stir over low heat until chocolate is melted. Add marshmallows; stir until melted and smooth. Pour chocolate mixture over cereal; mix until evenly coated. Press firmly into prepared pan. Place semisweet and white chocolates into separate bowls. Add 1 teaspoon shortening to each bowl. Place bowls over very warm water; stir until chocolates are melted. Spread top of bars with melted semisweet chocolate; cool until chocolate is set. Turn bars out of pan onto a sheet of waxed paper, chocolate side down. Remove waxed paper from bottom of bars; spread white chocolate over surface. Cool until chocolate is set. Cut into 2×1½-inch bars using a sharp, thin knife.

Makes about 3 dozen bars

Clockwise from top: Double Chocolate Crispy Bars, Chocolate Macadamia Bars (page 554), Naomi's Revel Bars (page 554)

CHOCOLATE MACADAMIA BARS

- 12 squares (1 ounce each) bittersweet chocolate *or* 1 package (12 ounces) semisweet chocolate chips
- 1 package (8 ounces) cream cheese, softened
- ⅔ cup whipping cream or undiluted evaporated milk
- 1 cup chopped macadamia nuts or almonds
- 1 teaspoon vanilla, divided
- 1 cup butter or margarine, softened
- 1½ cups sugar
- 1 egg
- 3 cups all-purpose flour
- 1 teaspoon baking powder
- ¼ teaspoon salt

Preheat oven to 375°F. Lightly grease a 13×9-inch pan. Combine chocolate, cream cheese and cream in large heavy saucepan. Stir over low heat until chocolate is melted and mixture is smooth. Remove from heat; stir in nuts and ½ teaspoon of the vanilla. Cream butter and sugar in large bowl. Beat in egg and remaining ½ teaspoon vanilla. Add flour, baking powder and salt, blending well. Press half of the butter mixture on bottom of prepared pan. Spread chocolate mixture evenly over the top. Sprinkle remaining butter mixture over chocolate. Bake 35 to 40 minutes or until golden brown. Cool in pan on wire rack. Cut into 2×1½-inch bars.

Makes about 3 dozen bars

NAOMI'S REVEL BARS

- 1 cup plus 2 tablespoons butter or margarine, softened
- 2 cups packed brown sugar
- 2 eggs
- 2 teaspoons vanilla
- 2½ cups all-purpose flour
- 1 teaspoon baking soda
- 3 cups uncooked rolled oats
- 1 package (12 ounces) semisweet chocolate chips
- 1 can (14 ounces) sweetened condensed milk

Preheat oven to 325°F. Lightly grease a 13×9-inch pan. Cream the 1 cup butter and the sugar in large bowl. Add eggs; beat until light. Blend in vanilla. Combine flour and baking soda; stir into creamed mixture. Blend in oats. Spread ¾ of the oat mixture evenly in prepared pan. Combine chocolate chips, milk and the 2 tablespoons butter in small heavy saucepan. Stir over low heat until chocolate is melted. Pour chocolate mixture evenly over mixture in pan. Dot with remaining oat mixture. Bake 20 to 25 minutes or until edges are browned and center feels firm. Cool in pan on wire rack. Cut into 2×1½-inch bars.

Makes about 3 dozen bars

NORMA D's COCOA BROWNIES

This large pan of cake-like brownies is perfect for a potluck supper or club meeting.

- 2 cups all-purpose flour
- 2 cups granulated sugar
- 1 cup butter or margarine
- 1 cup hot coffee
- ¼ cup unsweetened cocoa
- ½ cup buttermilk
- 2 eggs, slightly beaten
- 1 teaspoon baking soda
- 1 teaspoon vanilla
- Cocoa Frosting (recipe follows)

Preheat oven to 400°F. Butter a 17½×11-inch jelly-roll pan. Combine flour and granulated sugar in large bowl. Combine butter, coffee and cocoa in small heavy saucepan. Bring to a boil over medium heat, stirring constantly. Combine buttermilk, eggs, baking soda and vanilla in small bowl. Stir cocoa mixture into flour mixture until smooth. Stir in buttermilk mixture until well blended. Pour batter into prepared pan. Bake 20 minutes or until center springs back when touched. Meanwhile, prepare Cocoa Frosting. Remove brownies from oven. Immediately pour warm frosting over hot brownies, spreading evenly. Cool in pan on wire rack. Cut into 2½-inch squares.

Makes about 30 brownies

COCOA FROSTING

- ½ cup butter or margarine
- 2 tablespoons unsweetened cocoa
- ¼ cup milk
- 3½ cups powdered sugar
- 1 teaspoon vanilla

Combine butter, cocoa and milk in large saucepan. Bring to a boil over medium heat. Remove from heat. Stir in powdered sugar and vanilla; beat until smooth.

CHOCOLATE CHIP & SOUR CREAM BROWNIES

- ½ cup butter or margarine, softened
- 1 cup packed light brown sugar
- 1 egg
- 1 cup sour cream
- 1 teaspoon vanilla
- ½ cup unsweetened cocoa
- ½ teaspoon baking soda
- ¼ teaspoon salt
- 2 cups all-purpose flour
- 1 cup (6 ounces) semisweet chocolate chips
- Powdered sugar

Preheat oven to 350°F. Butter a 13×9-inch pan. Cream butter and brown sugar in large bowl until blended. Add egg, sour cream and vanilla; beat until light. Add cocoa, baking soda and salt; beat until smooth. Blend in flour until well mixed. Stir in chocolate chips; spread batter evenly in prepared pan. Bake 25 to 30 minutes or until center springs back when touched. Cool in pan on wire rack. Sift powdered sugar over the top. Cut into 2½×1½-inch bars.

Makes about 30 brownies

MARBLED PEANUT-BUTTER BROWNIES

Swirls of peanut butter and chocolate form an unbeatable flavor combination.

- **½ cup butter or margarine, softened**
- **¼ cup peanut butter**
- **1 cup packed light brown sugar**
- **½ cup granulated sugar**
- **3 eggs**
- **1 teaspoon vanilla**
- **2 cups all-purpose flour**
- **2 teaspoons baking powder**
- **⅛ teaspoon salt**
- **1 cup chocolate-flavored syrup**
- **½ cup coarsely chopped salted mixed nuts**

Preheat oven to 350°F. Lightly grease a 13×9-inch pan. Cream butter and peanut butter in large bowl until blended; stir in sugars. Beat in eggs, one at a time, until batter is light. Blend in vanilla. Combine flour, baking powder and salt in small bowl. Stir into creamed mixture. Spread half of the batter evenly in prepared pan. Spread syrup over the top. Spoon remaining batter over syrup. Swirl with knife or spatula to create a marbled effect. Sprinkle chopped nuts over the top. Bake 35 to 40 minutes or until lightly browned. Cool in pan on wire rack. Cut into 2-inch squares.

Makes about 2 dozen brownies

WEST HAVEN DATE BARS

- **1 cup boiling water**
- **1 cup chopped pitted dates**
- **½ cup butter or margarine, softened**
- **1 cup sugar**
- **2 eggs**
- **1 teaspoon vanilla**
- **1½ cups all-purpose flour**
- **2 tablespoons unsweetened cocoa**
- **1 teaspoon baking soda**
- **1 cup (6 ounces) semisweet chocolate chips**
- **½ cup chopped walnuts or pecans**

Preheat oven to 350°F. Lightly grease a 13×9-inch pan. Pour boiling water over dates in small bowl; let stand until cooled. Cream butter with sugar in large bowl. Add eggs and vanilla; beat until light. Blend in flour, cocoa and baking soda to make a smooth dough. Stir in date mixture. Spread batter evenly in prepared pan. Sprinkle chocolate chips and nuts over the top. Bake 25 to 30 minutes or just until center feels firm. Cut into 2×1½-inch bars while still warm.

Makes about 3 dozen bars

Marbled Peanut-Butter Brownies

Chocolate Chippers

Clockwise from top right: White Chocolate and Cocoa Chippers (page 560), Aloha Chippers (page 560), Peanutty Double Chip Cookies (page 561)

ALOHA CHIPPERS

½ cup butter or margarine, softened
⅓ cup granulated sugar
⅓ cup packed light brown sugar
1 egg
1 tablespoon dark rum or water
1 teaspoon vanilla
½ teaspoon baking soda
⅛ teaspoon salt
1¼ cups all-purpose flour
½ cup semisweet chocolate chips
1 cup (6 ounces) white chocolate chips
½ cup flaked coconut
½ cup coarsely chopped macadamia nuts
Flaked coconut

Preheat oven to 375°F. Line cookie sheets with parchment paper or leave ungreased. Cream butter, sugars, egg, rum, vanilla, baking soda and salt in large bowl until light and fluffy. Blend in flour until dough is smooth and stiff. Stir in semisweet and white chocolate chips, ½ cup coconut and the macadamia nuts. Drop dough by teaspoonfuls 2 inches apart onto cookie sheets. Sprinkle tops of cookies with additional coconut. Bake 8 to 10 minutes or until just firm in center. Do not overbake. Remove to wire racks to cool.

Makes about 3 dozen cookies

WHITE CHOCOLATE & COCOA CHIPPERS

¾ cup butter or margarine, softened
½ cup granulated sugar
½ cup packed brown sugar
1 egg
2 tablespoons water
½ cup unsweetened cocoa
¾ teaspoon baking soda
½ teaspoon vanilla
¼ teaspoon salt
1⅓ cups all-purpose flour
1½ cups (10 to 12 ounces) large white chocolate chips
1 cup coarsely chopped pecans or walnuts

Preheat oven to 375°F. Line cookie sheets with parchment paper or leave ungreased. Cream butter, sugars, egg and water in large bowl until light and fluffy. Blend in cocoa, baking soda, vanilla and salt. Blend in flour until well mixed. Stir in white chocolate chips and nuts. Drop dough by rounded tablespoonfuls 3 inches apart onto cookie sheets. Bake 8 to 10 minutes or until firm in center. Do not overbake. Remove to wire racks to cool.

Makes about 4 dozen cookies

PEANUTTY DOUBLE CHIP COOKIES

- ½ cup butter or margarine, softened
- ¾ cup packed light brown sugar
- ¾ cup granulated sugar
- 2 eggs
- 1 teaspoon baking soda
- 1 teaspoon vanilla
- 2 cups all-purpose flour
- 1 cup chunky peanut butter
- 1 cup (6 ounces) semisweet or milk chocolate chips
- 1 cup (6 ounces) peanut butter chips

Preheat oven to 350°F. Lightly grease cookie sheets or line with parchment paper. Cream butter and sugars in large bowl until blended. Add eggs, baking soda and vanilla; beat until light. Blend in flour and peanut butter until dough is stiff and smooth. Stir in chocolate and peanut butter chips. Drop dough by teaspoonfuls 2 inches apart onto prepared cookie sheets. Press cookies down with tines of fork to flatten slightly. Bake 12 minutes or until just barely done. Do not overbake. Remove to wire racks to cool.

Makes about 5 dozen cookies

MRS. J'S CHIP COOKIES

Crispy rice cereal, pulverized into a flour, adds flavor and texture to these cookies.

- 4 cups crispy rice cereal
- 1 milk chocolate crunch bar (5 ounces), broken into squares
- 2 cups all-purpose flour
- 1 teaspoon baking powder
- 1 teaspoon baking soda
- ¼ teaspoon salt
- 1 cup butter or margarine, softened
- 1 cup granulated sugar
- 1 cup packed light brown sugar
- 2 eggs
- 1 teaspoon vanilla
- 1 package (12 ounces) semisweet chocolate chips
- 1½ cups chopped walnuts

Preheat oven to 375°F. Line cookie sheets with parchment paper or leave ungreased. Process cereal in blender or food processor until pulverized. Add chocolate bar; continue processing until both chocolate and cereal are completely ground. Add flour, baking powder, baking soda and salt; process until blended. Cream butter and sugars in large bowl. Add eggs; beat until light. Blend in vanilla. Add flour mixture; blend until smooth. Stir in chocolate chips and walnuts until blended. Shape dough into walnut-sized balls. Place 2 inches apart on cookie sheets. Bake 10 to 12 minutes or until firm in center. Do not overbake. Remove to wire racks to cool.

Makes about 8 dozen cookies

DOUBLE CHOCOLATE CHUNK COOKIES

- 2 squares (1 ounce each) unsweetened chocolate
- 3 eggs
- 1 cup vegetable oil
- ¾ cup packed brown sugar
- 1 teaspoon baking powder
- 1 teaspoon vanilla
- ¼ teaspoon baking soda
- ¼ teaspoon salt
- 2⅓ cups all-purpose flour
- 1 package (12 ounces) semisweet chocolate chunks

Preheat oven to 350°F. Lightly grease cookie sheets or line with parchment paper. Melt unsweetened chocolate in top of double boiler over hot, not boiling, water. Remove from heat; cool. Beat eggs in large bowl until foamy. Add the oil and sugar; continue beating until light and frothy. Blend in baking powder, vanilla, baking soda, salt and melted chocolate. Mix in flour until smooth. Stir in chocolate chunks. Shape dough into walnut-sized balls. Place 2 inches apart on prepared cookie sheets. Bake 10 to 12 minutes or until firm in center. Do not overbake. Remove to wire racks to cool.

Makes about 4½ dozen cookies

White Chocolate Chunk Cookies: Substitute one package (12 ounces) white chocolate chunks *or* two white chocolate candy bars (5 to 6 ounces each), cut into chunks, for the semisweet chocolate chunks.

CHOCOLATE CHUNK COOKIES

- 3 eggs
- 1 cup vegetable oil
- ¾ cup packed brown sugar
- 1 teaspoon baking powder
- 1 teaspoon vanilla
- ¼ teaspoon baking soda
- ¼ teaspoon salt
- 2½ cups all-purpose flour
- 1 package (12 ounces) semisweet chocolate chunks

Preheat oven to 350°F. Lightly grease cookie sheets or line with parchment paper. Beat eggs in large bowl until foamy. Add oil and sugar; beating until light and frothy. Blend in baking powder, vanilla, baking soda and salt. Mix in flour until dough is smooth. Stir in chocolate chunks. Shape dough into walnut-sized balls. Place 2 inches apart on prepared cookie sheets. Bake 10 to 12 minutes or until lightly browned. Remove to wire racks to cool.

Makes about 4½ dozen cookies

White Chocolate Chunk Co

THE YALE
SHAKESPEARE
KING HENRY
THE FIFTH
EDITED BY
ROBERT D. FRENCH
UNIVERSITY
PRESS

WHOLE GRAIN CHIPPERS

Whole wheat flour, rolled oats and sunflower seeds add nutrients, crunch and flavor to after-school cookies.

- 1 cup butter or margarine, softened
- ⅔ cup granulated sugar
- 1 cup packed light brown sugar
- 2 eggs
- 1 teaspoon baking soda
- 1 teaspoon vanilla
- Pinch salt
- 1 cup whole wheat flour
- 1 cup all-purpose flour
- 2 cups uncooked rolled oats
- 1 package (12 ounces) semisweet chocolate chips
- 1 cup sunflower seeds

Preheat oven to 375°F. Lightly grease cookie sheets or line with parchment paper. Cream butter with sugars and eggs in large bowl until light and fluffy. Beat in baking soda, vanilla and salt. Blend in flours and oats to make a stiff dough. Stir in chocolate chips. Shape rounded teaspoonfuls of dough into balls; roll in sunflower seeds. Place 2 inches apart on prepared cookie sheets. Bake 8 to 10 minutes or until firm. Do not overbake. Cool a few minutes on cookie sheet, then remove to wire racks to cool completely

Makes about 6 dozen cookies

WHITE CHOCOLATE CHIP & MACADAMIA COOKIES

Bake these for someone special. Macadamia nuts give them a sensational crunch.

- 2 squares (1 ounce each) unsweetened chocolate
- ½ cup butter or margarine, softened
- 1 cup packed light brown sugar
- 1 egg
- 1 teaspoon vanilla
- 1¼ cups all-purpose flour
- ½ teaspoon baking soda
- 1 cup (6 ounces) white chocolate chips
- ¾ cup macadamia nuts, chopped

Preheat oven to 350°F. Lightly grease cookie sheets or line with parchment paper. Melt unsweetened chocolate in top of double boiler over hot, not boiling, water. Remove from heat; cool. Cream butter, melted chocolate and sugar in large bowl until blended. Add egg and vanilla; beat until light. Blend in flour, baking soda, chocolate chips and macadamia nuts. Drop dough by rounded teaspoonfuls 2 inches apart onto prepared cookie sheets. Bake 10 to 12 minutes or until firm. Do not overbake. Remove to wire racks to cool.

Makes about 4 dozen cookies

Whole Grain Chippers

Special-Day Cookies

Top left to bottom right: Mocha pecan Pinwheels (page 568), Chocolate Pistachio Fingers (page 578), Chocolate Cherry Cookies (page 569), Orange & Chocolate Ribbon Cookies (page 571), Chocolate Spritz (page 582)

MOCHA PECAN PINWHEELS

- 1 square (1 ounce) unsweetened chocolate
- ½ cup (1 stick) butter or margarine, softened
- ¾ cup packed brown sugar
- 1 egg
- 1 teaspoon vanilla
- ¼ teaspoon baking soda
- 1¾ cups all-purpose flour
- ½ cup chopped pecans
- 1 teaspoon instant espresso coffee powder

Melt chocolate in small bowl over hot water. Stir until smooth. Cream butter, sugar, egg, vanilla and baking soda in large bowl, blending well. Stir in flour to make a stiff dough. Remove half of the dough; place in another bowl. Blend pecans and coffee powder into half of the dough. Stir melted chocolate into remaining dough. Cover doughs; refrigerate 30 minutes. Roll out light-colored dough to a 15×8-inch rectangle between 2 sheets of plastic wrap. Roll chocolate dough out to same dimensions between 2 more sheets of plastic wrap. Remove top sheets of plastic. Place light-colored dough on top of chocolate dough. Roll up firmly, jelly-roll fashion, starting with a long side. Wrap in plastic; freeze. (Dough can be frozen up to 6 weeks.) Preheat oven to 350°F. Line cookie sheets with parchment paper or leave ungreased. Cut frozen dough into ¼-inch-thick slices; place 2 inches apart on cookie sheets. Bake 9 to 12 minutes or until set. Remove to wire racks to cool.

Makes about 5 dozen cookies

CHOCOLATE-COCONUT MACAROONS

- 4 egg whites
- 1 teaspoon vanilla
- Dash salt
- 1½ cups sugar
- 2⅔ cups flaked coconut
- 2 tablespoons ground chocolate with sugar added*

*This type of ground chocolate is available in specialty food stores.

Preheat oven to 325°F. Line cookie sheets with parchment paper or lightly grease and dust with flour. In large clean, dry bowl, beat egg whites with vanilla and salt until stiff, but not dry. Beat in sugar, one tablespoon at a time, until mixture becomes stiff and glossy. Gently fold in coconut and ground chocolate until blended. Drop by rounded teaspoonfuls 2 inches apart onto prepared cookie sheets. Bake 20 minutes or until firm. Remove to wire racks to cool. Store in airtight containers.

Makes about 6 dozen cookies

CHOCOLATE CHERRY COOKIES

- 2 squares (1 ounce each) unsweetened chocolate
- ½ cup butter or margarine, softened
- ½ cup sugar
- 1 egg
- 2 cups cake flour
- 1 teaspoon vanilla
- ¼ teaspoon salt
- Maraschino cherries, well drained (about 48)
- 1 cup (6 ounces) semisweet or milk chocolate chips

Melt unsweetened chocolate in top of double boiler over hot, not boiling, water. Remove from heat; cool. Cream butter and sugar in large bowl until light. Add egg and melted chocolate; beat until fluffy. Stir in cake flour, vanilla and salt until well blended. Cover; refrigerate until firm, about 1 hour.

Preheat oven to 400°F. Lightly grease cookie sheets or line with parchment paper. Shape dough into 1-inch balls. Place 2 inches apart on prepared cookie sheets. With knuckle of a finger, make a deep indentation in center of each ball. Place a cherry into each indentation. Bake 8 minutes or just until set. Meanwhile, melt chocolate chips in small bowl over hot water. Stir until melted. Remove cookies to wire racks. Drizzle melted chocolate over tops while still warm. Refrigerate until chocolate is set.

Makes about 4 dozen cookies

FUDGE KISSES

Flavored with coconut, nuts and swirls of chocolate, these meringue-based cookies are called kisses—maybe because they crumble when you bite into them.

- 1 cup (6 ounces) semisweet chocolate chips
- 2 egg whites
- Dash salt
- ½ teaspoon cider vinegar
- ½ teaspoon vanilla
- ½ cup sugar
- ½ cup flaked coconut
- ¼ cup chopped walnuts or pecans

Preheat oven to 350°F. Line cookie sheets with parchment paper or lightly grease and sprinkle with flour. Melt chocolate chips in top of double boiler over hot, not boiling, water. Remove from heat; cool. In large clean, dry bowl, beat egg whites with salt until frothy. Beat in vinegar and vanilla. Beat in sugar, one tablespoon at a time, until mixture becomes stiff and glossy. Gently fold in coconut, nuts and melted chocolate until mixture is marbled. Drop mixture by rounded teaspoonfuls 2 inches apart onto prepared cookie sheets. Bake 12 to 15 minutes or until dry on top. Cool completely on cookie sheets. Store in airtight containers.

Makes 3 dozen cookies

ORANGE & CHOCOLATE RIBBON COOKIES

Use an empty 12×2×2-inch food wrap box to shape these cookies as they chill. A foil, plastic wrap, or waxed paper box is ideal.

- 1 cup butter or margarine, softened
- ½ cup sugar
- 3 egg yolks
- 2 teaspoons grated orange zest
- 1 teaspoon orange extract
- 2¼ cups all-purpose flour, divided
- 3 tablespoons unsweetened cocoa
- 1 teaspoon vanilla
- 1 teaspoon chocolate extract

Cream butter, sugar and egg yolks in large bowl until light and fluffy. Remove half of the mixture; place in another bowl. Add orange zest, orange extract and 1¼ cups of the flour to one half of the mixture; mix until blended and smooth. Shape into a ball. Add cocoa, vanilla and chocolate extract to second half of the mixture; beat until smooth. Stir in remaining 1 cup flour; mix until blended and smooth. Shape into a ball. Cover doughs; refrigerate 10 minutes.

Empty a 12×2×2-inch food wrap box, such as foil or plastic wrap; set aside. Roll out each dough separately on lightly floured surface to a 12×4-inch rectangle. Pat edges of dough to straighten; use rolling pin to level off thickness. Place one of the doughs on top of the other. Using a sharp knife, make a lengthwise cut through center of doughs. Lift half of the dough onto the other to make a long, 4-layer strip of dough. With hands, press dough strips together. Wrap in plastic wrap; fit into food wrap box, pressing down at the top. Close box; refrigerate at least 1 hour or up to 3 days. (For longer storage, freeze up to 6 weeks.)

Preheat oven to 350°F. Lightly grease cookie sheets or line with parchment paper. Cut dough crosswise into ¼-inch-thick slices; place 2 inches apart on prepared cookie sheets. Bake 10 to 12 minutes or until very lightly browned. Remove to wire racks to cool.

Makes about 5 dozen cookies

Orange & Chocolate Ribbon Cookies, Chocolate-Mint Sandwiches (page 78), Cinnamon-Chocolate Cutouts (page 79)

CHOCOLATE-MINT SANDWICHES

- 2 squares (1 ounce each) unsweetened chocolate
- ½ cup butter or margarine, softened
- 1 cup packed light brown sugar
- 1 teaspoon vanilla
- 1 egg
- ⅛ teaspoon baking soda
- 2 cups all-purpose flour
- Creamy Mint Filling (recipe follows)

Melt chocolate in top of double boiler over hot, not boiling, water. Remove from heat; cool. Cream butter and brown sugar in large bowl. Beat in vanilla, egg, melted chocolate and baking soda until light and fluffy. Stir in flour to make a stiff dough. Divide dough into 4 parts. Shape each part into a roll, about 1½ inches in diameter. Wrap in plastic wrap; refrigerate at least 1 hour or up to 2 weeks. (For longer storage, freeze up to 6 weeks.)

Preheat oven to 375°F. Line cookie sheets with parchment paper or leave ungreased. Cut rolls into ⅛-inch-thick slices; place 2 inches apart on cookie sheets. Bake 6 to 7 minutes or until firm. Remove to wire racks to cool. Prepare Creamy Mint Filling. Spread filling on bottoms of half the cookies. Top with remaining cookies, bottom sides down, forming sandwiches.

Makes about 3 dozen sandwich cookies

CREAMY MINT FILLING

- 2 tablespoons butter or margarine, softened
- 1½ cups powdered sugar
- 3 to 4 tablespoons light cream or half-and-half
- ¼ teaspoon peppermint extract
- Few drops green food coloring

Cream butter with powdered sugar and cream in small bowl until smooth and blended. Stir in peppermint extract and food coloring, blending well.

CINNAMON-CHOCOLATE CUTOUTS

- 2 squares (1 ounce each) unsweetened chocolate
- ½ cup butter or margarine, softened
- 1 cup granulated sugar
- 1 egg
- 1 teaspoon vanilla
- 3 cups all-purpose flour
- 2 teaspoons ground cinnamon
- ½ teaspoon baking soda
- ¼ teaspoon salt
- ½ cup sour cream
- Decorator Icing (recipe follows)

Melt chocolate in top of double boiler over hot, not boiling, water. Remove from heat; cool. Cream butter, melted chocolate, granulated sugar, egg and vanilla in large bowl until light. Combine flour, cinnamon, baking soda and salt in small bowl. Stir into creamed mixture with sour cream until smooth. Cover; refrigerate at least 30 minutes.

Preheat oven to 400°F. Lightly grease cookie sheets or line with parchment paper. Roll out dough, one fourth at a time, ¼ inch thick on lightly floured surface. Cut out with cookie cutters. Place 2 inches apart on prepared cookie sheets. Bake 10 minutes or until lightly browned, but not dark. Remove to wire racks to cool. Prepare Decorator Icing. Spoon into pastry bag fitted with small tip or small heavy-duty plastic bag. (If using plastic bag, close securely. With scissors, snip off small corner from one side of bag.) Decorate cookies with icing.

Makes about 6 dozen cookies

DECORATOR ICING

- 1 egg white*
- 3½ cups powdered sugar
- 1 teaspoon almond or lemon extract
- 2 to 3 tablespoons water

Beat egg white in large bowl until frothy. Gradually beat in powdered sugar until blended. Add almond extract and enough water to moisten. Beat until smooth and glossy.

*Use clean, uncracked egg.

SPUMONI BARS

These pretty tri-colored cookies will remind you of the popular Italian ice cream.

¾ cup butter or margarine, softened
⅔ cup sugar
3 egg yolks
1 teaspoon vanilla
¼ teaspoon baking powder
⅛ teaspoon salt
2 cups all-purpose flour
12 maraschino cherries, well drained and chopped
¼ cup chopped walnuts
¼ cup mint-flavored or plain semisweet chocolate chips
2 teaspoons water, divided

Preheat oven to 350°F. Cream butter and sugar in large bowl until blended. Beat in egg yolks, vanilla, baking powder and salt until light. Stir in flour to make a stiff dough. Divide dough into 3 equal parts; place each part in small bowl. Add cherries and walnuts to one part, blending well. Melt chocolate chips in small bowl over hot water. Stir until smooth. Add melted chocolate and 1 teaspoon of the water to second part, blending well. Stir remaining 1 teaspoon water into third part. (If doughs are soft, refrigerate 10 minutes.)

Divide each color dough into 4 equal parts. Shape each part into a 6-inch rope by rolling on lightly floured surface. Place one rope of each color side by side on ungreased cookie sheet. Flatten ropes so they attach together making 1 strip of 3 colors. With rolling pin, roll strip directly on cookie sheet until it measures 12×3 inches. With straight edge of knife, score strip crosswise at 1-inch intervals. Repeat with remaining ropes to make a total of 4 tri-colored strips of dough. Bake 12 to 13 minutes or until set but not completely browned; remove from oven. While cookies are still warm, trim lengthwise edges to make them even and cut into individual cookies along score marks. (Cookies will bake together but are easy to cut apart while still warm.) Cool on cookie sheets.

Makes 4 dozen cookies

Spumoni Bars, Chocolate Pistachio Fingers (page 84), Chocolate-Dipped Oat Cookies (page 84)

DOUBLE-DIPPED HAZELNUT CRISPS

- ¾ cup semisweet chocolate chips
- 1¼ cups all-purpose flour
- ¾ cup powdered sugar
- ⅔ cup whole hazelnuts, toasted, hulled and pulverized*
- ¼ teaspoon instant espresso coffee powder
- Dash salt
- ½ cup butter or margarine, softened
- 2 teaspoons vanilla
- 4 squares (1 ounce each) bittersweet or semisweet chocolate
- 4 ounces white chocolate
- 2 teaspoons shortening, divided

Preheat oven to 350°F. Lightly grease cookie sheets or line with parchment paper. Melt chocolate chips in top of double boiler over hot, not boiling, water. Remove from heat; cool. Blend flour, sugar, hazelnuts, coffee powder and salt in large bowl. Blend in butter, melted chocolate and vanilla until dough is stiff but smooth. (If dough is too soft to handle, cover and refrigerate until firm.) Roll out dough, one fourth at a time, ⅛ inch thick on lightly floured surface. Cut out with 2-inch scalloped round cutters. Place 2 inches apart on prepared cookie sheets. Bake 8 minutes or until not quite firm. (Cookies should not brown. They will puff up during baking and then fall again.) Remove to wire racks to cool.

Place bittersweet and white chocolates into separate small bowls. Add 1 teaspoon shortening to each bowl. Place bowls over hot water; stir until chocolate is melted and smooth. Dip cookies, one at a time, halfway into bittersweet chocolate. Place on waxed paper; refrigerate until chocolate is set. Dip other halves of cookies into white chocolate; refrigerate until set. Store cookies in airtight container in cool place. (If cookies are frozen, chocolate may discolor.)

Makes about 4 dozen cookies

*To pulverize hazelnuts, place in food processor or blender. Process until thoroughly ground with a dry, not pasty, texture.

Left to right: Double-Dipped Hazelnut Crisps, Pecan Florentines (page 579)

CHOCOLATE-DIPPED OAT COOKIES

- 2 cups uncooked rolled oats
- ¾ cup packed brown sugar
- ½ cup vegetable oil
- ½ cup finely chopped walnuts
- 1 egg
- 2 teaspoons grated orange rind
- ¼ teaspoon salt
- 1 package (12 ounces) milk chocolate chips

Combine oats, sugar, oil, walnuts, egg, orange rind and salt in large bowl until blended. Cover; refrigerate overnight. Preheat oven to 350°F. Lightly grease cookie sheets or line with parchment paper. Melt chocolate chips in top of double boiler over hot, not boiling, water; set aside. Shape oat mixture into large-marble-sized balls. Place 2 inches apart on prepared cookie sheets. Bake 10 to 12 minutes or until golden and crisp. Cool 10 minutes on wire racks. Dip tops of cookies, one at a time, into melted chocolate. Place on waxed paper; cool until chocolate is set.

Makes about 6 dozen cookies

CHOCOLATE PISTACHIO FINGERS

Both ends of these buttery, finger-shaped cookies are dipped into melted chocolate. Then, for an elegant finish, the chocolate ends are covered with chopped pistachios.

- ¾ cup butter or margarine, softened
- ⅓ cup sugar
- 3 ounces (about ⅓ cup) almond paste
- 1 egg yolk
- 1⅔ cups all-purpose flour
- 1 cup (6 ounces) semisweet chocolate chips
- ½ cup finely chopped natural pistachios

Preheat oven to 350°F. Line cookie sheets with parchment paper or lightly grease and dust with flour. Cream butter and sugar in large bowl until blended. Add almond paste and egg yolk; beat until light. Blend in flour to make a smooth dough. (If dough is too soft to handle, cover and refrigerate until firm.) Turn out onto lightly floured board. Divide into 8 equal pieces; divide each piece in half. Roll each half into a 12-inch rope; cut each rope into 2-inch lengths. Place 2 inches apart on prepared cookie sheets. Bake 10 to 12 minutes or until edges just begin to brown. Remove to wire racks to cool. Melt chocolate chips in small bowl over hot water. Stir until smooth. Dip both ends of cookies about ½ inch into melted chocolate, then dip the chocolate ends into pistachios. Place on waxed paper; let stand until chocolate is set.

Makes 8 dozen cookies

PECAN FLORENTINES

Florentines are lacy confections that require a bit more skill than the average drop cookie. When baked on foil as directed, they are much easier to handle.

¾ cup pecan halves, pulverized*
½ cup all-purpose flour
⅓ cup packed brown sugar
¼ cup light corn syrup
¼ cup butter or margarine
2 tablespoons milk
⅓ cup semisweet chocolate chips

Preheat oven to 350°F. Line cookie sheets with foil; lightly grease foil. Combine pecans and flour in small bowl. Combine sugar, syrup, butter and milk in medium saucepan. Stir over medium heat until mixture comes to a boil. Remove from heat; stir in flour mixture. Drop batter by teaspoonfuls about 3 inches apart onto prepared cookie sheets. Bake 10 to 12 minutes or until lacy and golden brown. (Cookies are soft when hot, but become crispy as they cool.) Cool completely on foil. Place chocolate chips in small heavy-duty plastic bag; close securely. Set bag in bowl of hot water until chips are melted, being careful not to let any water into bag. (Knead bag lightly to check that chips are completely melted.) Pat bag dry. With scissors, snip off a small corner from one side of bag. Squeeze melted chocolate over cookies to decorate. Let stand until chocolate is set. Peel foil off cookies.

Makes about 3 dozen cookies

*To pulverize pecans, place in food processor or blender. Process until thoroughly ground with a dry, not pasty, texture.

TRIPLE CHOCOLATE PRETZELS

Buttery pretzel-shaped chocolate cookies are glazed with dark chocolate, then decorated with white chocolate for a triple chocolate treat.

- 2 squares (1 ounce each) unsweetened chocolate
- ½ cup butter or margarine, softened
- ½ cup granulated sugar
- 1 egg
- 2 cups cake flour
- 1 teaspoon vanilla
- ¼ teaspoon salt
- Mocha Glaze (recipe follows)
- 2 ounces white chocolate, chopped

Melt unsweetened chocolate in top of double boiler over hot, not boiling, water. Remove from heat; cool. Cream butter and granulated sugar in large bowl until light. Add egg and melted chocolate; beat until fluffy. Stir in cake flour, vanilla and salt until well blended. Cover; refrigerate until firm, about 1 hour.

Preheat oven to 400°F. Lightly grease cookie sheets or line with parchment paper. Divide dough into 4 equal parts. Divide each part into 12 pieces. To form pretzels, knead each piece briefly to soften dough. Roll into a rope about 6 inches long. Form each rope on prepared cookie sheet into a pretzel shape. Repeat with all pieces of dough, spacing cookies 2 inches apart. Bake 7 to 9 minutes or until firm. Remove to wire racks to cool. Prepare Mocha Glaze. Dip pretzels, one at a time, into glaze to coat completely. Place on waxed paper, right side up. Let stand until glaze is set. Melt white chocolate in small bowl over hot water. Squeeze melted chocolate through pastry bag or drizzle over pretzels to decorate. Let stand until chocolate is completely set.

Makes 4 dozen cookies

MOCHA GLAZE

- 1 cup (6 ounces) semisweet chocolate chips
- 1 teaspoon light corn syrup
- 1 teaspoon shortening
- 1 cup powdered sugar
- 3 to 5 tablespoons hot coffee or water

Combine chocolate chips, corn syrup and shortening in small heavy saucepan. Stir over low heat until chocolate is melted. Stir in powdered sugar and enough coffee to make a smooth glaze.

Top: Chocolate Spritz (page 582) and Chocolate Cherry Cookies (page 569), bottom: Triple Chocolate Pretzels

CHOCOLATE SPRITZ

- 2 squares (1 ounce each) unsweetened chocolate
- 1 cup butter, softened
- ½ cup granulated sugar
- 1 egg
- 1 teaspoon vanilla
- ¼ teaspoon salt
- 2¼ cups all-purpose flour
- Powdered sugar

Preheat oven to 400°F. Line cookie sheets with parchment paper or leave ungreased. Melt chocolate in top of double boiler over hot, not boiling, water. Remove from heat; cool. Cream butter, granulated sugar, egg, vanilla and salt in large bowl until light. Blend in melted chocolate and flour until stiff. Fit cookie press with your choice of plate. Load press with dough; press cookies out onto cookie sheets, spacing 2 inches apart. Bake 5 to 7 minutes or just until very slightly browned around edges. Remove to wire racks to cool. Dust with powdered sugar.

Makes about 5 dozen cookies

CHOCOLATE-FROSTED ALMOND SHORTBREAD

This shortbread keeps quite well in the refrigerator. Simply slip the whole pan into a plastic bag and seal securely.

- ¾ cup butter, softened
- ¼ cup packed light brown sugar
- ¼ cup powdered sugar
- 1 egg yolk
- 1 teaspoon almond extract
- 1½ cups all-purpose flour
- ⅛ teaspoon baking soda
- 7 ounces (about 1 cup) almond paste
- ½ cup granulated sugar
- 1 egg
- ½ cup milk chocolate chips

Preheat oven to 350°F. Cover bottom of a 9-inch pie pan with parchment or waxed paper. Cream butter, brown sugar, powdered sugar, egg yolk and almond extract in large bowl. Blend in flour and baking soda until smooth. Press half of the dough into prepared pie pan. Beat almond paste, granulated sugar and whole egg in small bowl until smooth. Spread over dough in pan. Roll out remaining half of dough on lightly floured surface into a circle to fit top of almond layer. Place over almond layer; press down to make smooth top. Bake 30 to 40 minutes or until top appears very lightly browned and feels firm. Remove from oven; sprinkle chocolate chips over the top. Let stand a few minutes until chips melt, then spread evenly over shortbread. Refrigerate until chocolate is set. Cut into slim wedges to serve.

Makes 16 to 20 cookies

DANISH RASPBERRY COOKIES

These fancy cookies look like you fussed all day making them. Only you know how easy and fun they were to prepare.

- 2 squares (1 ounce each) unsweetened chocolate
- ½ cup butter or margarine, softened
- ½ cup sugar
- 1 egg
- 2 cups cake flour
- 1 teaspoon vanilla
- ¼ teaspoon salt
- 1 cup (6 ounces) milk chocolate or white chocolate chips *or* ½ cup of each
- 1 to 1¼ cups seedless raspberry preserves or jam

Melt unsweetened chocolate in top of double boiler over hot, not boiling, water. Remove from heat; cool. Cream butter and sugar in large bowl until light. Add egg and melted chocolate; beat until fluffy. Stir in cake flour, vanilla and salt until well blended. Cover; refrigerate until firm, about 1 hour.

Preheat oven to 400°F. Lightly grease cookie sheets or line with parchment paper. Divide dough into 4 equal parts. Divide each part into 2 pieces. Roll each piece into a rope 12 inches long on lightly floured board. (The ropes should be about the thickness of a finger.) Place 2 inches apart on prepared cookie sheets. With side of finger, make an indentation along length of each rope. Bake 8 minutes or until firm. Meanwhile, melt chocolate chips in small bowl over hot water. Stir until smooth. (If using both kinds of chips, melt separately.) Stir preserves; spoon into pastry bag fitted with ¼-inch tip or into small heavy-duty plastic bag. (If using plastic bag, snip off a small corner from one side of bag.) Remove cookies from oven. Press preserves down length of each cookie strip. Return to oven for 2 minutes, then remove to wire racks. While cookies are still warm, drizzle melted chocolate over the tops, then cut strips into 1-inch diagonal pieces. Refrigerate until chocolate is set.

Makes 8 dozen cookies

CHOCOLATE COOKIE PRINTS

Cookie stamps imprint cookies with a raised design. Usually made of ceramic or glass, they are available in specialty shops or large department stores.

2 squares (1 ounce each) unsweetened chocolate
½ cup butter or margarine, softened
¾ cup sugar
1 egg
2 cups cake flour
1 tcaspoon vanilla
¼ teaspoon salt
Sugar

Melt chocolate in top of double boiler over hot, not boiling, water. Remove from heat; cool. Cream butter and sugar in large bowl until light. Add egg and melted chocolate; beat until fluffy. Stir in cake flour, vanilla and salt until well blended. Cover; refrigerate until firm, about 1 hour.

Preheat oven to 400°F. Lightly grease cookie sheets or line with parchment paper. Divide dough into 4 equal parts. Divide each part into 12 pieces. Roll each piece into a smooth round ball. Place 2 inches apart on prepared cookie sheets. Dip cookie stamp into water, then into sugar. Press down firmly onto a dough ball; remove. (Cookie will have imprint of stamp on it.) Repeat for each cookie, dipping stamp into water and sugar each time. Bake 7 to 9 minutes or until firm. Remove to wire racks to cool.

Makes 4 dozen cookies

CHOCOLATE RUM BALLS

½ cup butter or margarine, softened
⅓ cup granulated sugar
1 egg yolk
1 tablespoon dark rum
1 teaspoon vanilla
1 cup all-purpose flour
¼ cup unsweetened cocoa
1 cup finely chopped walnuts or pecans
Powdered sugar

Cream butter, granulated sugar and egg yolk in large bowl until light and fluffy. Blend in rum and vanilla. Stir in flour, cocoa and nuts; mix well. Cover; refrigerate until firm, about 1 hour. Preheat oven to 350°F. Lightly grease cookie sheets or line with parchment paper. Shape dough into 1-inch balls. Place 2 inches apart on prepared cookie sheets. Bake 15 to 20 minutes or until firm. Remove to wire racks to cool. Roll in powdered sugar.

Makes about 3 dozen cookies

Clockwise form center: Chocolate Tassies (page 587), Chocolate-Dipped Almond Crescents (page 586), Chocolate Cookie Prints

CHOCOLATE-DIPPED ALMOND CRESCENTS

One end of these crescent-shaped cookies is dipped into melted chocolate—a decorative touch that makes them look special.

- **1 cup butter or margarine, softened**
- **1 cup powdered sugar**
- **2 egg yolks**
- **2½ cups all-purpose flour**
- **1½ teaspoons almond extract**
- **1 cup (6 ounces) semisweet chocolate chips**

Preheat oven to 375°F. Line cookie sheets with parchment paper or leave ungreased. Cream butter, sugar and egg yolks in large bowl. Beat in flour and almond extract until well mixed. Shape dough into 1-inch balls. (If dough is too soft to handle, cover and refrigerate until firm.) Roll balls into 2-inch long ropes, tapering both ends. Curve ropes into crescent shapes. Place 2 inches apart on cookie sheets. Bake 8 to 10 minutes or until set, but not browned. Remove to wire racks to cool. Melt chocolate chips in top of double boiler over hot, not boiling, water. Dip one end of each crescent in melted chocolate. Place on waxed paper; cool until chocolate is set.

Makes about 5 dozen cookies

COCOA GINGERBREAD COOKIES

- **¼ cup butter or margarine, softened**
- **2 tablespoons shortening**
- **⅓ cup packed brown sugar**
- **¼ cup dark molasses**
- **1 egg**
- **1½ cups all-purpose flour**
- **¼ cup unsweetened cocoa**
- **½ teaspoon baking soda**
- **½ teaspoon ground ginger**
- **½ teaspoon ground cinnamon**
- **¼ teaspoon salt**
- **¼ teaspoon ground nutmeg**
- **⅛ teaspoon ground cloves**
- **Decorator Icing (page 573)**

Preheat oven to 400°F. Lightly grease cookie sheets or line with parchment paper. Cream butter, shortening, brown sugar and molasses in large bowl. Add egg; beat until light. Combine flour, cocoa, baking soda, ginger, cinnamon, salt, nutmeg and cloves in small bowl. Blend into creamed mixture until smooth. (If dough is too soft to handle, cover and refrigerate until firm.) Roll out dough ¼ inch thick on lightly floured surface. Cut out with cookie cutters. Place 2 inches apart on prepared cookie sheets. Bake 8 to 10 minutes or until firm. Remove to wire racks to cool. Prepare Decorator Icing. Spoon into pastry bag fitted with small tip. Decorate cookies with icing.

Makes about 6 dozen cookies

CHOCOLATE TASSIES

Tassies are old-fashioned cookies that resemble miniature pecan tarts. Here, the pecan filling is enriched with chocolate.

PASTRY
- 2 cups all-purpose flour
- 2 packages (3 ounces each) cream cheese, cold, cut into chunks
- 1 cup butter or margarine, cold, cut into chunks

FILLING
- 2 tablespoons butter or margarine
- 2 squares (1 ounce each) unsweetened chocolate
- 1½ cups packed brown sugar
- 2 teaspoons vanilla
- 2 eggs, beaten
- Dash salt
- 1½ cups chopped pecans

To prepare Pastry: Place flour in large bowl. Cut in cream cheese and butter. Continue to mix until dough can be shaped into a ball. Wrap dough in plastic wrap; refrigerate 1 hour. Shape dough into 1-inch balls. Press each ball into ungreased miniature (1¾-inch) muffin pan cup, covering bottom and side of cup with dough. Preheat oven to 350°F.

To prepare Filling: Melt butter and chocolate in medium-sized heavy saucepan over low heat. Remove from heat. Blend in sugar, vanilla, eggs and salt; beat until thick. Stir in pecans. Spoon about 1 teaspoon filling into each unbaked pastry shell. Bake 20 to 25 minutes or until lightly browned and filling is set. Cool in pans on wire racks. Remove from pans; store in airtight containers.

Makes about 5 dozen cookies

ALMOND FUDGE CUPS

PASTRY
- ¾ cup butter or margarine, softened
- ⅓ cup sugar
- 2 cups all-purpose flour
- 1 tablespoon almond- or fruit-flavored liqueur *or* water
- 1 teaspoon vanilla

FILLING
- 1 cup (6 ounces) semisweet chocolate chips
- ¾ cup blanched almonds
- 2 eggs
- ½ cup sugar
- Dash salt

To prepare Pastry: Lightly grease 3 dozen miniature (1¾-inch) muffin pan cups or small tart shells. Cream butter and sugar in large bowl until blended. Add flour, liqueur and vanilla; stir to make moist crumbs. Divide crumbs evenly among muffin cups; press to cover bottoms and sides of cups completely. Preheat oven to 350°F.

To prepare Filling: Place chocolate chips and almonds in food processor or blender. Process until finely ground. Beat eggs in medium bowl until thick; stir in sugar and salt. Blend in chocolate mixture. Spoon filling into unbaked pastry shells. Bake 20 minutes or until filling is set. Cool in pans on wire racks. Store in airtight containers.

Makes 3 dozen cookies

INDEX

A

B

C

D

E

F

G

H

I

J

K

L

M

N

O

P

Q

R

S

T

V

W

Y

Z

METRIC CONVERSION CHART

VOLUME MEASUREMENT (dry)

⅛ teaspoon = .5 mL
¼ teaspoon = 1 mL
½ teaspoon = 2 mL
¾ teaspoon = 4 mL
1 teaspoon = 5 mL
1 tablespoon = 15 mL
2 tablespoons = 25 mL
¼ cup = 50 mL
⅓ cup = 75 mL
⅔ cup = 150 mL
¾ cup = 175 mL
1 cup = 250 mL
2 cups = 1 pint = 500 mL
3 cups = 750 mL
4 cups = 1 quart = 1 L

VOLUME MEASUREMENT (fluid)

1 fluid ounce (2 tablespoons) = 30 mL
4 fluid ounces (½ cup) = 125 mL
8 fluid ounces (1 cup) = 250 mL
12 fluid ounces (1½ cups) = 375 mL
16 fluid ounces (2 cups) = 500 mL

WEIGHT (MASS)

½ ounce = 15 g
1 ounce = 30 g
3 ounces = 85 g
3.75 ounces = 100 g
4 ounces = 115 g
8 ounces = 225 g
12 ounces = 340 g
16 ounces = 1 pound = 450 g

DIMENSION

1/16 inch = 2 mm
⅛ inch = 3 mm
¼ inch = 6 mm
½ inch = 1.5 cm
¾ inch = 2 cm
1 inch = 2.5 cm

OVEN TEMPERATURES

250°F = 120°C
275°F = 140°C
300°F = 150°C
325°F = 160°C
350°F = 180°C
375°F = 190°C
400°F = 200°C
425°F = 220°C
450°F = 230°C

BAKING PAN SIZES

Utensil	Size in Inches/Quarts	Metric Volume	Size in Centimeters
Baking or	8×8×2	2 L	20×20 ×5
Cake pan	9×9×2	2.5 L	22×22 ×5
(square or	12×8×2	3 L	30×20 ×5
rectangular)	13×9×2	3.5 L	33×23 ×5
Loaf Pan	8×4×3	1.5 L	20×10 ×7
	9×5×3	2 L	23×13 ×7
Round Layer	8×1½	1.2 L	20×4
Cake Pan	9×1½	1.5 L	23×4
Pie Plate	8×1¼	750 mL	20×3
	9×1¼	1 L	23×3
Baking Dish	1 quart	1 L	
or Casserole	1½ quart	1.5 L	
	2 quart	2 L	

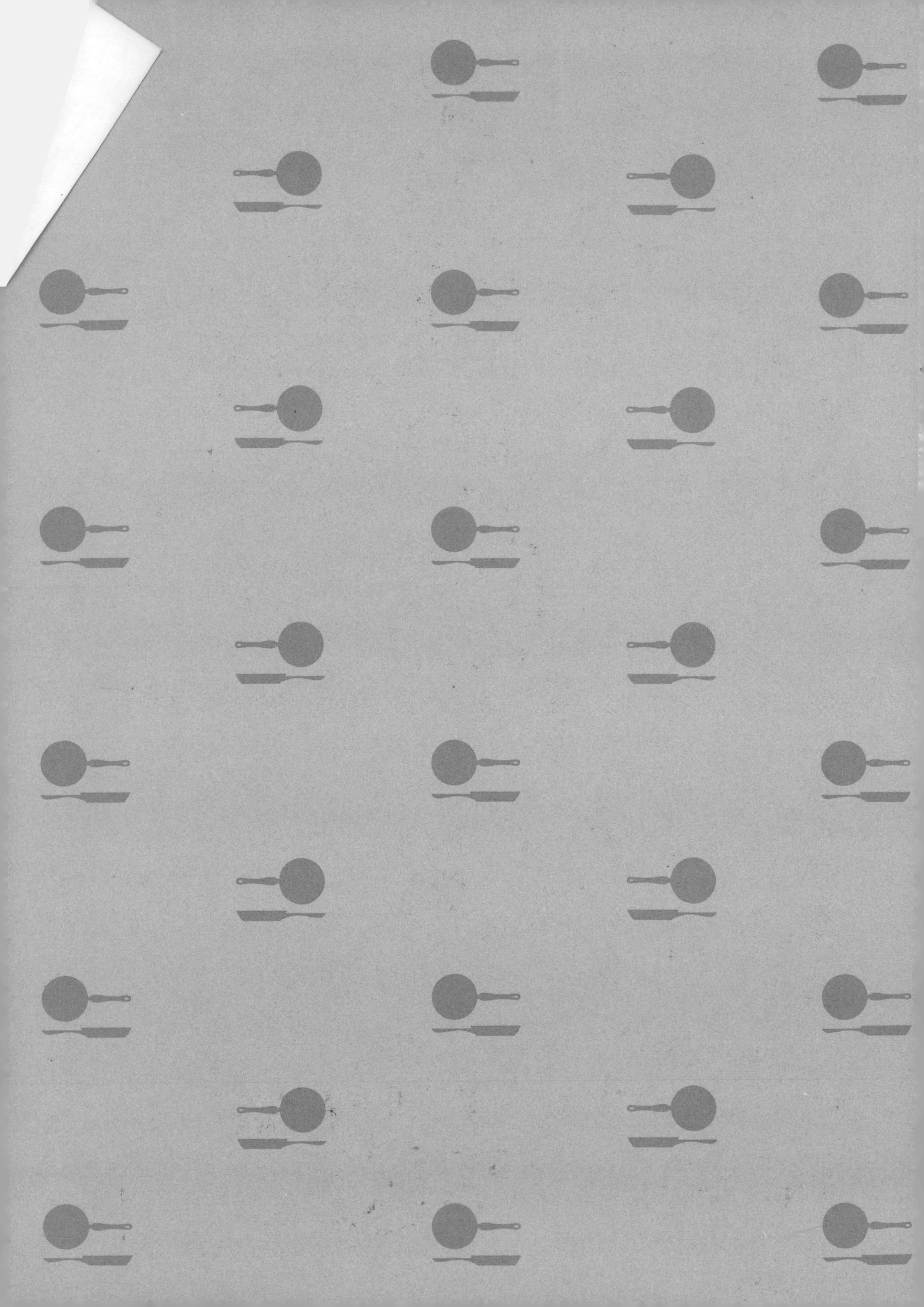